LET US C

Eighth Edition

By
Yashavant Kanetkar

INFINITY SCIENCE PRESS LLC
Hingham, Massachusetts
New Delhi

Original Copyright 2008 by BPB PUBLICATIONS PVT. LTD. All rights reserved.
Let Us C® is a Registered Trademark of BPB PUBLICATIONS PVT. LTD, New Delhi under Registration No. 135514

INFINITY SCIENCE PRESS LLC
11 Leavitt Street
Hingham, MA 02043
Tel. 877-266-5796 (toll free)
Fax 781-740-1677
info@infinitysciencepress.com
www.infinitysciencepress.com

This book is printed on acid-free paper.

Let Us C, Eighth Edition
ISBN: 978-1-934015-25-4

Library of Congress Cataloging-in-Publication Data

Kanetkar, Yashavant P.
   Let us C / Yashavant P. Kanetkar. —8th ed.
      p. cm.
   ISBN 978-1-934015-25-4 (pbk.)
   1. C (Computer program language)   I. Title.
   QA76.73.C15K36 2007
   005.13'3—dc22
                                   2008001937
8 9 4 3 2

Our titles are available for adoption, license or bulk purchase by institutions, corporations, etc. For additional information, please contact the Customer Service Dept. at 877-266-5796 (toll free in US).

Requests for replacement of a defective CD-ROM must be accompanied by the original disc, your mailing address, telephone number, date of purchase and purchase price. Please state the nature of the problem, and send the information to INFINITY SCIENCE PRESS, 11 Leavitt Street, Hingham, MA 02043.

The sole obligation of INFINITY SCIENCE PRESS to the purchaser is to replace the disc, based on defective materials or faulty workmanship, but not based on the operation or functionality of the product.

LET US C

Eighth Edition

Dedicated to baba
Who couldn't be here to see this day . . .

ABOUT THE AUTHOR

Through his books and Quest! Video Courses on C, C++, Data Structures, VC++, .NET, Embedded Systems, etc., Yashavant Kanetkar has created, moulded, and groomed many IT careers in the last decade and half. In recognition of his immense contribution to IT education, he was awarded the "Best .NET Technical Contributor" and "Most Valuable Professional" awards by Microsoft. His current passions are Internet Technologies, Device Drivers, and Embedded Systems. He is currently scripting a book titled *Go Embedded!* Yashavant holds a BE from VJTI Mumbai and an M.Tech. from IIT Kanpur. Yashavant's current affiliation is Director of KICIT and KSET. He can be reached at kanetkar@kicit.com or through *www.kicit.com.*

ACKNOWLEDGMENTS

*L*et Us C has become an important part of my life. I have created and nurtured it for the last decade or so. While doing so, I have received, in addition to the compliments, many suggestions from students, developers, professors, publishers, and authors. Their input has helped me in taking this book up to this eighth edition, and ideally I should put their names on the cover page too.

The seven editions of this book saw several changes. During this course many people helped in executing programs, spotting bugs, drawing figures, and preparing the index.

I thank Seema, my wife, for enduring the late nights, the clicking keyboard, and the noisy printer, and mostly for putting up with yet another marathon book effort.

And, finally, my heartfelt gratitude to the countless students who made me look into every nook and cranny of C. I remain in their debt.

PREFACE

The aim of *Let Us C* for its first few editions was to teach C programming in its entirety in as simple a manner as possible. From the fifth edition onward it took a slightly different turn. It started talking about use of the C language in different programming environments like Windows and Linux. From this edition onward I have decided to also address the issues and topics where I find that many students and professionals face difficulties while doing real-life programming. One topic that came to my mind immediately is Internet programming. So you will find in this edition a complete chapter devoted to it. It discusses the TCP/IP model and usage of different protocols, such as HTTP, Whois, Time, SMTP, POP3, etc. I sincerely believe that if you try the programs in this chapter, you will grow in confidence for doing larger projects in Internet programming.

Armed with the knowledge of language elements, the C programmer enters the second phase. Here he wishes to use all that he has learned to create programs that match the ability of programs that he comes across in today's world. I am pointing toward programs in the Windows and Linux world. Chapters 16 to 20 are devoted to this. I would like to bring to your attention the fact that if you want to program Windows or Linux you need to have a very good grasp over the programming model used by each of these OSs. Windows messaging architecture and Linux signaling mechanism are the cases in point. Once you understand these thoroughly, the rest is just a matter of time. Chapters 16 to 20 have been written with this motive.

In Linux programming, the basic hurdle is in choosing the Linux distribution, compiler, editor, shell, libraries, etc. To get a head-start, you can follow the choices that I found most reasonable and simple. They have been mentioned in Chapter 20 and Appendix F. Once you are comfortable with Linux, you can explore the other choices on your own.

In the fourth edition of *Let Us C*, there were chapters on 'Disk Basics,' 'VDU Basics,' 'Graphics,' 'Mouse Programming,' and 'C and Assembly.' Although I used to like these chapters a lot, I had to make the decision to drop them since most of them were DOS-centric and would not be that useful in modern-day programming. Modern counterparts of all of these have been covered in Chapters 16 to 20. However, if you still need the chapters from previous editions they are available at *www.kicit.com/books/letusc/fourthedition*.

Also, all the programs present in the book are available in source code form at *www.kicit.com/books/letusc/sourcecode*. You are free to download them, improve them, change them, do whatever with them. If you wish to get solutions for the Exercises in the book, they are available in another book titled *Let Us C Solutions*.

If you like *Let Us C* and want to hear the complete video-recorded lectures created by me on C language (and other subjects like C++, VC++, .NET, Embedded Systems, etc.), then you can visit *quest.ksetindia.com* for more details.

Let Us C is as much your book as it is mine. So if you feel that I could have done a job better than what I have, or if you have any suggestions about what you would like to see in the next edition, please drop a line to *letuscsuggestions@kicit.com*.

All the best and happy programming!

CONTENTS

GETTING STARTED

Before we can begin to write serious programs in C, it would be interesting to find out what C really is, how it came into existence, and how it compares with other computer languages. In this chapter, we will briefly outline these issues.

Four important aspects of any language are the way it stores data, the way it operates upon this data, how it accomplishes input and output, and how it lets you control the sequence of execution of instructions in a program. We will discuss the first three of these building blocks in this chapter.

WHAT IS C?

C is a programming language developed at AT&T's Bell Laboratories in 1972. It was designed and written by a man named Dennis Ritchie. In the late seventies, C began to replace the more familiar languages of that time like PL/I, ALGOL, etc. No one pushed C. It wasn't made the 'official' Bell Labs language. Thus, without any advertisement, C's reputation spread and its pool of users grew. Ritchie seems to have been rather surprised that so many programmers preferred C to older languages like FORTRAN or PL/I, or the newer ones like Pascal and APL. But, that's what happened.

Possibly, C seems so popular is because it is reliable, simple, and easy to use. Moreover, in an industry where newer languages, tools, and technologies emerge and vanish day in and day out, a language that has survived for more than three decades has to be really good.

An opinion that is often heard today is, "C has already been superseded by languages like C++, C#, and Java, so why bother to learn C today." This is not true. There are several reasons for this:

(a) It is difficult for anyone to learn C++ or Java directly. This is because while learning these languages you have things like classes, objects, inheritance, polymorphism, templates, exception handling, references, etc., to deal with apart from knowing the actual language elements. Learning these complicated concepts when you are not even comfortable with the basic language elements is like putting the cart before the horse. Hence, one should first learn all the language elements very thoroughly using C language before migrating to C++, C#, or Java. Though this two-step learning process may take more time, at the end of it you will definitely find it worth the trouble.

(b) C++, C#, and Java make use of a principle called Object Oriented Programming (OOP) to organize the program. This organizing principle has lots of advantages to offer. But even while using this organizing principle you would still need a good hold over the language elements of C and the basic programming skills.

(c) Though many C++ and Java-based programming tools and frameworks have evolved over the years, the importance of C is still unchallenged because knowingly or unknowingly, while using these frameworks and tools, you would be still required to use the core C language elements—another good reason why one should learn C before C++, C#, or Java.

(d) Major parts of popular operating systems like Windows, UNIX, and Linux are still written in C. This is because even today, when it comes to performance (speed of execution) nothing beats C. Moreover, if one is to extend the operating system to work with new devices one needs to write device driver programs. These programs are exclusively written in C.

(e) Mobile devices, like cellular phones and palmtops, have become all the rage today. Also, common consumer devices, like microwave ovens, washing machines, and digital cameras are getting smarter by the day. This smartness comes from a microprocessor, an operating system, and a program embedded in these devices. These programs not only have to run fast but also have to work in limited amount of memory. No wonder such programs are written in C. With these constraints on time and space, C is the language of choice while building such operating systems and programs.

(f) You must have seen several professional 3D computer games where the user navigates some object, like a spaceship, and fires bullets at the invaders. The essence of all such games is speed. Needless to say, such games won't become popular if they takes a long time to move the spaceship or to fire a bullet. To match the expectations of the player the game has to react fast to the user inputs. This is where C language scores over other languages. Many popular gaming frameworks have been built using C language.

(g) At times, one is required to very closely interact with hardware devices. Since C provides several language elements that make this interaction feasible without compromising the performance it is the preferred choice of the programmer.

These should be very convincing reasons why you should adopt C as the first and the very important step in your quest for learning programming languages.

Steps in learning English language:

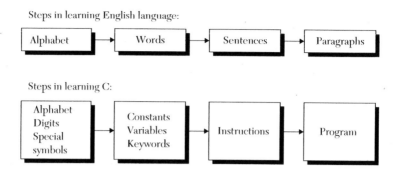

FIGURE 1.1

GETTING STARTED WITH C

Communicating with a computer involves speaking the language the computer understands, which immediately rules out English as the language of communication with a computer. However, there is a close analogy between learning the English language and learning C language. The classical method of learning English is to first learn the alphabet used in the language, then learn to combine these letters to form words, which, in turn, are combined to form sentences and sentences are combined to form paragraphs. Learning C is similar and easier. Instead of straight-away learning how to write programs, we must first know what alphabet, numbers, and special symbols are used in C, then how using them, constants, variables, and keywords are constructed, and finally, how are these combined to form an instruction. A group of instructions will be combined later on to form a program. This is illustrated in Figure 1.1.

The C Character Set

A character denotes any alphabet, digit, or special symbol used to represent information. Figure 1.2 shows the valid alphabets, numbers, and special symbols allowed in C.

Constants, Variables, and Keywords

The alphabets, numbers, and special symbols, when properly combined form constants, variables, and keywords. Let us see what 'constants' and 'variables' are in C. A constant is an entity that doesn't change, whereas, a variable is an entity that may change.

In any program we typically do lots of calculations. The results of these calculations are stored in a computer's memory. Like human memory, the

Alphabets	A, B, ..., Y, Z a, b, ..., y, z
Digits	0, 1, 2, 3, 4, 5, 6, 7, 8, 9
Special symbols	~ ' ! @ # % ^ & * ( ) _ - + = ! \ { } [ ] : ; " ' < > , . ? /

FIGURE 1.2

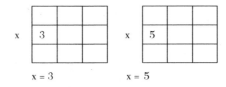

x = 3   x = 5

FIGURE 1.3

computer's memory also consists of millions of cells. The calculated values are stored in these memory cells. To make the retrieval and usage of these values easy, these memory cells (also called memory locations) are given names. Since the value stored in each location may change, the names given to these locations are called variable names. Consider the example shown in Figure 1.3.

Here, 3 is stored in a memory location and a name **x** is given to it. Then, we have assigned a new value 5 to the same memory location **x**. This would overwrite the earlier value 3, since a memory location can hold only one value at a time.

Since the location whose name is **x** can hold different values at different times, **x** is known as a variable. As compared to this, 3 or 5 do not change, and hence are known as constants.

Types of C Constants

C constants can be divided into two major categories:

(a) Primary Constants
(b) Secondary Constants

These constants are further categorized as shown in Figure 1.4.

At this stage, we would restrict our discussion to only Primary constants, namely, Integer, Real, and Character constants. Let us see the details of

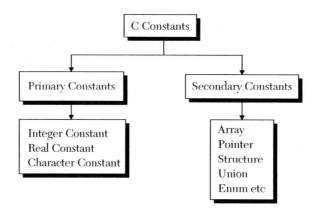

FIGURE 1.4

each of these constants. For constructing these different types of constants, certain rules have been laid down. These rules are as follows:

Rules for Constructing Integer Constants

(a) An integer constant must have at least one digit.
(b) It must not have a decimal point.
(c) It can be either positive or negative.
(d) If no sign precedes an integer constant, it is assumed to be positive.
(e) No commas or blanks are allowed within an integer constant.
(f) The allowable range for integer constants is −32768 to 32767.

Truly speaking, the range of an Integer constant depends upon the compiler. For a 16-bit compiler like Turbo C or Turbo C++, the range is −32768 to 32767. For a 32-bit compiler, the range would be even greater. Questions such as, what exactly do you mean by a 16-bit or a 32-bit compiler, what does the range of an Integer constant have to do with the type of compiler, etc., are discussed in detail in Chapter 16. Until that time it should be assumed that we are working with a 16-bit compiler.

```
Ex.:  426
      +782
      -8000
      -7605
```

Rules for Constructing Real Constants

Real constants are often called Floating Point constants. The real constants could be written in two forms—Fractional form and Exponential form.

The following rules must be observed while constructing real constants expressed in fractional form:

(a) A real constant must have at least one digit.
(b) It must have a decimal point.
(c) It could be either positive or negative.
(d) Default sign is positive.
(e) No commas or blanks are allowed within a real constant.

```
Ex.: +325.34
     426.0
     -32.76
     -48.5792
```

The exponential form of representation of real constants is usually used if the value of the constant is either too small or too large. It, however, doesn't restrict us in any way from using an exponential form of representation for other real constants.

In exponential form of representation, the real constant is represented in two parts. The part appearing before 'e' is called the mantissa, whereas the part following 'e' is called the exponent. Thus, 0.000342 can be represented in exponential form as 3.42e-4.

The following rules must be observed while constructing real constants expressed in exponential form:

(a) The mantissa part and the exponential part should be separated by a letter e or E.
(b) The mantissa part may have a positive or negative sign.
(c) The default sign of the mantissa part is positive.
(d) The exponent must have at least one digit, which must be a positive or negative integer. The default sign is positive.
(e) The range of real constants expressed in exponential form is −3.4e38 to 3.4e38.

```
Ex.: +3.2e-5
     4.1e8
     -0.2E+3
     -3.2e-5
```

Rules for Constructing Character Constants

(a) A character constant is a single alphabet, a single digit, or a single special symbol enclosed within single inverted quotes. Both the inverted commas should point to the left. For example, 'A' is a valid character constant whereas 'A' is not.

(b) The maximum length of a character constant is 1 character.

```
Ex.: 'A'
     'I'
     '5'
     '='
```

Types of C Variables

As we saw earlier, an entity that may vary during program execution is called a variable. Variable names are names given to locations in memory. These locations can contain integer, real, or character constants. In any language, the types of variables that it can support depend on the types of constants that it can handle. This is because a particular type of variable can hold only the same type of constant. For example, an integer variable can hold only an integer constant, a real variable can hold only a real constant, and a character variable can hold only a character constant.

The rules for constructing different types of constants are different. However, for constructing variable names of all types, the same set of rules apply. These rules are given as follows.

Rules for Constructing Variable Names

(a) A variable name is any combination of 1 to 31 alphabets, digits, or underscores. Some compilers allow variable names whose length could be up to 247 characters. Still, it would be safer to stick to the rule of 31 characters. Do not create unnecessarily long variable names as it adds to your typing effort.

(b) The first character in the variable name must be an alphabet or underscore.

(c) No commas or blanks are allowed within a variable name.

(d) No special symbol other than an underscore (as in **gross_sal**) can be used in a variable name.

```
Ex.: si_int
     m_hra
     pop_e_89
```

These rules remain the same for all the types of primary and secondary variables. Naturally, the question follows ... how is C able to differentiate between these variables? This is a rather simple matter. The C compiler is able to distinguish between the variable names by making it compulsory for you to declare the type of any variable name that you wish to use in a program. This type declaration is done at the beginning of the program. Following are some examples of type declaration statements:

```
Ex.: int si, m_hra ;
     float bassal ;
     char code ;
```

Since the maximum allowable length of a variable name is 31 characters, an enormous number of variable names can be constructed using the previously mentioned rules. It is a good practice to exploit this enormous choice in naming variables by using meaningful variable names.

Thus, if we want to calculate simple interest, it is always advisable to construct meaningful variable names like **prin**, **roi**, and **noy** to represent Principle, Rate of interest, and Number of years rather than using the variables **a**, **b**, **c**.

C Keywords

Keywords are the words whose meaning has already been explained to the C compiler (or in a broad sense to the computer). The keywords **cannot** be used as variable names because if we do so, we are trying to assign a new meaning to the keyword, which is not allowed by the computer. Some C compilers allow you to construct variable names that exactly resemble the keywords. However, it would be safer not to mix up the variable names and the keywords. The keywords are also called 'Reserved words.'

There are only 32 keywords available in C. Figure 1.5 gives a list of these keywords for your reference. A detailed discussion of each of these keywords will be taken up in later chapters wherever their use is relevant.

Note that compiler vendors (like Microsoft, Borland, etc.) provide their own keywords apart from the ones mentioned in Figure 1.5. These include extended keywords like **near**, **far**, **asm**, etc. Though it has been suggested

auto	double	int	struct
break	else	long	switch
case	enum	register	typedef
char	extern	return	union
const	float	short	unsigned
continue	for	signed	void
default	goto	sizeof	volatile
do	if	static	while

FIGURE 1.5

by the ANSI committee that every such compiler-specific keyword should be preceded by two underscores (as in __**asm**), not every vendor follows this rule.

THE FIRST C PROGRAM

Armed with the knowledge about the types of variables, constants, and keywords, the next logical step is to combine them to form instructions. However, instead of this, we will write our first C program now. Once we have done that we will see in detail the instructions that it made use of.

Before we begin with our first C program, do remember the following rules that are applicable to all C programs:

(a) Each instruction in a C program is written as a separate statement. Therefore, a complete C program will comprise a series of statements.

(b) The statements in a program must appear in the same order in which we wish them to be executed; unless of course the logic of the problem demands a deliberate 'jump' or transfer of control to a statement, which is out of sequence.

(c) Blank spaces may be inserted between two words to improve the readability of the statement. However, no blank spaces are allowed within a variable, constant, or keyword.

(d) All statements are entered in lower case letters.

(e) C has no specific rules for the position at which a statement is written. That's why it is often called a free-form language.

(f) Every C statement must end with a ;. Thus ; acts as a statement terminator.

Let us write down our first C program. It will simply calculate simple interest for a set of values representing principle, number of years, and rate of interest.

```
/* Calculation of simple interest */
/* Author gekay Date: 25/05/2006 */
# include <stdio.h>

void main( )
{
    int p, n ;
    float r, si ;
```

```
p = 1000 ;
n = 3 ;
r = 8.5 ;

/* formula for simple interest */
si = p * n * r / 100 ;
printf ( "%f" , si ) ;
}
```

Now a few useful tips about the program:

- Comments about the program should be enclosed within /* */. For example, the first two statements in our program are comments.
- Though comments are not necessary, it is a good practice to begin a program with a comment indicating the purpose of the program, its author, and the date on which the program was written.
- Any number of comments can be written at any place in the program. For example, a comment can be written before the statement, after the statement, or within the statement as shown below:

```
/* formula */ si = p * n * r / 100 ;
si = p * n * r / 100 ; /* formula */
si = p * n * r / /* formula */ 100 ;
```

- Sometimes it is not very obvious as to what a particular statement in a program accomplishes. At such times it is worthwhile mentioning the purpose of the statement (or a set of statements) using a comment. For example:

```
/* formula for simple interest */
si = p * n * r / 100 ;
```

- Often programmers seem to ignore the writing of comments. But when a team is building big software, well-commented code is almost essential for other team members to understand it.
- Although a lot of comments are probably not necessary in this program, it is usually the case that programmers tend to use too few comments rather than too many. An adequate number of comments can save hours of misery and suffering when you later try to figure out what the program does.
- The normal language rules do not apply to text written within /* .. */. Thus we can type this text in lower case, upper case, or a combination. This is because the comments are solely given for the understanding

of the programmer, or fellow programmers, and are completely ignored by the compiler.

— Comments cannot be nested. For example,

```
/* Cal of SI /* sam date 01/05/2005 */ */
```

is invalid.

— A comment can be split over more than one line, as in,

```
/* This is
   a jazzy
   comment */
```

Such a comment is often called a multiline comment.

— **main( )** is a collective name given to a set of statements. This name has to be **main( )**, it cannot be anything else. All statements that belong to **main( )** are enclosed within a pair of braces { } as shown below.

```
void main( )
{
    statement 1 ;
    statement 2 ;
    statement 3 ;
}
```

— Technically speaking, **main( )** is a function. Every function has a pair of parentheses ( ) associated with it.

— The way functions in a calculator return a value, similarly, functions in C also return a value. If we want that the **main( )** function should not return any value, then we should preced it with the keyword **void**. We will discuss functions and their working in great detail in Chapter 5.

— Any variable used in the program must be declared before using it. For example,

```
int p, n ;          /* declaration */
float r, si ;       /* declaration */
si = p * n * r / 100 ; /* usage */
```

— Any C statement always ends with a ;
    For example,

```
float r, si ;
r = 8.5 ;
```

- In the statement,

```
si = p * n * r / 100 ;
```

* and **/** are the arithmetic operators. The arithmetic operators available in C are **+**, **-**, *****, and **/**. C is very rich in operators. There are about 45 operators available in C. Surprisingly, there is no operator for exponentiation— a slip, which can be forgiven considering the fact that C has been developed by an individual, not by a committee.

- Once the value of **si** is calculated it needs to be displayed on the screen. Unlike other languages, C does not contain any instruction to display output on the screen. All output to screen is achieved using ready-made library functions. One such function is **printf( )**. We use it to display on the screen the value contained in **si**.

- For us to be able to use the **printf( )** function, it is necessary to use **# include <stdio.h>** at the beginning of the program. **# include** is a preprocessor directive. Its purpose will be clarified in Chapter 7. For now, use it whenever you use **printf( )**.

- The general form of the **printf( )** function is,

```
printf ( "<format string>", <list of variables> ) ;
```

```
<format string> can contain,
```

%f for printing real values
%d for printing integer values
%c for printing character values

In addition to format specifiers like **%f**, **%d**, and **%c**, the format string may also contain many other characters. These characters are printed as they are when the **printf( )** is executed.

The following are some examples of usage of the **printf( )** function:

```
printf ( "%f", si ) ;
printf ( "%d %d %f %f", p, n, r, si ) ;
printf ( "Simple interest = Rs. %f", si ) ;
printf ( "Prin = %d \nRate = %f", p, r ) ;
```

The output of the last statement would look like this:

```
Prin = 1000
Rate = 8.500000
```

What is '\n' doing in this statement? It is called newline and it takes the cursor to the next line. Therefore, you get the output split over two lines. '\n' is one of the several Escape Sequences available in C. These are discussed in detail in Chapter 11. Right now, all that we can say is '\n' comes in handy when we want to format the output properly on separate lines.

printf( ) can not only print values of variables, it can also print the result of an expression. An expression is nothing but a valid combination of constants, variables, and operators. Thus, 3, 3 + 2, c, and $a + b*c - d$ all are valid expressions. The results of these expressions can be printed as shown below:

```
printf ( "%d %d %d %d", 3, 3 + 2, c, a + b * c - d ) ;
```

Note that **3** and **c** also represent valid expressions.

COMPILATION AND EXECUTION

Once you have written the program, you need to type it and instruct the machine to execute it. To type your C program you need another program, called an Editor. Once the program has been typed, it needs to be converted to machine language (0s and 1s) before the machine can execute it. To carry out this conversion, we need another program, called a Compiler. Compiler vendors provide an Integrated Development Environment (IDE) which consists of an Editor as well as the Compiler.

There are several such IDEs available in the market targeted toward different operating systems. For example, Turbo C, Turbo C++, and Microsoft C are some of the popular compilers that work under MS-DOS; Visual C++ and Borland C++ are the compilers that work under Windows, whereas the gcc compiler works under Linux. Note that Turbo C++, Microsoft C++, and Borland C++ software also contain a C compiler bundled with them. If you are a beginner, you will be better off using a simple compiler like Turbo C or Turbo C++. Once you have mastered the language elements you can then switch over to more sophisticated compilers, like Visual C++ under Windows or gcc under Linux. Most of the programs in this book will work with all the compilers. Wherever there is a deviation, it will be mentioned.

Assuming that you are using a Turbo C or Turbo C++ compiler, here are the steps that you need to follow to compile and execute your first C program:

(a) Start the compiler at the **C>** prompt. The compiler (TC.EXE) is usually present in the **C:\TC\BIN** directory.

(b) Select **New** from the **File** menu.
(c) Type the program.
(d) Save the program using **F2** under a proper name (Program1.c).
(e) Use **Ctrl + F9** to compile and execute the program.
(f) Use **Alt + F5** to view the output.

Note that on compiling the program its machine language equivalent is stored as an EXE file (Program1.EXE) on the disk. This file is called an executable file. If we copy this file to another machine we can execute it there without being required to recompile it. In fact, the other machine need not even have a compiler to be able to execute the file.

A word of caution! If you run this program in the Turbo C++ compiler, you may get an error—"The function printf should have a prototype." To get rid of this error, perform the following steps and then recompile the program.

(a) Select the 'Options' menu and then select 'Compiler | C++ Options.' In the dialog box that pops up, select 'CPP always' in the 'Use C++ Compiler' options.
(b) Again select, the 'Options' menu and then select 'Environment | Editor.' Make sure that the default extension is 'C' rather than 'CPP.'

RECEIVING INPUT

In the program we just discussed we assumed the values of **p**, **n**, and **r** to be 1000, 3, and 8.5. Every time we run the program we will get the same value for simple interest. If we want to calculate simple interest for some other set of values, then we are required to make the relevant change in the program, and again compile and execute it. Thus the program is not general enough to calculate simple interest for any set of values without being required to make a change in the program. Moreover, if you distribute the EXE file of this program to somebody they would not be able to make changes in the program. Hence, it is a good practice to create a program that is general enough to work for any set of values.

To make the program general, the program itself should ask the user to supply the values of **p**, **n**, and **r** through the keyboard during execution. This can be achieved using a function called **scanf( )**. This function is a counterpart of the **printf( )** function. **printf( )** outputs the values to the screen whereas **scanf( )** receives them from the keyboard. This is illustrated in the following program.

```
/* Calculation of simple interest */
/* Author gekay Date 25/05/2005 */
# include <stdio.h>
void main( )
{
    int p, n ;
    float r, si ;
    printf ( "Enter values of p, n, r" ) ;
    scanf ( "%d %d %f", & p, & n, & r ) ;

    si = p * n * r / 100 ;
    printf ( "%f" , si ) ;
}
```

The first **printf( )** outputs the message 'Enter values of p, n, r' on the screen. Here we have not used any expression in **printf( )**, which means that using expressions in **printf( )** is optional.

Note that the ampersand (**&**) before the variables in the **scanf( )** function is a must. **&** is an 'Address of' operator. It gives the location number used by the variable in memory. When we say **& a**, we are telling **scanf( )** at which memory location it should store the value supplied by the user from the keyboard. The detailed working of the **&** operator will be taken up in Chapter 5.

Note that a blank, a tab, or a new line must separate the values supplied to **scanf( )**. Note that a blank is created using a spacebar, tab using the Tab key, and new line using the Enter key. This is shown below:

Ex.: The three values separated by a blank

```
1000 5 15.5
```

Ex.: The three values separated by a tab.

```
1000 5 15.5
```

Ex.: The three values separated by a new line.

```
1000
5
15.5
```

So much for the tips. How about another program to give you a feel of things?

```
/* Just for fun. Author: Bozo */
# include <stdio.h>
void main( )
```

```
{
    int num ;

    printf ( "Enter a number" ) ;
    scanf ( "%d", & num ) ;

    printf ( "Now I am letting you on a secret..." ) ;
    printf ( "You have just entered the number %d", num ) ;
}
```

C INSTRUCTIONS

Now that we have written a few programs, let us look at the instructions that we used in these programs. There are basically three types of instructions in C:

  (a) Type Declaration Instruction
  (b) Arithmetic Instruction
  (c) Control Instruction

The purpose of each of these instructions is as follows:

  (a) Type declaration instruction – To declare the type of variables used in a C program.
  (b) Arithmetic instruction – To perform arithmetic operations between con-stants and variables.
  (c) Control instruction – To control the sequence of execution of various state-ments in a C program.

Since the elementary C programs will usually contain only the type declaration and the arithmetic instructions; we will discuss only these two instructions at this stage. The other types of instructions will be discussed in detail in the subsequent chapters.

Type Declaration Instruction

This instruction is used to declare the type of variables being used in the program. Any variable used in the program must be declared before using it in any statement. The type declaration statement is written at the beginning of the **main( )** function.

```
Ex.: int bas ;
     float rs, grosssal ;
     char name, code ;
```

There are several subtle variations of the type declaration instruction. These are discussed as follows:

(a) While declaring the type of variable we can also initialize it as shown here:

```
int i = 10, j = 25 ;
float a = 1.5, b = 1.99 + 2.4 * 1.44 ;
```

(b) The order in which we define the variables is sometimes important, sometimes not. For example,

```
int i = 10, j = 25 ;
```

is the same as

```
int j = 25, j = 10 ;
```

However,

```
float a = 1.5, b = a + 3.1 ;
```

is alright, but

```
float b = a + 3.1, a = 1.5 ;
```

is not. This is because here we are trying to use **a** even before defining it.

(c) The following statements would work

```
int a, b, c, d ;
a = b = c = 10 ;
```

However, the following statement would not work

```
int a = b = c = d = 10 ;
```

Once again, we are trying to use **b** (to assign to **a**) before defining it.

Arithmetic Instruction

A C arithmetic instruction consists of a variable name on the left-hand side of = and variable names and constants on the right-hand side of =. The variables and constants appearing on the right-hand side of = are connected by arithmetic operators like **+**, **-**, *, and **/**.

```
Ex.: int ad ;
     float kot, deta, alpha, beta, gamma ;
     ad = 3200 ;
     kot = 0.0056 ;
     deta = alpha * beta / gamma + 3.2 * 2 / 5 ;
```

Here,

*, /, -, + are the arithmetic operators.
= is the assignment operator.
2, 5, and 3200 are integer constants.
3.2 and 0.0056 are real constants.
ad is an integer variable.
kot, **deta**, **alpha**, **beta**, and **gamma** are real variables.

The variables and constants are together called 'operands' that are operated upon by the 'arithmetic operators' and the result is assigned, using the assignment operator, to the variable on the left-hand side.

A C arithmetic statement could be of three types. These are as follows:

(a) Integer mode arithmetic statement—This is an arithmetic statement in which all operands are either integer variables or integer constants.

```
Ex.: int i, king, issac, noteit ;
     i = i + 1 ;
     king = issac * 234 + noteit - 7689 ;
```

(b) Real mode arithmetic statement—This is an arithmetic statement in which all operands are either real constants or real variables.

```
Ex.: float qbee, antink, si, prin, anoy, roi ;
     qbee = antink + 23.123 / 4.5 * 0.3442 ;
     si = prin * anoy * roi / 100.0 ;
```

(c) Mixed mode arithmetic statement—This is an arithmetic statement in which some of the operands are integers and some of the operands are real.

```
Ex.: float si, prin, anoy, roi, avg ;
     int a, b, c, num ;
     si = prin * anoy * roi / 100.0 ;
     avg = ( a + b + c + num ) / 4 ;
```

It is very important to understand how the execution of an arithmetic statement takes place. First, the right-hand side is evaluated using constants and the numerical values stored in the variable names. This value is then assigned to the variable on the left-hand side.

Although arithmetic instructions look easy to use, one often commits mistakes in writing them. Let us take a closer look at these statements. Note the following points carefully.

(a) C allows only one variable on the left-hand side of **=**. That is, **z = k ∗ l** is legal, whereas **k ∗ l = z** is illegal.

(b) In addition to the division operator, C also provides a modular division operator. This operator returns the remainder on dividing one integer with another. Thus, the expression 10 / 2 yields 5, whereas, 10 % 2 yields 0. Note that the modulus operator (**%**) cannot be applied on a float. Also, note that on using % the sign of the remainder is always the same as the sign of the numerator. Thus, −5 % 2 yields −1, whereas, 5 % −2 yields 1.

(c) An arithmetic instruction is at times used for storing character constants in character variables.

```
char a, b, d ;
a = 'F' ;
b = 'G' ;
d = '+' ;
```

When we do this, the ASCII values of the characters are stored in the variables. ASCII values are used to represent any character in memory. The ASCII values of 'F' and 'G' are 70 and 71 (refer to the ASCII Table in Appendix E).

(d) Arithmetic operations can be performed on **int**s, **float**s, and **char**s. Thus the statements,

```
char x, y ;
int z ;
x = 'a' ;
y = 'b' ;
z = x + y ;
```

are perfectly valid, since the addition is performed on the ASCII values of the characters and not on the characters themselves. The ASCII values of 'a' and 'b' are 97 and 98, and therefore can definitely be added.

(e) No operator is assumed to be present. It must be written explicitly. In the following example, the multiplication operator after b must be explicitly written.

```
a = c.d.b(xy)                    usual arithmetic statement
b = c * d * b * ( x * y )    C statement
```

(f) Unlike other high-level languages, there is no operator for performing exponentiation operation. Thus, the following statements are
invalid.

```
a = 3 ** 2 ;
b = 3 ˆ 2 ;
```

If we want to do the exponentiation, we can get it done this way:

```
# include <math.h>
# include <stdio.h>

void main( )
{
    int a ;
    a = pow ( 3, 2 ) ;
    printf ( "%d", a ) ;
}
```

Here, the **pow( )** function is a standard library function. It is being
used to raise 3 to the power of 2. **# include <math.h>** is a prepro-
cessor directive. It is being used here to ensure that the **pow( )**
function works correctly. We would learn more about standard
library functions in Chapter 5 and about preprocessors in Chapter 7.

(g) In addition to +, -, *, and /, there exists one more arithmetic operator
in C. It is called a modular division operator, and it is represented
using the symbol % . Unlike /, which returns the quotient, % returns
the remainder. Thus 5 % 3 yields 2 as the remainder.

Integer and Float Conversions

In order to effectively develop C programs, it will be necessary to understand
the rules that are used for the implicit conversion of floating point and integer
values in C. These are mentioned in the following list. Note them carefully.

(a) An arithmetic operation between an integer and integer always yields
an integer result.

(b) An operation between a real and real always yields a real result.

(c) An operation between an integer and real always yields a real result.
In this operation, the integer is first promoted to a real and then the
operation is performed. Hence, the result is real.

Operation	Result	Operation	Result
5 / 2	2	2 / 5	0
5.0 / 2	2.500000	2.0 / 5	0.400000
5 / 2.0	2.500000	2 / 5.0	0.400000
5.0 / 2.0	2.500000	2.0 / 5.0	0.400000

FIGURE 1.6

A few practical examples shown in Figure 1.6 will put the issue beyond doubt.

Type Conversion in Assignments

It may so happen that the type of the expression and the type of the variable on the left-hand side of the assignment operator may not be the same. In such a case, the value of the expression is promoted or demoted depending on the type of the variable on the left-hand side of =.

For example, consider the following assignment statements.

```
int i ;
float b ;
i = 3.5 ;
b = 30 ;
```

Here, in the first assignment statement, although the expression's value is a **float** (3.5), it cannot be stored in **i** since it is an **int**. In such a case, the **float** is demoted to an **int** and then its value is stored. Therefore, what gets stored in **i** is 3. The exact opposite happens in the next statement. Here, 30 is promoted to 30.000000 and then stored in **b**, since **b** being a **float** variable cannot hold anything except a **float** value.

Instead of a simple expression used in the above examples, if a complex expression occurs, the same rules still apply. For example, consider the following program fragment.

```
float a, b, c ;
int s ;
s = a * b * c / 100 + 32 / 4 - 3 * 1.1 ;
```

Here, in the assignment statement, some operands are **int**s whereas others are **float**s. As we know, during evaluation of the expression, the **int**s will be promoted to **float**s and the result of the expression will be a **float**. But when this **float** value is assigned to **s** it is again demoted to an **int** and then stored in **s**.

Arithmetic Instruction	Result	Arithmetic Inst.	Result
k = 2 / 9	0	a = 2 / 9	0.000000
k = 2.0 / 9	0	a = 2.0 / 9	0.222222
k = 2 / 9.0	0	a = 2 / 9.0	0.222222
k = 2.0 / 9.0	0	a = 2.0 / 9.0	0.222222
k = 9 / 2	4	a = 9 / 2	4.000000
k = 9.0 / 2	4	a = 9.0 / 2	4.500000
k = 9 / 2.0	4	a = 9 / 2.0	4.500000
k = 9.0 / 2.0	4	a = 9.0 / 2.0	4.500000

FIGURE 1.7

Observe the results of the arithmetic statements shown in Figure 1.7. It has been assumed that **k** is an integer variable and **a** is a real variable.

Note that although the following statements give the same result, 0, the results are obtained differently.

```
k = 2 / 9 ;
k = 2.0 / 9 ;
```

In the first statement, since both 2 and 9 are integers, the result is an integer, i.e., 0. This 0 is then assigned to **k**. In the second statement, 9 is promoted to 9.0 and then the division is performed. Division yields 0.222222. However, this cannot be stored in **k**, **k** being an **int**. Hence, it gets demoted to 0 and then stored in **k**.

HIERARCHY OF OPERATIONS

While executing an arithmetic statement that has two or more operators, we may have some problems as to how exactly it gets executed. For example, does the expression $2* \times -3* y$ correspond to $(2x) - (3y)$ or to $2(x - 3y)$? Similarly, does A / B * C correspond to A / (B * C) or to (A / B) * C? To answer these questions satisfactorily, one has to understand the 'hierarchy' of operations. The priority or precedence in which the operations in an arithmetic statement are performed is called the hierarchy of operations. The hierarchy of commonly used operators is shown in Figure 1.8.

Now a few tips about usage of operators in general.

(a) Within parentheses the same hierarchy as mentioned in Figure 1.8 is operative. Also, if there are more than one set of parentheses, the operations within the innermost parentheses will be performed first, followed by the operations within the second innermost pair, and so on.

Priority	Operators	Description
1st	* / %	multiplication, division, modular division
2nd	+ -	addition, subtraction
3rd	=	Assignment

FIGURE 1.8

(b) We must always remember to use pairs of parentheses. A careless imbalance of the right and left parentheses is a common error. The best way to avoid this error is to type ( ) and then type an expression inside it.

A few examples will clarify the issue further.

Example 1.1: Determine the hierarchy of operations and evaluate the following expression, assuming that **i** is an integer variable:

```
i = 2 * 3 / 4 + 4 / 4 + 8 - 2 + 5 / 8
```

A stepwise evaluation of this expression is shown below:

```
i = 2 * 3 / 4 + 4 / 4 + 8 - 2 + 5 / 8
i = 6 / 4 + 4 / 4 + 8 - 2 + 5 / 8        operation: *
i = 1 + 4 / 4 + 8 - 2 + 5 / 8           operation: /
i = 1 + 1+ 8 - 2 + 5 / 8                operation: /
i = 1 + 1 + 8 - 2 + 0                   operation: /
i = 2 + 8 - 2 + 0                       operation: +
i = 10 - 2 + 0                          operation: +
i = 8 + 0                              operation: -
i = 8                                  operation: +
```

Note that 6 / 4 gives 1 and not 1.5. This happens because 6 and 4 are both integers and therefore would evaluate to only an integer constant. Similarly 5 / 8 evaluates to zero, since 5 and 8 are integer constants and therefore must return an integer value.

Example 1.2: Determine the hierarchy of operations and evaluate the following expression, assuming that **kk** is a float variable:

```
kk = 3 / 2 * 4 + 3 / 8 + 3
```

A stepwise evaluation of this expression is shown below:

```
kk = 3 / 2 * 4 + 3 / 8 + 3
kk = 1 * 4 + 3 / 8 + 3        operation: /
```

Algebric Expression	C Expression
a x b – c x d	a * b – c * d
(m + n) (a + b)	(m + n) * (a + b)
$3x^2 + 2x + 5$	3 * x * x + 2 * x + 5
$\dfrac{(a + b + c)}{d + e}$	(a + b + c) / (d + e)
$\left[\dfrac{2BY}{d + 1} - \dfrac{x}{3(z + y)}\right]$	2 * b * y / (d + 1) – x / 3 * (z + y)

FIGURE 1.9

```
kk = 4 + 3 / 8 + 3          operation: *
kk = 4 + 0 + 3              operation: /
kk = 4 + 3                  operation: +
kk = 7                      operation: +
```

Note that 3 / 8 gives zero, again for the same reason mentioned in the previous example.

All operators in C are ranked according to their precedence. And mind you, there are as many as 45 odd operators in C, and these can affect the evaluation of an expression in subtle and unexpected ways if we aren't careful. Unfortunately, there are no simple rules that one can follow, such as "BODMAS," that tells algebra students in which order does an expression evaluate. We have not encountered many out of these 45 operators, so we won't pursue the subject of precedence any further here. However, it can be realized at this stage that it would be almost impossible to remember the precedence of all these operators. So a full-fledged list of all operators and their precedence is given in Appendix A. This may sound daunting, but when its contents are absorbed in small bites, it becomes more palatable.

So far we have seen how the computer evaluates an arithmetic statement written in C. But our knowledge would be incomplete unless we know how to convert a general arithmetic statement to a C statement. C can handle any complex expression with ease. Some of the examples of C expressions are shown in Figure 1.9.

Associativity of Operators

When an expression contains two operators of equal priority the tie between them is settled using the associativity of the operators. Associativity can be of two types—Left to Right or Right to Left. Left to Right associativity means that the left operand must be unambiguous. Unambiguous in what sense? It must not be involved in the evaluation of any other subexpression. Similarly, in the case of Right to Left associativity, the right operand must be unambiguous. Let us understand this with an example.

Consider the expression

```
a = 3 / 2 * 5 ;
```

Here there is a tie between operators of same priority, that is between / and *. This tie is settled using the associativity of / and *. But both enjoy Left to Right associativity. Figure 1.10 shows for each operator which operand is unambiguous and which is not.

Since both / and * have L to R associativity and only / has an unambiguous left operand (necessary condition for L to R associativity) it is performed earlier.

Consider one more expression

```
a = b = 3 ;
```

Here, both assignment operators have the same priority and same associativity (Right to Left). Figure 1.11 shows for each operator which operand is unambiguous and which is not.

Operator	Left	Right	Remark
/	3	2 or 2 *t 5	Left operand is unambiguous, Right is not
*	3 / 2 or 2	5	Right operand is unambiguous, Left is not

FIGURE 1.10

Operator	Left	Right	Remark
=	a	b or b = 3	Left operand is unambiguous, Right is not
=	b or a = b	3	Right operand is unambiguous, Left is not

FIGURE 1.11

Operator	Left	Right	Remark
*	a	B	Both operands are unambiguous
/	c	D	Both operands are unambiguous

FIGURE 1.12

Since both = have R to L associativity and only the second = has an unambiguous right operand (necessary condition for R to L associativity) the second = is performed earlier.

Consider yet another expression

```
z = a * b + c / d;
```

Here, * and / enjoy same priority and same associativity (Left to Right). Figure 1.12 shows for each operator which operand is unambiguous and which is not.

Here, since the left operands for both operators are unambiguous, the Compiler is free to perform the * or / operation as per its convenience since no matter which is performed earlier the result will be same.

Appendix A gives the associativity of all the operators available in C.

CONTROL INSTRUCTIONS IN C

As the name suggests, the 'Control Instructions' enable us to specify the order in which the various instructions in a program are executed by the computer. In other words, the control instructions determine the 'flow of control' in a program. There are four types of control instructions in C. They are:

(a) Sequence Control Instruction
(b) Selection or Decision Control Instruction
(c) Repetition or Loop Control Instruction
(d) Case Control Instruction

The Sequence control instruction ensures that the instructions are executed in the same order in which they appear in the program. Decision and Case control instructions allow the computer to make a decision as to which instruction is executed next. The Loop control instruction helps the computer to execute a group of statements repeatedly. In the following chapters, we are going to learn these instructions in detail. Try your hand at the Exercises presented on the following pages before proceeding to the next chapter, which discusses the decision control instruction.

SUMMARY

(a) The three primary constants and variable types in C are integer, float, and character.
(b) A variable name can be a maximum 31 characters.
(c) Do not use a keyword as a variable name.
(d) An expression may contain any sequence of constants, variables, and operators.
(e) Operators having equal precedence are evaluated using associativity.
(f) Left to right associativity means that the left operand of an operator must be unambiguous whereas right to left associativity means that the right operand of an operator must be unambiguous.
(g) Input/output in C can be achieved using **scanf( )** and **printf( )** functions.

EXERCISES

[A] Which of the following are invalid variable names and why?

```
BASICSALARY          _basic       basic-hra
#MEAN                group.       422
population in 2006   over time    mindovermatter
FLOAT                hELLO        queue.
team'svictory        Plot #3      2015_DDay
```

[B] Point out the errors, if any, in the following C statements:

(a) int = 314.562*150;
(b) name = 'Ajay';
(c) varchar = '3';
(d) $3.14 * r * r * h = vol\_of\_cyl$;
(e) $k = (a * b)(c + (2.5a + b)(d + e)$;
(f) m_inst = rate of interest ° amount in rs;
(g) si = principal * rate of interest * number of years/100;
(h) area = $3.14 * r * *2$;
(i) volume = $3.14 * r^2 * h$;

(j) k = ((a * b) + c)(2.5 * a + b);
(k) a = b = 3 = 4;
(l) count = count + 1;
(m) date = '2 Mar 04';

[C] Evaluate the following expressions and show their hierarchy.

(a) g = big/2 + big*4/big − big + abc/3;
     (abc = 2.5, big = 2, assume **g** to be a float)

(b) on = ink * act/2 + 3/2*act + 2 + tig;
     (ink = 4, act = 1, tig = 3.2, assume **on** to be an int)

(c) s = qui * add/4 − 6/2 + 2/3*6/god;
     (qui = 4, add = 2, god = 2, assume **s** to be an int)

(d) s = 1/3 * a/4 − 6/2 + 2/3*6/g;
     (a = 4, g = 3, assume **s** to be an int)

[D] Fill the following table for the expressions given and then evaluate the result. A sample entry has been filled in the table for expression (a).

Operator	Left	Right	Remark
/	10	5 or 5/2/1	Left operand is unambiguous, Right is not
..	..	..	..

(a) g = 10/5/2/1;
(b) b = 3/2 + 5*4/3;
(c) a = b = c = 3 + 4;

[E] Convert the following equations into corresponding C statements.

(a) $Z = \dfrac{8.8(a + b)2/c − 0.5 + 2a/(q + r)}{(a + b)*(1/m)}$

(b) $X = \dfrac{−b + (b*b) + 24ac}{2a}$

(c) $R = \dfrac{2v + 6.22(c + d)}{g + v}$

(d) $A = \dfrac{7.7b(xy + a)/c − 0.8 + 2b}{(x + a)(1/y)}$

[F] What will be the output of the following programs:

(a)
```
# include <stdio.h>
void main( )
{
    int i = 2, j = 3, k, l ;
    float a, b ;
    k = i / j * j ;
    l = j / i * i ;
    a = i / j * j ;
    b = j / i * i ;
    printf( "%d %d %f %f", k, l, a, b ) ;
}
```

(b)
```
# include <stdio.h>
void main( )
{
    int a, b ;
    a = -3 - - 3 ;
    b = -3 - - ( - 3 ) ;
    printf ( "a = %d b = %d", a, b ) ;
}
```

(c)
```
# include <stdio.h>
void main( )
{
    float a = 5, b = 2 ;
    int c ;
    c = a % b ;
    printf ( "%d", c ) ;
}
```

(d)
```
# include <stdio.h>
void main( )
{
    printf ( "nn \n\n nn\n" ) ;
    printf ( "nn /n/n nn/n" ) ;
}
```

(e)
```
# include <stdio.h>
void main( )
{
    int a, b ;
    printf ( "Enter values of a and b" ) ;
```

```
    scanf ( " %d %d ", &a, &b ) ;
    printf ( "a = %d b = %d", a, b ) ;
}
```

[G] Pick the correct answer for each of the following questions:

(a) C language has been developed by
    (1) Ken Thompson
    (2) Dennis Ritchie
    (3) Peter Norton
    (4) Martin Richards

(b) C can be used on
    (1) Only MS-DOS operating systems
    (2) Only Linux operating systems
    (3) Only Windows operating systems
    (4) All the above

(c) C programs are converted into machine language with the help of
    (1) An Editor
    (2) A compiler
    (3) An operating system
    (4) None of the above

(d) The real constant in C can be expressed in which of the following forms
    (1) Fractional form only
    (2) Exponential form only
    (3) ASCII form only
    (4) Both Fractional and Exponential forms

(e) A character variable can at a time store
    (1) 1 character
    (2) 8 characters
    (3) 254 characters
    (4) None of the above

(f) The statement **char ch** = '**Z**' will store in **ch**
    (1) The character Z
    (2) ASCII value of Z
    (3) Z along with the single inverted commas
    (4) Both (1) and (2)

(g) Which of the following is NOT a character constant
    (1) 'Thank You'
    (2) 'Enter values of P, N, R'
    (3) '23.56E-03'
    (4) All the above

(h) The maximum value that an integer constant can have is
  (1) −32767
  (2) 32767
  (3) 1.7014e + 38
  (4) −1.7014e + 38

(i) A C variable cannot start with
  (1) An alphabet
  (2) A number
  (3) A special symbol other than underscore
  (4) Both (2) and (3) above

(j) Which of the following statements is wrong
  (1) mes = 123.56 ;
  (2) con = 'T' ° 'A';
  (3) this = 'T' ° 20;
  (4) 3 + a = b;

(k) Which of the following shows the correct hierarchy of arithmetic operators in C
  (1) **, * or /, + or −
  (2) **, *, /, +, −
  (3) **, /, *, +, −
  (4) / or *, − or +

(l) In b = 6.6/a + 2 * n; which operation will be performed first?
  (1) 6.6 / a
  (2) a + 2
  (3) 2 * n
  (4) Depends upon the compiler

(m) Which of the following is allowed in a C Arithmetic instruction
  (1) [ ]
  (2) { }
  (3) ( )
  (4) None of the above

(n) Which of the following statements is FALSE
  (1) Each new C instruction has to be written on a separate line
  (2) Usually all C statements are entered in lower case letters
  (3) Blank spaces may be inserted between two words in a C statement
  (4) Blank spaces cannot be inserted within a variable name

(o) If a is an integer variable, a = 5/2; will return a value
  (1) 2.5
  (2) 3
  (3) 2
  (4) 0

(p) The expression, a = 7/22 * (3.14 + 2) * 3/5; evaluates to
    (1) 8.28
    (2) 6.28
    (3) 3.14
    (4) 0

(q) The expression, a = 30 * 1000 + 2768; evaluates to
    (1) 32768
    (2) −32768
    (3) 113040
    (4) 0

(r) The expression x = 4 + 2% − 8 evaluates to
    (1) −6
    (2) 6
    (3) 4
    (4) None of the above

(s) Hierarchy decides which operator
    (1) is most important
    (2) is used first
    (3) is fastest
    (4) operates on largest numbers

(t) An integer constant in C must have
    (1) At least one digit
    (2) At least one decimal point
    (3) A comma along with digits
    (4) Digits separated by commas

(u) In C, a variable cannot contain
    (1) Blank spaces
    (2) Hyphen
    (3) Decimal point
    (4) All the above

(v) Which of the following is FALSE in C
    (1) Keywords can be used as variable names
    (2) Variable names can contain a digit
    (3) Variable names do not contain a blank space
    (4) Capital letters can be used in variable names

(w) In C, arithmetic instruction cannot contain
    (1) variables
    (2) constants
    (3) variable names on the right side of =
    (4) constants on the left side of =

(x) Which of the following is the odd one out
   (1) +
   (2) −
   (3) /
   (4) **
(y) What will be the value of **d** (assume **d** to be a **float**) after the operation **d = 2/7.0**?
   (1) 0
   (2) 0.2857
   (3) Cannot be determined
   (4) None of the above

[**H**] Write C programs for the following:

(a) Ramesh's base salary is input through the keyboard. His hospitaliza-tion allowance is 40% of base salary, and rent allowance is 20% of base salary. Write a program to calculate his gross salary.
(b) The distance between two cities (in km.) is input through the key-board. Write a program to convert and print this distance in meters, feet, inches, and centimeters.
(c) If the marks obtained by a student in five different subjects are input through the keyboard, find out the aggregate marks and percentage marks obtained by the student. Assume that the maximum marks that can be obtained by a student in each subject is 100.
(d) The temperature of a city in Fahrenheit degrees is input through the keyboard. Write a program to convert this temperature into Centigrade degrees.
(e) The length and breadth of a rectangle and radius of a circle are input through the keyboard. Write a program to calculate the area and perimeter of the rectangle, and the area and circumference of the circle.
(f) Two numbers are input through the keyboard into two locations, C and D. Write a program to interchange the contents of C and D.
(g) If a five-digit number is input through the keyboard, write a program to calculate the sum of its digits.
   (Hint: Use the modulus operator '%')
(h) If a five-digit number is input through the keyboard, write a program to reverse the number.
(i) If a four-digit number is input through the keyboard, write a program to obtain the sum of the first and last digit of this number.

(j) In a town, the percentage of men is 52. The percentage of total literacy is 48. If total percentage of literate men is 35 of the total population, write a program to find the total number of illiterate men and women if the population of the town is 80,000.

(k) A cashier has currency notes in denominations of 10, 50, and 100. If the amount to be withdrawn is input through the keyboard in hundreds, find the total number of currency notes of each denomination the cashier will have to give to the withdrawer.

(l) If the total selling price of 15 items and the total profit earned on them is input through the keyboard, write a program to find the cost price of one item.

(m) If a five-digit number is input through the keyboard, write a program to print a new number by adding one to each of its digits. For example, if the number that is input is 12391, then the output should be displayed as 23502.

Chapter 2

THE DECISION CONTROL STRUCTURE

W e all need to alter our actions in the face of changing circumstances. If the weather is fine, then we can go for a stroll. If the highway is busy, we can take a different route. If the pitch takes a spin, we could win the match. If she says no, you will look elsewhere. If you like this book, there will be another edition. You may notice that all these decisions depend on some condition being met.

C language must also be able to perform different sets of actions depending on the circumstances. In fact, this is what makes it worth its salt. C has three major decision-making instructions—the **if** statement, the **if-else** statement, and the **switch** statement. A fourth, somewhat less-important structure is the one that uses conditional operators. In this chapter, we will explore all these ways (except **switch**, which has a separate chapter devoted to it) in which a C program can react to changing circumstances.

DECISIONS! DECISIONS!

In the programs written in Chapter 1, we used sequence control structure in which the various steps are executed sequentially, i.e., in the same order in which they appear in the program. In fact, to execute the instructions sequentially, we don't have to do anything at all. By default, the instructions in a program are executed sequentially. However, in serious programming situations, seldom do we want the instructions to be executed sequentially. Many a time we want a set of instructions executed in one situation, and an entirely different set of instructions executed in another situation. This kind of situation is dealt with in C programs using a decision control instruction. As mentioned earlier, a decision control instruction can be implemented in C using:

(a) The **if** statement
(b) The **if-else** statement
(c) The conditional operators

Now let us learn each of these and their variations in turn.

THE *IF* STATEMENT

Like most languages, C uses the keyword **if** to implement the decision control instruction. The general form of the **if** statement looks like this:

```
if ( this condition is true )
    execute this statement;
```

this expression	is true if
x == y	x is equal to y
x != y	x is not equal to y
x < y	x is less than y
x > y	x is g reater than y
x <= y	x is less than or equal to y
x >= y	x is g reater than or equal to y

FIGURE 2.1

The keyword **if** tells the compiler that what follows is a decision control instruction. The condition following the keyword **if** is always enclosed within a pair of parentheses. If the condition, whatever it is, is true, then the statement is executed. If the condition is not true, then the statement is not executed; instead the program skips past it. But how do we express the condition itself in C? And how do we evaluate its truth or falsity? As a general rule, we express a condition using C's 'relational' operators. The relational operators allow us to compare two values to see whether they are equal to each other, unequal, or whether one is greater than the other. Figure 2.1 shows how they look and how they are evaluated in C.

The relational operators should be familiar to you except for the equality operator == and the inequality operator !=. Note that = is used for assignment, whereas == is used for comparison of two quantities. Here is a simple program, which demonstrates the use of **if** and the relational operators.

```
/* Demonstration of if statement */
# include <stdio.h>
main( )
{
    int num;

    printf ("Enter a number less than 10") ;
    scanf ( "%d", &num ) ;

    if( num < 10 )
        printf ( "What an obedient servant you are !" ) ;
}
```

On execution of this program, if you type a number less than 10, you get a message on the screen through **printf( )**. If you type some other number the

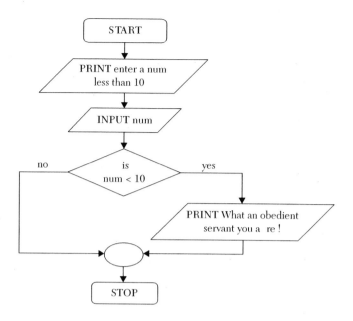

FIGURE 2.2

program doesn't do anything. The flowchart given in Figure 2.2 will help you understand the flow of control in the program.

To make you comfortable with the decision control instruction, the following example has been given. Study it carefully before reading further. To help you understand it easily, the program is accompanied by an appropriate flowchart in Figure 2.3.

Example 2.1: While purchasing certain items, a discount of 10% is offered if the quantity purchased is more than 1000. If quantity and price per item are input through the keyboard, write a program to calculate the total expenses.

```
/* Calculation of total expenses */
# include <stdio.h>
main( )
{
    int qty, dis = 0;
    float rate, tot;
    printf ( "Enter quantity and rate" ) ;
    scanf ( "%d %f", &qty, &rate ) ;

    if( qty > 1000 )
        dis = 10;
```

```
    tot = ( qty * rate ) - ( qty * rate * dis / 100 ) ;
    printf ( "Total expenses = Rs. %f", tot ) ;
}
```

Here is some sample interaction with the program.

```
Enter quantity and rate 1200 15.50
Total expenses = Rs. 16740.000000

Enter quantity and rate 200 15.50
Total expenses = Rs. 3100.000000
```

In the first run of the program, the condition evaluates to true, as 1200 (value of **qty**) is greater than 1000. Therefore, the variable **dis**, which was earlier set to 0, now gets a new value 10. Using this new value, total expenses are calculated and printed.

In the second run, the condition evaluates to false, as 200 (the value of **qty**) isn't greater than 1000. Thus, **dis**, which is earlier set to 0, remains 0,

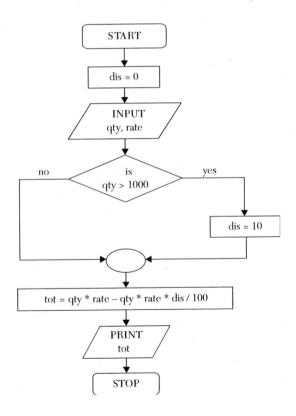

FIGURE 2.3

and hence the expression after the minus sign evaluates to zero, thereby offering no discount.

Is the statement **dis = 0** necessary? The answer is yes, since in C, a variable, if not specifically initialized, contains some unpredictable value (garbage value).

The Real Thing

We mentioned earlier that the general form of the **if** statement is as follows:

```
if ( condition )
    statement ;
```

Truly speaking, the general form is as follows:

```
if ( expression )
    statement ;
```

Here the expression can be any valid expression, including a relational expression. We can even use arithmetic expressions in the **if** statement. For example, all of the following **if** statements are valid:

```
if ( 3 + 2 % 5 )
    printf ( "This works" ) ;

if ( a = 10 )
    printf ( "Even this works" ) ;

if ( -5 )
    printf ( "Surprisingly even this works" ) ;
```

Note that in C, a nonzero value is considered true, whereas a 0 is considered false. In the first **if**, the expression evaluates to **5** and since **5** is nonzero it is considered true. Hence, the **printf( )** gets executed.

In the second **if**, 10 gets assigned to **a** so the **if** is now reduced to **if (a)** or **if (10)**. Since 10 is nonzero, it is true, therefore, **printf( )** goes to work again.

In the third **if**, −5 is a nonzero number, hence it is true. So, again, **printf( )** goes to work. In place of −5, even if a float like 3.14 were used it would be considered true. So the issue is not whether the number is an integer or float, or whether it is positive or negative. The issue is whether it is zero or nonzero.

Multiple Statements within *if*

It may so happen that in a program we want more than one statement to be executed if the expression following **if** is satisfied. If such multiple statements are executed, then they must be placed within a pair of braces, as illustrated in the following example.

Example 2.2: The current year and the year in which the employee joined the organization are entered through the keyboard. If the number of years for which the employee has served the organization is greater than 3, then a bonus of Rs. 2500/- is given to the employee. If the years of service are not greater than 3, then the program should do nothing (see Fig. 2.4).

```
/* Calculation of bonus */
# include <stdio.h>
main( )
{
    int bonus, cy, yoj, yos ;

    printf ( "Enter current year and year of joining" ) ;
    scanf ( "%d %d", &cy, &yoj ) ;

    yos = cy - yoj;

    if( yos > 3 )
    {
        bonus = 2500 ;
        printf ( "Bonus = Rs. %d", bonus ) ;
    }
}
```

Observe that here the two statements to be executed, on satisfaction of the condition, that have been enclosed within a pair of braces. If a pair of braces is not used, then the C compiler assumes that the programmer wants only the next immediate statement after the **if** to be executed on satisfaction of the condition. In other words, we can say that the default scope of the **if** statement is the next immediate statement after it.

THE *IF-ELSE* STATEMENT

The **if** statement by itself will execute a single statement, or a group of statements, when the expression following **if** evaluates to true. It does nothing when the expression evaluates to false. Can we execute one group of

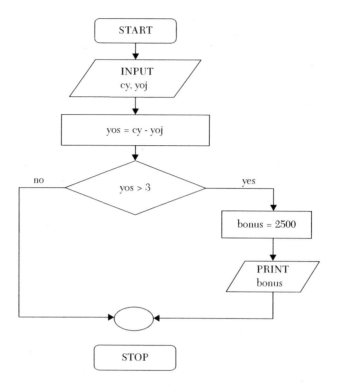

FIGURE 2.4

statements if the expression evaluates to true and another group of state-ments if the expression evaluates to false? Of course! This is the purpose of the **else** statement that is demonstrated in the following example:

Example 2.3: In an Indian company, an employee is paid as follows (see Fig. 2.5):

If his base salary is less than Rs. 1500, then HRA = 10% of base salary and HA = 90% of base salary. If his salary is either equal to or above Rs. 1500, then HRA = Rs. 500 and HA = 98% of base salary. If the employee's salary is input through the keyboard, write a program to find his gross salary. (NOTE: Rs. = rupees; HRA = Housing/Rent Allowance; HA = Hospitalization Allowance.)

```
/* Calculation of gross salary */
# include <stdio.h>
main( )
{
    float bs, gs, da, hra;
```

```
printf ( "Enter basic salary" ) ;
scanf ( "%f", &bs ) ;

if ( bs < 1500 )
{
    hra = bs * 10 / 100 ;
    da = bs * 90 / 100 ;
}
else
{
    hra = 500 ;
    da = bs * 98 / 100 ;
}

gs = bs + hra + da;
printf ( "gross salary = Rs. %f", gs ) ;
}
```

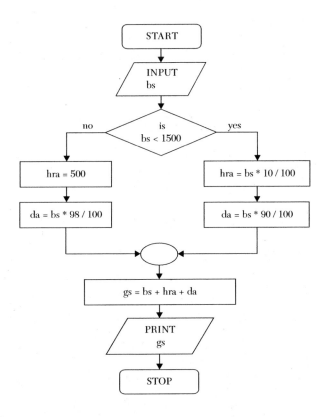

FIGURE 2.5

A few points worth noting:

(a) The group of statements after the **if**, up to but not including the **else**, is called an 'if block.' Similarly, the statements after the **else** form the 'else block.'

(b) Notice that the **else** is written exactly below the **if**. The statements in the if block and those in the else block have been indented to the right. This formatting convention is followed throughout the book to enable you to understand the working of the program better.

(c) Had there been only one statement to be executed in the if block and only one statement in the else block, we could have dropped the pair of braces.

(d) As with the **if** statement, the default scope of **else** is also the statement immediately after the **else**. To override this default scope, a pair of braces, as shown in the previous example, must be used.

Nested *if -else*s

It is perfectly all right if we write an entire **if-else** construct within either the body of an **if** statement or the body of an **else** statement. This is called 'nesting' of **if**s. This is shown in the following program.

```
/* A quick demo of nested if-else */
# include <stdio.h>
main( )
{
    int i ;

    printf ( "Enter either 1 or 2" ) ;
    scanf ( "%d", &i ) ;

    if ( i == 1 )
          printf ( "You would go to heaven !" ) ;
    else
    {
        if ( i == 2 )
              printf ( "Hell was created with you in mind" );
        else
              printf ( "How about mother earth !" ) ;
    }
}
```

Note that the second **if-else** construct is nested in the first **else** statement. If the condition in the first **if** statement is false, then the condition in the second

if statement is checked. If it is false as well, then the final **else** statement is executed.

You can see in the program how each time an **if-else** construct is nested within another **if-else** construct, it is also indented to add clarity to the program. Inculcate this habit of indentation; otherwise, you will end up writing programs that nobody (you included) can understand easily at a later date. Note that whether we indent or do not indent the program, it doesn't alter the flow of execution of instructions in the program.

In the previous program, an **if-else** occurs within the **else** block of the first **if** statement. Similarly, in some other program, an **if-else** may occur in the **if** block as well. There is no limit on how deeply the **if**s and the **else**s can be nested.

Forms of *if*

The **if** statement can take any of the following forms:

```
(a)  if ( condition )
         do this ;
(b)  if ( condition )
     {
         do this ;
         and this ;
     }
(c)  if ( condition )
         do this ;
     else
         do this ;
(d)  if ( condition )
     {
         do this ;
         and this ;
     }
     else
     {
         do this ;
         and this ;
     }
(e)  if ( condition )
         do this ;
     else
     {
         if ( condition )
             do this ;
```

```
        else
        {
            do this ;
            and this ;
        }
    }
(f)  if ( condition )
    {
        if ( condition )
            do this ;
        else
        {
            do this ;
            and this ;
        }
    }
    else
        do this ;
```

USE OF LOGICAL OPERATORS

C allows usage of three logical operators, namely, && , ||, and !. These are read as 'AND,' 'OR,' and 'NOT' respectively.

There are several things to note about these logical operators. Most obviously, two of them are composed of double symbols: || and **&&** . Don't use the single symbol | and **&** . These single symbols also have a meaning. They are bitwise operators, which we will examine in Chapter 14.

The first two operators, **&&** and ||, allow two or more conditions to be combined in an **if** statement. Let us see how they are used in a program. Consider the following example.

Example 2.4: The marks obtained by a student in 5 different subjects are input through the keyboard. The student gets a division as per the following rules:

Percentage above or equal to 60—First division
Percentage between 50 and 59—Second division
Percentage between 40 and 49—Third division
Percentage less than 40—Fail

Write a program to calculate the division obtained by the student.

There are two ways in which we can write a program for this example. These methods are given as follows.

```c
/* Method -- I */
# include <stdio.h>
main( )
{
    int m1, m2, m3, m4, m5, per ;

    printf( "Enter marks in five subjects" ) ;
    scanf ( "%d %d %d %d %d", &m1, &m2, &m3, &m4, &m5 ) ;
    per = ( m1 + m2 + m3 + m4 + m5 ) / 500 * 100 ;
    if ( per >= 60 )
        printf ( "First division" ) ;
    else
    {
        if ( per >= 50 )
            printf ( "Second division" ) ;
        else
        {
            if ( per >= 40 )
                printf ( "Third division" ) ;
            else
                printf ( "Fail" ) ;
        }
    }
}
```

This is a straightforward program. Observe that the program uses nested **if-else**s. This leads to three disadvantages:

(a) As the number of conditions go on increasing, the level of indentation also goes on increasing. As a result, the whole program creeps to the right.

(b) Care needs to be exercised to match the corresponding **if**s and **else**s.

(c) Care needs to be exercised to match the corresponding pair of braces.

All three of these problems can be eliminated by usage of 'Logical operators.' The following program illustrates this.

```c
/* Method -- II */
main( )
{
    int m1, m2, m3, m4, m5, per ;
```

```
printf ( "Enter marks in five subjects" ) ;
scanf ( "%d %d %d %d %d", &m1, &m2, &m3, &m4, &m5 ) ;
per = (m1 + m2 + m3 + m4 + m5) / 500 * 100;

if ( per >= 60 )
    printf ( "First division" ) ;

if (( per >= 50 ) && ( per < 60 ) )
    printf ( "Second division" ) ;

if (( per >= 40 ) && ( per < 50 ) )
    printf ( "Third division" ) ;

if ( per < 40 )
    printf ( "Fail" ) ;
}
```

As can be seen from the second **if** statement, the **&&** operator is used to combine two conditions. 'Second division' gets printed if both the conditions evaluate to true. If one of the conditions evaluate to false, then the whole thing is treated as false.

Two distinct advantages can be cited in favor of this program:

(a) The matching (or mismatching) of the **if**s with their corresponding **else**s gets avoided, since there are no **else**s in this program.
(b) In spite of using several conditions, the program doesn't creep to the right. In the previous program the statements went on creeping to the right. This effect becomes more pronounced as the number of conditions goes on increasing. This would make the task of matching the **if**s with their corresponding **else**s and matching of opening and closing braces much more difficult.

There is a negative side to the program, too. Even if the first condition turns out to be true, all other conditions are still checked. This will increase the time of execution of the program. This can be avoided using the **else-if** clause discussed in the next section.

The *else-if* Clause

There is one more way in which we can write program for Example 2.4. This involves usage of **else-if** blocks as shown here:

```
/* else if ladder demo */
# include <stdio.h>
main( )
{
    int m1, m2, m3, m4, m5, per;

    per = ( m1+ m2 + m3 + m4+ m5) / 500 * 100 ;

    if ( per >= 60 )
        printf( "First division" ) ;
    else if( per >= 50 )
        printf ( "Second division" ) ;
    else if( per >= 40 )
        printf ( "Third division" ) ;
    else
        printf ( "fail" );
}
```

You can note that this program reduces the indentation of the statements. In this case, every **else** is associated with its previous **if**. The last **else** goes to work only if all the conditions fail. Also, if the first condition is satisfied, other conditions are not checked. Even in an **else-if** ladder, the last **else** is optional.

Note that the **else-if** clause is nothing different. It is just a way of rearranging the **else** with the **if** that follows it. This would be evident if you look at the following code:

```
if(i == 2)
    printf( "With you..." );
else
{
    if( j == 2 )
        printf ( "... All the time" );
}
```

```
if(i == 2)
    printf ( "With you..." ) ;
else if (j == 2 )
    printf ( "... All the time" ) ;
```

Another place where logical operators are useful is when we want to write programs for complicated logics that ultimately boil down to only two answers. For example, consider the following:

Example 2.5: A company insures its drivers in the following cases:

- If the driver is married.
- If the driver is unmarried, male, and above 30 years of age.
- If the driver is unmarried, female, and above 25 years of age.

In all other cases, the driver is not insured. If the marital status, sex, and age of the driver are the inputs, write a program to determine whether the driver is to be insured or not.

Here, after checking a complicated set of instructions, the final output of the program would be one of the two—either the driver should be ensured or the driver should not be ensured. As mentioned, these are the only two outcomes this problem can have using logical operators. But before we do that, let us write a program that does not make use of logical operators.

```
/* Insurance of driver - without using logical operators */
# include <stdio.h>
main( )
{
    char sex, ms ;
    int age ;

    printf ( "Enter age, sex, marital status" ) ;
    scanf ("%d %c %c", &age, &sex, &ms ) ;

    if ( ms == 'M' )
        printf ( "Driver is insured" ) ;
    else
    {
        if ( sex == 'M' )
        {
            if ( age > 30 )
                printf ( "Driver is insured" ) ;
            else
                printf ( "Driver is not insured" ) ;
        }
        else
        {
            if ( age > 25 )
                printf ( "Driver is insured" ) ;
            else
                printf ( "Driver is not insured" ) ;
        }
    }
}
```

From the program it is evident that we are required to match several **if**s and **else**s and several pairs of braces. In a more real-life situation there would be more conditions to check leading to the program creeping to the right. Let us now see how to avoid these problems by using logical operators.

As mentioned earlier in this example, we expect the answer to be either 'Driver is insured' or 'Driver is not insured.' If we list down all those cases in which the driver is insured, then they would be:

(a) Driver is married.
(b) Driver is an unmarried male above 30 years of age.
(c) Driver is an unmarried female above 25 years of age.

Since all these cases lead to the driver being insured, they can be combined together using **&&** and || as shown in the following program:

```
/* Insurance of driver - using logical operators */
# include <stdio.h>
main( )
{
    char sex, ms ;
    int age ;

    printf ( "Enter age, sex, marital status " ) ;
    scanf ( "%d %c %c" &age, &sex, &ms ) ;

    if ( ( ms == 'M') || ( ms == 'U' && sex == 'M' && age > 30 ) ||
                ( ms == 'U' && sex == 'F' && age > 25 ) )
            printf ( "Driver is insured" ) ;
    else
            printf ( "Driver is not insured" ) ;

}
```

In this program, it is important to note that:

–   The driver will be insured only if one of the conditions enclosed in parentheses evaluates to true.
–   For the second pair of parentheses to evaluate to true, each condition in the parentheses separated by **&&** must evaluate to true.
–   Even if one of the conditions in the second parentheses evaluates to false, then the whole of the second parentheses evaluates to false.
–   The last two of the above arguments apply to the third pair of parentheses as well.

Thus, we can conclude that the **&&** and || are useful in the following programming situations:

(a) When it is to be tested whether a value falls within a particular range or not.
(b) When after testing several conditions, the outcome is only one of the two answers (this problem is often called a yes/no problem).

Gender	Years of Service	Qualifications	Salary
Male	>= 10	Postgraduate	15000
	>= 10	Graduate	10000
	< 10	Postgraduate	10000
	< 10	Graduate	7000
Female	>= 10	Postgraduate	12000
	>= 10	Graduate	9000
	< 10	Postgraduate	10000
	< 10	Graduate	6000

FIGURE 2.6

There can be one more situation other than checking ranges or yes/no problems, where you might find logical operators useful. The following program demonstrates it.

Example 2.6: Write a program to calculate the salary as per the following table in Figure 2.6:

```c
# include <stdio.h>
main( )
{
    char g ;
    int yos, qual, sal = 0 ;

    printf ( "Enter Gender, Years of Service and
             Qualifications ( 0 = G, 1 = PG ):" ) ;
    scanf ( "%c%d%d", &g, &yos, &qual ) ;

    if ( g == 'm' && yos >= 10 && qual == 1 )
        sal = 15000 ;
    else if ( ( g == 'm' && yos >= 10 && qual == 0 )||
        ( g == 'm' && yos < 10 && qual == 1 ) )
        sal = 10000 ;
    else if ( g == 'm' && yos < 10 && qual == 0 )
        sal = 7000 ;
    else if ( g == 'f' && yos >= 10 && qual == 1 )
        sal = 12000 ;
    else if ( g == 'f' && yos >= 10 && qual == 0 )
        sal = 9000 ;
```

```
    else if ( g == 'f' && yos < 10 && qual == 1 )
        sal = 10000 ;
    else if ( g == 'f' && yos < 10 && qual == 0 )
        sal = 6000 ;

    printf ( "\nSalary of Employee = %d", sal ) ;
}
```

The ! Operator

So far, we have only used the logical operators **&&** and **||**. The third logical operator is the NOT operator, written as **!**. This operator reverses the result of the expression it operates on. For example, if the expression evaluates to a nonzero value, then applying the **!** operator to it results into a 0. Vice versa, if the expression evaluates to zero then on applying the **!** operator to it makes it 1, a nonzero value. The final result (after applying **!**), 0 or 1, is considered false or true respectively. Here is an example of the NOT operator applied to a relational expression:

```
! ( y < 10 )
```

This means "not **y** less than 10." In other words, if **y** is less than 10, the expression will be false, since (**y < 10**) is true. We can express the same condition as (**y >= 10**).

The NOT operator is often used to reverse the logical value of a single variable, as in the expression

```
if ( ! flag )
```

This is another way of saying

```
if ( flag == 0 )
```

Does the NOT operator sound confusing? Avoid it if you want, as the same thing can be achieved without using the NOT operator.

Hierarchy of Operators Revisited

Since we have now added the logical operators to the list of operators we know, it is time to review these operators and their priorities. Figure 2.7 summarizes the operators we have seen so far. The higher the position of an operator in the table, the higher is its priority. (A complete precedence table of operators is given in Appendix A.)

Operators	Type
!	Logical NOT
* / %	Arithmetic and modulus
+ -	Arithmetic
< > <= >=	Relational
== !=	Relational
&&	Logical AND
||	Logical OR
=	Assignment

FIGURE 2.7

A WORD OF CAUTION

What will be the output of the following program:

```
# include <stdio.h>
main( )
{
    int i ;

    printf ( "Enter value of i " ) ;
    scanf ( "%d", &i ) ;
    if ( i = 5 )
            printf ( "You entered 5" ) ;
    else
            printf ( "You entered something other than 5" ) ;
}
```

And here is the output of two runs of this program:

```
Enter value of i 200
You entered 5

Enter value of i 9999
You entered 5
```

Surprising? You have entered 200 and 9999, and still you find in either case the output is 'You entered 5.' This is because we have written the condition wrong. We have used the assignment operator = instead of the relational operator ==. As a result, the condition gets reduced to **if (5)**, regardless of what you supply as the value of **i**. And remember that in C, 'truth' is always non-zero, whereas 'falsity' is always zero. Therefore, **if (5)** always evaluates to true and hence the result.

Another common mistake while using the **if** statement is to write a semicolon (;) after the condition, as shown below:

```
# include <stdio.h>
main( )
{
    int i ;

    printf ( "Enter value of i " ) ;
    scanf ( "%d", &i ) ;

    if ( i == 5 ) ;
            printf ( "You entered 5" ) ;
}
```

The ; makes the compiler interpret the statement as if you have written it in following manner:

```
if ( i == 5 )
      ;
printf ( "You entered 5" ) ;
```

Here, if the condition evaluates to true, the ; (null statement, which does nothing on execution) gets executed, following which the **printf( )** gets executed. If the condition fails, then straightaway the **printf( )** gets executed. Thus, regardless of whether the condition evaluates to true or false, the **printf( )** is bound to get executed. Remember that the compiler will not point out this as an error, since as far as the syntax is concerned, nothing has gone wrong, but the logic has certainly gone awry. Moral is, beware of such pitfalls.

Figure 2.8 summarizes the working of all three logical operators.

Operands		Results			
x	y	!x	!y	x && y	x ‖ y
0	0	1	1	0	0
0	non-zero	1	0	0	1
non-zero	0	0	1	0	1
non-zero	non-zero	0	0	1	1

FIGURE 2.8

THE CONDITIONAL OPERATORS

The conditional operators **?** and **:** are sometimes called ternary operators since they take three arguments. In fact, they form a kind of foreshortened if-then-else. Their general form is,

```
expression 1 ? expression 2 : expression 3
```

What this expression says is: "if **expression 1** is true (that is, if its value is nonzero), then the value returned will be **expression 2**, otherwise the value returned will be **expression 3**." Let us understand this with the help of a few examples:

(a)
```
int x, y ;
scanf ( "%d", &x ) ;
y = ( x > 5 ? 3 : 4 ) ;
```
This statement will store 3 in **y** if **x** is greater than 5, otherwise it will store 4 in y.

The equivalent **if** statement will be,

```
if ( x > 5 )
     y = 3 ;
else
     y = 4 ;
```

(b)
```
char a ;
int y ;
scanf ( "%c", &a ) ;
y = ( a >= 65 && a <= 90 ? 1 : 0 ) ;
```

Here 1 would be assigned to **y** if **a >= 65 && a <= 90** evaluates to true, otherwise 0 would be assigned.

The following points should be noted about the conditional operators:

(a) It's not necessary that the conditional operators should be used only in arithmetic statements. This is illustrated in the following examples:

```
Ex.:    int i ;
        scanf ( "%d", &i ) ;
        ( i == 1 ? printf ( "Amit" ) : printf ( "All and sundry" ) ) ;

Ex.:    char a = 'z' ;
        printf ( "%c" , ( a >= 'a' ? a : '!' ) ) ;
```

(b) The conditional operators can be nested as shown here:

```
int big, a, b, c ;
big = ( a > b ? ( a > c ? 3: 4 ) : ( b > c ? 6: 8 ) ) ;
```

(c) Check out the following conditional expression:

```
a > b ? g = a : g = b ;
```

This will give you an error 'Lvalue Required.' The error can be overcome by enclosing the statement in the **:** part within a pair of parentheses. This is shown here:

```
a > b ? g = a : ( g = b ) ;
```

In absence of parentheses, the compiler believes that **b** is being assigned to the result of the expression to the left of the second =. Therefore, it reports an error.

The limitation of the conditional operators is that after the **?** or after the **:**, only one C statement can occur. In practice, rarely is this the requirement. Therefore, in serious C programming, conditional operators aren't as frequently used as the **if-else**.

SUMMARY

(a) There are three ways for making decisions in a program. The first way is to use the **if-else** statement, the second way is to use the conditional operators, and the third way is to use the **switch** statement.

(b) The default scope of the **if** statement is only the next statement. So, to execute more than one statement they must be written in a pair of braces.

(c) An **if** block need not always be associated with an **else** block. However, an **else** block is always associated with an **if** statement.

(d) If the outcome of an **if-else** ladder is only one of two answers, then the ladder should be replaced either with an **else-if** clause or by logical operators.

(e) **&&** and **||** are binary operators, whereas **!** is a unary operator.

(f) In C every test expression is evaluated in terms of zero and nonzero values. A zero value is considered false and a nonzero value is considered true.

(g) Assignment statements used with conditional operators must be enclosed within a pair of parentheses.

EXERCISES

if, if-else, Nested *if-elses*

[A] What will be the output of the following programs:

(a)
```c
# include <stdio.h>
main( )
{
    int a = 300, b, c ;
    if ( a >= 400 )
        b = 300 ;
        c = 200 ;
        printf ( "\n%d %d", b, c ) ;
}
```

(b)
```c
# include <stdio.h>
main( )
{
    int a = 500, b, c ;
    if ( a >= 400 )
        b = 300 ;
        c = 200 ;
        printf ( "\n%d %d", b, c ) ;
}
```

(c)
```c
main( )
{
    int x = 10, y = 20 ;
    if ( x == y ) ;
        printf ( "\n%d %d", x, y ) ;
}
```

(d)
```c
# include <stdio.h>
main( )
{
    int x = 3, y = 5 ;
    if ( x == 3 )
        printf ( "\n%d", x ) ;
    else ;
        printf ( "\n%d", y ) ;
}
```

(e)
```c
# include <stdio.h>
main( )
{
    int x = 3 ;
    float y = 3.0 ;

    if ( x == y )
            printf ( "\nx and y are equal" ) ;
    else
            printf ( "\nx and y are not equal" ) ;
}
```
(f)
```c
# include <stdio.h>
main( )
{
    int x = 3, y, z ;
    y = x = 10 ;
    z = x < 10 ;
    printf ( "\nx = %d y = %d z = %d", x, y, z ) ;
}
```
(g)
```c
main( )
{
    int k = 35 ;
    printf ( "\n%d %d %d", k == 35, k = 50, k > 40 ) ;
}
```
(h)
```c
# include <stdio.h>
main( )
{
    int i = 65 ;
    char j = `A' ;
    if ( i == j )
            printf ( "C is WOW" ) ;
    else
            printf( "C is a headache" ) ;
}
```
(i)
```c
# include <stdio.h>
main( )
{
    int a = 5, b, c ;
    b = a = 15 ;
    c = a < 15 ;
    printf ( "\na = %d b = %d c = %d", a, b, c ) ;
}
```

```
(j)  # include <stdio.h>
     main( )
     {
         int x = 15 ;
         printf ( "\n%d %d %d", x != 15, x = 20, x < 30 ) ;
     }
```

[B] Point out the errors, if any, in the following programs:

```
(a)  # include <stdio.h>
     main( )
     {
         float a = 12.25, b = 12.52 ;
         if ( a = b )
             printf ( "\na and b are equal" ) ;
     }
```

```
(b)  # include <stdio.h>
     main( )
     {
         int j = 10, k = 12 ;
         if ( k >= j )
         {
             {
                 k = j ;
                 j = k ;
             }
         }
     }
```

```
(c)  # include <stdio.h>
     main( )
     {
         if ( 'X' < 'x' )
                 printf ( "\nascii value of X is smaller than that of x" ) ;
     }
```

```
(d)  # include <stdio.h>
     main( )
     {
         int x = 10 ;
         if ( x >= 2 ) then
                 printf ( "\n%d", x ) ;
     }
```

(e)
```
# include <stdio.h>
main( )
{
    int x = 10, y = 15 ;
    if ( x % 2 = y % 3 )
            printf ( "\nCarpathians" ) ;
}
```
(f)
```
# include <stdio.h>
main( )
{
    int x = 30 , y = 40 ;
    if ( x == y )
            printf( "x is equal to y" ) ;
    elseif ( x > y )
            printf( "x is greater than y" ) ;
    elseif ( x < y )
            printf( "x is less than y" ) ;
}
```
(g)
```
# include <stdio.h>
main( )
{
    int a, b ;
    scanf ( "%d %d", a, b ) ;
    if ( a > b ) ;
            printf ( "This is a game" ) ;
    else
            printf ( "You have to play it" ) ;
}
```

[C] Attempt the following:

(a) If cost price and selling price of an item is input through the keyboard, write a program to determine whether the seller has made profit or incurred loss. Also, determine how much profit he made or loss he incurred.

(b) Any integer is input through the keyboard. Write a program to find out whether it is an odd number or even number.

(c) Any year is input through the keyboard. Write a program to determine whether the year is a leap year or not. (Hint: Use the % (modulus) operator.)

(d) According to the Gregorian calendar, it was Monday on the date 01/01/01. If any year is input through the keyboard, write a program to find out what is the day on January 1st of this year.

(e) A five-digit number is entered through the keyboard. Write a program to obtain the reversed number and to determine whether the original and reversed numbers are equal or not.

(f) If the ages of Rolfe, Sharon, and Ajay, are input through the keyboard, write a program to determine the youngest of the three.

(g) Write a program to check whether a triangle is valid or not when the three angles of the triangle are entered through the keyboard. A triangle is valid if the sum of all three angles is equal to 180 degrees.

(h) Find the absolute value of a number entered through the keyboard.

(i) Given the length and breadth of a rectangle, write a program to find whether the area of the rectangle is greater than its perimeter. For example, the area of the rectangle with length $= 5$ and breadth $= 4$ is greater than its perimeter.

(j) Given three points $(x1, y1)$, $(x2, y2)$, and $(x3, y3)$, write a program to check if all three points fall on one straight line.

(k) Given the coordinates (x, y) of a center of a circle and it's radius, write a program that will determine whether a point lies inside the circle, on the circle, or outside the circle.

(Hint: Use **sqrt( )** and **pow( )** functions.)

(l) Given a point (x, y), write a program to find out if it lies on the x-axis, y-axis, or on the origin, viz. $(0, 0)$.

Logical Operators

[D] If $a = 10, b = 12, c = 0$, find the values of the expressions in the following table:

Expression	Value
a! $= 6$ && b > 5	1
a $== 9\|\|$b < 3	
!(a < 10)	
!(a > 5 && c)	
5 && c! $= 8\|\|$!c	

[E] What will be the output of the following programs:

```
(a) # include <stdio.h>
    main( )
    {
        int i = 4, z = 12 ;
```

```
            if ( i = 5 || z > 50 )
                    printf ( "\nDean of students affairs" ) ;
            else
                    printf ( "\nDosa" ) ;
        }
(b) # include <stdio.h>
    main( )
    {
        int i = 4, z = 12 ;
        if ( i = 5 && z > 5 )
                printf ( "\nLet us C" ) ;
        else
                printf ( "\nWish C was free !" ) ;
    }
(c) main( )
    {
        int i = 4, j = -1, k = 0, w, x, y, z ;
        w = i || j || k ;
        x = i && j && k ;
        y = i || j && k ;
        z = i && j || k ;
        printf ( "\nw = %d x = %d y = %d z = %d", w, x, y, z ) ;
    }
(d) # include <stdio.h>
    main( )
    {
        int i = 4, j = -1, k = 0, y, z ;
        y = i + 5 && j + 1 || k + 2 ;
        z = i + 5 || j + 1 && k + 2 ;
        printf ( "\ny = %d z = %d", y, z ) ;
    }
(e) # include <stdio.h>
    main( )
    {
        int i = -3, j = 3 ;
        if ( !i + !j * 1 )
                printf ( "\nMassaro" ) ;
        else
                printf ( "\nBennarivo" ) ;
    }
(f) # include <stdio.h>
    main( )
    {
        int a = 40 ;
```

```
        if ( a > 40 && a < 45 )
                printf ( "a is greater than 40 and less than 45" ) ;
        else
                printf ( "%d", a ) ;
    }
(g) # include <stdio.h>
    main( )
    {
        int p = 8, q = 20 ;
        if ( p == 5 && q > 5 )
                printf ( "\nWhy not C" ) ;
        else
                printf ( "\nDefinitely C !" ) ;
    }
(h) # include <stdio.h>
    main( )
    {
        int i = -1, j = 1, k ,l ;
        k = i && j ;
        l = i || j ;
        printf ( "%d %d", i, j ) ;
    }
(i) # include <stdio.h>
    main( )
    {
        int x = 20 , y = 40 , z = 45 ;
        if ( x > y && x > z )
                printf( "x is big" ) ;
        else if ( y > x && y > z )
                printf( "y is big" ) ;
        else if ( z > x && z > y )
                printf( "z is big" ) ;
    }
(j) # include <stdio.h>
    main( )
    {
        int i = -1, j = 1, k ,l ;
        k = !i && j ;
        l = !i || j ;
        printf ( "%d %d", i, j ) ;
    }
```

(k)
```
# include <stdio.h>
main( )
{
    int j = 4, k ;
    k = !5 && j ;
    printf ( "\nk = %d", k ) ;
}
```

[F] Point out the errors, if any, in the following programs:

(a)
```
/* This program
/* is an example of
/* using Logical operators */
# include <stdio.h>
main( )
{
    int i = 2, j = 5 ;
    if ( i == 2 && j == 5 )
        printf ( "\nSatisfied at last" ) ;
}
```
(b)
```
# include <stdio.h>
main( )
{
    int code, flag ;
    if ( code == 1 & flag == 0 )
        printf ( "\nThe eagle has landed" ) ;
}
```
(c)
```
# include <stdio.h>
main( )
{
    char spy = 'a', password = 'z' ;
    if ( spy == 'a' or password == 'z' )
        printf ( "\nAll the birds are safe in the nest" ) ;
}
```
(d)
```
# include <stdio.h>
main( )
{
    int i = 10, j = 20 ;
    if ( i = 5 ) && if ( j = 10 )
        printf ( "nHave a nice day" ) ;
}
```

```
(e)  # include <stdio.h>
     main( )
     {
        int x = 10 , y = 20;
        if ( x >= 2 and y <=50 )
                printf ( "\n%d", x ) ;
     }
(f)  # include <stdio.h>
     main( )
     {
        int a, b ;
        if ( a == 1 & b == 0 )
                printf ( "\nGod is Great" ) ;
     }
(g)  # include <stdio.h>
     main( )
     {
        int x = 2;
        if ( x == 2 && x != 0 ) ;
        {
                printf ( "\nHi" ) ;
                printf( "\nHello" ) ;
        }
        else
                printf( "Bye" ) ;
     }
(h)  # include <stdio.h>
     main( )
     {
        int i = 10, j = 10 ;
        if ( i && j == 10)
                printf ( "\nHave a nice day" ) ;
     }
```

[G] Attempt the following:

(a) Any year is entered through the keyboard, write a program to determine whether the year is leap or not. Use the logical operators **&&** and ||.

(b) Any character is entered through the keyboard, write a program to determine whether the character entered is an uppercase letter, a lower case letter, a digit, or a special symbol.

The following table shows the range of ASCII values for various characters.

Characters	ASCII Values
A–Z	65–90
a–z	97–122
0–9	48–57
special symbols	0–47, 58–64, 91–96, 123–127

(c) A certain grade of steel is graded according to the following conditions:

   (i)   Hardness must be greater than 50
   (ii) Carbon content must be less than 0.7
   (iii) Tensile strength must be greater than 5600

The grades are as follows:

Grade is 10 if all three conditions are met
Grade is 9 if conditions (i) and (ii) are met
Grade is 8 if conditions (ii) and (iii) are met
Grade is 7 if conditions (i) and (iii) are met
Grade is 6 if only one condition is met
Grade is 5 if none of the conditions are met

     Write a program, which will require the user to give values of hardness, carbon content, and tensile strength of the steel under consideration and output the grade of the steel.

(d) A library charges a fine for every book returned late. For the first 5 days the fine is 50 cents, for 6–10 days the fine is 10 cents and above 10 days the fine is 5 cents. If you return the book after 30 days your membership will be cancelled. Write a program to accept the number of days the member is late to return the book and display the fine or the appropriate message.

(e) If the three sides of a triangle are entered through the keyboard, write a program to check whether the triangle is valid or not. The triangle is valid if the sum of two sides is greater than the largest of the three sides.

(f) If the three sides of a triangle are entered through the keyboard, write a program to check whether the triangle is isosceles, equilateral, scalene, or right angled.

(g) In a company, worker efficiency is determined on the basis of the time required for a worker to complete a particular job. If the time taken by the worker is 2–3 hours, then the worker is said to be highly efficient. If the time required by the worker is 3–4 hours, then the worker is ordered to improve speed. If the time taken is 4–5 hours, the worker is given training to improve his speed, and if the time taken by the worker is more than 5 hours, then the worker has to leave the company. If the time taken by the worker is input through the keyboard, write a program to find the efficiency of the worker.

(h) The policy followed by a company to process customer orders is given by the following rules:

(a) If a customer order quantity is less than or equal to that in stock and his credit is OK, supply his requirement.

(b) If his credit is not OK do not supply. Send him an intimation.

(c) If his credit is OK but the item in stock is less than his order, supply what is in stock. Intimate to him the date on which the balance will be shipped.

Write a C program to implement the company policy.

Conditional Operators

[H] What will be the output of the following programs:

(a)
```c
# include <stdio.h>
main( )
{
    int i = -4, j, num ;
    j = ( num < 0 ? 0 : num * num ) ;
    printf ( "\n% d", j ) ;
}
```

(b)
```c
# include <stdio.h>
main( )
{
    int k, num = 30 ;
    k = ( num > 5 ? ( num <= 10 ? 100 : 200 ) : 500 ) ;
    printf ( "\n% d", num ) ;
}
```

(c)
```c
# include <stdio.h>
main( )
{
    int j = 4 ;
    ( ! j != 1 ? printf ( "\nWelcome") : printf ( "\nGood Bye") ) ;
}
```

[I] Point out the errors, if any, in the following programs:

(a)
```
# include <stdio.h>
main( )
{
    int tag = 0, code = 1 ;
    if ( tag == 0 )
            ( code > 1 ? printf ( "\nHello" ) ? printf ( "\nHi" ) ) ;
    else
            printf ( "\nHello Hi !!" ) ;
}
```

(b)
```
# include <stdio.h>
main( )
{
    int ji = 65 ;
    printf ( "\nji >= 65 ? %d : %c", ji ) ;
}
```

(c)
```
# include <stdio.h>
main( )
{
    int i = 10, j ;
    i >= 5 ? ( j = 10 ) : ( j = 15 ) ;
    printf ( "\n%d %d", i, j ) ;
}
```

(d)
```
# include <stdio.h>
main( )
{
    int a = 5 , b = 6 ;
    ( a == b ? printf ( "%d",a ) ) ;
}
```

(e)
```
# include <stdio.h>
main( )
{
    int n = 9 ;
    ( n == 9 ? printf ( "You are correct" ) ; :
    printf ( "You are wrong" ) ; ) ;
}
```

(f)
```
# include <stdio.h>
main( )
{
    int kk = 65 ,ll ;
    ll = ( kk == 65 : printf ( "\n kk == 65" ) :
    printf ("\n kk != 65" ) ) ; printf( "%d", ll ) ;
}
```

```
(g) # include <stdio.h>
    main( )
    {
        int x = 10, y = 20 ;
        x == 20 && y != 10 ? printf ( "True" ) : printf ( "False" ) ;
    }
```

[J] Rewrite the following programs using conditional operators.

```
(a) # include <stdio.h>
    main( )
    {
        int x, min, max ;
        scanf ( "%d %d", &max, &x ) ;
        if ( x > max )
                max = x ;
        else
                min = x ;
    }
```

```
(b) # include <stdio.h>
    main( )
    {
        int code ;
        scanf ( "%d", &code ) ;
        if ( code > 1 )
                printf ( "\nJerusalem" ) ;
        else
                if ( code < 1 )
                        printf ( "\nEddie" ) ;
                else
                        printf ( "\nC Brain" ) ;
    }
```

```
(c) # include <stdio.h>
    main( )
    {
        float sal ;
        printf ( "Enter the salary" ) ;
        scanf ( "% f", &sal ) ;
        if ( sal < 40000 && sal > 25000 )
                printf ( "Manager" ) ;
        else
```

```
if ( sal < 25000 && sal > 15000 )
        printf ( "Accountant" ) ;
else
        printf ( "Clerk" ) ;
}
```

[K] Attempt the following:

(a) Using conditional operators, determine:
 (1) Whether the character entered through the keyboard is a lower-case letter or not.
 (2) Whether a character entered through the keyboard is a special symbol or not.
(b) Write a program using conditional operators to determine whether a year entered through the keyboard is a leap year or not.
(c) Write a program to find the greatest of the three numbers entered through the keyboard using conditional operators.

# Chapter 3

THE LOOP CONTROL STRUCTURE

The programs that we have developed so far used either a sequential or a decision control instruction. In the sequential ones, the calculations were carried out in a fixed order, while in the decision control ones, an appropriate set of instructions were executed depending upon the outcome of the condition being tested (or a logical decision being taken).

These programs were of limited nature, because when executed, they always performed the same series of actions, in the same way, exactly once. Almost always, if something is worth doing, it's worth doing more than once. You can probably think of several examples of this from real life, such as eating a good dinner or going to a movie. Programming is the same; we frequently need to perform an action over and over, often with variations in the details each time. The mechanism that meets this need is the 'loop,' and loops are the subject of this chapter.

LOOPS

The versatility of the computer lies in its ability to perform a set of instructions repeatedly. This involves repeating some portion of the program either a specified number of times or until a particular condition is satisfied. This repetitive operation is done through a loop control instruction.

There are three methods by way of which we can repeat a part of a program. They are:

(a) Using a **for** statement
(b) Using a **while** statement
(c) Using a **do-while** statement

Each of these methods is discussed in the following pages.

THE *WHILE* LOOP

It is often the case in programming that you want to do something a fixed number of times. Perhaps you want to calculate the gross salaries of ten different people, or you want to convert temperatures from centigrade to fahrenheit for 15 different cities. The **while** loop is ideally suited for such cases. Let us look at a simple example that uses a **while** loop. The flowchart shown in Figure 3.1 will help you to understand the operation of the **while** loop.

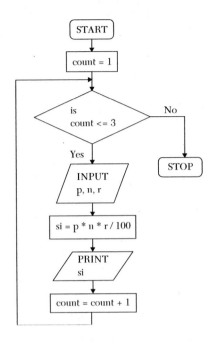

FIGURE 3.1

```
/* Calculation of simple interest for 3 sets of p, n and r */
# include <stdio.h>
void main( )
{
    int p, n, count ;
    float r, si ;

    count = 1 ;
    while ( count <= 3 )
    {
        printf ( "\nEnter values of p, n and r " ) ;
        scanf ( "%d %d %f", &p, &n, &r ) ;
        si = p * n * r / 100 ;
        printf ( "Simple interest = Rs. %f", si ) ;

        count = count + 1 ;
    }
}
```

And here are a few sample runs:

```
Enter values of p, n and r 1000 5 13.5
Simple interest = Rs. 675.000000
```

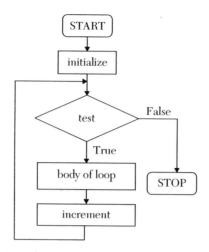

FIGURE 3.2

```
Enter values of p, n and r 2000 5 13.5
Simple interest = Rs. 1350.000000
Enter values of p, n and r 3500 5 3.5
Simple interest = Rs. 612.500000
```

The program executes all statements after the **while** 3 times. The logic for calculating the simple interest is written within a pair of braces immediately after the **while** keyword. These statements form what is called the 'body' of the **while** loop. The parentheses after the **while** contain a condition. So long as this condition remains true, all statements within the body of the **while** loop keep getting executed repeatedly. To begin with, the variable **count** is initialized to 1 and every time the simple interest logic is executed, the value of **count** is incremented by one. The variable **count** is often called either a 'loop counter' or an 'index variable.'

The operation of the **while** loop is illustrated in Figure 3.2.

Tips and Traps

The general form of **while** is as shown:

```
initialize loop counter ;
while ( test loop counter using a condition )
{
    do this ;
    and this ;
    increment loop counter ;
}
```

Note the following points about **while**:

− The statements within the **while** loop will keep on getting executed until the condition being tested remains true. When the condition becomes false, the control passes to the first statement that follows the body of the **while** loop.

In place of the condition there can be any other valid expression. So long as the expression evaluates to a nonzero value, the statements within the loop will get executed.

− The condition being tested may use relational or logical operators as shown in the following examples:

```
while ( i <= 10 )
while ( i >= 10 & & j <= 15 )
while ( j > 10 & & ( b < 15 || c < 20 ) )
```

− The statements within the loop may be a single line or a block of statements. In the first case, the braces are optional. For example,

```
while ( i <= 10 )
    i = i + 1 ;
```

is the same as

```
while ( i <= 10 )
{
    i = i + 1 ;
}
```

− Almost always, the **while** must test a condition that will eventually become false, otherwise the loop would be executed forever.

```
# include <stdio.h>
void main( )
{
    int i = 1 ;
    while ( i <= 10 )
        printf ( "%d\n", i ) ;
}
```

This is an indefinite loop, since **i** remains equal to 1 forever. The correct form would be:

```
# include <stdio.h>
void main( )
```

```
{
    int i = 1 ;
    while ( i <= 10 )
    {
        printf ( "%d\n", i ) ;
        i = i + 1 ;

    }
}
```

- Instead of incrementing a loop counter, we can even decrement it and still manage to get the body of the loop executed repeatedly. This is shown here:

```
# include <stdio.h>
void main( )
{
    int i = 5 ;
    while ( i >= 1 )
    {
        printf ( "\nMake the computer literate!" ) ;
        i = i - 1 ;
    }
}
```

- It is not necessary that a loop counter must only be an int. It can even be a float.

```
# include <stdio.h>
void main( )
{
    float a = 10.0 ;
    while ( a <= 10.5 )
    {
        printf ( "\nRaindrops on roses..." ) ;
        printf ( "...and whiskers on kittens" ) ;
        a = a + 0.1 ;
    }
}
```

- Even floating point loop counters can be decremented. Once again, the increment and decrement could be by any value, not necessarily 1.

What do you think would be the output of the following program?

```
# include <stdio.h>
void main( )
{
    int i = 1 ;
    while ( i <= 32767 )
    {
        printf ( "%d\n", i ) ;
        i = i + 1 ;
    }
}
```

No, it doesn't print numbers from 1 to 32767. It's an indefinite loop. To begin with, it prints out numbers from 1 to 32767. After that, the value of **i** is incremented by 1, therefore it tries to become 32768, which falls outside the valid integer range, so it goes to other side and becomes −32768 which would certainly satisfy the condition in the **while**. This process goes on indefinitely.

What will be the output of the following program?

```
# include <stdio.h>
void main( )
{
    int i = 1 ;
    while ( i <= 10 ) ;
    {
        printf ( "%d\n", i ) ;
        i = i + 1 ;
    }
}
```

This is another indefinite loop, and it doesn't give any output at all. The reason is, we have carelessly given a **;** after the **while**. This would make the loop work like this:

```
while ( i <= 10 )
    ;
{
    printf ( "%d\n", i ) ;
    i = i + 1 ;
}
```

Since the value of **i** is not getting incremented, the control will keep rotating within the loop, forever. Note that enclosing **printf( )** and i = i + 1 within a pair of braces is not an error. In fact, we can put a pair of braces around any individual statement or set of statements without affecting the execution of the program.

More Operators

There are varieties of operators that are frequently used with **while**. To illustrate their usage, let us consider a problem wherein numbers from 1 to 10 are to be printed on the screen. The program for performing this task can be written using **while** in the following different ways:

(a)
```
# include <stdio.h>
void main( )
{
    int i = 1 ;
    while ( i <= 10 )
    {
        printf ( "%d\n", i ) ;
        i = i + 1 ;
    }
}
```

(b)
```
# include <stdio.h>
void main( )
{
    int i = 1 ;
    while ( i <= 10 )
    {
        printf ( "%d\n", i ) ;
        i++ ;
    }
}
```

Note that the increment operator **++** increments the value of **i** by 1 every time the statement **i++** gets executed. Similarly, to reduce the value of a variable by 1, a decrement operator **--** is also available.

However, never use **n+++** to increment the value of **n** by 2, since C doesn't recognize the operator **+++**.

(c)
```
# include <stdio.h>
void main( )
{
    int i = 1 ;
    while ( i <= 10 )
```

```
    {
        printf ( "%d\n", i ) ;
        i += 1 ;
    }
}
```

Note that **+=** is a compound assignment operator. It increments the value of **i** by 1. Similarly, **j** = **j** + **10** can also be written as **j** += **10**. Other compound assignment operators are -=, *=, / =, and %=.

(d)
```
# include <stdio.h>
void main( )
{
    int i = 0 ;
    while ( i++ < 10 )
        printf ( "%d\n", i ) ;
}
```

In the statement **while (i++ < 10)**, first the comparison of value of **i** with 10 is performed, and then the incrementation of **i** takes place. Since the incrementation of **i** happens after its usage, here the **++** operator is called a post-incrementation operator. When the control reaches **printf( )**, **i** has already been incremented, hence **i** must be initialized to 0.

(e)
```
# include <stdio.h>
void main( )
{
    int i = 0 ;
    while ( ++i <= 10 )
        printf ( "%d\n", i ) ;
}
```

In the statement **while (++i <= 10)**, first the incrementation of **i** takes place, then the comparison of value of **i** with 10 is performed. Since the incrementation of **i** happens before its usage, here the **++** operator is called a pre-incrementation operator.

THE *FOR* LOOP

Perhaps one reason why few programmers use **while** is that they are too busy using the **for**, which is probably the most popular looping instruction. The

for allows us to specify three things about a loop in a single line:

(a) Setting a loop counter to an initial value.
(b) Testing the loop counter to determine whether its value has reached the number of repetitions desired.
(c) Increasing the value of the loop counter each time the program segment within the loop has been executed.

The general form of a **for** statement is:

```
for ( initialise counter ; test counter ; increment counter )
{
    do this ;
    and this ;
    and this ;
}
```

Let us write down the simple interest program using **for**. Compare this program with the one we wrote using **while**. The flowchart in Figure 3.3 is also given for a better understanding.

```
/* Calculation of simple interest for 3 sets of p, n and r */
# include <stdio.h>
void main( )
{
    int p, n, count ;
    float r, si ;

    for ( count = 1 ; count <= 3 ; count = count + 1 )
    {
        printf ( "Enter values of p, n, and r " ) ;
        scanf ( "%d %d %f", &p, &n, &r ) ;

        si = p * n * r / 100 ;
        printf ( "Simple Interest = Rs.%f\n", si ) ;
    }
}
```

If this program is compared with the one written using **while**, it can be seen that the three steps required for the loop construct—initialization, testing, and incrementation—have now been incorporated in the **for** statement.

Let us now examine how the **for** statement gets executed:

— When the **for** statement is executed for the first time, the value of **count** is set to an initial value 1.

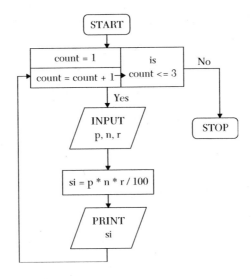

FIGURE 3.3

- Now the condition **count** <= **3** is tested. Since **count** is 1, the condition is satisfied and the body of the loop is executed for the first time.
- Upon reaching the closing brace of **for**, control is sent back to the **for** statement, where the value of **count** gets incremented by 1.
- Again the test is performed to check whether the new value of **count** exceeds 3.
- If the value of **count** is less than or equal to 3, the statements within the braces of **for** are executed again.
- The body of the **for** loop continues to get executed until **count** doesn't exceed the final value 3.
- When **count** reaches the value 4, the control exits from the loop and is transferred to the statement (if any) immediately after the body of **for**.

Figure 3.4 will help in further clarifying the concept of execution of the **for** loop.

It is important to note that the initialization, testing, and incrementation part of a **for** loop can be replaced by any valid expression. Thus, the following **for** loops are perfectly OK.

```
for ( i = 10 ; i ; i -- )
    printf ( "%d", i ) ;
for ( i < 4 ; j = 5 ; j = 0 )
    printf ( "%d", i ) ;
```

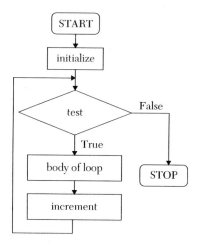

FIGURE 3.4

```
for ( i = 1; i <=10 ; printf ( "%d",i++ )
    ;
for ( scanf ( "%d", &i ) ; i <= 10 ; i++ )
    printf ( "%d", i ) ;
```

Let us now write down the program to print numbers from 1 to 10 in different ways. This time we will use a **for** loop instead of a **while** loop.

(a)
```
# include <stdio.h>
void main( )
{
    int i ;
    for ( i = 1 ; i <= 10 ; i = i + 1 )
        printf ( "%d\n", i ) ;
}
```

Note that the initialisation, testing, and incrementation of the loop counter is done in the **for** statement itself. Instead of $i = i + 1$, the statements $i + +$ or $i+ = 1$ can also be used.

Since there is only one statement in the body of the **for** loop, the pair of braces have been dropped. As with the **while**, the default scope of **for** is the next immediate statement after **for**.

(b)
```
# include <stdio.h>
void main( )
{
    int i ;
    for ( i = 1 ; i <= 10 ; )
```

```
    {
        printf ( "%d\n", i ) ;
        i = i + 1 ;
    }
}
```

Here, the incrementation is done within the body of the **for** loop and not in the **for** statement. Note that, in spite of this, the semicolon after the condition is necessary.

(c)
```
# include <stdio.h>
void main( )
{
    int i = 1 ;
    for ( ; i <= 10 ; i = i + 1 )
        printf ( "%d\n", i ) ;
}
```

Here the initialization is done in the declaration statement itself, but still the semicolon before the condition is necessary.

(d)
```
# include <stdio.h>
void main( )
{
    int i = 1 ;
    for ( ; i <= 10 ; )
    {
        printf ( "%d\n", i ) ;
        i = i + 1 ;
    }
}
```

Here, neither the initialization, nor the incrementation is done in the **for** statement, but still the two semicolons are necessary.

(e)
```
# include <stdio.h>
void main( )
{
    int i ;
    for ( i = 0 ; i++ < 10 ; )
        printf ( "%d\n", i ) ;
}
```

Here, the comparison as well as the incrementation is done through the same statement, **i++ < 10**. Since the **++** operator comes after **i**, first a comparison is done, followed by incrementation. Note that it is necessary to initialize **i** to 0.

(f)
```c
# include <stdio.h>
void main( )
{
    int i ;
    for ( i = 0 ; ++i <= 10 ; )
        printf ( "%d\n", i ) ;
}
```

Here again, both the comparison and the incrementation are done through the same statement, **++i <= 10**. Since **++** precedes **i**, incrementation is done first, followed by comparison. Note that it is necessary to initialize **i** to 0.

Nesting of Loops

The same way **if** statements can be nested, **while**s and **for**s can also be nested. To understand how nested loops work, look at the following program:

```c
/* Demonstration of nested loops */
# include <stdio.h>
void main( )
{
    int r, c, sum ;
    for ( r = 1 ; r <= 3 ; r++ ) /* outer loop */
    {
        for ( c = 1 ; c <= 2 ; c++ ) /* inner loop */
        {
            sum = r + c ;
            printf ( "r = %d c = %d sum = %d\n", r, c, sum ) ;
        }
    }
}
```

When you run this program, you will get the following output:

```
r = 1 c = 1 sum = 2
r = 1 c = 2 sum = 3
r = 2 c = 1 sum = 3
r = 2 c = 2 sum = 4
r = 3 c = 1 sum = 4
r = 3 c = 2 sum = 5
```

Here, for each value of **r**, the inner loop is cycled through twice, with the variable **c** taking values from 1 to 2. The inner loop terminates when the value of **c** exceeds 2, and the outer loop terminates when the value of **r** exceeds 3.

As you can see, the body of the outer **for** loop is indented, and the body of the inner **for** loop is further indented. These multiple indentations make the program easier to understand.

Instead of using two statements, one to calculate **sum** and another to print it out, we can compact this into one single statement by saying:

```
printf ( "r = %d c = %d sum = %d\n", r, c, r + c ) ;
```

The way **for** loops have been nested here, similarly, two **while** loops can also be nested. Not only this, a **for** loop can occur within a **while** loop, or a **while** within a **for**.

Multiple Initializations in the *for* Loop

The initialization expression of the **for** loop can contain more than one statement separated by a comma. For example,

```
for ( i = 1, j = 2 ; j <= 10 ; j++ )
```

Multiple statements can also be used in the incrementation expression of a **for** loop; i.e., you can increment (or decrement) two or more variables at the same time. However, only one statement is allowed in the test expression. This expression may contain several conditions linked together using logical operators.

Use of multiple statements in the initialization expression also demonstrates why semicolons are used to separate the three expressions in the **for** loop. If commas had been used, they could not have also been used to separate multiple statements in the initialisation expression without confusing the compiler.

THE ODD LOOP

The loops that we have used so far executed the statements within them a finite number of times. However, in real-life programming, one comes across a situation when it is not known beforehand how many times the statements in the loop are to be executed. This situation can be programmed as shown here:

```
/* Execution of a loop an unknown number of times */
# include <stdio.h>
void main( )
```

```
{
    char another ;
    int num ;
    do
    {
        printf ( "Enter a number " ) ;
        scanf ( "%d", &num ) ;
        printf ( "square of %d is %d", num, num * num ) ;
        printf ( "\nWant to enter another number y/n " ) ;
        scanf ( " %c", &another ) ;
    } while ( another == 'y' ) ;
}
```

And here is the sample output:

```
Enter a number 5
square of 5 is 25
Want to enter another number y/n y
Enter a number 7
square of 7 is 49
Want to enter another number y/n n
```

In this program, the **do-while** loop will keep getting executed until the user continues to answer y. The moment he answers n, the loop terminates, since the condition (**another ==** ' **y** ') fails. Note that this loop ensures that statements within it are executed at least once even if **n** is supplied the first time.

Though it is simpler to program such a requirement using a **do-while** loop, the same functionality, if required, can also be accomplished using **for** and **while** loops as shown here:

```
/* odd loop using a for loop */
# include <stdio.h>
void main( )
{
    char another = 'y' ;
    int num ;
    for ( ; another == 'y' ; )
    {
        printf ( "Enter a number " ) ;
        scanf ( "%d", &num ) ;
        printf ( "square of %d is %d", num, num * num ) ;
        printf ( "\nWant to enter another number y/n " ) ;
        scanf ( " %c", &another ) ;
    }
}
```

```
/* odd loop using a while loop */
# include <stdio.h>
void main( )
{
    char another = 'y' ;
    int num ;

    while ( another == 'y' )
    {
        printf ( "Enter a number " ) ;
        scanf ( "%d", &num ) ;
        printf ( "square of %d is %d", num, num * num ) ;
        printf ( "\nWant to enter another number y/n " ) ;
        scanf ( " %c", &another ) ;
    }
}
```

THE *BREAK* STATEMENT

We often come across situations where we want to jump out of a loop instantly, without waiting to get back to the conditional test. The keyword **break** allows us to do this. When **break** is encountered inside any loop, control automatically passes to the first statement after the loop. A **break** is usually associated with an **if**. As an example, let's consider the following:

Example 3.1: Write a program to determine whether a number is prime or not. A prime number is one that is divisible only by 1 or itself.

All we have to do to test whether a number is prime or not, is to divide it successively by all numbers from 2 to one less than itself. If the remainder of any of these divisions is zero, the number is not a prime. If no division yields a zero then the number is a prime number. The following program implements this logic.

```
# include <stdio.h>
void main( )
{
    int num, i ;

    printf ( "Enter a number " ) ;
    scanf ( "%d", &num ) ;
```

```
i = 2 ;
while ( i <= num - 1 )
{
    if ( num %i == 0 )
    {
        printf ( "Not a prime number" ) ;
        break ;
    }
    i++ ;
}

if ( i == num )
    printf ( "Prime number" ) ;
}
```

In this program, the moment **num % i** turns out to be zero, (i.e., **num** is exactly divisible by **i**), the message "Not a prime number" is printed and the control breaks out of the **while** loop. Why does the program require the **if** statement after the **while** loop at all? Well, there are two ways the control could have reached outside the **while** loop:

(a) It jumped out because the number proved to not be a prime.
(b) The loop came to an end because the value of **i** became equal to **num**.

When the loop terminates in the second case, it means that there was no number between 2 to **num - 1** that could exactly divide **num**. That is, **num** is indeed a prime. If this is true, the program should print out the message "Prime number."

The keyword **break**, breaks the control only from the **while** in which it is placed. Consider the following program, which illustrates this fact.

```
# include <stdio.h>
void main( )
{
    int i = 1 , j = 1 ;

    while ( i++ <= 100 )
    {
        while ( j++ <= 200 )
        {
            if ( j == 150 )
                break ;
            else
```

```
                    printf ( "%d %d\n", i, j ) ;
            }
        }
    }
```

In this program when **j** equals 150, **break** takes the control outside the inner **while** only, since it is placed inside the inner **while**.

THE *CONTINUE* STATEMENT

In some programming situations, we want to take the control to the beginning of the loop, bypassing the statements inside the loop that have not yet been executed. The keyword **continue** allows us to do this. When **continue** is encountered inside any loop, control automatically passes to the beginning of the loop.

A **continue** is usually associated with an **if**. As an example, let's consider the following program.

```
# include <stdio.h>
void main( )
{
    int i,j ;

    for ( i = 1 ; i <= 2 ; i++ )
    {
        for ( j = 1 ; j <= 2 ; j++ )
        {
            if ( i == j )
                    continue ;
                    printf ( "\n%d %d", i,j ) ;
        }
    }
}
```

The output of the above program would be:

```
1 2
2 1
```

Note that when the value of **i** equals that of **j**, the **continue** statement takes the control of the **for** loop (inner), bypassing the rest of the statements pending execution in the **for** loop (inner).

THE *DO-WHILE* LOOPS

The **do-while** loop looks like this:

```
do
{
    this ;
    and this ;
    and this ;
    and this ;
} while ( this condition is true ) ;
```

There is a minor difference between the working of **while** and **do-while** loops. This difference is the place where the condition is tested. The **while** tests the condition before executing any of the statements within the **while** loop whereas the **do-while** tests the condition after having executed the statements within the loop. Figure 3.5 will clarify the execution of a **do-while** loop even further.

This means that **do-while** will execute its statements at least once, even if the condition fails for the first time. The **while**, on the other hand, will not execute its statements if the condition fails for the first time. This difference is brought about more clearly by the following program.

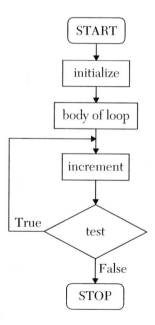

FIGURE 3.5

```
# include <stdio.h>
void main( )
{
    while ( 4 < 1 )
        printf ( "Hello there \n") ;
}
```

Here, since the condition fails the first time, the **printf( )** will not get executed at all. Let's now write the same program using a **do-while** loop.

```
# include <stdio.h>
void main( )
{
    do
    {
        printf ( "Hello there \n") ;
    } while ( 4 < 1 ) ;
}
```

In this program, the **printf( )** would be executed once, since first the body of the loop is executed and then the condition is tested.

There are some occasions when we want to execute a loop at least once no matter what. This is illustrated in the following example:

break and **continue** are used with **do-while** just as they would be in a **while** or a **for** loop. A **break** takes you out of the **do-while** bypassing the conditional test. A **continue** sends you straight to the test at the end of the loop.

SUMMARY

(a) The three type of loops available in C are **for, while,** and **do-while.**

(b) A **break** statement takes the execution control out of the loop.

(c) A **continue** statement skips the execution of the statements after it and takes the control to the beginning of the loop.

(d) A **do-while** loop is used to ensure that the statements within the loop are executed at least once.

(e) The ++ operator increments the operand by 1, whereas, the - - operator decrements it by 1.

(f) The operators +=, -=, *=, /=, and % = are compound assignment operators. They modify the value of the operand to the left of them.

EXERCISES

while Loop

[A] What will be the output of the following programs:

(a)
```
# include <stdio.h>
void main( )
{
    int i = 1 ;
    while ( i <= 10 ) ;
    {
        printf ( "\n%d", i ) ;
        i++ ;
    }
}
```

(b)
```
# include <stdio.h>
void main( )
{
    int x = 4 ;
    while ( x == 1 )
    {
        x = x - 1 ;
        printf ( "\n%d", x ) ;
        -- x ;
    }
}
```

(c)
```
# include <stdio.h>
void main( )
{
    int x = 4, y, z ;
    y = --x ;
    z = x-- ;
    printf ( "\n%d %d %d",x,y,z ) ;
}
```

(d)
```
# include <stdio.h>
void main( )
{
    int x = 4, y = 3, z ;
    z = x-- -y ;
    printf ( "\n%d %d %d", x,y,z ) ;
}
```

(e)
```c
# include <stdio.h>
void main( )
{
    while ( 'a' < 'b' )
    printf ( "\nmalayalam is a palindrome" ) ;
}
```

(f)
```c
# include <stdio.h>
void main( )
{
    int i ;
    while ( i = 10 )
    {
        printf ( "\n%d", i ) ;
        i = i + 1 ;
    }
}
```

(g)
```c
# include <stdio.h>
void main( )
{
    float x = 1.1 ;
    while ( x == 1.1 )
    {
        printf ( "\n%f", x ) ;
        x = x -- 0.1 ;
    }
}
```

(h)
```c
# include <stdio.h>
void main( )
{
    int x = 4, y = 0, z ;
    while ( x >= 0 )
    {
        x-- ;
        y++ ;
        if ( x == y )
                continue ;
        else
                printf ( "\n%d %d", x,y ) ;
    }
}
```

```
(i)  # include <stdio.h>
     void main( )
     {
         int x = 4, y = 0, z ;
         while ( x >= 0 )
         {
              if ( x == y )
                    break ;
              else
                    printf ( ``\n%d %d'', x,y ) ;
              x-- ;
              y++ ;
         }
     }
```

[B] Attempt the following:

(a) Write a program to calculate overtime pay of 10 employees. Overtime is paid at the rate of $12.00 per hour for every hour worked above 40 hours. Assume that employees do not work for a fractional part of an hour.

(b) Write a program to find the factorial value of any number entered through the keyboard.

(c) Two numbers are entered through the keyboard. Write a program to find the value of one number raised to the power of another.

(d) Write a program to print all the ASCII values and their equivalent characters using a **while** loop. The ASCII values vary from 0 to 255.

(e) Write a program to print out all Armstrong numbers between 1 and 500. If the sum of cubes of each digit of the number is equal to the number itself, then the number is called an Armstrong number. For example, $153 = (1 * 1 * 1) + (5 * 5 * 5) + (3 * 3 * 3)$

(f) Write a program for a matchstick game being played between the computer and a user. Your program should ensure that the computer always wins. Rules for the game are as follows:
  – There are 21 matchsticks.
  – The computer asks the player to pick 1, 2, 3, or 4 matchsticks.
  – After the person picks, the computer does its picking.
  – Whoever is forced to pick up the last matchstick loses the game.

(g) Write a program to enter numbers until the user wants to stop and at the end it should display the count of positive, negative, and zeros entered.

(h) Write a program to receive an integer and find its octal equivalent.

(i) Write a program to find the range of a set of numbers. Range is the difference between the smallest and biggest number in the list.

for, break, continue, do-while

[C] What will be the output of the following programs:

(a)
```
# include <stdio.h>
void main( )
{
    int i = 0 ;
    for ( ; i ; )
            printf ( "\nHere is some mail for you" ) ;
}
```

(b)
```
# include <stdio.h>
void main( )
{
    int i ;
    for ( i = 1 ; i <= 5 ; printf ( "\n%d", i ) ) ;
        i++ ;
}
```

(c)
```
# include <stdio.h>
void main( )
{
    int i = 1, j = 1 ;
    for ( ; ; )
    {
            if(i > 5 )
                break ;
            else
                j += i ;
            printf ( "\n%d", j ) ;
            i += j ;
    }
}
```

[D] Answer the following:

(a) The three parts of the loop expression in the **for** loop are:
     the i_____ expression
     the t_____ expression
     the i_____ expression

(b) An expression contains relational operators, assignment operators, and arithmetic operators. In the absence of parentheses, they will be evaluated in which of the following order:

1. assignment, relational, arithmetic
2. arithmetic, relational, assignment
3. relational, arithmetic, assignment
4. assignment, arithmetic, relational

(c) The **break** statement is used to exit from:

1. an **if** statement
2. a **for** loop
3. a program
4. the **main( )** function

(d) A **do-while** loop is useful when we want the statements within the loop executed:

1. Only once
2. At least once
3. More than once
4. None of the above

(e) In what sequence is the initialization, testing, and execution of body done in a **do-while** loop

1. Initialization, execution of body, testing
2. Execution of body, initialization, testing
3. Initialization, testing, execution of body
4. None of the above

(f) Which of the following is not an infinite loop.

```
1. int i = 1 ;              2. for ( ; ; ) ;
   while ( 1 )
   {
       i++ ;
   }


3. int True = 0, false ;    4. int y, x = 0 ;
   while ( True )              do
   {                          {
     False = 1 ;                 y = x ;
   }                          } while ( x == 0 ) ;
```

(g) Which of the following statements is used to take the control to the beginning of the loop?

1. exit
2. break

3. continue
4. None of the above

(h) How many times in the while loop will the following Ansi C code get executed?

```
# include <stdio.h>
void main( )
{
    int j = 1 ;
    while ( j <= 255 ) ;
    {
        printf ( "%c %d ", j,j ) ;
        j++;
    }
}
```

(i) Which of the following statements is true for the following program?

```
# include <stdio.h>
void main()
{
    int x=10, y = 100%90;
    for (i=1; i <= 10; i++);
    if (x != y);
            printf ("x = %d y = %d", x,y);
}
```

(i)   The **printf( )** function is called 10 times.
(ii) The program will produce the output $x = 10$ $y = 10$.
(iii) The ; after the **if (x!=y)** would NOT produce an error.
(iv) The program will not produce any output.
(v)   The **printf( )** function is called infinite times.

(j) Which of the following statements is true about a for loop used in an Ansi C program?
(i)   **for** loop works faster than a **while** loop.
(ii) All things that can be done using a **for** loop can also be done using a **while** loop.
(iii) **for (; ;)** implements an infinite loop.
(iv) **for** loop can be used if we want statements in a loop to get executed at least once.
(v)   **for** loop works faster than a **do-while** loop.

[E] Attempt the following:

(a) Write a program to print all prime numbers from 1 to 300. (Hint: Use nested loops, **break**, and **continue**)

(b) Write a program to fill the entire screen with a smiling face. The smiling face has an ASCII value 1.

(c) Write a program to add the first seven terms of the following series using a **for** loop:

$$\frac{1}{1!} + \frac{2}{2!} + \frac{3}{3!} + \dots$$

(d) Write a program to generate all combinations of 1, 2, and 3 using a **for** loop.

(e) According to a study, the approximate level of intelligence of a person can be calculated using the following formula:

```
i = 2 + ( y + 0.5 x )
```

Write a program that will produce a table of values of **i**, **y**, and **x**, where **y** varies from 1 to 6, and, for each value of **y**, **x** varies from 5.5 to 12.5 in steps of 0.5.

(f) Write a program to produce the following output:

```
A  B  C  D  E  F  G  F  E  D  C  B  A
A  B  C  D  E  F     F  E  D  C  B  A
A  B  C  D  E           E  D  C  B  A
A  B  C  D                 D  C  B  A
A  B  C                       C  B  A
A  B                             B  A
A                                   A
```

(g) Write a program to print the multiplication table of the number entered by the user. The table should get displayed in the following form:

```
29 * 1 = 29
29 * 2 = 58
...
```

(h) Write a program to produce the following output:

```
            1
         2     3
      4     5     6
   7     8     9     10
```

(i) Write a program to produce the following output:

$$
\begin{array}{ccccccccc}
 & & & & 1 & & & & \\
 & & & 1 & & 1 & & & \\
 & & 1 & & 2 & & 1 & & \\
 & 1 & & 3 & & 3 & & 1 & \\
1 & & 4 & & 6 & & 4 & & 1
\end{array}
$$

(j) A machine is purchased which will produce earning of $1000 per year while it lasts. The machine costs $6000 and will have a salvage value of $2000 when it is condemned. If 12 percent per annum can be earned on alternate investments, what will be the minimum life of the machine to make it a more attractive investment compared to an alternative investment?

(k) When interest compounds **q** times per year at an annual rate of **r** % for **n** years, the principle **p** compounds to an amount **a** as per the following formula:

```
a = p ( 1 + r / q )nq
```

Write a program to read 10 sets of **p**, **r**, **n**, & **q** and calculate the corresponding as.

(l) The natural logarithm can be approximated by the following series.

$$
\frac{x-1}{x} + \frac{1}{2}\left(\frac{x-1}{x}\right)^2 + \frac{1}{2}\left(\frac{x-1}{x}\right)^3 + \frac{1}{2}\left(\frac{x-1}{x}\right)^3 + \ldots
$$

If **x** is input through the keyboard, write a program to calculate the sum of first seven terms of this series.

Chapter 4

THE CASE
CONTROL
STRUCTURE

In real life, we are often faced with situations where we are required to make a choice between a number of alternatives rather than only one or two. For example, which school to join or which hotel to visit or, still harder, which girl to marry (you almost always ending up making a wrong decision is a different matter altogether!). Serious C programming is the same; the choices we are asked to make are more complicated than merely selecting between two alternatives. C provides a special control statement that allows us to handle such cases effectively; rather than using a series of **if** statements. This control instruction is, in fact, the topic of this chapter. Toward the end of the chapter, we will also study a keyword, called **goto**, and understand why we should avoid its usage in C programming.

DECISIONS USING *SWITCH*

The control statement that allows us to make a decision from the number of choices is called a **switch**, or more correctly a **switch-case-default**, since these three keywords go together to make up the control statement. They most often appear as follows:

```
switch ( integer expression )
{
    case constant 1 :
        do this;
    case constant 2 :
        do this ;
    case constant 3 :
        do this ;
    default :
        do this ;
}
```

The integer expression following the keyword **switch** is any C expression that will yield an integer value. It could be an integer constant like 1, 2, or 3, or an expression that evaluates to an integer. The keyword **case** is followed by an integer or a character constant. Each constant in each **case** must be different from all the others. The "do this" lines in the previous form of **switch** represent any valid C statement.

What happens when we run a program containing a **switch**? First, the integer expression following the keyword **switch** is evaluated. The value it gives is then matched, one by one, against the constant values that follow the **case** statements. When a match is found, the program executes the statements following that **case**, and all subsequent **case** and **default** statements as well. If no match is found with any of the **case** statements, only the statements following the **default** are executed. A few examples will show how this control structure works.

Consider the following program:

```
# include <stdio.h>
void main( )
{
    int i = 2;

    switch ( i )
    {
        case 1 :
            printf ( "I am in case 1 \n" ) ;
        case 2 :
            printf ( "I am in case 2 \n" ) ;
        case 3 :
            printf ( "I am in case 3 \n" ) ;
        default :
            printf ( "I am in default \n" ) ;
    }
}
```

The output of this program will be:

```
I am in case 2
I am in case 3
I am in default
```

The output is definitely not what we expected! We didn't expect the second and third line in the output. The program prints case 2 and 3 and the default case. Well, yes—we said the **switch** executes the case where a match is found and all the subsequent **cases** and the **default** as well.

If you want that only case 2 should get executed, it is up to you to get out of the **switch** then and there by using a **break** statement. The following example shows how this is done. Note that there is no need for a **break** statement after the **default**, since the control comes out of the **switch** anyway.

```
# include <stdio.h>
void main( )
{
    int i = 2 ;
    switch ( i )
```

```
    {
        case 1 :
            printf ( "I am in case 1 \n" ) ;
            break ;
        case 2 :
            printf ( "I am in case 2 \n" ) ;
            break ;
        case 3 :
            printf ( "I am in case 3 \n" ) ;
            break ;
        default :
            printf ( "I am in default \n" ) ;
    }
}
```

The output of this program will be:

```
I am in case 2
```

The operation of **switch** is shown in Figure 4.1 in the form of a flowchart for a better understanding.

The Tips and Traps

A few useful tips about the usage of **switch** and a few pitfalls to be avoided:

(a) The earlier program that used **switch** may give you the wrong impression that you can use only cases arranged in ascending order, 1, 2, 3, and default. You can, in fact, put the cases in any order you please. Here is an example of scrambled case order:

```
# include <stdio.h>
void main( )
{
    int i = 22 ;

    switch ( i )
    {
        case 121 :
            printf ( "I am in case 121 \n" ) ;
            break ;
        case 7 :
            printf ( "I am in case 7 \n" ) ;
            break ;
```

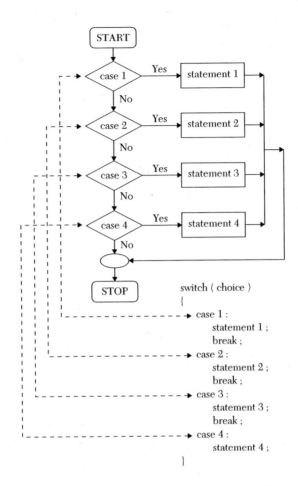

FIGURE 4.1

```
        case 22 :
            printf ( "I am in case 22 \n" ) ;
            break ;
        default :
            printf ( "I am in default \n" ) ;

    }
}
```

The output of this program will be:

```
I am in case 22
```

(b) You are also allowed to use **char** values in **case** and **switch** as shown in the following program:

```
# include <stdio.h>
void main( )
{
    char c = 'x' ;

    switch ( c )
    {
        case 'v' :
            printf ( "I am in case v \n" ) ;
            break ;
        case 'a' :
            printf ( "I am in case a \n" ) ;
            break ;
        case 'x' :
            printf ( "I am in case x \n" ) ;
            break ;
        default :
            printf ( "I am in default \n" ) ;
    }
}
```

The output of this program will be:

```
I am in case x
```

In fact, here when we use 'v', 'a', and 'x,' they are actually replaced by the ASCII values (118, 97, and 120) of these character constants.

(c) At times we may want to execute a common set of statements for multiple **case**s. How this can be done is shown in the following example:

```
# include <stdio.h>
void main( )
{
    char ch ;

    printf ( "Enter any one of the alphabets a, b, or c " );
    scanf ( "%c", &ch );

    switch ( ch )
    {
        case 'a' :
```

```
        case 'A' :
            printf ( "a as in ashar" ) ;
            break ;
        case 'b' :
        case 'B' :
            printf ( "b as in brain" ) ;
            break ;
        case 'c' :
        case 'C' :
            printf ( "c as in cookie" ) ;
            break ;
        default :
            printf ( "wish you knew what are alphabets" ) ;
    }
}
```

Here, we are making use of the fact that once a **case** is satisfied, the control simply falls through the **case** until it doesn't encounter a **break** statement. That is why if a letter **a** is entered, the **case 'a'** is satisfied, and since there are no statements to be executed in this **case**, the control automatically reaches the next **case** i.e., **case 'A'** and executes all the statements in this **case**.

(d) Even if there are multiple statements to be executed in each **case**, there is no need to enclose them within a pair of braces (unlike **if** and **else**).

(e) Every statement in a **switch** must belong to some **case** or the other. If a statement doesn't belong to any **case**, the compiler won't report an error. However, the statement will never get executed. For example, in the following program, the **printf( )** never goes to work.

```
# include <stdio.h>
void main( )
{
    int i, j ;

    printf ( "Enter value of i" ) ;
    scanf ( "%d", &i ) ;

    switch ( i )
    {
        printf ( "Hello" ) ;
        case 1 :
            j = 10 ;
            break ;
```

```
            case 2 :
                j = 20 ;
                break ;
        }
    }
```

(f) If we have no **default** case, then the program simply falls through the entire **switch** and continues with the next instruction (if any) that follows the closing brace of **switch**.

(g) Is **switch** a replacement for **if**? Yes and no. Yes, because it offers a better way of writing programs as compared to **if**, and no, because, in certain situations, we are left with no choice but to use **if**. The disadvantage of **switch** is that one cannot have a case in a **switch** that looks like:

```
case i <= 20 :
```

All that we can have after the case is an **int** constant or a **char** constant or an expression that evaluates to one of these constants. Even a **float** is not allowed.

The advantage of **switch** over **if** is that it leads to a more structured program and the level of indentation is manageable, more so if there are multiple statements within each **case** of a **switch**.

(h) We can check the value of any expression in a **switch**. Thus, the following **switch** statements are legal.

```
switch ( i + j * k )
switch ( 23 + 45 % 4 * k )
switch ( a < 4 && b > 7 )
```

Expressions can also be used in cases provided they are constant expressions. Thus, **case 3 + 7** is correct, however, **case a + b** is incorrect.

(i) The **break** statement, when used in a **switch**, takes the control outside the **switch**. However, use of **continue** will not take the control to the beginning of **switch** as one is likely to believe. This is because **switch** is not a looping statement unlike **while**, **for**, and **do-while**.

(j) In principle, a **switch** may occur within another, but in practice, it is rarely done. Such statements would be called nested **switch** statements.

(k) The **switch** statement is very useful while writing menu-driven programs. This aspect of **switch** is discussed in the exercise at the end of this chapter.

SWITCH VERSUS IF-ELSE LADDER

There are some things that you simply cannot do with a **switch**. These are:

(a) A float expression cannot be tested using a **switch**.

(b) Cases can never have variable expressions (for example, it is wrong to say **case a +3:**).

(c) Multiple cases cannot use the same expressions. Thus, the following **switch** is illegal:

```
switch ( a )
{
    case 3 :
        ...
    case 1 + 2 :
        ...
}
```

(a), (b), and (c) may lead you to believe that these are obvious disadvantages with a **switch**, especially since there weren't any such limitations with **if-else**. Then why use a **switch** at all? For speed—**switch** works faster than an equivalent **if-else** ladder. How come? This is because the compiler generates a jump table for a **switch** during compilation. As a result, during execution it simply refers to the jump table to decide which case should be executed rather than actually checking which case is satisfied. Compared to this, **if-else**s are slower because the conditions in them are evaluated at execution time. Thus, a **switch** with 10 cases would work faster than an equivalent **if-else** ladder. If the 10th **case** is satisfied, then the jump table would be referred to and statements for the 10th **case** would be executed. Compared to this, in an **if-else** ladder, 10 conditions would be evaluated at execution time, which makes it slow. Note that a lookup in the jump table is faster than evaluation of a condition, especially if the condition is complex.

If, on the other hand, the conditions in the **if-else** were simple and less in number, then **if-else** would work out faster than the lookup mechanism of a **switch**. Hence, a **switch** with two **case**s would work slower than an equivalent **if-else**. Thus, you as a programmer should make a decision on which of the two should be used when.

THE GOTO KEYWORD

Avoid the **goto** keyword! They make a C programmer's life miserable. There is seldom a legitimate reason for using **goto**, and its use is one of the reasons that programs become unreliable, unreadable, and hard to debug. And yet many programmers find **goto** seductive.

In a difficult programming situation, it seems so easy to use a **goto** to take the control where you want. However, almost always, there is a more elegant way of writing the same program using **if**, **for**, **while**, and **switch**. These constructs are far more logical and easy to understand.

The big problem with **goto**s is that when we do use them we can never be sure how we got to a certain point in our code. They obscure the flow of control. So as far as possible, skip them. You can always get the job done without them. With good programming skills **goto** can always be avoided. This is the first and last time that we are going to use **goto** in this book. However, for sake of completeness, the following program shows how to use **goto**.

```c
# include <stdio.h>
void main( )
{
    int goals ;

    printf ( "Enter the number of goals scored against India" ) ;
    scanf ( "%d", &goals ) ;

    if ( goals <= 5 )
        goto sos ;
    else
    {
        printf ( "About time soccer players learnt C\n" ) ;
        printf ( "and said goodbye! adieu! to soccer" ) ;
        exit( ) ; /* terminates program execution */
    }

    sos :
        printf ( "To err is human!" ) ;
}
```

And here are two sample runs of the program:

```
Enter the number of goals scored against India 3
To err is human!
Enter the number of goals scored against India 7
About time soccer players learnt C
and said goodbye! adieu! to soccer
```

A few remarks about the program will make the things clearer.

- If the condition is satisfied, the **goto** statement transfers control to the label 'sos,' causing **printf( )** following **sos** to be executed.
- The label can be on a separate line or on the same line as the statement following it, as in,

```
sos : printf ( "To err is human!" ) ;
```

- Any number of **goto**s can take the control to the same label.
- The **exit( )** function is a standard library function that terminates the execution of the program. It is necessary to use this function since we don't want the statement

```
printf ( "To err is human!" )
```

to get executed after execution of the **else** block.
- The only programming situation in favor of using **goto** is when we want to take the control out of the loop that is contained in several other loops. The following program illustrates this.

```
# include <stdio.h>
void main( )
{
    int i, j, k ;

    for ( i = 1 ; i <= 3 ; i++ )
    {
        for ( j = 1 ; j <= 3 ; j++ )
        {
            for ( k = 1 ; k <= 3 ; k++ )
            {
                if (i == 3 && j == 3 && k == 3)
                    goto out ;
                else
                    printf ( "%d %d %d\n", i, j, k ) ;
            }
        }
    }
    out :
        printf ( "Out of the loop at last!" ) ;
}
```

Go through the program carefully and find out how it works. Also, write down the same program without using **goto**.

SUMMARY

(a) When we need to choose one among a number of alternatives, a **switch** statement is used.

(b) The **switch** keyword is followed by an integer or an expression that evaluates to an integer.

(c) The **case** keyword is followed by an integer or a character constant.

(d) The control falls through all the cases unless the **break** statement is given.

(e) The usage of the **goto** keyword should be avoided as it usually violates the normal flow of execution.

EXERCISES

[A] What will be the output of the following programs:

(a)
```c
# include <stdio.h>
void main( )
{
    char suite = 3 ;
    switch ( suite )
    {
        case 1  :
            printf ( "\nDiamond" ) ;
        case 2  :
            printf ( "\nSpade" ) ;
        default :
            printf ( "\nHeart") ;
    }
    printf ( "\nI thought one wears a suite" ) ;
}
```

(b)
```c
# include <stdio.h>
void main( )
{
    int c = 3 ;
    switch ( c )
    {
        case '3' :
            printf ( "You never win the silver prize" ) ;
            break ;
```

```
            case 3 :
                printf ( "You always lose the gold prize" ) ;
                break ;
            default :
                printf ( "Of course provided you win a prize" ) ;
        }
    }
```

(c)
```
# include <stdio.h>
void main( )
{
    int i = 3 ;
    switch ( i )
    {
        case 0 :
            printf ( "\nCustomers are dicey" ) ;
        case 1 + 0 :
            printf ( "\nMarkets are pricey" ) ;
        case 4 / 2 :
            printf ( "\nInvestors are moody" ) ;
        case 8 % 5 :
            printf ( "\nAt least employees are good" ) ;
    }
}
```

(d)
```
# include <stdio.h>
void main( )
{
    int k ;
    float j = 2.0 ;
    switch ( k = j + 1 )
    {
        case 3 :
            printf ( "\nTrapped" ) ;
            break ;
        default :
            printf ( "\nCaught!" ) ;
    }
}
```

(e)
```
# include <stdio.h>
void main( )
{
    int ch = 'a' + 'b' ;
    switch ( ch )
```

```
        {
            case 'a' :
            case 'b' :
                printf ( "\nYou entered b" ) ;
            case 'A' :
                printf ( "\na as in ashar" ) ;
            case 'b' + 'a' :
                printf ( "\nYou entered a and b" ) ;
        }
    }
```

(f)
```
    # include <stdio.h>
    void main( )
    {
        int i = 1 ;
        switch ( i - 2 )
        {
            case -1 :
                printf ( "\nFeeding fish" ) ;
            case 0 :
                printf ( "\nWeeding grass" ) ;
            case 1 :
                printf ( "\nmending roof" ) ;
            default :
                printf ( "\nJust to survive" ) ;
        }
    }
```

[B] Point out the errors, if any, in the following programs:

(a)
```
    # include <stdio.h>
    void main( )
    {
        int suite = 1 ;
        switch ( suite ) ;
        {
            case 0 ;
                printf ( "\nClub" ) ;
            case 1 ;
                printf ( "\nDiamond" ) ;
        }
    }
```

(b)
```c
# include <stdio.h>
void main( )
{
    int temp ;
    scanf ( "%d", &temp ) ;
    switch ( temp )
    {
        case ( temp <= 20 ) :
            printf ( "\nOooooooohhhh! Damn cool!" ) ;
        case ( temp > 20 && temp <= 30 ) :
            printf ( "\nRain rain here again!" ) ;
        case ( temp > 30 && temp <= 40 ) :
            printf ( "\nWish I am on Everest" ) ;
        default :
            printf ( "\nGood old nagpur weather" ) ;
    }
}
```

(c)
```c
# include <stdio.h>
void main( )
{
    float a = 3.5 ;
    switch ( a )
    {
        case 0.5 :
            printf ( "\nThe art of C" ) ;
            break ;
        case 1.5 :
            printf ( "\nThe spirit of C" ) ;
            break ;
        case 2.5 :
            printf ( "\nSee through C" ) ;
            break ;
        case 3.5 :
            printf ( "\nSimply c" ) ;
    }
}
```

(d)
```c
# include <stdio.h>
void main( )
{
    int a = 3, b = 4, c ;
    c = b -- a ;
    switch ( c )
```

```
        {
            case 1 || 2 :
                printf ( "God give me an opportunity to change things" ) ;
                break ;

            case a || b :
                printf ( "God give me an opportunity to run my show" ) ;
                break ;
        }
    }
```

[C] Write a menu-driven program that has following options:

1. Factorial of a number
2. Prime or not
3. Odd or even
4. Exit

Once a menu item is selected, the appropriate action should be taken and once this action is finished, the menu should reappear. Unless the user selects the 'Exit' option, the program should continue to work.

Hint: Make use of an infinite **while** and a **switch** statement.

Chapter 5

FUNCTIONS AND POINTERS

121

K nowingly or unknowingly, we rely on so many people for so many things. Man is an intelligent species, but still cannot perform all of life's tasks alone. He has to rely on others. You may call a mechanic to fix up your car, hire a gardener to mow your lawn, or rely on a store to supply you groceries every month. A computer program (except for the simplest one) finds itself in a similar situation. It cannot handle all the tasks by itself. Instead, it requests other program-like entities—called 'functions' in C—to get its tasks done. In this chapter we will study these functions. We will look at a variety of features of these functions, starting with the simplest one, and then working toward those that demonstrate the power of C functions.

WHAT IS A FUNCTION?

A function is a self-contained block of statements that perform a coherent task of some kind. Every C program can be thought of as a collection of these functions. As we noted earlier, using a function is something like hiring a person to do a specific job for you. Sometimes the interaction with this person is very simple; sometimes it's complex.

Suppose you have a task that is always performed in exactly the same way—say a bimonthly servicing of your motorbike. When you want it to be done, you go to the service station and say, "It's time, do it now." You don't need to give instructions, because the mechanic knows his job. You don't need to be told how the job is done. You assume the bike will be serviced in the usual way, the mechanic does it, and that's that.

Let us now look at a simple C function that operates in much the same way as the mechanic. Actually, we will be looking at two things—a function that calls or activates the function and the function itself.

```
# include <stdio.h>
void message( ) ; /* function prototype declaration */
void main()
{
    message( ) ; /* function call */
    printf ( "\nCry, and you stop the monotony!" ) ;

}
void message( ) /* function definition */
{
    printf ( "\nSmile, and the world smiles with you..." ) ;
}
```

And here's the output:

```
Smile, and the world smiles with you...
Cry, and you stop the monotony!
```

Here, we have defined two functions—**main( )** and **message( )**. In fact we have used the word **message** at three places in the program. Let us understand the meaning of each.

The first is the function prototype and is written as:

```
void message( ) ;
```

This prototype declaration indicates that **message( )** is a function, which, after completing its execution, does not return anything. This 'does not return anything' is indicated using the keyword **void**. It is necessary to mention the prototype of every function that we intend to define in the program.

The second usage of **message** is:

```
void message( )
{
    printf ( "\nSmile, and the world smiles with you..." ) ;
}
```

This is the function definition. In this definition right now we have only **printf( )**, but we can also use **if**, **for**, **while**, **switch**, etc., within this function definition.

The third usage is:

```
message( ) ;
```

Here, the function **message( )** is being called by **main( )**. What do we mean when we say that **main( )** 'calls' the function **message( )**? We mean that the control passes to the function **message( )**. The activity of **main( )** is temporarily suspended; it falls asleep while the **message( )** function wakes up and goes to work. When the **message( )** function runs out of statements to execute, the control returns to **main( )**, which comes to life again and begins executing its code at the exact point where it left off. Thus, **main( )** becomes the 'calling' function, whereas **message( )** becomes the 'called' function.

If you have grasped the concept of 'calling' a function, you are prepared for a call to more than one function. Consider the following example:

```
# include <stdio.h>
void italy( ) ;
void brazil( ) ;
void argentina( ) ;
void main( )
```

```
{
    printf ( "\nI am in main" ) ;
    italy( ) ;
    brazil( ) ;
    argentina( ) ;
}
void italy( )
{
    printf ( "\nI am in italy" )
}
void brazil( )
{
    printf ( "\nI am in brazil" ) ;
}
void argentina( )
{
    printf ( "\nI am in argentina") ;
}
```

The output of the above program, when executed, would be:

```
I am in main
I am in italy
I am in brazil
I am in argentina
```

A number of conclusions can be drawn from this program:

- A C program is a collection of one or more functions.
- If a C program contains only one function, it must be **main( )**.
- If a C program contains more than one function, then one (and only one) of these functions must be **main( )**, because program execution always begins with **main( )**.
- There is no limit on the number of functions that might be present in a C program.
- Each function in a program is called in the sequence specified by the function calls in **main( )**.
- After each function has done its thing, control returns to **main( )**. When **main( )** runs out of statements and function calls, the program ends.

As we have noted earlier, the program execution always begins with **main( )**. Except for this fact, all C functions enjoy a state of perfect equality. No precedence, no priorities, nobody is anybody's boss. One function can call another function it has already called but has, in the meantime, temporarily left in order to call a third function, which will sometime later call the function that has called it. Understand what that means? No? Well, let's illustrate with an example.

```c
# include <stdio.h>
void italy( ) ;
void brazil( ) ;
void argentina( ) ;
void main( )
{
    printf( "\nI am in main" ) ;
    italy( ) ;
    printf ( "\nI am finally back in main" ) ;
}
void italy( )
{
    printf ( "\nI am in italy" ) ;
    brazil( ) ;
    printf ( "\nI am back in italy" ) ;
}
void brazil( )
{
    printf ( "\nI am in brazil" ) ;
    argentina( ) ;
}
void argentina( )
{
    printf ( "\nI am in argentina" ) ;
}
```

And the output would look like:

```
I am in main
I am in italy
I am in brazil
I am in argentina
I am back in italy
I am finally back in main
```

Here, **main( )** calls other functions, which in turn call still other functions. Trace carefully the way control passes from one function to another. Since the compiler always begins the program execution with **main( )**, every function in a program must be called directly or indirectly by **main( )**. In other words, the **main( )** function drives other functions.

Let us now summarize what we have learned so far.

(a) A function gets called when the function name is followed by a semicolon. For example,

```
void main( )
{
    argentina( ) ;
}
```

(b) A function is defined when function name is followed by a pair of braces in which one or more statements may be present. For example,

```
void argentina( )
{
    statement 1 ;
    statement 2 ;
    statement 3 ;
}
```

(c) Any function can be called from any other function. Even **main( )** can be called from other functions. For example,

```
# include <stdio.h>
void message( ) ;
void main( )
{
    message( ) ;
}
void message( )
{
    printf ( "\nCan't imagine life without C" ) ;
    main( ) ;
}
```

(d) A function can be called any number of times. For example,

```
# include <stdio.h>
void message( ) ;
void main( )
{
    message( ) ;
    message( ) ;
}
void message( )
```

```
{
    printf ( "\nJewel Thief!!" ) ;
}
```

(e) The order in which the functions are defined in a program and the order in which they get called need not necessarily be the same. For example,

```
# include <stdio.h>
void message1( ) ;
void message2( ) ;
void main( )
{
    message1( ) ;
    message2( ) ;
}
void message2( )
{
    printf ( "\nBut the butter was bitter" ) ;
}
void message1( )
{
    printf ( "\nMary bought some butter" ) ;
}
```

Here, even though **message1( )** is getting called before **message2( )**, still, **message1( )** has been defined after **message2( )**. However, it is advisable to define the functions in the same order in which they are called. This makes the program easier to understand.

(f) A function can call itself. Such a process is called 'recursion.' We will discuss this aspect of C functions later in this chapter.

(g) A function can be called from another function, but a function cannot be defined in another function. Thus, the following program code would be wrong, since **argentina( )** is being defined inside another function, **main( )**.

```
void main( )
{
    printf ( "\nI am in main" ) ;
    void argentina( )
    {
        printf ( "\nI am in argentina" ) ;
    }
}
```

(h) There are basically two types of functions:

Library functions Ex. **printf( )**, **scanf( )**, etc.
User-defined functions Ex. **argentina( )**, **brazil( )**, etc.

As the name suggests, library functions are nothing but commonly required functions grouped together and stored in what is called a Library. This library of functions is present on the disk and is written for us by people who write compilers. Almost always, a compiler comes with a library of standard functions. The procedure of calling both types of functions is exactly same.

Why Use Functions?

Why write separate functions at all? Why not squeeze the entire logic into one function, **main( )**? Two reasons:

(a) Writing functions avoids rewriting the same code over and over. Suppose you have a section of code in your program that calculates the area of a triangle. If later in the program you want to calculate the area of a different triangle, you won't like it if you are required to write the same instructions all over again. Instead, you would prefer to jump to a 'section of code' that calculates area and then jump back to the place from where you left off. This section of code is nothing but a function.

(b) By using functions, it becomes easier to write programs and keep track of what they are doing. If the operation of a program can be divided into separate activities, and each activity placed in a different function, then each could be written and checked more or less independently. Separating the code into modular functions also makes the program easier to design and understand.

What is the moral of the story? Don't try to cram the entire logic in one function. It is a very bad style of programming. Instead, break a program into small units and write functions for each of these isolated subdivisions. Don't hesitate to write functions that are called only once. What is important is that these functions perform some logically isolated task.

PASSING VALUES BETWEEN FUNCTIONS

The functions that we have used so far haven't been very flexible. We call them and they do what they are designed to do. Like our mechanic who always services the motorbike in exactly the same way, we haven't been able to influence the functions in the way they carry out their tasks. It would be nice to have a little more control over what functions do, in the same way it would be nice to be able to tell the mechanic, "Also, change the engine oil, I am going on a trip." In short, now we want to communicate between the 'calling' and the 'called' functions.

The mechanism used to convey information to the function is the 'argument.' You have unknowingly used the arguments in the **printf( )** and **scanf( )** functions; the format string and the list of variables used inside the parentheses in these functions are arguments. The arguments are sometimes also called 'parameters.'

Consider the following program. In this program, in **main( )**, we receive the values of **a**, **b**, and **c** through the keyboard and then output the sum of **a**, **b**, and **c**. However, the calculation of sum is done in a different function called **calsum( )**. If the sum is to be calculated in **calsum( )** and values of **a**, **b**, and **c** are received in **main( )**, then we must pass on these values to **calsum( )**, and once **calsum( )** calculates the sum, we must return it from **calsum( )** back to **main( )**.

```c
/* Sending and receiving values between functions */
\# include <stdio.h>
int calsum ( int x, int y, int z ) ;
void main( )
{
    int a, b, c, sum ;
    printf ( "\nEnter any three numbers " ) ;
    scanf ( "%d %d %d", &a, &b, &c ) ;
    sum = calsum ( a, b, c ) ;
    printf ( "\nSum = %d", sum ) ;
}
int calsum ( int x, int y, int z )
{
    int d ;

    d = x + y + z ;
    return ( d ) ;
}
```

And here is the output:

```
Enter any three numbers 10 20 30
Sum = 60
```

There are a number of things to note about this program:

(a) In this program, from the function **main( )**, the values of **a**, **b**, and **c** are passed on to the function **calsum( )** by making a call to the function **calsum( )** and mentioning **a**, **b**, and **c** in the parentheses:

```
sum = calsum ( a, b, c ) ;
```

In the **calsum( )** function, these values get collected in three variables **x**, **y**, and **z**:

```
int calsum ( int x, int y, int z )
```

(b) The variables **a**, **b**, and **c** are called 'actual arguments,' whereas the variables **x**, **y**, and **z** are called 'formal arguments.' Any number of arguments can be passed to a function being called. However, the type, order, and number of the actual and formal arguments must always be the same.

Instead of using different variable names **x**, **y**, and **z**, we could have used the same variable names **a**, **b**, and **c**. But the compiler would still treat them as different variables since they are in different functions.

(c) Note the function prototype declaration of **calsum( )**. Instead of the usual **void**, we are using **int**. This indicates that **calsum( )** is going to return a value of the type **int**. It is not compulsory to use variable names in the prototype declaration. Hence, we could as well have written the prototype as

```
int calsum ( int, int, int ) ;
```

Also, in the definition of **calsum**, **void** has been replaced by **int**.

(d) In the earlier programs, the moment the closing brace (**}**) of the called function was encountered, the control returned to the calling function. No separate **return** statement was necessary to send back to the control.

This approach is fine if the called function is not going to return any meaningful value to the calling function. In the earlier program, however, we want to return the sum of **x**, **y**, and **z**. Therefore, it is necessary to use the **return** statement.

The **return** statement serves two purposes:

(1) On executing the **return** statement, it immediately transfers the control back to the calling function.
(2) It returns the value present in the parentheses after **return** to the calling function. In the earlier program, the value of sum of three numbers is being returned.

(e) There is no restriction on the number of **return** statements that may be present in a function. Also, the **return** statement need not always be present at the end of the called function. The following program illustrates these facts.

```
int fun( )
{
    int n ;
    printf ( "\nEnter any number " ) ;
    scanf ( "%d", &n ) ;
    if ( n >= 10 && n <= 90 )
            return ( n ) ;
    else
            return ( n + 32 ) ;
}
```

In this function, different **return** statements will be executed depending on whether **ch** is capital or not.

(f) Whenever the control returns from a function, the sum being returned is collected in the calling function by equating the called function to some variable. For example,

```
sum = calsum ( a, b, c ) ;
```

(g) All the following are valid **return** statements.

```
return ( a ) ;
return ( 23 ) ;
return ;
```

In the last statement, a garbage value is returned to the calling function since we are not returning any specific value. Note that, in this case, the parentheses after **return** are dropped. Also, in the other **return** statements, the parentheses can be dropped.

(h) A function can return only one value at a time. Thus, the following statements are invalid.

```
return ( a, b ) ;
return ( x, 12 ) ;
```

There is a way to get around this limitation, which will be discussed later in this chapter when we learn pointers.

(i)   If the value of a formal argument is changed in the called function, the corresponding change does not take place in the calling function. For example,

```
# include <stdio.h>
void fun ( int ) ;
void main( )
{
    int a = 30 ;
    fun ( a ) ;
    printf ( "\n%d", a ) ;
}
void fun ( int b )
{
    b = 60 ;
    printf ( "\n%d", b ) ;
}
```

The output of the above program would be:

```
60
30
```

Thus, even though the value of **b** is changed in **fun( )**, the value of **a** in **main( )** remains unchanged. This means that when values are passed to a called function, the values present in actual arguments are not physically moved to the formal arguments; just a photocopy of values in actual argument is made into formal arguments.

SCOPE RULE OF FUNCTIONS

Look at the following program:

```
# include <stdio.h>
void display ( int ) ;
void main( )
{
    int i = 20 ;
    display ( i ) ;
}
void display ( int j )
```

```
{
    int k = 35 ;
    printf ( "\n%d", j ) ;
    printf ( "\n%d", k ) ;
}
```

In this program, is it necessary to pass the value of the variable **i** to the function **display( )**? Will it not become automatically available to the function **display( )**? No. Because, by default, the scope of a variable is local to the function in which it is defined. The presence of **i** is known only to the function **main( )** and not to any other function. Similarly, the variable **k** is local to the function **display( )** and therefore it is not available to **main( )**. That is why to make the value of **i** available to **display( )**, we have to explicitly pass it to **display( )**. Likewise, if we want **k** to be available to **main( )**, we will have to return it to **main( )** using the **return** statement. In general, we can say that the scope of a variable is local to the function in which it is defined.

CALLING CONVENTION

Calling convention indicates two things:

(a) The order in which the arguments are passed to the function.
(b) Which function (calling function or called function) performs the cleanup of variables when the control returns from the function.

When a function call is encountered and the arguments are to be passed to a function, two possibilities exist:

(a) Arguments can be passed from left to right.
(b) Arguments can be passed from right to left.

The formal arguments and the local variables defined inside a function are created at a place in memory called 'Stack.' When the control returns from the function, the stack is cleaned up. Either the calling function or the called function clears the stack. Which function will do this is decided by the calling convention.

There are different calling conventions available. The most common amongst them is a convention called standard calling convention. In this convention the arguments are passed to a function in right to left order and the stack is cleaned up by the called function.

Consider the following function call:

```
fun (a, b, c, d ) ;
```

In this call, it doesn't matter whether the arguments are passed from left to right or from right to left. However, in some function calls, the order of passing arguments becomes an important consideration. For example:

```
int a = 1 ;
printf ( "%d %d %d", a, ++a, a++ ) ;
```

It appears that this **printf( )** would output 1 2 2.

This, however, is not the case. Surprisingly, it outputs 3 3 1. This is because C's calling convention is from right to left. That is, first 1 is passed through the expression **a++** and then **a** is incremented to 2. Then the result of **++a** is passed. That is, **a** is incremented to 3 and then passed. Finally, the latest value of **a**, i.e., 3, is passed. Thus, in right to left order, 1, 3, 3 get passed. Once **printf( )** collects them, it prints them in the order in which we have asked it to get them printed (and not the order in which they were passed). Thus 3 3 1 gets printed.

ONE DICEY ISSUE

Consider the following function calls:

```
# include <conio.h>
clrscr( ) ;
gotoxy ( 10, 20 ) ;
ch = getch ( a ) ;
```

Here we are calling three standard library functions. As we know, before calling any function, we must declare its prototype. This helps the compiler in checking whether the values being passed and returned are as per the prototype declaration. But since we don't define the library functions (we merely call them), we may not know the prototypes of library functions. Hence, when the library of functions is provided, a set of '.h' files is also provided. These files contain the prototypes of library functions. But why multiple files? Because the library functions are divided into different groups and one file is provided for each group. For example, prototypes of all input/output functions are provided in the file 'stdio.h,' prototypes of all mathematical functions are provided in the file 'math.h,' etc.

Prototypes of functions **clrscr( )**, **gotoxy( )**, and **getch( )** are declared in the file 'conio.h.' You can even open this file and look at the prototypes. They would appear as shown here:

```
void clrscr( ) ;
void gotoxy ( int, int ) ;
int getch( ) ;
```

Now consider the following function calls:

```
# include <stdio.h>
int i = 10, j = 20 ;

printf ( "%d %d %d ", i, j ) ;
printf ( "%d", i, j ) ;
```

These functions get successfully compiled, even though there is a mismatch in the format specifiers and the variables in the list. This is because **printf( )** accepts *variable* number of arguments (sometimes 2 arguments, sometimes 3 arguments, etc.), and even with the mismatch shown, the call still matches with the prototype of **printf( )** present in 'stdio.h.' At runtime, when the first **printf( )** is executed, since there is no variable matching with the last specifier **%d**, a garbage integer gets printed. Similarly, in the second **printf( )**, since the format specifier for **j** has not been mentioned, its value does not get printed.

ADVANCED FEATURES OF FUNCTIONS

With a sound basis of the preliminaries of C functions, let us now get into their intricacies. The following advanced topics will be considered here.

(a) Return type of function
(b) Calling functions by value or by reference
(c) Recursion

Let us understand these features one by one.

Return Type of Function

Suppose we want to find the square of a floating point number using a function. This is how this simple program would look:

```
# include <stdio.h>
float square ( float ) ;
```

```
void main( )
{
    float a, b ;
    printf ( "\nEnter any number " ) ;
    scanf ( "%f", &a ) ;
    b = square ( a ) ;
    printf ( "\nSquare of %f is %f", a, b ) ;
}
float square ( float x )
{
    float y ;
    y = x * x ;
    return ( y ) ;
}
```

And here are three sample runs of this program:

```
Enter any number 3
Square of 3 is 9.000000
Enter any number 1.5
Square of 1.5 is 2.250000
Enter any number 2.5
Square of 2.5 is 6.250000
```

Since we are returning a **float** value from this function, we have indicated the return type of the **square( )** function as **float** in the prototype declaration as well as in the function definition. Had we dropped **float** from the prototype and the definition, the compiler would have assumed that **square( )** is supposed to return an integer value.

Call by Value and Call by Reference

By now we are very familiar with how to call functions. But, if you observe carefully, whenever we called a function and passed something to it we have always passed the 'values' of variables to the called function. Such function calls are called 'calls by value.' What we mean by this is, on calling a function, we are passing values of variables to it. The examples of call by value are shown here:

```
sum = calsum ( a, b, c ) ;
f = factr ( a ) ;
```

We have also learned that variables are stored somewhere in memory. So instead of passing the value of a variable, can we not pass the location number (also called address) of the variable to a function? If we were able to do so, it would become a 'call by reference.' What purpose a 'call by reference' serves we will find out a little later. First we must equip ourselves with the knowledge of how to make a 'call by reference.' This feature of C functions needs at least an elementary knowledge of a concept called 'pointers.' So let us first acquire the basics of pointers after which we will take up this topic once again.

An Introduction to Pointers

Which feature of C do beginners find the most difficult to understand? The answer is easy: pointers. Other languages have pointers but few use them as frequently as C does. And why not? It is C's clever use of pointers that makes it the excellent language it is.

The difficulty beginners have with pointers has much to do with C's pointer terminology than the actual concept. For instance, when a C programmer says that a certain variable is a "pointer," what does that mean? It is hard to see how a variable can point to something, or in a certain direction.

It is hard to get a grip on pointers just by listening to programmer's jargon. In our discussion of C pointers, therefore, we will try to avoid this difficulty by explaining pointers in terms of programming concepts we already understand. The first thing we want to do is explain the rationale of C's pointer notation.

Pointer Notation

Consider the declaration,

```
int i = 3 ;
```

This declaration tells the C compiler to:

(a) Reserve space in memory to hold the integer value.
(b) Associate the name **i** with this memory location.
(c) Store the value 3 at this location.

We may represent **i**'s location in memory by the following memory map, shown in Figure 5.1.

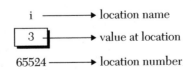

i ———→ location name
3 ———→ value at location
65524 ———→ location number

FIGURE 5.1

We see that the computer has selected memory location 65524 as the place to store the value 3. The location number 65524 is not a number to be relied upon, because some other time the computer may choose a different location for storing the value 3. The important point is, **i**'s address in memory is a number.

We can print this address number through the following program:

```
# include <stdio.h>
void main( )
{
    int i = 3 ;
    printf ( "\nAddress of i = %u", &i ) ;
    printf ( "\nValue of i = %d", i ) ;
}
```

The output of the program will be:

```
Address of i = 65524
Value of i = 3
```

Look at the first **printf( )** statement carefully. '&' used in this statement is C's 'address of' operator. The expression **& i** returns the address of the variable **i**, which in this case happens to be 65524. Since 65524 represents an address, there is no question of a sign being associated with it. Hence it is printed out using **% u**, which is a format specifier for printing an unsigned integer. We have been using the '& ' operator all the time in the **scanf( )** statement.

The other pointer operator available in C is '*****,' called the 'value at address' operator. It gives the value stored at a particular address. The 'value at address' operator is also called the 'indirection' operator.

Observe carefully the output of the following program:

```
# include <stdio.h>
void main( )
{
    int i = 3 ;
    printf ( "\nAddress of i = %u", &i ) ;
    printf ( "\nValue of i = %d", i ) ;
    printf ( "\nValue of i = %d", *( &i ) );
}
```

The output of the program will be:

```
Address of i = 65524
Value of i = 3
Value of i = 3
```

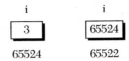

i   i

```
┌─────┐          ┌───────┐
│  3  │          │ 65524 │
└─────┘          └───────┘
 65524             65522
```

FIGURE 5.2

Note that printing the value of ***(& i)** is the same as printing the value of **i**.

The expression **& i** gives the address of the variable **i**. This address can be collected in a variable, by saying,

```
j = &i ;
```

But remember that **j** is not an ordinary variable like any other integer variable. It is a variable that contains the address of another variable (**i** in this case). Since **j** is a variable, the compiler must provide it space in the memory. Once again, the following memory map in Figure 5.2 will illustrate the contents of **i** and **j**.

As you can see, **i**'s value is 3 and **j**'s value is **i**'s address.

But wait, we can't use **j** in a program without declaring it. And since **j** is a variable that contains the address of **i**, it is declared as,

```
int *j ;
```

This declaration tells the compiler that **j** will be used to store the address of an integer value. In other words, **j** points to an integer. How do we justify the usage of ***** in the declaration,

```
int *j ;
```

Let us go by the meaning of *****. It stands for 'value at address.' Thus, **int *j** would mean the value at the address contained in **j** is an **int**.

Here is a program that demonstrates the relationships we have been discussing.

```
# include <stdio.h>
void main( )
{
    int i = 3 ;
    int *j ;

    j = &i ;
    printf ( "\nAddress of i = %u", &i ) ;
    printf ( "\nAddress of i = %u", j ) ;
    printf ( "\nAddress of j = %u", &j ) ;
    printf ( "\nValue of j = %u", j ) ;
```

```
        printf ( "\nValue of i = %d", i ) ;
        printf ( "\nValue of i = %d", *( &i ) ) ;
        printf ( "\nValue of i = %d", *j ) ;
}
```

The output of the program will be:

```
Address of i = 65524
Address of i = 65524
Address of j = 65522
Value of j = 65524
Value of i = 3
Value of i = 3
Value of i = 3
```

Work through the previous program carefully, taking note of the memory locations of **i** and **j** shown earlier. This program summarizes everything that we have discussed so far. If you don't understand the program's output, or the meanings of **& i**, **& j**, ***j**, and ***(& i)**, reread the last few pages. Everything we say about pointers from here onward will depend on your understanding these expressions thoroughly.

Look at the following declarations:

```
int *alpha ;
char *ch ;
float *s ;
```

Here, **alpha, ch**, and **s** are declared as pointer variables, i.e., variables capable of holding addresses. Remember that addresses (location nos.) are always going to be whole numbers, therefore pointers always contain whole numbers. Now we can put these two facts together and say—pointers are variables that contain addresses, and since addresses are always whole numbers, pointers will always contain whole numbers.

The declaration **float *s** does not mean that **s** is going to contain a floating-point value. What it means is, **s** is going to contain the address of a floating-point value. Similarly, **char *ch** means that **ch** is going to contain the address of a **char** value. Or, in other words, the value of the address stored in **ch** is going to be a **char**.

The concept of pointers can be further extended. A pointer, we know, is a variable that contains the address of another variable. Now this variable itself might be another pointer. Thus, we now have a pointer that contains another pointer's address. The following example should make this point clear.

```
# include <stdio.h>
void main( )
```

```
{
    int i = 3, *j, **k ;

    j = &i ;
    k = &j ;
    printf ( "\nAddress of i = %u", &i ) ;
    printf ( "\nAddress of i = %u", j ) ;
    printf ( "\nAddress of i = %u", *k ) ;
    printf ( "\nAddress of j = %u", &j ) ;
    printf ( "\nAddress of j = %u", k ) ;
    printf ( "\nAddress of k = %u", &k ) ;
    printf ( "\nValue of j = %u", j ) ;
    printf ( "\nValue of k = %u", k ) ;
    printf ( "\nValue of i = %d", i ) ;
    printf ( "\nValue of i = %d", * ( &i ) ) ;
    printf ( "\nValue of i = %d", *j ) ;
    printf ( "\nValue of i = %d", **k ) ;
}
```

The output of the program will be:

```
Address of i = 65524
Address of i = 65524
Address of i = 65524
Address of j = 65522
Address of j = 65522
Address of k = 65520
Value of j = 65524
Value of k = 65522
Value of i = 3
Value of i = 3
Value of i = 3
Value of i = 3
```

Figure 5.3 will help you in tracing out how the program prints the output.

Remember that when you run this program, the addresses that get printed might turn out to be something different than the ones shown in

FIGURE 5.3

the figure. However, even with these addresses, the relationship between **i**, **j**, and **k** can be easily established.

Observe how the variables **j** and **k** have been declared,

```
int i, *j, **k ;
```

Here, **i** is an ordinary **int**, **j** is a pointer to an **int** (often called an integer pointer), whereas **k** is a pointer to an integer pointer. We can extend the earlier program further still by creating a pointer to a pointer to an integer pointer. In principle, you will agree that likewise there could exist a pointer to a pointer to a pointer to a pointer to a pointer. There is no limit on how far can we go on extending this definition. Possibly, until the point we can comprehend it. And that point of comprehension is usually a pointer to a pointer. Beyond this, one rarely requires to extend the definition of a pointer. But just in case...

Back to Function Calls

Having had the first tryst with pointers, let us now get back to what we had originally set out to learn—the two types of function calls—call by value and call by reference. Arguments can generally be passed to functions in one of two ways:

(a) sending the values of the arguments
(b) sending the addresses of the arguments

In the first method, the 'value' of each of the actual arguments in the calling function is copied into corresponding formal arguments of the called function. With this method, the changes made to the formal arguments in the called function have no effect on the values of actual arguments in the calling function. The following program illustrates the 'call by value.'

```
# include <stdio.h>
void swapv ( int x, int y ) ;
void main( )
{
    int a = 10, b = 20 ;
    swapv ( a, b ) ;
    printf ( "\na = %d b = %d", a, b ) ;
}
void swapv ( int x, int y )
{
    int t ;
    t = x ;
```

```
        x = y ;
        y = t ;
        printf ( "\nx = %d y = %d", x, y ) ;
}
```

The output of the program will be:

```
x = 20 y = 10
a = 10 b = 20
```

Note that values of **a** and **b** remain unchanged even after exchanging the values of **x** and **y**.

In the second method (call by reference), the addresses of actual arguments in the calling function are copied into the formal arguments of the called function. This means that, using these addresses, we will have an access to the actual arguments and therefore we will be able to manipulate them. The following program illustrates this fact.

```
# include <stdio.h>
void swapr ( int *, int * ) ;
void main( )
{
        int a = 10, b = 20 ;
        swapr ( &a, &b ) ;
        printf ( "\na = %d b = %d", a, b ) ;
}
void swapr ( int *x, int *y )
{
        int t ;
        t = *x ;
        *x = *y ;
        *y = t ;
}
```

The output of the program will be:

```
a = 20 b = 10
```

Note that this program manages to exchange the values of **a** and **b** using their addresses stored in **x** and **y**.

Usually, in C programming, we make a call by value. This means that, in general, you cannot alter the actual arguments. But if desired, it can always be achieved through a call by reference.

Using a call by reference intelligently, we can make a function return more than one value at a time, which is not possible ordinarily. This is shown in the following program.

```
# include <stdio.h>
void areaperi ( int, float *, float * ) ;
void main( )
{
    int radius ;
    float area, perimeter ;

    printf ( "\nEnter radius of a circle " ) ;
    scanf ( "%d", &radius ) ;
    areaperi ( radius, &area, & perimeter ) ;

    printf ( "Area = %f", area ) ;
    printf ( "\nPerimeter = %f", perimeter ) ;
}
void areaperi ( int r, float *a, float *p )
{
    *a = 3.14 * r * r ;
    *p = 2 * 3.14 * r ;
}
```

And here is the output:

```
Enter radius of a circle 5
Area = 78.500000
Perimeter = 31.400000
```

Here we are making a mixed call in the sense that we are passing the value of **radius** and the addresses of **area** and **perimeter**. And since we are passing the addresses, any change that we make in values stored at addresses contained in the variables **a** and **p** will make the change effective in **main( )**. That is why, when the control returns from the function **areaperi( )**, we are able to output the values of **area** and **perimeter**.

Thus, we have been able to indirectly return two values from a called function, and hence, have overcome the limitation of the **return** statement, which can return only one value from a function at a time.

Conclusions

From the programs that we discussed here, we can draw the following conclusions:

(a) If we want that the value of an actual argument should not get changed in the function being called, pass the actual argument by value.

(b) If we want that the value of an actual argument should get changed in the function being called, pass the actual argument by reference.

(c) If a function is made to return more than one value at a time, then return these values indirectly by using a call by reference.

Recursion

In C, it is possible for the functions to call themselves. A function is called 'recursive' if a statement within the body of a function calls the same function. Sometimes called 'circular definition,' recursion is thus the process of defining something in terms of itself.

Let us now see a simple example of recursion. Suppose we want to calculate the factorial value of an integer. As we know, the factorial of a number is the product of all the integers between 1 and that number. For example, 4 factorial is $4 * 3 * 2 * 1$. This can also be expressed as $4! = 4 * 3!$ where '!' stands for factorial. Thus, the factorial of a number can be expressed in the form of itself. Therefore, this can be programmed using recursion. However, before we try to write a recursive function for calculating factorial, let us take a look at the nonrecursive function for calculating the factorial value of an integer.

```
# include <stdio.h>
int factorial ( int ) ;
void main( )
{
    int a, fact ;

    printf ( "\nEnter any number " ) ;
    scanf ( "%d", &a ) ;

    fact = factorial ( a ) ;
    printf ( "Factorial value = %d", fact ) ;
}
int factorial ( int x )
{
    int f = 1, i ;

    for ( i = x ; i >= 1 ; i-- )
        f = f * i ;

    return ( f ) ;
}
```

And here is the output:

```
Enter any number 3
Factorial value = 6
```

Work through the program carefully until you understand the logic of the program properly. Recursive factorial function can be understood only if you are thorough with the above logic.

Following is the recursive version of the function to calculate the factorial value.

```
# include <stdio.h>
int rec ( int ) ;
void main( )
{
    int a, fact ;
    printf ( "\nEnter any number " ) ;
    scanf ( "%d", &a ) ;

    fact = rec ( a ) ;
    printf ( "Factorial value = %d", fact ) ;
}
int rec ( int x )
{
    int f ;

    if ( x == 1 )
        return ( 1 ) ;
    else
        f = x * rec ( x - 1 ) ;

    return ( f ) ;
}
```

And here is the output for four runs of the program:

```
Enter any number 1
Factorial value = 1
Enter any number 2
Factorial value = 2
Enter any number 3
Factorial value = 6
Enter any number 5
Factorial value = 120
```

Let us understand this recursive factorial function thoroughly. In the first run, when the number entered through **scanf( )** is 1, let us see what action **rec( )** takes. The value of **a** (i.e., 1) is copied into **x**. Since **x** turns out to be 1, the condition **if (x == 1)** is satisfied and hence 1 (which indeed is the value of 1 factorial) is returned through the **return** statement.

When the number entered through **scanf( )** is 2, the **(x == 1)** test fails, so we reach the statement,

```
f = x * rec ( x - 1 ) ;
```

And here is where we meet recursion. How do we handle the expression **x * rec (x − 1)**? We multiply **x** by **rec (x − 1)**. Since the current value of **x** is 2, it is the same as saying that we must calculate the value (2 * rec (1)). We know that the value returned by **rec (1)** is 1, so the expression reduces to (2 * 1), or simply 2. Thus the statement,

```
x * rec ( x - 1 ) ;
```

evaluates to 2, which is stored in the variable **f**, and is returned to **main( )**, where it is duly printed as

```
Factorial value = 2
```

Now perhaps you can see what would happen if the value of **a** is 3, 4, 5 and so on.

In case the value of **a** is 5, **main( )** would call **rec( )** with 5 as its actual argument, and **rec( )** will send back the computed value. But before sending the computed value, **rec( )** calls **rec( )** and waits for a value to be returned. It is possible for the **rec( )** that has just been called to call yet another **rec( )**, the argument **x** being decreased in value by 1 for each of these recursive calls. We speak of this series of calls to **rec( )** as being different invocations of **rec( )**. These successive invocations of the same function are possible because the C compiler keeps track of which invocation calls which. These recursive invocations finally end when the last invocation gets an argument value of 1, which the preceding invocation of **rec( )** now uses to calculate its own **f** value and so on up the ladder. So we might say what happens is,

```
rec ( 5 ) returns ( 5 times rec ( 4 ),
     which returns ( 4 times rec ( 3 ),
         which returns ( 3 times rec ( 2 ),
             which returns ( 2 times rec ( 1 ),
                 which returns ( 1 ) ) ) ) )
```

Confused? Well, that is recursion for you in its simplest garbs. It's difficult to visualize how the control flows from one function call to another. Figure 5.4 may make things a bit clearer.

Assume that the number entered through **scanf( )** is 3. Using Figure 5.4, let's visualize exactly what happens when the recursive function **rec( )** gets called. Go through the figure carefully. The first time **rec( )** is called from **main( )**, **x** collects 3. From here, since **x** is not equal to 1, the **if** block is

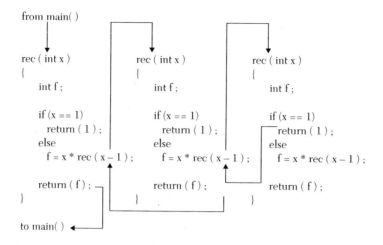

FIGURE 5.4

skipped and **rec( )** is called again with the argument (**x − 1**), i.e., 2. This is a recursive call. Since **x** is still not equal to 1, **rec( )** is called yet another time, with the argument (2 − 1). This time as **x** is 1, control goes back to the previous **rec( )** with the value 1, and **f** is evaluated as 2.

Similarly, each **rec( )** evaluates its **f** from the returned value, and finally, 6 is returned to **main( )**. The sequence can be grasped better by following the arrows shown in Figure 5.4. Let it be clear that while executing the program, so many copies of the function **rec( )** do not exist. These have been shown in the figure just to help you keep track of how the control flows during successive recursive calls.

Recursion may seem strange and complicated at first glance, but it is often the most direct way to code an algorithm, and once you are familiar with recursion, the clearest way of doing so.

Recursion and Stack

There are different ways in which data can be organized. For example, if you are going to store five numbers, then we can store them in five different variables, an array, a linked list, a binary tree, etc. All these different ways of organizing the data are known as data structures. The compiler uses one such data structure called stack for implementing normal as well as recursive function calls.

A stack is a Last In First Out (LIFO) data structure. This means that the last item to get stored on the stack (often called a Push operation) is the first one to get out of it (often called a Pop operation). You can compare this to the stack of plates in a cafeteria—the last plate that goes on the stack is the first one to get out of it. Now let us see how the stack works in the case of the following program.

```c
# include <stdio.h>
int add ( int, int ) ;
void main( )
{
    int a = 5, b = 2, c ;
    c = add ( a, b ) ;
    printf ( "sum = %d", c ) ;
}
int add ( int i, int j )
{
    int sum ;
    sum = i + j ;
    return sum ;
}
```

In this program, before transferring the execution control to the function **add( )**, the values of parameters **a** and **b** are pushed on the stack. Following this, the address of the statement **printf( )** is pushed on the stack and the control is transferred to **add( )**. It is necessary to push this address on the stack. In **add( )**, the values of **a** and **b** that were pushed on the stack are referred to as **i** and **j**. Once inside **add( )**, the local variable **sum** gets pushed on the stack. When the value of **sum** is returned, **sum** is popped off from the stack. Next, the address of the statement where the control should be returned is popped off from the stack. Using this address, the control returns to the **printf( )** statement in **main( )**. Before execution of **printf( )** begins, the two integers that were earlier pushed on the stack are now popped off.

How are the values are being pushed and popped even though we didn't write any code to do so? Simple—the compiler, on encountering the function call, will generate code to push the parameters and the address. Similarly, it will generate code to clear the stack when the control returns back from **add( )**. Figure 5.5 shows the contents of the stack at different stages of execution.

Note that in this program, the popping of **sum** and address is done by **add( )**, whereas, the popping of the two integers is done by **main( )**. When it is done this way, it is known as the 'CDecl Calling Convention.' There are other calling conventions as well, where instead of **main( )**, **add( )** itself clears the two integers. The calling convention also decides whether the parameters

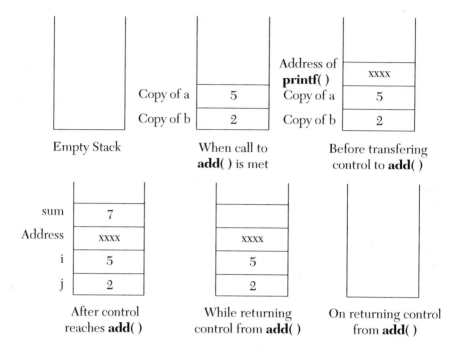

FIGURE 5.5

being passed to the function are pushed on the stack in left-to-right or right-to-left order. The standard calling convention always uses the right-to-left order. Thus, during the call to **add( )**, first the value of **b** is pushed to the stack, followed by the value of **a**.

The recursive calls are no different. Whenever we make a recursive call the parameters and the return address gets pushed on the stack. The stack gets unwound when the control returns from the called function. Thus, during every recursive function call we are working with a fresh set of parameters.

Also, note that while writing recursive functions, you must have an **if** statement somewhere in the recursive function to force the function to return without a recursive call being executed. If you don't do this and you call the function, you will fall into an indefinite loop, and the stack will keep on getting filled with parameters and the return address each time there is a call. Soon the stack will become full and you will get a runtime error indicating that the stack has become full. This is a very common error while writing recursive functions. You can use a **printf( )** statement liberally during the development of recursive function so that you can watch what is going on and can abort execution if you see that you have made a mistake.

ADDING FUNCTIONS TO THE LIBRARY

Most times, we either use the functions present in the standard library or we define our own functions and use them. Can we not add our functions to the standard library? And would it make any sense in doing so? We can add user-defined functions to the library. It makes sense in doing so as the functions that are added to the library are first compiled and then added. When we use these functions (by calling them), we save on their compilation time as they are available in the library in the compiled form.

Let us now see how to add user-defined functions to the library. Different compilers provide different utilities to add/delete/modify functions in the standard library. For example, Turbo C/C++ compilers provide a utility called 'tlib.exe' (Turbo Librarian). Let us use this utility to add the function **factorial( )** to the library.

The following are the steps to do so:

(a) Write the function definition of **factorial( )** in some file, say 'fact.c.'

```
int factorial ( int num )
{
    int i, f = 1 ;
    for  ( i = 1 ; i <= num ; i++ )
            f = f * i ;
    return ( f ) ;
}
```

(b) Compile the 'fact.c' file using Alt F9. A new file called 'fact.obj' will get created containing the compiled code in machine language.

(c) Add the function to the library 'maths.lib' by issuing the command

```
C:\tlib maths.lib + c:\fact.obj
```

Here, 'maths.lib' is a library filename, + is a switch, which means we want to add a new function to the library and 'c:\ fact.obj' is the path of the '.obj' file.

(d) Declare the prototype of the **factorial( )** function in the header file, say 'fact.h.' This file should be included while calling the function.

(e) To use the function present inside the library, create a program as shown here:

```
# include "c:\fact.h"
# include <stdio.h>
```

```
void main( )
{
    int f ;
    f = factorial ( 5 ) ;
    printf ( "%d", f ) ;
}
```

(f) Compile and execute the program using Ctrl F9.

If we wish we can delete the existing functions present in the library using the minus (−) switch.

Instead of modifying the existing libraries, we can create our own library. Let's see how to do this. Let us assume that we wish to create a library containing the functions **factorial( )**, **prime( )**, and **fibonacci( )**. As their names suggest, **factorial( )** calculates and returns the factorial value of the integer passed to it, **prime( )** reports whether the number passed to it is a prime number or not, and **fibonacci( )** prints the first **n** terms of the Fibonacci series, where **n** is the number passed to it. Here are the steps that need to be carried out to create this library. Note that these steps are specific to the Turbo C/C++ compiler and will vary for other compilers.

(a) Define the functions **factorial( )**, **prime( )**, and **fibonacci( )** in a file, say 'myfuncs.c.' Do not define **main( )** in this file.

(b) Create a file 'myfuncs.h' and declare the prototypes of **factorial( )**, **prime( )**, and **fibonacci( )** in it as shown here:

```
int factorial ( int ) ;
int prime ( int ) ;
void fibonacci ( int ) ;
```

(c) From the Options menu select the menu item 'Application.' From the dialog that pops up select the option 'Library.' Select OK.

(d) Compile the program using Alt F9. This will create the library file called 'myfuncs.lib.'

That's it. The library now stands created. Now we have to use the functions defined in this library. Here is how it can be done.

(a) Create a file, say 'sample.c,' and type the following code in it.

```
# include "myfuncs.h"
# include <stdio.h>
```

```
void main( )
{
    int f, result ;
    f = factorial ( 5 ) ;
    result = prime ( 13 ) ;
    fibonacci ( 6 ) ;
    printf ( "\n%d %d", f, result ) ;
}
```

Note that the file 'myfuncs.h' should be in the same directory as the file 'sample.c.' If not, then while including 'myfuncs.h' mention the appropriate path.

(b) Go to the 'Project' menu and select the 'Open Project...' option. On doing so a dialog will pop up. Give the name of the project, say 'sample.prj,' and select OK.

(c) From the 'Project' menu select 'Add Item.' On doing so a file dialog will appear. Select the file 'sample.c' and then select 'Add.' Also, add the file 'myfuncs.lib' in the same manner. Finally, select 'Done.'

(d) Compile and execute the project using Ctrl F9.

SUMMARY

(a) To avoid repetition of code and bulky programs, functionally related statements are isolated into a function.

(b) Function declaration specifies the return type of the function and the types of parameters it accepts.

(c) Function definition defines the body of the function.

(d) Variables declared in a function are not available to other functions in a program. So there won't be any clash even if we give the same name to the variables declared in different functions.

(e) Pointers are variables that hold addresses of other variables.

(f) A function can be called either by value or by reference.

(g) Pointers can be used to make a function return more than one value simultaneously.

(h) Recursion is difficult to understand, but in some cases offer a better solution than loops.

(i) Adding too many functions and calling them frequently may slow down the program execution.

EXERCISES

Simple Functions, Passing Values between Functions

[A] What will be the output of the following programs:

(a)
```c
# include <stdio.h>
void display( ) ;
void main( )
{
    printf ( "\nOnly stupids use C?" ) ;
    display( ) ;
}
void display( )
{
    printf ( "\nFools too use C!" ) ;
    main( ) ;
}
```

(b)
```c
# include <stdio.h>
void main( )
{
    printf ( "\nC to it that C survives" ) ;
    main( ) ;
}
```

(c)
```c
# include <stdio.h>
int check ( int ) ;
void main( )
{
    int i = 45, c ;
    c = check ( i ) ;
    printf ( "\n%d", c ) ;
}
int check ( int ch )
{
    if ( ch >= 45 )
            return ( 100 ) ;
    else
            return ( 10 * 10 ) ;
}
```

(d)
```c
# include <stdio.h>
int check ( int ) ;
void main( )
{
    int i = 45, c ;
    c = multiply ( i * 1000 ) ;
    printf ( "\n%d", c ) ;
}
int check ( int ch )
{
    if ( ch >= 40000 )
            return ( ch / 10 ) ;
    else
            return ( 10 ) ;
}
```

[B] Point out the errors, if any, in the following programs:

(a)
```c
# include <stdio.h>
int addmult ( int, int )
void main( )
{
    int i = 3, j = 4, k, l ;
    k = addmult ( i, j ) ;
    l = addmult ( i, j ) ;
    printf ( "\n%d %d", k, l ) ;
}
int addmult ( int ii, int jj )
{
    int kk, ll ;
    kk = ii + jj ;
    ll = ii * jj ;
    return ( kk, ll ) ;
}
```

(b)
```c
# include <stdio.h>
void message( ) ;
void main( )
{
    int a ;
    a = message( ) ;
}
```

```
     void message( )
     {
        printf ( "\nViruses are written in C" ) ;
        return ;
     }
```

(c)
```
     # include <stdio.h>
     void main( )
     {
        float a = 15.5 ;
        char ch = 'C' ;
        printit ( a, ch ) ;
     }
        printit ( a, ch )
     {
           printf ( "\n%f %c", a, ch ) ;
     }
```

(d)
```
     # include <stdio.h>
     void message( ) ;
     void main( )
     {
        message( ) ;
        message( ) ;
     }
     void message( ) ;
     {
        printf ( "\nPraise worthy and C worthy are synonyms" ) ;
     }
```

(e)
```
     # include <stdio.h>
     void main( )
     {
        let_us_c( )
        {
           printf ( "\nC is a Cimple minded language !") ;
           printf ( "\nOthers are of course no match !" ) ;
        }
     }
```

(f)
```
     # include <stdio.h>
     void message( ) ;
     void main( )
```

```
{
    message ( message( ) ) ;
}
void message( )
{
    printf ( "\nIt's a small world after all... " ) ;
}
```

[C] Answer the following:

(a)   Is this a correctly written function:

```
int sqr ( int a ) ;
{
    return ( a * a ) ;
}
```

(b) State whether the following statements are True or False:
1.   The variables commonly used in C functions are available to all the functions in a program.
2.   To return the control back to the calling function we must use the keyword **return**.
3.   The same variable names can be used in different functions without any conflict.
4.   Every called function must contain a **return** statement.
5.   A function may contain more than one **return** statement.
6.   Each **return** statement in a function may return a different value.
7.   A function can still be useful even if you don't pass any arguments to it and the function doesn't return any value back.
8.   Same names can be used for different functions without any conflict.
9.   A function may be called more than once from any other function.
10. It is necessary for a function to return some value.

[D] Answer the following:

(a) Write a function to calculate the factorial value of any integer entered through the keyboard.
(b) Write a function **power (a, b)**, to calculate the value of **a** raised to **b**.
(c) Write a general-purpose function to convert any given year into its Roman equivalent. The following table shows the Roman equivalents of decimal numbers:

Decimal	Roman	Decimal	Roman
1	i	100	c
5	v	500	d
10	x	1000	m
50	l		

Example:

Roman equivalent of 1988 is mdccclxxxviii

Roman equivalent of 1525 is mdxxv

(d) Any year is entered through the keyboard. Write a function to determine whether the year is a leap year or not.

(e) A positive integer is entered through the keyboard. Write a function to obtain the prime factors of this number.

For example, prime factors of 24 are 2, 2, 2, and 3, whereas prime factors of 35 are 5 and 7.

Function Prototypes, Call by Value/Reference, Pointers

[E] What will be the output of the following programs:

(a)
```
# include <stdio.h>
float circle ( int ) ;
void main( )
{
    float area ;
    int radius = 1 ;
    area = circle ( radius ) ;
    printf ( "\n%f", area ) ;
}
float circle ( int r )
{
    float a ;
    a = 3.14 * r * r ;
    return ( a ) ;
}
```

(b)
```
main( )
{
    void slogan( ) ;
    int c = 5 ;
```

```
    c = slogan( ) ;
    printf ( "\n%d", c ) ;
}
void slogan( )
{
    printf ( "\nOnly He men use C!" ) ;
}
```

[F] Answer the following:

(a) Write a function that receives a **float** and an **int** from **main( )**, finds the product of these two, and returns the product which is printed through **main( )**.

(b) Write a function that receives 5 integers and returns the sum, average, and standard deviation of these numbers. Call this function from **main( )** and print the results in **main( )**.

(c) Write a function that receives marks received by a student in 3 subjects and returns the average and percentage of these marks. Call this function from **main( )** and print the results in **main( )**.

[G] What will be the output of the following programs:

(a)
```
# include <stdio.h>
void fun ( int, int ) ;
void main( )
{
    int i = 5, j = 2 ;
    fun ( i, j ) ;
    printf ( "\n%d %d", i, j ) ;
}
void fun ( int i, int j )
{
    i = i * i ;
    j = j * j ;
}
```

(b)
```
# include <stdio.h>
void fun ( int *, int * ) ;
void main( )
{
    int i = 5, j = 2 ;
    fun ( &i, &j ) ;
    printf ( "\n%d %d", i, j ) ;
}
```

```
                 void fun ( int *i, int *j )
                 {
                    *i = *i * *i ;
                    *j = *j * *j ;
                 }
```

(c) ```
     # include <stdio.h>
     void fun (int *x, int y)
     void main( )
     {
        int i = 4, j = 2 ;
        fun (&i, j) ;
        printf ("\n%d %d", i, j) ;
     }
     void fun (int *i, int j)
     {
        *i = *i * *i ;
        j = j * j ;
     }
     ```

(d)  ```
     # include <stdio.h>
     void main( )
     {
        float a = 13.5 ;
        float *b, *c ;
        b = &a ; /* suppose address of a is 1006 */
        c = b ;
        printf ( "\n%u %u %u", &a, b, c ) ;
        printf ( "\n%f %f %f %f %f", a, *(& a), *&a, *b, *c ) ;
     }
     ```

[H] Point out the errors, if any, in the following programs:

(a) ```
     # include <stdio.h>
     void pass (int, int) ;
     void main( )
     {
        int i = 135, a = 135, k ;
        k = pass (i, a) ;
        printf ("\n%d", k) ;
     }
     void pass (int j, int b)
     int c ;
     ```
     ```

```
        {
           c = j + b ;
           return ( c ) ;
        }
```

(b)
```
        # include <stdio.h>
        void jiaayjo ( int , int )
        void main( )
        {
           int p = 23, f = 24 ;
           jiaayjo ( &p, &f ) ;
           printf ( "\n%d %d", p, f ) ;
        }
        void jiaayjo ( int q, int g )
        {
           q = q + q ;
           g = g + g ;
        }
```

(c)
```
        # include <stdio.h>
        void check ( int ) ;
        void main( )
        {
           int k = 35, z ;
           z = check ( k ) ;
           printf ( "\n%d", z ) ;
        }
        void check ( m )
        {
           int m ;
           if ( m > 40 )
                   return ( 1 ) ;
           else
                   return ( 0 ) ;
        }
```

(d)
```
        # include <stdio.h>
        void function ( int * ) ;
        void main( )
        {
           int i = 35, *z ;
           z = function ( &i ) ;
           printf ( "\n%d", z ) ;
        }
```

```
void function ( int *m )
{
    return ( m + 2 ) ;
}
```

[I] What will be the output of the following programs:

(a)
```
# include <stdio.h>
void main( )
{
    int i = 0 ;
    i++ ;
    if ( i <= 5 )
    {
        printf ( "\nC adds wings to your thoughts" ) ;
        exit( ) ;
        main( ) ;
    }
}
```

(b)
```
# include <stdio.h>
void main( )
{
    static int i = 0 ;
    i++ ;
    if ( i <= 5 )
    {
        printf ( "\n%d", i ) ;
        main( ) ;
    }
    else
        exit( ) ;
}
```

[J] Attempt the following:

(a) A 5-digit positive integer is entered through the keyboard, write a function to calculate the sum of the digits of the 5-digit number:
   (1) Without using recursion
   (2) Using recursion

(b) A positive integer is entered through the keyboard, write a program to obtain the prime factors of the number. Modify the function suitably to obtain the prime factors recursively.

(c) Write a recursive function to obtain the first 25 numbers of a Fibonacci sequence. In a Fibonacci sequence the sum of two successive terms gives the third term. Following are the first few terms of the Fibonacci sequence:

$$1 \quad 1 \quad 2 \quad 3 \quad 5 \quad 8 \quad 13 \quad 21 \quad 34 \quad 55 \quad 89 \ldots$$

(d) A positive integer is entered through the keyboard, write a function to find the binary equivalent of this number using recursion.

(e) Write a recursive function to obtain the running sum of the first 25 natural numbers.

(f) Write a C function to evaluate the series

$$\sin(x) = x - (x^3/3!) + (x^5/5!) - (x^7/7!) + \cdots$$

to five significant digits.

(g) Given three variables **x**, **y**, **z** write a function to circularly shift their values to right. In other words, if $x = 5, y = 8, z = 10$ after a circular shift $y = 5, z = 8, x = 10$, after another circular shift $y = 5, z = 8$ and $x = 10$. Call the function with variables **a**, **b**, **c** to circularly shift values.

(h) Write a function to find the binary equivalent of a given decimal integer and display it.

(i) If the lengths of the sides of a triangle are denoted by **a**, **b**, and **c**, then the area of a triangle is given by

$$area = \sqrt{S(S-a)(S-b)(S-c)}$$

where, $S = (a+b+c)/2$

(j) Write a function to compute the distance between two points and use it to develop another function that will compute the area of the triangle whose vertices are **A(x1, y1)**, **B(x2, y2)**, and **C(x3, y3)**. Use these functions to develop a function that returns a value 1 if the point **(x, y)** lines inside the triangle ABC, otherwise a value 0.

(k) Write a function to compute the greatest common divisor given by Euclid's algorithm, exemplified for $J = 1980, K = 1617$ as follows:

$$1980/1617 = 1 \quad 1980 - 1*1617 = 363$$
$$1617/363 = 4 \quad 1617 - 4*363 = 165$$
$$363/165 = 2 \quad 363 - 2*165 = 33$$
$$5/33 = 5 \quad 165 - 5*33 = 0$$

Thus, the greatest common divisor is 33.

Chapter **6**

DATA TYPES REVISITED

As seen in the first chapter, the primary data types can be of three varieties—**char**, **int**, and **float**. It may seem odd to many, how C programmers manage with such a tiny set of data types. Fact is, the C programmers aren't really deprived. They can derive many data types from these three types. In fact, the number of data types that can be derived in C, is in principle, unlimited. A C programmer can always invent whatever data type he needs, as we will see later in Chapter 10.

Not only this, but the primary data types themselves can be of several types. For example, a **char** can be an **unsigned char** or a **signed char**. Or an **int** can be a **short int** or a **long int**. Sufficiently confusing? Well, let us take a closer look at these variations of primary data types in this chapter.

To fully define a variable, one needs to mention not only its type but also its storage class. In this chapter we will explore the different storage classes and their relevance in C programming.

INTEGERS, *LONG* AND *SHORT*

We have seen earlier that the range of an Integer constant depends upon the compiler. For a 16-bit compiler, like Turbo C or Turbo C++, the range is −32768 to 32767. For a 32-bit compiler, the range would be −2147483648 to +2147483647. Here, a 16-bit compiler means that when it compiles a C program it generates machine language code that is targeted toward working on a 16-bit microprocessor like the Intel 8086/8088. Likewise, a 32-bit compiler like VC++ generates machine language code that is targeted toward a 32-bit microprocessor like the Intel Pentium. Note that this does not mean that a program compiled using Turbo C would not work on 32-bit processor. It would run successfully, but the 32-bit processor would work as if it were a 16-bit processor. This happens because a 32-bit processor provides support for programs compiled using 16-bit compilers. If this backward compatibility support is not provided, the 16-bit program would not run on it. This is precisely what happens on the new Intel Itanium processors, which have withdrawn support for 16-bit code.

Remember that out of the two/four bytes used to store an integer, the highest bit (16th/32nd bit) is used to store the sign of the integer. This bit is 1 if the number is negative, and 0 if the number is positive.

C offers a variation of the integer data type that provides what are called **short** and **long** integer values. The intention of providing these variations is to provide integers with different ranges wherever possible. Though not a rule, **short** and **long** integers will usually occupy two and four bytes, respectively.

Compiler	short	int	long
16-bit (Turbo C/C++)	2	2	4
32-bit (Visual C++)	2	4	4

FIGURE 6.1

Each compiler can decide appropriate sizes depending on the operating system and hardware for which it is being written, subject to the following rules:

   (a) **short**s are at least 2 bytes big
   (b) **long**s are at least 4 bytes big
   (c) **short**s are never bigger than **int**s
   (d) **int**s are never bigger than **long**s

Figure 6.1 shows the sizes of different integers based upon the OS used.
   long variables that hold **long** integers are declared using the keyword **long**, as in,

```
long int i ;
long int abc ;
```

long integers cause the program to run a bit slower, but the range of values that we can use is expanded tremendously. The value of a **long** integer typically can vary from -2147483648 to $+2147483647$. You should not need more than this unless you are taking a world census.
   If there are such things as **long**s, symmetry requires **short**s as well—integers that need less space in memory and thus help speed up program execution. **short** integer variables are declared as,

```
short int j ;
short int height ;
```

C allows the abbreviation of **short int** to **short** and of **long int** to **long**. So the previous declarations can be written as,

```
long i ;
long abc ;
short j ;
short height ;
```

Naturally, most C programmers prefer this shortcut.

Sometimes we come across situations where the constant is small enough to be an **int**, but still we want to give it as much storage as a **long**. In such cases, we add the suffix 'L' or 'l' at the end of the number, as in 23L.

INTEGERS, *SIGNED* **AND** *UNSIGNED*

Sometimes we know in advance that the value stored in a given integer variable will always be positive—when it is being used to only count things, for example. In such a case we can declare the variable to be **unsigned**, as in,

```
unsigned int num_students ;
```

With such a declaration, the range of permissible integer values (for a 16-bit OS) will shift from the range −32768 to +32767 to the range 0 to 65535. Thus, declaring an integer as **unsigned** almost doubles the size of the largest possible value that it can otherwise take. This so happens because on declaring the integer as **unsigned**, the left-most bit is now free and is not used to store the sign of the number. Note that an **unsigned** integer still occupies two bytes. This is how an **unsigned** integer can be declared:

```
unsigned int i ;
unsigned i ;
```

Like an **unsigned int**, there also exists a **short unsigned int** and a **long unsigned int**. By default, a **short int** is a **signed short int** and a **long int** is a **signed long int**.

CHARS, *SIGNED* **AND** *UNSIGNED*

Parallel to **signed** and **unsigned int**s (either **short** or **long**), there also exist **signed** and **unsigned char**s, both occupying one byte each, but having different ranges. To begin with, it might appear strange as to how a **char** can have a sign. Consider the statement

```
char ch = 'A' ;
```

Here, what gets stored in **ch** is the binary equivalent of the ASCII value of 'A' (i.e., binary of 65). And if 65's binary can be stored, then −54's binary can also be stored (in a **signed char**).

A **signed char** is the same as an ordinary **char** and has a range from −128 to +127; whereas an **unsigned char** has a range from 0 to 255. Let us now see a program that illustrates this range:

```
# include <stdio.h>
void main( )
{
    char ch = 291 ;
    printf ( "\n%d %c", ch, ch ) ;
}
```

What output do you expect from this program? Possibly, 291 and the character corresponding to it. Well, not really. Surprised? The reason is that **ch** has been defined as a **char**, and a **char** cannot take a value bigger than +127. Therefore, when the value of **ch** exceeds +127, an appropriate value from the other side of the range is picked up and stored in **ch**. This value in our case happens to be 35, hence 35 and its corresponding character #, gets printed out.

Here is another program that will make the concept clearer.

```
# include <stdio.h>
void main( )
{
    char ch ;

    for ( ch = 0 ; ch <= 255 ; ch++ )
        printf ( "\n%d %c", ch, ch ) ;
}
```

This program should output ASCII values and their corresponding characters. Well, No! This is an indefinite loop. The reason is that **ch** has been defined as a **char**, and a **char** cannot take values bigger than +127. Therefore, when the value of **ch** is +127 and we perform **ch++**, it becomes −128 instead of +128. −128 is less than 255, hence the condition is still satisfied. Here onward **ch** will take values like −127, −126, −125, . . . − 2, −1, 0, +1, +2, . . . + 127, −128, −127, etc. Thus, the value of **ch** will keep oscillating between −128 to +127, thereby ensuring that the loop never gets terminated. How do you overcome this difficulty? Would declaring **ch** as an **unsigned char** solve the problem? Even this would not serve the purpose since when **ch** reaches a value 255, **ch++** would try to make it 256, which cannot be stored in an **unsigned char**. Thus, the only alternative is to declare **ch** as an **int**. However, if we are bent upon writing the program using **unsigned char**, it can be done as follows. The program is definitely less elegant, but workable all the same.

```
# include <stdio.h>
void main( )
```

```
{
    unsigned char ch ;

    for ( ch = 0 ; ch <= 254 ; ch++ )
        printf ( "\n%d %c", ch, ch ) ;
    printf ( "\n%d %c", ch, ch ) ;
}
```

FLOATS AND DOUBLES

A **float** occupies four bytes in memory and can range from $-3.4e38$ to $+3.4e38$. If this is insufficient, then C offers a **double** data type that occupies 8 bytes in memory and has a range from $-1.7e308$ to $+1.7e308$. A variable of type **double** can be declared as,

```
double a, population ;
```

If the situation demands usage of real numbers that lie even beyond the range offered by **double** data type, then there exists a **long double** that can range from $-1.7e4932$ to $+1.7e4932$. A **long double** occupies 10 bytes in memory.

You will see that most of the time in C programming, one is required to use either **char**s or **int**s and cases where **float**s, **double**s, or **long double**s are used are indeed rare.

Let us now write a program that puts to use all the data types that we have learned in this chapter. Go through the following program carefully, which shows how to use these different data types. Note the format specifiers used to input and output these data types.

```
# include <stdio.h>
void main( )
{
    char c ;
    unsigned char d ;
    int i ;
    unsigned int j ;
    short int k ;
    unsigned short int l ;
    long int m ;
    unsigned long int n ;
    float x ;
    double y ;
    long double z ;
```

```
/* char */
scanf ( "%c %c", &c, &d ) ;
printf ( "%c %c", c, d ) ;

/* int */
scanf ( "%d %u", &i, &j ) ;
printf ( "%d %u", i, j ) ;

/* short int */
scanf ( "%d %u", &k, &l ) ;
printf ( "%d %u", k, l ) ;

/* long int */
scanf ( "%ld %lu", &m, &n ) ;
printf ( "%ld %lu", m, n ) ;

/* float, double, long double */
scanf ( "%f %lf %Lf", &x, &y, &z ) ;
printf ( "%f %lf %Lf", x, y, z ) ;
}
```

The essence of all the data types that we have learned so far has been captured in Figure 6.2.

A FEW MORE ISSUES. . .

Having seen all the variations of the primary types, let us take a look at some more related issues.

(a) We saw earlier that the size of an integer is compiler dependent. This is even true in the case of **char**s and **float**s. Also, depending upon the microprocessor for which the compiler targets its code, the accuracy of floating point calculations may change. For example, the result of 22.0/7.0 would be reported more accurately by a VC++ compiler as compared to TC/TC++ compilers. This is because TC/TC++ targets its compiled code to 8088/8086 (16-bit) microprocessors. Since these microprocessors do not offer floating point support, TC/TC++ performs all float operations using a software piece called Floating Point Emulator. This emulator has limitations and therefore produces less accurate results. Also, this emulator becomes part of the EXE file, thereby increasing its size. In addition to this increased size there is

Data Type	Range	Bytes	Format
signed char	-128 to + 127	1	%c
unsigned char	0 to 255	1	%c
short signed int	-32768 to +32767	2	%d
short unsigned int	0 to 65535	2	%u
signed int	-32768 to +32767	2	%d
unsigned int	0 to 65535	2	%u
long signed int	-2147483648 to +2147483647	4	%ld
long unsigned int	0 to 4294967295	4	%lu
float	-3.4e38 to +3.4e38	4	%f
double	-1.7e308 to +1.7e308	8	%lf
long double	-1.7e4932 to +1.7e4932	10	%Lf

Note: The sizes and ranges of int, short, and long are compiler dependent. Sizes in this figure are for a 16-bit compiler

FIGURE 6.2

a performance penalty since this bigger code will take more time to execute.

(b) If you look at ranges of **char**s and **int**s there seems to be one extra number on the negative side. This is because a negative number is always stored as 2's complement of its binary. For example, let us see how −128 is stored. First, binary of 128 is calculated (10000000), then its 1's complement is obtained (01111111). A 1's complement is obtained by changing all 0s to 1s and 1s to 0s. Finally, 2's complement of this number, i.e., 10000000, gets stored. A 2's complement is obtained by adding 1 to the 1's complement. Thus, for −128, 10000000 gets stored. This is an 8-bit number and it can be easily accommodated in a **char**, whereas +128 cannot be stored in a **char** because its binary 010000000 (left-most 0 is for a positive sign) is a 9-bit number. However, +127 can be stored as its binary 01111111 turns out to be an 8-bit number.

(c) What happens when we attempt to store +128 in a **char**? The first number on the negative side, i.e., −128 gets stored. This is because from the 9-bit binary of +128, 010000000, only the rightmost 8 bits get stored. But when 10000000 is stored, the leftmost bit is 1 and it is treated as a sign bit. Thus the value of the number becomes −128 since it is indeed the binary of −128, as can be understood from (b) earlier. Similarly, you can verify that an attempt to store +129 in a **char** results in storing −127 in it. In general, if we exceed the range from the positive side we end up on the negative side. Vice versa is also true. If we exceed the range from the negative side we end up on the positive side.

STORAGE CLASSES IN C

We have already said all that needs to be said about constants, but we are not finished with variables. To fully define a variable, one needs to mention not only its 'type' but also its 'storage class.' In other words, not only do all variables have a data type, they also have a 'storage class.'

We have not mentioned storage classes yet, though we have written several programs in C. We were able to get away with this because storage classes have defaults. If we don't specify the storage class of a variable in its declaration, the compiler will assume a storage class depending on the context in which the variable is used. Thus, variables have certain default storage classes.

From the C compiler's point of view, a variable name identifies some physical location within the computer where the string of bits representing the variable's value is stored. There are basically two kinds of locations in a computer where such a value may be kept—Memory and CPU registers. It is the variable's storage class that determines in which of these two types of locations the value is stored.

Moreover, a variable's storage class tells us:

(a) Where the variable will be stored.
(b) What is the initial value of the variable, if the initial value is not specifically assigned (i.e., the default initial value).
(c) What is the scope of the variable; i.e., in which functions the value of the variable will be available.
(d) What is the life of the variable; i.e., how long will the variable exist.

There are four storage classes in C:

(a) Automatic storage class
(b) Register storage class
(c) Static storage class
(d) External storage class

Let us examine these storage classes one by one.

Automatic Storage Class

The features of a variable defined to have an automatic storage class are:

Storage	—	Memory.
Default initial value	—	An unpredictable value, which is often called a garbage value.
Scope	—	Local to the block in which the variable is defined.
Life	—	Until the control remains within the block in which the variable is defined.

The following program shows how an automatic storage class variable is declared, and the fact that if the variable is not initialized, it contains a garbage value.

```
# include <stdio.h>
void main( )
{
    auto int i, j ;
    printf ( "\n%d %d", i, j ) ;
}
```

The output of the program could be:

```
1211 221
```

where 1211 and 221 are garbage values of **i** and **j**. When you run this program, you may get different values, since garbage values are unpredictable. So always make it a point that you initialize the automatic variables properly, otherwise you are likely to get unexpected results. Note that the keyword for this storage class is **auto**, and not automatic.

Scope and life of an automatic variable is illustrated in the following program.

```
# include <stdio.h>
void main( )
{
    auto int i = 1 ;
    {
        {
            {
                printf ( "\n%d ", i ) ;
            }
```

```
          printf ( "%d ", i ) ;
      }
      printf ( "%d", i ) ;
  }
}
```

The output of the program is:

1 1 1

This is because all **printf( )** statements occur within the outermost block (a block is all statements enclosed within a pair of braces) in which **i** has been defined. It means the scope of **i** is local to the block in which it is defined. The moment the control comes out of the block in which the variable is defined, the variable and its value is irretrievably lost. This is shown in the following program.

```
# include <stdio.h>
void main( )
{
    auto int i = 1 ;
    {
        auto int i = 2 ;
        {
            auto int i = 3 ;
            printf ( "\n%d ", i ) ;
        }
        printf ( "%d ", i ) ;
    }
    printf ( "%d", i ) ;
}
```

The output of the program will be:

3 2 1

Note that the compiler treats the three **i**'s as totally different variables, since they are defined in different blocks. Once the control comes out of the innermost block, the variable **i** with value 3 is lost, and hence the **i** in the second **printf( )** refers to **i** with value 2. Similarly, when the control comes out of the next innermost block, the third **printf( )** refers to the **i** with value 1.

Understand the concept of life and scope of an automatic storage class variable thoroughly before proceeding with the next storage class.

Register Storage Class

The features of a variable defined to be of the **register** storage class are:

Storage   — CPU registers.
Default initial value — Garbage value.
Scope   — Local to the block in which the variable is defined.
Life   — Until the control remains within the block in which
                           the variable is defined.

A value stored in a CPU register can always be accessed faster than the one that is stored in memory. Therefore, if a variable is used at many places in a program, it is better to declare its storage class as **register**. A good example of frequently used variables is loop counters. We can name their storage class as **register**.

```
# include <stdio.h>
void main( )
{
    register int i ;

    for ( i = 1 ; i <= 10 ; i++ )
        printf ( "\n%d", i ) ;
}
```

Here, even though we have declared the storage class of **i** as **register**, we cannot say for sure that the value of **i** will be stored in a CPU register. Why? Because the number of CPU registers are limited, and they may be busy doing some other task. What happens in such an event? The variable works as if its storage class is **auto**.

Not every type of variable can be stored in a CPU register. For example, if the microprocessor has 16-bit registers then they cannot hold a **float** value or a **double** value, which require 4 and 8 bytes respectively. However, if you use the **register** storage class for a **float** or a **double** variable, you won't get any error messages. All that would happen is the compiler would treat the variables to be of **auto** storage class.

Static Storage Class

The features of a variable defined to have a **static** storage class are:

Storage   — Memory.
Default initial value — Zero.

Scope   — Local to the block in which the variable is defined.
Life   — Value of the variable persists between different
                 function calls.

Compare the two programs and their output given in Figure 6.3 to understand the difference between the **automatic** and **static** storage classes.

The programs in Figure 6.3 consist of two functions **main( )** and **increment( )**. The function **increment( )** gets called from **main( )** thrice. Each time it prints the value of **i** and then increments it. The only difference in the two programs is that one uses an **auto** storage class for variable **i**, whereas the other uses **static** storage class.

Like **auto** variables, **static** variables are also local to the block in which they are declared. The difference between them is that **static** variables don't disappear when the function is no longer active. Their values persist. If the control comes back to the same function again, the **static** variables have the same values they had last time around.

In the example in Figure 6.3, when variable **i** is **auto**, each time **increment( )** is called, it is re-initialized to one. When the function terminates, **i** vanishes and its new value of 2 is lost. The result: no matter how many times we call **increment( )**, **i** is initialized to 1 every time.

```
# include <stdio.h>                  # include <stdio.h>
void increment( ) ;                  void increment( ) ;
void main( )                         void main( )
{                                    {
    increment( ) ;                       increment( ) ;
    increment( ) ;                       increment( ) ;
    increment( ) ;                       increment( ) ;
}                                    }
void increment( )                    void increment( )
{                                    {
    auto int i = 1 ;                     static int i = 1 ;
    printf ( "%d\n", i ) ;               printf ( "%d\n", i ) ;
    i = i + 1 ;                          i = i + 1 ;
}                                    }
```

The output of the above programs will be:

```
    1                                    1
    1                                    2
    1                                    3
```

FIGURE 6.3

On the other hand, if **i** is **static**, it is initialized to 1 only once. It is never initialized again. During the first call to **increment( )**, **i** is incremented to 2. Because **i** is static, this value persists. The next time **increment( )** is called, **i** is not re-initialized to 1; on the contrary, its old value 2 is still available. This current value of **i** (i.e., 2) gets printed and then **i = i + 1** adds 1 to **i** to get a value of 3. When **increment( )** is called the third time, the current value of **i** (i.e., 3) gets printed and once again **i** is incremented. In short, if the storage class is **static**, then the statement **static int i = 1** is executed only once, regardless of how many times the same function is called.

Consider one more program.

```
# include <stdio.h>

int * fun( ) ;
void main( )
{
    int *j ;
    int * fun( ) ;
    j = fun( ) ;
    printf ( "\n%d", *j ) ;
}
int *fun( )
{
    int k = 35 ;
    return ( &k ) ;
}
```

Here we are returning an address of **k** from **fun( )** and collecting it in **j**. Thus, **j** becomes pointer to **k**. Then, using this pointer, we are printing the value of **k**. This correctly prints out 35. Now try calling any function (even **printf( )**) immediately after the call to **fun( )**. This time **printf( )** prints a garbage value. Why does this happen? In the first case, when the control returned from **fun( )** although **k** went dead, it was still left on the stack. We then accessed this value using its address that was collected in **j**. But when we precede the call to **printf( )** by a call to any other function, the stack is now changed, hence we get the garbage value. If we want to get the correct value each time then we must declare **k** as **static**. By doing this when the control returns from **fun( )**, **k** would not die.

All this having been said, a word of advice—avoid using **static** variables unless you really need them. Because their values are kept in memory when the variables are not active, which means they take up space in memory that could otherwise be used by other variables.

External Storage Class

The features of a variable whose storage class has been defined as external are as follows:

Storage — Memory.
Default initial value — Zero.
Scope — Global.
Life — As long as the program's execution doesn't come to an end.

External variables differ from those we have already discussed in that their scope is global, not local. External variables are declared outside all functions, yet are available to all functions that care to use them. Here is an example to illustrate this fact.

```
# include <stdio.h>

int i ;
void increment( ) ;
void decrement( ) ;

void main( )
{

    printf ( "\ni = %d", i ) ;
    increment( ) ;
    increment( ) ;
    decrement( ) ;
    decrement( ) ;
}

void increment( )
{
    i = i + 1 ;
    printf ( "\non incrementing i = %d", i ) ;
}

void decrement( )
{
    i = i - 1 ;
    printf ( "\non decrementing i = %d", i ) ;
}
```

The output will be:

```
i = 0
on incrementing i = 1
on incrementing i = 2
on decrementing i = 1
on decrementing i = 0
```

As is obvious from the output, the value of **i** is available to the functions **increment( )** and **decrement( )** since **i** has been declared outside all functions.

Look at the following program.

```
# include <stdio.h>
int x = 21 ;

void main( )
{
    extern int y ;
    printf ( "\n%d %d", x, y ) ;
}
int y = 31 ;
```

Here, **x** and **y** both are global variables. Since both of them have been defined outside all the functions, both enjoy external storage class. Note the difference between the following:

```
extern int y ;
int y = 31 ;
```

Here the first statement is a declaration, whereas the second is the definition. When we declare a variable, no space is reserved for it, whereas, when we define it space gets reserved for it in memory. We had to declare **y** since it is being used in **printf( )** before it's definition is encountered. There was no need to declare **x** since its definition is done before its usage. Also, remember that a variable can be declared several times but can be defined only once.

Another small issue—what will be the output of the following program?

```
# include <stdio.h>
int x = 10 ;
void display( ) ;
void main( )
{
    int x = 20 ;
    printf ( "\n%d", x ) ;
```

```
    display( ) ;
}

void display( )
{
    printf ( "\n%d", x ) ;
}
```

Here, **x** is defined at two places, once outside **main( )** and once inside it. When the control reaches the **printf( )** in **main( )** which **x** gets printed? Whenever such a conflict arises, it's the local variable that gets preference over the global variable. Hence the **printf( )** outputs 20. When **display( )** is called and control reaches the **printf( )** there is no such conflict. Hence, this time, the value of the global **x**, i.e., 10, gets printed.

One last thing—a **static** variable can also be declared outside all the functions. For all practical purposes it will be treated as an **extern** variable. However, the scope of this variable is limited to the same file in which it is declared. This means that the variable will not be available to any function that is defined in a file other than the file in which the variable is defined.

A Few Subtle Issues

Let us now look at some subtle issues about storage classes.

(a) All variables that are defined inside a function are normally created on the stack each time the function is called. These variables die as soon as control goes back from the function. However, if the variables inside the function are defined as **static** then they *do not* get created on the stack. Instead they are created in a place in memory called 'Data Segment.' Such variables die only when program execution comes to an end.

(b) If a variable is defined outside all functions, then not only is it available to all other functions in the file in which it is defined, but is also available to functions defined in other files. In the other files the variable should be declared as **extern**. This is shown in the following program:

```
/* PR1.C */
# include <stdio.h>
# include <functions.c>

int i = 35 ;
int fun1( ) ;
int fun2( ) ;
```

```
void main( )
{
    printf ( "%d", I ) ;
    fun1( ) ;
    fun2( ) ;
}

/* FUNCTIONS.C */
extern int i ;
int fun1( )
{
    i++ ;
    printf ( "\n%d", i ) ;
    return 0 ;
}
int fun2( )
{
    i-- ;
    printf ( "\n%d", i ) ;
    return 0 ;
}
```

The output of the program will be:

```
35
36
35
```

However, if we place the word **static** in front of an external variable (**i** in our case) it makes the variable private and not accessible to use in any other file.

(c) In the following statements the first three are definitions, whereas, the last one is a declaration.

```
auto int i ;
static int j ;
register int k ;
extern int l ;
```

Which to Use When

Dennis Ritchie has made available to the C programmer a number of storage classes with varying features, believing that the programmer is in the best position to decide which one of these storage classes to use and when. We can make a few ground rules for usage of different storage classes in different programming situations with a view to:

(a) economise the memory space consumed by the variables

(b) improve the speed of execution of the program

The rules are as follows:

— Use the **static** storage class only if you want the value of a variable to persist between different function calls.

— Use the **register** storage class for only those variables that are being used very often in a program. The reason is, there are very few CPU registers at our disposal and many of them might be busy doing something else. Make careful utilization of the scarce resources. A typical application of **register** storage class is loop counters, which get used a number of times in a program.

— Use the **extern** storage class for only those variables that are being used by almost all the functions in the program. This would avoid unnecessary passing of these variables as arguments when making a function call. Declaring all the variables as **extern** would amount to a lot of wasted memory space because these variables would remain active throughout the life of the program.

— If you don't have any of the express needs mentioned earlier, then use the **auto** storage class. In fact, most of the times, we end up using the **auto** variables, because often it so happens that once we have used the variables in a function, we don't mind losing them.

SUMMARY

(a) We can use different variations of the primary data types, namely **signed** and **unsigned char**, **long** and **short int**, **float**, **double** and **long double**. There are different format specifications for all these data types when they are used in **scanf( )** and **printf( )** functions.

(b) The maximum value a variable can hold depends upon the number of bytes it occupies in memory.

(c) By default, all the variables are **signed**. We can declare a variable as **unsigned** to accommodate greater value without increasing the bytes occupied.

(d) We can make use of proper storage classes like **auto**, **register**, **static**, and **extern** to control four properties of the variable—storage, default initial value, scope, and life.

EXERCISES

[A] What will be the output of the following programs:

(a)
```c
# include <stdio.h>
void main( )
{
    int i ;
    for ( i = 0 ; i <= 50000 ; i++ )
            printf ( "\n%d", i ) ;
}
```

(b)
```c
# include <stdio.h>
void main( )
{
    float a = 13.5 ;
    double b = 13.5 ;
    printf ( "\n%f %lf", a, b ) ;
}
```

(c)
```c
# include <stdio.h>
int i = 0 ;
void val( ) ;
void main( )
{
    printf ( "\nmain's i = %d", i ) ;
    i++ ;
    val( ) ;
    printf ( "\nmain's i = %d", i ) ;
    val( ) ;
}
void val( )
{
    i = 100 ;
    printf ( "\nval's i = %d", i ) ;
    i++ ;
}
```

(d)
```c
# include <stdio.h>
int f ( int ) ;
int g ( int ) ;
void main( )
```

```
    {
        int x, y, s = 2 ;
        s *= 3 ;
        y = f ( s ) ;
        x = g ( s ) ;
        printf ( "\n%d %d %d", s, y, x ) ;
    }
    int t = 8 ;

    int f ( int a )
    {
        a += -5 ;
        t -= 4 ;
        return ( a + t ) ;
    }

    int g ( int a )
    {
        a = 1 ;
        t += a ;
        return ( a + t ) ;
    }
```

(e)
```
    # include <stdio.h>
    void main( )
    {
        static int count = 5 ;
        printf ( "\ncount = %d", count-- ) ;
        if ( count != 0 )
            main( ) ;
    }
```

(f)
```
    # include <stdio.h>
    int g ( int ) ;
    void main( )
    {
        int i, j ;
        for ( i = 1 ; i < 5 ; i++ )
        {
            j = g ( i ) ;
            printf ( "\n%d", j ) ;
        }
    }
```

```
    int g ( int x )
    {
        static int v = 1 ;
        int b = 3 ;
        v += x ;
        return ( v + x + b ) ;
    }
```

(g) # include <stdio.h>
```
    float x = 4.5 ;
    float f ( float ) ;
    void main( )
    {
        float y, float f ( float ) ;
        x *= 2.0 ;
        y = f ( x ) ;
        printf ( "\n%f %f", x, y ) ;
    }
    float f ( float a )
    {
        a += 1.3 ;
        x -= 4.5 ;
        return ( a + x ) ;
    }
```

(h) # include <stdio.h>
```
    void main( )
    {
        func( ) ;
        func( ) ;
    }
    void func( )
    {
        auto int i = 0 ;
        register int j = 0 ;
        static int k = 0 ;
        i++ ; j++ ; k++ ;
        printf ( "\n %d %d %d", i, j, k ) ;
    }
```

(i) # include <stdio.h>
```
    int x = 10 ;
    void main( )
```

```
    {
        int x = 20 ;
        {
            int x = 30 ;
            printf ( "\n%d", x ) ;
        }
        printf ("\n%d", x ) ;
    }
```

[B] Point out the errors, if any, in the following programs:

(a)
```
# include <stdio.h>
void main( )
{
    long num ;
    num = 2 ;
    printf ( "\n%ld", num ) ;
}
```

(b)
```
# include <stdio.h>
void main( )
{
    char ch = 200 ;
    printf ( "\n%d", ch ) ;
}
```

(c)
```
# include <stdio.h>
void main( )
{
    unsigned a = 25 ;
    long unsigned b = 251 ;
    printf ( "\n%lu %u", a, b ) ;
}
```

(d)
```
# include <stdio.h>
void main( )
{
    long float a = 25.345e454 ;
    unsigned double b = 25 ;
    printf ( "\n%lf %d", a, b ) ;
}
```

(e)
```
# include <stdio.h>
void main( )
```

```
    {
        float a = 25.345 ;
        float *b ;
        b = &a ;
        printf ( "\n%f %u", a, b ) ;
    }


(f)  # include <stdio.h>
     static int y ;
     void main( )
     {
         static int z ;
         printf ("%d %d", y, z ) ;
     }
```

[C] State whether the following statements are True or False:

(a) Storage for a register storage class variable is allocated each time the control reaches the block in which it is present.

(b) An extern storage class variable is not available to the functions that precede its definition, unless the variable is explicitly declared in these functions.

(c) The value of an automatic storage class variable persists between various function invocations.

(d) If the CPU registers are not available, the register storage class variables are treated as static storage class variables.

(e) The register storage class variables cannot hold float values.

(f) If we try to use the register storage class for a **float** variable the compiler will flash an error message.

(g) If the variable **x** is defined outside all functions and a variable **x** is also defined as a local variable of some function, then the global variable gets preference over the local variable.

(h) The default value for an automatic variable is zero.

(i) The life of a static variable is until the control remains within the block in which it is defined.

(j) If a global variable is defined, then the **extern** keyword is necessary in its declaration.

(k) The address of a register variable is not accessible.

(l) A variable that is defined outside all functions can also have a static **storage** class.

(m) One variable can have multiple storage classes.

[D] The following program calculates the sum of digits of the number 12345. Go through it and find out why is it necessary to declare the storage class of the variable **sum** as **static**.

```c
# include <stdio.h>
void main( )
{
    int a ;
    a = sumdig ( 12345 ) ;
    printf ( "\n%d", a ) ;
}

int sumdig ( int num )
{

static int sum ;
int a, b ;
a = num % 10 ;
b = ( num - a ) / 10 ;
sum = sum + a ;
if ( b != 0 )
        sumdig ( b ) ;
else
        return ( sum ) ;

}
```

Chapter **7**

THE C PREPROCESSOR

The C preprocessor is exactly what its name implies. It is a program that processes our source program before it is passed to the compiler. Preprocessor commands (often known as directives) form what can almost be considered a language within C language. We can certainly write C programs without knowing anything about the preprocessor or its facilities. But the preprocessor is such a great convenience that virtually all C programmers rely on it. This chapter explores the preprocessor directives and discusses the pros and cons of using them in programs.

FEATURES OF THE C PREPROCESSOR

There are several steps involved from the stage of writing a C program to the stage of getting it executed. The combination of these steps is known as the 'Build Process.' The detailed build process is discussed in the last section of this chapter. At this stage it would be sufficient to note that before a C program is compiled it is passed through another program called 'Preprocessor.' The C program is often known as 'Source Code.' The Preprocessor works on the source code and creates 'Expanded Source Code.' If the source code is stored in a file PR1.C, then the expanded source code gets stored in a file PR1.I. It is this expanded source code that is sent to the compiler for compilation.

The preprocessor offers several features called preprocessor directives. Each of these preprocessor directives begins with a # symbol. The directives can be placed anywhere in a program but are most often placed at the beginning of a program, before the first function definition. We will learn the following preprocessor directives here:

(a) Macro expansion
(b) File inclusion
(c) Conditional Compilation
(d) Miscellaneous directives

Let us understand these features of preprocessor one by one.

MACRO EXPANSION

Have a look at the following program.

```
# include <stdio.h>
# define UPPER 25
```

```
void main( )
{
    int i ;
    for ( i = 1 ; i <= UPPER ; i++ )
            printf ( "\n%d", i ) ;
}
```

In this program, instead of writing 25 in the **for** loop we are writing it in the form of UPPER, which has already been defined before **main( )** through the statement,

```
# define UPPER 25
```

This statement is called 'macro definition' or more commonly, just a 'macro.' What purpose does it serve? During preprocessing, the preprocessor replaces every occurrence of UPPER in the program with 25. Here is another example of macro definition.

```
# include <stdio.h>
# define PI 3.1415
void main( )
{
    float r = 6.25 ;
    float area ;

    area = PI * r * r ;
    printf ( "\nArea of circle = %f", area ) ;

}
```

UPPER and PI in the previous programs are often called 'macro templates,' whereas, 25 and 3.1415 are called their corresponding 'macro expansions.'

When we compile the program, before the source code passes to the compiler, it is examined by the C preprocessor for any macro definitions. When it sees the **#define** directive, it goes through the entire program in search of the macro templates; wherever it finds one, it replaces the macro template with the appropriate macro expansion. Only after this procedure has been completed, is the program handed over to the compiler.

In C programming, it is customary to use capital letters for a macro template. This makes it easy for programmers to pick out all the macro templates when reading through the program.

Note that a macro template and its macro expansion are separated by blanks or tabs. A space between # and **define** is optional. Remember that a macro definition is never to be terminated by a semicolon.

And now the million dollar question—why use **#define** in the earlier programs? What have we gained by substituting PI for 3.1415 in our program? Probably, we have made the program easier to read. Even though 3.1415 is such a common constant that it is easily recognizable, there are many instances where a constant doesn't reveal its purpose so readily. For example, if the phrase "\x1B[2J" causes the screen to clear, which would you find easier to understand in the middle of your program, "\x1B[2J" or "CLEARSCREEN"? Thus, we would use the macro definition

```
# define CLEARSCREEN "\x1B[2J"
```

Then wherever CLEARSCREEN appears in the program, it would automatically be replaced by "\x1B[2J" before compilation begins.

There is perhaps a more important reason for using macro definition than mere readability. Suppose a constant like 3.1415 appears many times in your program. This value may have to be changed some day to 3.141592. Ordinarily, you would need to go through the program and manually change each occurrence of the constant. However, if you have defined PI in a **#define** directive, you only need to make one change, in the **#define** directive itself:

```
\# define PI 3.141592
```

Beyond this, the change will be made automatically to all occurrences of PI before the beginning of compilation.

In short, it is nice to know that you can change values of a constant at all the places in the program by just making a change in the **#define** directive. This convenience may not matter for small programs shown previously, but with large programs, macro definitions are almost indispensable.

But the same purpose could have been served had we used a variable **pi** instead of a macro template **PI**. A variable could also have provided a meaningful name for a constant and permitted one change to effect many occurrences of the constant. It's true that a variable can be used in this way. Then, why not use it? For three reasons it's a bad idea.

First, it is inefficient, since the compiler can generate faster and more compact code for constants than it can for variables. Secondly, using a variable for what is really a constant encourages sloppy thinking and makes the program more difficult to understand: if something never changes, it is hard to imagine it as a variable. And third, there is always a danger that the variable may inadvertently get altered somewhere in the program. So it's no longer the constant that you think it is.

Thus, using **#define** can produce more efficient and more easily understandable programs. This directive is used extensively by C programmers, as you will see in many programs in this book.

The following three examples show popular places where a **#define** directive is used by C programmers.

A **#define** directive is many a time used to define operators as shown here:

```
# include <stdio.h>
# define AND &&
# define OR ||
void main( )
{
    int f = 1, x = 4, y = 90 ;

    if ( ( f < 5 ) AND ( x <= 20 OR y <= 45 ) )
            printf ( "\nYour PC will always work fine..." ) ;
    else
            printf ( "\nIn front of the maintenance man" ) ;

}
```

A **#define** directive could be used to replace a condition, as shown here:

```
# include <stdio.h>
# define AND &&
# define ARANGE ( a > 25 AND a < 50 )

void main( )
{
    int a = 30 ;

    if ( ARANGE )
            printf ( "within range" ) ;
    else
            printf ( "out of range" ) ;
}
```

A **#define** directive could be used to replace an entire C statement. This is shown here:

```
# include <stdio.h>
# define FOUND printf ( "The Yankee Doodle Virus" ) ;

void main( )
{
    char signature ;
```

```
         if ( signature == 'Y' )
                 FOUND
         else
                 printf ( "Safe... as yet !" ) ;
}
```

Macros with Arguments

The macros that we have used so far are called simple macros. Macros can have arguments, just as functions can. Here is an example that illustrates this fact.

```
# include <stdio.h>
# define AREA(x) ( 3.14 * x * x )

void main( )
{
    float r1 = 6.25, r2 = 2.5, a ;

    a = AREA ( r1 ) ;
    printf ( "\nArea of circle = %f", a ) ;
    a = AREA ( r2 ) ;
    printf ( "\nArea of circle = %f", a ) ;
}
```

Here's the output of the program:

```
Area of circle = 122.656250
Area of circle = 19.625000
```

In this program, wherever the preprocessor finds the phrase **AREA(x)** it expands it into the statement (**3.14** * **x** * **x**). However, that's not all that it does. The **x** in the macro template **AREA(x)** is an argument that matches the **x** in the macro expansion (**3.14** * **x** * **x**). The statement **AREA(r1)** in the program causes the variable **r1** to be substituted for **x**. Thus the statement **AREA(r1)** is equivalent to:

```
( 3.14 * r1 * r1 )
```

After the source code has passed through the preprocessor, what the compiler gets to work on will be this:

```
# include <stdio.h>
void main( )
{
    float r1 = 6.25, r2 = 2.5, a ;
```

```
    a = 3.14 * r1 *r1 ;
    printf ( "Area of circle = %f\n", a ) ;
    a = 3.14 *r2 * r2 ;
    printf ( "Area of circle = %f", a ) ;
}
```

Here is another example of macros with arguments:

```
# include <stdio.h>
# define ISDIGIT(y) ( y >= 48 && y <= 57 )

void main( )
{
    char ch ;

    printf ( "Enter any digit " ) ;
    scanf ( "%c", &ch ) ;

    if ( ISDIGIT ( ch ) )
            printf ( "\nYou entered a digit" ) ;
    else
            printf ( "\nIllegal input" ) ;
}
```

Here are some important points to remember while writing macros with arguments:

(a) Be careful not to leave a blank between the macro template and its argument while defining the macro. For example, there should be no blank between **AREA** and **(x)** in the definition, #define AREA(x) (3.14 * x * x).

  If we were to write **AREA (x)** instead of **AREA(x)**, the **(x)** would become a part of macro expansion, which we certainly don't want. What would happen is, the template would be expanded to

```
( r1 ) ( 3.14 * r1 * r1 )
```

  which won't run. Not at all what we wanted.

(b) The entire macro expansion should be enclosed within parentheses. Here is an example of what would happen if we fail to enclose the macro expansion within parentheses.

```
# include <stdio.h>
# define SQUARE(n) n * n
```

```
void main( )
{
    int j ;
    j = 64 / SQUARE ( 4 ) ;
    printf ( "j = %d", j ) ;
}
```

The output of the program would be:

```
j = 64
```

whereas, what we expected was j = 4.

What went wrong? The macro was expanded into

```
j = 64 / 4 * 4 ;
```

which yielded 64.

(c) Macros can be split into multiple lines, with a '\' (back slash) present at the end of each line. The following program shows how we can define and use multiple line macros.

```
# include <stdio.h>
# define HLINE for ( i = 0 ; i < 79 ; i++ ) \
                       printf ( "%c", 196 ) ;

# define VLINE( X, Y ) { \
                          gotoxy ( X, Y ) ; \
                          printf ( "%c", 179 ) ; \
                       }

void main( )
{
    int i, y ;
    clrscr( ) ;

    gotoxy ( 1, 12 ) ; /* positions cursor in row x and column y */
    HLINE
    for ( y = 1 ; y < 25 ; y++ )
          VLINE ( 39, y ) ;
}
```

This program draws a vertical and a horizontal line in the center of the screen.

(d) If, for any reason, you are unable to debug a macro, then you should view the expanded code of the program to see how the macros are getting expanded. If your source code is present in the file PR1.C, then the expanded source code would be stored in PR1.I. You need to generate this file at the command prompt by saying:

```
cpp pr1.c
```

Here, CPP stands for C PreProcessor. It generates the expanded source code and stores it in a file called PR1.I. You can now open this file and see the expanded source code. Note that the file PR1.I gets generated in the C:\TC\BIN directory. The procedure for generating expanded source code for compilers other than Turbo C/C++ might be a little different.

Macros Versus Functions

In the previous example, a macro was used to calculate the area of the circle. As we know, even a function can be written to calculate the area of the circle. Though macro calls are 'like' function calls, they are not really the same things. Then what is the difference between the two?

In a macro call, the preprocessor replaces the macro template with its macro expansion, in a stupid, unthinking, literal way, whereas, in a function call, the control is passed to a function along with certain arguments, some calculations are performed in the function, and a useful value is returned back from the function.

This brings us to a question: when is it best to use macros with arguments and when is it better to use a function? Usually, macros make the program run faster but increase the program size, whereas functions make the program smaller and compact.

If we use a macro a hundred times in a program, the macro expansion goes into our source code at a hundred different places, thus increasing the program size. On the other hand, if a function is used, then even if it is called from a hundred different places in the program, it would take the same amount of space in the program.

But passing arguments to a function and getting back the returned value does take time and would therefore slow down the program. This gets avoided with macros since they have already been expanded and placed in the source code before compilation. Thus the trade-off is between memory space and time.

Moral of the story is—if the macro is simple and sweet like in our examples, it makes nice shorthand and avoids the overheads associated with function calls. On the other hand, if we have a fairly large macro and it is used fairly often, perhaps we ought to replace it with a function.

If memory space in the machine in which the program is being executed is less (like a mobile phone or a PDA), then it may make sense to use functions instead of macros. By doing so, the program may run slower, but will need less memory space.

FILE INCLUSION

The second preprocessor directive we'll explore in this chapter is file inclusion. This directive causes one file to be included in another. The preprocessor command for file inclusion looks like this:

```
# include "filename"
```

and it simply causes the entire contents of **filename** to be inserted into the source code at that point in the program. Of course, this presumes that the file being included exists. When and why is this feature used? It can be used in two cases:

(a) If we have a very large program, the code is best divided into several different files, each containing a set of related functions. It is a good programming practice to keep different sections of a large program separate. These files are **#include** at the beginning of a main program file.

(b) There are some functions and some macro definitions that we need almost in all programs that we write. These commonly needed functions and macro definitions can be stored in a file, and that file can be included in every program we write, which would add all the statements in this file to our program as if we have typed them in.

It is common for the files that are to be included to have a .h extension. This extension stands for 'header file,' possibly because it contains statements that when included go to the head of your program. The prototypes of all the library functions are grouped into different categories and then stored in different header files. For example, prototypes of all mathematics related functions are stored in the header file 'math.h,' prototypes of console input/output functions are stored in the header file 'conio.h,' and so on.

Actually there exist two ways to write **#include** statement. These are:

```
# include "filename"
# include <filename>
```

The meaning of each of these forms is given here:

`# include "goto.h"`   This command will look for the file **goto.h** in the current directory as well as the specified list of directories as mentioned in the include search path that might have been set up.

`# include <goto.h>`   This command will look for the file **goto.h** in the specified list of directories only.

The include search path is nothing but a list of directories that would be searched for the file being included. Different C compilers let you set the search path in different manners. If you are using the Turbo C/C++ compiler, then the search path can be set up by selecting 'Directories' from the 'Options' menu. On doing this, a dialog box appears. In this dialog box under 'Include Directories,' we can specify the search path. We can also specify multiple include paths separated by a ';' (semicolon) as shown below:

`c:\tc\lib ; c:\mylib ; d:\libfiles`

The path can contain a maximum of 127 characters. Both relative and absolute paths are valid. For example, '..\dir\incfiles' is a valid path.

CONDITIONAL COMPILATION

We can, if we want, have the compiler skip over part of a source code by inserting the preprocessing commands **#ifdef** and **#endif**, which have the general form:

```
# ifdef macroname
    statement 1 ;
    statement 2 ;
    statement 3 ;
# endif
```

If **macroname** has been **#define**d, the block of code will be processed as usual; otherwise not.

Where would **#ifdef** be useful? When would you like to compile only a part of your program? In three cases:

(a) To "comment out" obsolete lines of code. It often happens that a program is changed at the last minute to satisfy a client. This involves rewriting some part of source code to the client's satisfaction and deleting the old code. But veteran programmers are familiar with the clients who change their mind and want the old code back again just the way it was. Now you would definitely not like to retype the deleted code again.

One solution in such a situation is to put the old code within a pair of /*   */ combination. But we might have already written a comment in the code that we are about to "comment out." This would mean we end up with nested comments. Obviously, this solution won't work since we can't nest comments in C.

Therefore, the solution is to use conditional compilation as shown here:

```
void main( )
{
    # ifdef OKAY
        statement 1 ;
        statement 2 ; /* detects virus */
        statement 3 ;
        statement 4 ; /* specific to stone virus */
    # endif

    statement 5 ;
    statement 6 ;
    statement 7 ;
}
```

Here, statements 1, 2, 3, and 4 would get compiled only if the macro OKAY has been defined, and we have purposefully omitted the definition of the macro OKAY. At a later date, if we want that these statements should also get compiled, all that we are required to do is delete the **#ifdef** and **#endif** statements.

(b) A more sophisticated use of **#ifdef** has to do with making the programs portable, i.e., to make them work on two totally different computers. Suppose an organization has two different types of computers and you are expected to write a program that works on both machines. You can do so by isolating the lines of code that must be different for each machine by marking them with **#ifdef**. For example:

```
void main( )
{
    # ifdef INTEL
        code suitable for an Intel PC
    # else
        code suitable for a Motorola PC
    # endif
```

```
        code common to both the computers
}
```

When you compile this program, it would compile only the code suitable for a Mototola PC and the common code. This is because the macro INTEL has not been defined. Note that, the working of **#ifdef - #else - #endif** is similar to the ordinary **if - else** control instruction of C.

If you want to run your program on a Motorola PC, just add a statement at the top saying,

```
# define INTEL
```

Sometimes, instead of **#ifdef**, the **#ifndef** directive is used. The **#ifndef** (which means 'if not defined') works exactly opposite to **#ifdef**. The previous example, if written using **#ifndef**, would look like this:

```
void main( )
{
    # ifndef INTEL
            code suitable for a Intel PC
    # else
            code suitable for a Motorola PC
    # endif
    code common to both the computers
}
```

(c) Suppose a function **myfunc( )** is defined in a file 'myfile.h,' which is **#include**d in a file 'myfile1.h.' Now in your program file, if you **#include** both 'myfile.h' and 'myfile1.h,' the compiler flashes an error 'Multiple declaration for **myfunc**.' This is because the same file 'myfile.h' gets included twice. To avoid this, we can write the following code in the 'myfile.h' header file.

```
/* myfile.h */
# ifndef __myfile_h
    # define __myfile_h

    myfunc( )
    {
        /* some code */
    }
# endif
```

The first time the file 'myfile.h' gets included, the preprocessor checks whether a macro called **__myfile_h** has been defined or not. If it has not been, then it gets defined and the rest of the code gets included. Next time we attempt to include the same file, the inclusion is prevented since **__myfile_h** already stands defined. Note that there is nothing special about **__myfile_h**. In its place, we can use any other macro as well.

#*if* AND #*elif* DIRECTIVES

The **#if** directive can be used to test whether an expression evaluates to a nonzero value or not. If the result of the expression is nonzero, then subsequent lines up to a **# else**, **#elif**, or **#endif** are compiled, otherwise they are skipped.

A simple example of the **#if** directive is shown here:

```
void main( )
{
    # if TEST <= 5
        statement 1 ;
        statement 2 ;
        statement 3 ;
    # else
        statement 4 ;
        statement 5 ;
        statement 6 ;
    # endif
}
```

If the expression, **TEST <= 5** evaluates to true, then statements 1, 2, and 3 are compiled, otherwise statements 4, 5, and 6 are compiled. In place of the expression **TEST <= 5**, other expressions like (**LEVEL == HIGH || LEVEL == LOW**) or **ADAPTER == VGA** can also be used.

If we so desire, we can have nested conditional compilation directives. An example that uses such directives is shown here:

```
# if ADAPTER == VGA
        code for video graphics array
# else
        # if ADAPTER == SVGA
            code for super video graphics array
        # else
```

```
        code for extended graphics adapter
    # endif
# endif
```

The program segment can be made more compact by using another conditional compilation directive called **#elif**. The same program using this directive can be rewritten as follows. Observe that by using the **#elif** directives, the number of **#endif**s used in the program get reduced.

```
# if ADAPTER == VGA
      code for video graphics array
# elif ADAPTER == SVGA
        code for super video graphics array
# else
        code for extended graphics adapter
# endif
```

MISCELLANEOUS DIRECTIVES

There are two more preprocessor directives available, though they are not commonly used. They are:

(a) #undef
(b) #pragma

#undef Directive

On some occasions, it may be desirable to cause a defined name to become 'undefined.' This can be accomplished by means of the **#undef** directive. In order to undefine a macro that has been earlier **#define**d, the directive,

```
# undef macro template
```

can be used. Thus the statement,

```
\# undef PENTIUM
```

would cause the definition of PENTIUM to be removed from the system. All subsequent **#ifdef PENTIUM** statements would evaluate to false. In practice, seldom are you required to undefine a macro, but if for some reason you are required to, then you know that there is something to fall back upon.

#pragma Directive

This directive is another special-purpose directive that you can use to turn on or off certain features. Pragmas vary from one compiler to another. There are certain pragmas available with Microsoft C compiler that deal with formatting source listings and placing comments in the object file generated by the compiler. Turbo C/C++ compiler has got a pragma that allows you to suppress warnings generated by the compiler. Some of these pragmas are discussed as follows.

(a) **#pragma startup** and **#pragma exit**: These directives allow us to specify functions that are called upon program startup (before **main( )**) or program exit (just before the program terminates). Their usage is as follows:

```
void fun1( ) ;
void fun2( ) ;

# pragma startup fun1
# pragma exit fun2

void main( )
{
    printf ( "\nInside maim" ) ;
}

void fun1( )
{
    printf ( "\nInside fun1" ) ;
}

void fun2( )
{
    printf ( "\nInside fun2" ) ;
}
```

And here is the output of the program:

```
Inside fun1
Inside main
Inside fun2
```

Note that the functions **fun1( )** and **fun2( )** should neither receive nor return any value. If we want two functions to get executed at startup, then their pragmas should be defined in the reverse order in which you want to get them called.

(b) **#pragma warn**: On compilation the compiler reports Errors and Warnings in the program, if any. Errors provide the programmer with no options, apart from correcting them. Warnings, on the other hand, offer the programmer a hint or suggestion that something may be *wrong* with a particular piece of code. The two most common situations when warnings are displayed are:

–   If you have written code that the compiler's designers (or the ANSI-C specification) consider bad C programming practice. For example, if a function does not return a value, then it should be declared as **void**.

–   If you have written code that might cause runtime errors, such as assigning a value to an uninitialized pointer.

The **#pragma warn** directive tells the compiler whether or not we want to suppress a specific warning. Usage of this pragma is shown here:

```c
# pragma warn -rvl /* return value */
# pragma warn -par /* parameter not used */
# pragma warn -rch /* unreachable code */

int f1( )
{
    int a = 5 ;
}

void f2 ( int x )
{
    printf ( "\nInside f2" ) ;
}

int f3( )
{
    int x = 6 ;
    return x ;
    x++ ;
}

void main( )
{
    f1( ) ;
    f2 ( 7 ) ;
    f3( ) ;
}
```

If you go through the program, you should notice three problems immediately. These are:

(a) Though promised, **f1( )** doesn't return a value.
(b) The parameter **x** that is passed to **f2( )** is not being used anywhere in **f2( )**.
(c) The control can never reach **x++** in **f3( )**.

If we compile the program, we should expect warnings indicating these problems. However, this does not happen since we have suppressed the warnings using the **#pragma** directives. If we replace the '−' sign with a '+,' then these warnings would be flashed on compilation. Though it is a bad practice to suppress warnings, at times, it becomes useful to suppress them. For example, if have written a huge program and are trying to compile it, then to begin with, you are more interested in locating the errors, rather than the warnings. At such times, you may suppress the warnings. Once you have located all errors, then you may turn on the warnings and sort them out.

THE BUILD PROCESS

There are many steps involved in converting a C program into an executable form. Figure 7.1 shows these different steps along with the files created during each stage.

Many software development tools, like say TC++ and VC++, hide many of the steps shown in Figure 7.1 from us. However, it is important to understand these steps for two reasons:

(a) It would help you to understand the process much better, rather than just believing that some kind of 'magic' generates the executable code.
(b) If you are to alter any of these steps, then you would know how to do it.

Let us now understand the steps mentioned in Figure 7.1 in detail.

Preprocessing

During this step, the C source code is expanded based on the preprocessor directives like **#define**, **#include**, **#ifdef**, etc. The expanded source code is stored in an intermediate file with **.i** extension. Thus, if our source code

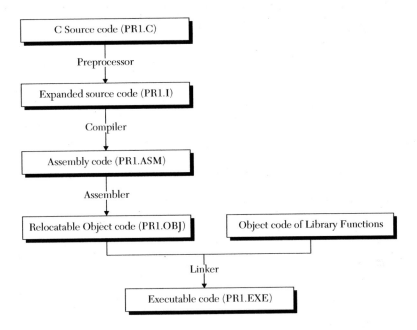

FIGURE 7.1

is stored in PR1.C, then the expanded source code is stored in PR1.I. The expanded source code is also in C language. Note that the '.I' extension may vary from one compiler to another.

Compilation

The expanded source code is then passed to the compiler, which identifies the syntax errors in the expanded source code. These errors are displayed along with warnings, if any. As we saw in the last section, using the **#pragma** directive we can control which warnings are displayed/hidden.

If the expanded source code is error-free, then the compiler translates the expanded source code in C into an equivalent assembly language program. Different processors (CPUs) support different sets of assembly instructions, using those they can be programmed with. Hence, the compiler targeted for an Intel Pentium III platform would generate the assembly code using the instructions understood by Intel Pentium III. Likewise, the same C program, when compiled using a compiler targeted for an Intel Pentium IV platform, is likely to generate a different assembly language code. The assembly code is typically stored in a .ASM file. Thus, for PR1.I the assembly code would be stored in PR1.ASM.

Assembling

The job of the Assembler is to translate .ASM programs into Relocatable Object code. Thus, if the assembly language instructions are present in PR1.ASM, then the relocatable object code gets stored in PR1.OBJ.

Here the word 'Relocatable' means that the program is complete except for one thing—no specific memory addresses have yet been assigned to the code and data sections in the relocatable code. All the addresses are relative offsets.

The .OBJ file that gets created is a specially formatted binary file. The object file contains a header and several sections. The header describes the sections that follow it. These sections are:

(a) Text section—This section contains machine language code equivalent to the expanded source code.

(b) Data Section—This section contains global variables and their initial values.

(c) Bss (Block Started by Symbol) section—This section contains uninitialized global variables.

(d) Symbol Table—This section contains information about symbols found during assembling of the program. Typical information present in the symbol table includes:
   – Names, types, and sizes of global variables
   – Names and addresses of functions defined in the source code
   – Names of external functions like **printf( )** and **scanf( )**

Although there are machine language instructions in the .OBJ file it cannot be executed directly. This is because of the following reasons:

(a) The external functions like **printf( )** are not present in the .OBJ file.

(b) The .OBJ file may use some global variables defined in another .OBJ file. For example, PR1.OBJ may use a global variable **count2**, which is defined in the file PR2.OBJ.

(c) The .OBJ file may use a function defined in another .OBJ file. For example, PR2.OBJ may use a function **display( )** defined in the file PR1.OBJ.

Note that parts of the symbol table may be incomplete because all the variables and functions may not be defined in the same file. The references to such variables and functions (symbols) that are defined in other source files are later on resolved by the linker.

Linking

Linking is the final stage in creating an executable program. It has to do the following important things:

   (a) Find definition of all external functions—those which are defined in other .OBJ files, and those which are defined in Libraries (like **printf( )**).

   (b) Find definition of all global variables—those which are defined in other .OBJ files, and those which are defined in Libraries (like 'errno,' which is a commonly used global variable that is defined in Standard C Library).

   (c) Combine Data Sections of different .OBJ files into a single Data Section.

   (d) Combine Code Sections of different .OBJ files into a single Code Section.

While combining different .OBJ files the linker has to address one problem—addresses of all variables and functions in the Symbol Table of the .OBJ file are Relative addresses. This means that the address of a Symbol (variable or function), is in fact only an offset from the start of the Section (Data or Code Section) to which it belongs. For example, if there are two 4-byte wide global integer variables **count1** and **index1** in PR1.OBJ, then the Symbol Table will have addresses 0 and 4 for them. Similarly, if PR2.OBJ has two similar variables **count2** and **index2**, then the Symbol Table in PR2.OBJ will have addresses 0 and 4 for these variables. The same addressing scheme is used with functions present in each .OBJ file.

When linker combines the two .OBJ files, it has to readjust the addresses of global variables and functions. Thus, the variables **count1**, **index1**, **count2**, and **index2** will now enjoy addresses 0, 4, 8, and 12 respectively. Similar readjustment of addresses will be done for functions. Even after readjustment, the addresses of variables and functions are still 'relative' in the combined Data and Code sections of the .EXE file.

In the .EXE file, machine language code from all of the input object files will be in the Text section. Similarly, all initialized and uninitialized variables will reside in the new Data and Bss sections, respectively.

During linking, if the linker detects errors such as misspelling the name of a library function in the source code, or using the incorrect number or type of parameters for a function, it stops the linking process and doesn't create the binary executable file.

Loading

Once the .EXE file is created and stored on the disk, it is ready for execution. When we execute it, it is first brought from the disk into the memory (RAM) by an Operating System component called Program Loader. Program Loader can place the .EXE anywhere in memory depending on its availability. Since all the addresses in the .EXE file are 'relative' addresses, exact 'position' where .EXE is loaded in memory doesn't matter. No further adjustment of addresses is necessary. Thus, the Code and Data in an .EXE file are 'Position Independent.' Once the loading process is completed, the execution begins from the first instruction in the Code section of the file loaded in memory.

Modern Operating Systems, like Windows and Linux, permit loading and execution of multiple programs in memory. One final word before we end this topic. Like a .OBJ file, a .EXE file is also a formatted binary file. The format of these binary files differ from one Operating System to another. For example, Windows Operating System use Portable Executable (PE) file format, whereas Linux uses Executable and Linking Format (ELF). Hence an .OBJ or .EXE file created for Windows cannot be used on Linux and vice versa.

Figure 7.2 summarizes the role played by each processor program during the build process.

Processor	Input	Output
Editor	Program typed from keyboard	C source code containing program and preprocessor commands
Prepro-cessor	C source code file	Source code file with the preprocessing commands properly sorted out
Compiler	Source code file with preprocessing commands sorted out	Assemby language code
Assembler	Assembly language code	Relocatable Oject code in machine language
Linker	Object code of our program and object code of library functions	Executable code in machine language
Loader	Executable file	

FIGURE 7.2

SUMMARY

(a) The preprocessor directives enable the programmer to write programs that are easy to develop, read, modify, and transport to a different computer system.

(b) We can make use of various preprocessor directives, such as **#define**, **#include**, **#ifdef** - **#else** - **#endif**, **#if**, and **#elif** in our program.

(c) The directives like **#undef** and **#pragma** are also useful although they are seldom used.

EXERCISES

[A] Answer the following:

(a) What is a preprocessor directive
  1. a message from the compiler to the programmer
  2. a message from the compiler to the linker
  3. a message from the programmer to the preprocessor
  4. a message from the programmer to the microprocessor

(b) Which of the following are correctly formed **# define** statements:

```
#define INCH PER FEET 12
#define SQR (X) ( X * X )
#define SQR(X) X * X
#define SQR(X) ( X * X )
```

(c) State True or False:
  1. A macro must always be written in capital letters.
  2. A macro should always be accomodated in a single line.
  3. After preprocessing, when the program is sent for compilation, the macros are removed from the expanded source code.
  4. Macros with arguments are not allowed.
  5. Nested macros are allowed.
  6. In a macro call, the control is passed to the macro.

(d) How many **#include** directives can there be in a given program file?

(e) What is the difference between the following two **#include** directives:

```
#include "conio.h"
#include <conio.h>
```

(f) A header file is:
1. A file that contains standard library functions
2. A file that contains definitions and macros
3. A file that contains user-defined functions
4. A file that is present in a current working directory
(g) Which of the following is not a preprocessor directive
1. #if
2. #elseif
3. #undef
4. #pragma
(h) All macro substitutions in a program are done
1. Before compilation of the program
2. After compilation
3. During execution
4. None of the above
(i) In a program, the statement:

```
#include "filename"
```

is replaced by the contents of the file "filename"
1. Before compilation
2. After compilation
3. During execution
4. None of the above

[B] What will be the output of the following programs:

(a)
```
# include <stdio.h>
void main( )
{
    int i = 2 ;
    # ifdef DEF
            i *= i ;
    # else
            printf ( "\n%d", i ) ;
    # endif
}
```

(b)
```
# include <stdio.h>
# define PRODUCT(x) ( x * x )
void main( )
{
    int i = 3, j ;
```

```
        j = PRODUCT( i + 1 ) ;
        printf ( "\n%d", j ) ;
    }
```

(c)
```
# include <stdio.h>
# define PRODUCT(x) ( x * x )
void main( )
{
    int i = 3, j, k ;
    j = PRODUCT( i++ ) ;
    k = PRODUCT ( ++i ) ;

    printf ( "\n%d %d", j, k ) ;
}
```

(d)
```
# include <stdio.h>
# define SEMI ;
void main( )
{
    int p = 3 SEMI ;
    printf ( "%d", p ) SEMI
}
```

(e)
```
# include <stdio.h>
# define PI 3.14
# define AREA( x, y, z ) ( PI * x * x + y * z ) ;
void main( )
{
    float a = AREA ( 1, 5, 8 ) ;
    float b = AREA ( AREA ( 1, 5, 8 ), 4, 5 ) ;
    printf ( "\n a = %f", a ) ;
    printf ( "\n b = %f", b ) ;
}
```

[C] Attempt the following:

(a) If a macro is not getting expanded as per your expectation, how will you find out how is it being expanded by the preprocessor.

(b) Write down macro definitions for the following:
1. To test whether a character is a lower case letter or not.
2. To test whether a character is an uppercase letter or not.
3. To test whether a character is a letter or not. Make use of the macros you defined in 1 and 2 above.
4. To obtain the bigger of two numbers.

(c) Write macro definitions with arguments for calculation of area and perimeter of a triangle, a square, and a circle. Store these macro definitions in a file called "areaperi.h." Include this file in your program, and call the macro definitions for calculating area and perimeter for different squares, triangles, and circles.

(d) Write down macro definitions for the following:
1. To find the arithmetic mean of two numbers.
2. To find the absolute value of a number.
3. To convert an uppercase letter to lowercase.
4. To obtain the bigger of two numbers.

(e) Write macro definitions with arguments for calculation of simple interest and amount. Store these macro definitions in a file called "interest.h." Include this file in your program, and use the macro definitions for calculating simple interest and amount.

Chapter 8

ARRAYS

The C language provides a capability that enables the user to design a set of similar data types, called arrays. This chapter describes how arrays can be created and manipulated in C.

We should note that, in many C books and courses, arrays and pointers are taught separately. We believe it is best to deal with these topics together. This is because pointers and arrays are so closely related that discussing arrays without discussing pointers would make the discussion incomplete and wanting. In fact, all arrays make use of pointers internally. Hence, it is all too relevant to study them together rather than as isolated topics.

WHAT ARE ARRAYS?

To understand arrays properly, let us consider the following program:

```
# include <stdio.h>
void main( )
{
    int x ;
    x = 5 ;
    x = 10 ;
    printf ( "\nx = %d", x ) ;
}
```

No doubt, this program will print the value of **x** as 10. Why so? Because, when a value 10 is assigned to **x**, the earlier value of **x**, i.e., 5, is lost. Thus, ordinary variables (the ones which we have used so far) are capable of holding only one value at a time (as in this example). However, there are situations in which we would want to store more than one value at a time in a single variable.

For example, suppose we wish to arrange the percentage marks obtained by 100 students in ascending order. In such a case, we have two options to store these marks in memory:

(a) Construct 100 variables to store percentage marks obtained by 100 different students, i.e., each variable containing one student's marks.
(b) Construct one variable (called an array or subscripted variable) capable of storing or holding all hundred values.

Obviously, the second alternative is better. A simple reason for this is, it would be much easier to handle one variable than handling 100 different variables. Moreover, there are certain logics that cannot be dealt with without the use of an array. Now a formal definition of an array—an array is a collective name given to a group of 'similar quantities.' These similar quantities could be percentage marks of 100 students, or salaries of 300 employees, or ages of 50 employees. What is important is that the quantities must be 'similar.' Each member in the group is referred to by its position in the group. For example, assume the following group of numbers, which represent percentage marks obtained by five students.

```
per = { 48, 88, 34, 23, 96 }
```

If we want to refer to the second number of the group, the usual notation used is per$_2$. Similarly, the fourth number of the group is referred to as per$_4$. However, in C, the fourth number is referred to as **per[3].** This is because, in C, the counting of elements begins with 0 and not with 1. Thus, in this example, **per[3]** refers to 23 and **per[4]** refers to 96. In general, the notation would be **per[i]**, where **i** can take a value 0, 1, 2, 3, or 4, depending on the position of the element being referred. Here, **per** is the subscripted variable (array), whereas **i** is its subscript.

Thus, an array is a collection of similar elements. These similar elements could be all **int**s, or all **float**s, or all **char**s, etc. Usually, the array of characters is called a 'string,' whereas an array of **int**s or **float**s is simply called an array. Remember that all elements of any given array must be of the same type, i.e., we cannot have an array of 10 numbers, of which 5 are **int**s and 5 are **float**s.

A Simple Program Using Arrays

Let us try to write a program to find the average mark obtained by a class of 30 students in a test.

```c
# include <stdio.h>
void main( )
{
    int avg, sum = 0 ;
    int i ;
    int marks[30] ; /* array declaration */

    for ( i = 0 ; i <= 29 ; i++ )
    {
        printf ( "\nEnter marks " ) ;
        scanf ( "%d", &marks[i] ) ; /* store data in array */
    }

    for ( i = 0 ; i <= 29 ; i++ )
        sum = sum + marks[i] ; /* read data from an array*/

    avg = sum / 30 ;
    printf ( "\nAverage marks = %d", avg ) ;
}
```

There is a lot of new material in this program, so let us take it apart slowly.

Array Declaration

To begin with, like other variables, an array needs to be declared so that the compiler will know what kind of an array and how large an array we want. In our program, we have done this with the statement:

```
int marks[30] ;
```

Here, **int** specifies the type of the variable, just as it does with ordinary variables and the word **marks** specifies the name of the variable. The **[30]**, however, is new. The number 30 tells how many elements of the type **int** will be in our array. This number is often called the 'dimension' of the array. The bracket ([ ]) tells the compiler that we are dealing with an array.

Accessing Elements of an Array

Once an array is declared, let us see how individual elements in the array can be referred. This is done with subscript, the number in the brackets following the array name. This number specifies the element's position in the array. All the array elements are numbered, starting with 0. Thus, **marks[2]** is not the second element of the array, but the third. In our program, we are using the variable **i** as a subscript to refer to various elements of the array. This variable can take different values and hence can refer to the different elements in the array in turn. This ability to use variables to represent subscripts is what makes arrays so useful.

Entering Data into an Array

Here is the section of code that places data into an array:

```
for ( i = 0 ; i <= 29 ; i++ )
{
    printf ( "\nEnter marks " ) ;
    scanf ( "%d", &marks[i] ) ;
}
```

The **for** loop causes the process of asking for and receiving a student's marks from the user to be repeated 30 times. The first time through the loop, **i** has a value 0, so the **scanf( )** function will cause the value typed to be stored in the array element **marks[0]**, the first element of the array. This process will be repeated until **i** becomes 29. This is last time through the loop, which is a good thing, because there is no array element **marks[30]**.

In the **scanf( )** function, we have used the "address of" operator **(&)** on the element **marks[i]** of the array, just as we have used it earlier on other variables **(& rate**, for example). In so doing, we are passing the address of this particular array element to the **scanf( )** function, rather than its value; which is what **scanf( )** requires.

Reading Data from an Array

The balance of the program reads the data back out of the array and uses it to calculate the average. The **for** loop is much the same, but now the body of the loop causes each student's marks to be added to a running total stored in a variable called **sum**. When all the marks have been added up, the result is divided by 30, the number of students, to get the average.

```
for ( i = 0 ; i <= 29 ; i++ )
        sum = sum + marks[i] ;

avg = sum / 30 ;
printf ( "\nAverage marks = %d", avg ) ;
```

Let us review what we have learned about arrays:

(a) An array is a collection of similar elements.
(b) The first element in the array is numbered 0, so the last element is 1 less than the size of the array.
(c) An array is also known as a subscripted variable.
(d) Before using an array, its type and dimension must be declared.
(e) However big an array, its elements are always stored in contiguous memory locations. This is a very important point which we will discuss in more detail later on.

MORE ON ARRAYS

An array is a very popular data type with C programmers. This is because of the convenience with which arrays lend themselves to programming. The features that make arrays so convenient to program will be discussed next, along with the possible pitfalls in using them.

Array Initialization

So far, we have used arrays that did not have any values in them to begin with. We managed to store values in them during program execution. Let us

12	34	66	-45	23	346	77	90

65508   65510   65512   65514   65516   65518   65520   65522

FIGURE 8.1

now see how to initialize an array while declaring it. The following are a few examples that demonstrate this.

```
int num[6] = { 2, 4, 12, 5, 45, 5 } ;
int n[ ] = { 2, 4, 12, 5, 45, 5 } ;
float press[ ] = { 12.3, 34.2 -23.4, -11.3 } ;
```

Note the following points carefully:

(a) Until the array elements are not given any specific values, they are supposed to contain garbage values.

(b) If the array is initialized where it is declared, mentioning the dimension of the array is optional as in the 2nd and 3rd example.

Array Elements in Memory

Consider the following array declaration:

```
int arr[8] ;
```

What happens in memory when we make this declaration? Sixteen bytes get immediately reserved in memory, 2 bytes each for the 8 integers (under Windows/Linux, the array would occupy 32 bytes as each integer would occupy 4 bytes). And since the array is not being initialized, all eight values present in it would be garbage values. This happens because the storage class of this array is assumed to be **auto**. If the storage class is declared to be **static**, then all the array elements would have a default initial value as zero. Whatever the initial values might be, all the array elements would always be present in contiguous memory locations. This arrangement of array elements in memory is shown in Figure 8.1.

Bounds Checking

In C, there is no check to see if the subscript used for an array exceeds the size of the array. Data entered with a subscript exceeding the array size will simply be placed in memory outside the array; probably on top of other data, or on the program itself. This will lead to unpredictable results to say the least, and there will be no error message to warn you that you are going beyond the array size. In some cases, the computer may just hang. Thus, the following program may turn out to be suicidal.

```c
# include <stdio.h>
void main( )
{
    int num[40], i ;

    for ( i = 0 ; i <= 100 ; i++ )
        num[i] = i ;
}
```

Thus, to see to it that we do not reach beyond the array size, is entirely the programmer's botheration and not the compiler's.

Passing Array Elements to a Function

Array elements can be passed to a function by calling the function by value, or by reference. In the call by value, we pass values of array elements to the function, whereas in the call by reference, we pass addresses of array elements to the function. These two calls are illustrated here:

```c
/* Demonstration of call by value */
# include <stdio.h>
void display ( int ) ;
void main( )
{
    int i ;
    int marks[ ] = { 55, 65, 75, 56, 78, 78, 90 } ;
    for ( i = 0 ; i <= 6 ; i++ )
        display ( marks[i] ) ;
}
void display ( int m )
{
    printf ( "%d ", m ) ;
}
```

And here's the output:

```
55 65 75 56 78 78 90
```

Here, we are passing an individual array element at a time to the function **display( )** and getting it printed in the function **display( )**. Note that, since one element at a time only is being passed, this element is collected in an ordinary integer variable **m**, in the function **display( )**.

And now the call by reference.

```
/* Demonstration of call by reference */
# include <stdio.h>
void disp ( int * ) ;
void main( )
{
    int i ;
    int marks[ ] = { 55, 65, 75, 56, 78, 78, 90 } ;
    for ( i = 0 ; i <= 6 ; i++ )
        disp ( &marks[i] ) ;
}
void disp ( int *n )
{
    printf ( "%d ", *n ) ;
}
```

And here's the output:

```
55 65 75 56 78 78 90
```

Here, we are passing addresses of individual array elements to the function **display( )**. Hence, the variable in which this address is collected (**n**), is declared as a pointer variable. And since **n** contains the address of the array element, to print out the array element, we are using the 'value at address' operator (*).

Read the following program carefully. The purpose of the function **disp( )** is just to display the array elements on the screen. The program is only partly complete. You are required to write the function **show( )** on your own. Try your hand at it.

```
# include <stdio.h>
void disp ( int * ) ;
void main( )
{
    int i ;
    int marks[ ] = { 55, 65, 75, 56, 78, 78, 90 } ;
    for ( i = 0 ; i <= 6 ; i++ )
        disp ( &marks[i] ) ;
}
void disp ( int *n )
{
    show ( &n ) ;
}
```

POINTERS AND ARRAYS

To be able to see what pointers have got to do with arrays, let us first learn some pointer arithmetic. Consider the following example:

```
# include <stdio.h>
void main( )
{
    int i = 3, *x ;
    float j = 1.5, *y ;
    char k = 'c', *z ;
    printf ( "\nValue of i = %d", i ) ;
    printf ( "\nValue of j = %f", j ) ;
    printf ( "\nValue of k = %c", k ) ;
    x = &i ;
    y = &j ;
    z = &k ;
    printf ( "\nOriginal address in x = %u", x ) ;
    printf ( "\nOriginal address in y = %u", y ) ;
    printf ( "\nOriginal address in z = %u", z ) ;
    x++ ;
    y++ ;
    z++ ;
    printf ( "\nNew address in x = %u", x ) ;
    printf ( "\nNew address in y = %u", y ) ;
    printf ( "\nNew address in z = %u", z ) ;
}
```

Here is the output of the program:

```
Value of i = 3
Value of j = 1.500000
Value of k = c
Original address in x = 65524
Original address in y = 65520
Original address in z = 65519
New address in x = 65526
New address in y = 65524
New address in z = 65520
```

Observe the last three lines of the output. 65526 is the original value in **x** plus 2, 65524 is the original value in **y** plus 4, and 65520 is the original value in **z** plus 1. This happens because every time a pointer is incremented, it points to the next immediate location of its type. That is why, when the integer pointer **x** is incremented, it points to an address two locations after the current location, since an **int** is always 2 bytes long (under Windows/Linux, since **int** is 4 bytes long, the new value of **x** would be 65528). Similarly, **y** points to an address 4 locations after the current location and **z** points 1 location after the current location. This is a very important result and can be effectively used while passing the entire array to a function.

The way a pointer can be incremented, it can be decremented as well, to point to earlier locations. Thus, the following operations can be performed on a pointer:

(a) Addition of a number to a pointer. For example,

```
int i = 4, *j, *k ;
j = &i ;
j = j + 1 ;
j = j + 9 ;
k = j + 3 ;
```

(b) Subtraction of a number from a pointer. For example,

```
int i = 4, *j, *k ;
j = &i ;
j = j - 2 ;
j = j - 5 ;
k = j - 6 ;
```

(c) Subtraction of one pointer from another.

One pointer variable can be subtracted from another provided both variables point to elements of the same array. The resulting value indicates the number of elements separating the corresponding array elements. This is illustrated in the following program.

```
# include <stdio.h>
void main( )
{
    int arr[ ] = { 10, 20, 30, 45, 67, 56, 74 } ;
    int *i, *j ;

    i = &arr[1] ;
    j = &arr[5] ;
    printf ( "%d %d", j - i, *j - *i ) ;
}
```

Here **i** and **j** have been declared as integer pointers holding addresses of first and fifth element of the array respectively.

Suppose the array begins at location 65502, then the elements **arr[1]** and **arr[5]** would be present at locations 65504 and 65512 respectively, since each integer in the array occupies two bytes in memory. The expression **j - i** would print a value 4 and not 8. This is because **j** and **i** are pointing to locations that are 4 integers apart. What will be the result of the expression ***j - *i**? 36, since ***j** and ***i** return the values present at addresses contained in the pointers **j** and **i**.

(d) Comparison of two pointer variables.

Pointer variables can be compared provided both variables point to objects of the same data type. Such comparisons can be useful when both pointer variables point to elements of the same array. The comparison can test for either equality or inequality. Moreover, a pointer variable can be compared with zero (usually expressed as NULL). The following program illustrates how the comparison is carried out.

```
# include <stdio..h>
void main( )
{
    int arr[ ] = { 10, 20, 36, 72, 45, 36 } ;
    int *j, *k ;

    j = &arr [ 4 ] ;
    k = ( arr + 4 ) ;
    if ( j == k )
        printf ( "The two pointers point to the same location" ) ;
    else
        printf ( "The two pointers do not point to the same location" ) ;
}
```

A word of caution! Do not attempt the following operations on pointers—they will never work out.

(a) Addition of two pointers
(b) Multiplication of a pointer with a constant
(c) Division of a pointer with a constant

Now we will try to correlate the following two facts, which we have previously learned:

(a) Array elements are always stored in contiguous memory locations.
(b) A pointer, when incremented, always points to the next immediate location of its type.

24	34	12	44	56	17

65512　　65514　　65516　　65518　　65520　　65522

FIGURE 8.2

Suppose we have an array **num[ ]** = { 24, 34, 12, 44, 56, 17 }. Figure 8.2 shows how this array is located in memory.

Here is a program that prints out the memory locations in which the elements of this array are stored.

```c
# include <stdio.h>
void main( )
{
    int num[ ] = { 24, 34, 12, 44, 56, 17 } ;
    int i ;
    for ( i = 0 ; i <= 5 ; i++ )
    {
        printf ( "\nelement no. %d ", i ) ;
        printf ( "address = %u", &num[i] ) ;
    }
}
```

The output of this program will look like this:

```
element no. 0 address = 65512
element no. 1 address = 65514
element no. 2 address = 65516
element no. 3 address = 65518
element no. 4 address = 65520
element no. 5 address = 65522
```

Note that the array elements are stored in contiguous memory locations, each element occupying two bytes, since it is an integer array. When you run this program, you may get different addresses, but what is certain is that each subsequent address will be 2 bytes (4 bytes under Windows/Linux) greater than its immediate predecessor.

Our next two programs show ways in which we can access the elements of this array.

```c
# include <stdio.h>
void main( )
{
    int num[ ] = { 24, 34, 12, 44, 56, 17 } ;
    int i ;
```

```
        for ( i = 0 ; i <= 5 ; i++ )
        {
                printf ( "\naddress = %u ", &num[i] ) ;
                printf ( "element = %d", num[i] ) ;
        }
}
```

The output of this program will be:

```
address = 65512 element = 24
address = 65514 element = 34
address = 65516 element = 12
address = 65518 element = 44
address = 65520 element = 56
address = 65522 element = 17
```

This method of accessing array elements by using subscripted variables is already known to us. This method has, in fact, been given here for easy comparison with the next method, which accesses the array elements using pointers.

```
# include <stdio.h>
void main( )
{
        int num[ ] = { 24, 34, 12, 44, 56, 17 } ;
        int i, *j ;

        j = &num[0] ; /* assign address of zeroth element */
        for ( i = 0 ; i <= 5 ; i++ )
        {
                printf ( "\naddress = %u ", j ) ;
                printf ( "element = %d", *j ) ;
                j++ ; /* increment pointer to point to next location */
        }
}
```

The output of this program will be:

```
address = 65512 element = 24
address = 65514 element = 34
address = 65516 element = 12
address = 65518 element = 44
address = 65520 element = 56
address = 65522 element = 17
```

In this program, to begin with, we have collected the base address of the array (address of the zeroth element) in the variable **j** using the statement,

```
j = &num[0] ; /* assigns address 65512 to j */
```

When we are inside the loop for the first time, **j** contains the address 65512, and the value at this address is 24. These are printed using the statements,

```
printf ( "\naddress = %u ", j ) ;
printf ( "element = %d", *j ) ;
```

On incrementing **j**, it points to the next memory location of its type (that is, location no. 65514). But location no. 65514 contains the second element of the array, therefore, when the **printf( )** statements are executed for the second time, they print out the second element of the array and its address (i.e., 34 and 65514), and so on until the last element of the array has been printed.

Obviously, a question arises as to which of these two methods should be used when? Accessing array elements by pointers is **always** faster than accessing them by subscripts. However, from the point of view of convenience in programming, we should observe the following:

Array elements should be accessed using pointers, if the elements are accessed in a fixed order, say from beginning to end, or from end to beginning, or every alternate element, or any such definite logic.

It would be easier to access the elements using a subscript if there is no fixed logic in accessing the elements. However, in this case also, accessing the elements by pointers would work faster than subscripts.

Passing an Entire Array to a Function

In the previous section, we saw two programs—one in which we passed individual elements of an array to a function, and another in which we passed addresses of individual elements to a function. Let us now see how to pass an entire array to a function rather than its individual elements. Consider the following example:

```
/* Demonstration of passing an entire array to a function */
# include <stdio.h>
void display ( int *, int ) ;
void main( )
{
    int num[ ] = { 24, 34, 12, 44, 56, 17 } ;
    dislpay ( &num[0], 6 ) ;
}
```

```
void display ( int *j, int n )
{
    int i ;
    for ( i = 0 ; i <= n - 1 ; i++ )
    {
        printf ( "\nelement = %d", *j ) ;
        j++ ; /* increment pointer to point to next element */
    }
}
```

Here, the **display( )** function is used to print out the array elements. Note that the address of the zeroth element is being passed to the **display( )** function. The **for** loop is the same as the one used in the earlier program to access the array elements using pointers. Thus, just passing the address of the zeroth element of the array to a function is as good as passing the entire array to the function. It is also necessary to pass the total number of elements in the array, otherwise the **display( )** function would not know when to terminate the **for** loop. Note that the address of the zeroth element (also called the base address) can also be passed by just passing the name of the array. Thus, the following two function calls are the same:

```
display ( &num[0], 6 ) ;
display ( num, 6 ) ;
```

The Real Thing

If you have grasped the concept of storage of array elements in memory and the arithmetic of pointers, here is some real food for thought. Once again, consider the following array shown in Figure 8.3.

This is how we would declare the array in C,

```
int num[ ] = { 24, 34, 12, 44, 56, 17 } ;
```

We also know, that on mentioning the name of the array, we get its base address. Thus, by saying ***num**, we would be able to refer to the zeroth element of the array, that is, 24. One can easily see that ***num** and *(**num + 0**) both refer to 24.

24	34	12	44	56	17
65512	65514	65516	65518	65520	65522

FIGURE 8.3

Similarly, by saying *(**num + 1**), we can refer to the first element of the array, that is, 34. In fact, this is what the C compiler does internally. When we say, **num[i]**, the C compiler internally converts it to *(**num + i**). This means that all the following notations are the same:

```
num[i]
*( num + i )
*( i + num )
i[num]
```

And here is a program to prove the point.

```
/* Accessing array elements in different ways */
# include <stdio.h>
void main( )
{
    int num[ ] = { 24, 34, 12, 44, 56, 17 } ;
    int i ;
    for ( i = 0 ; i <= 5 ; i++ )
    {
        printf ( "\naddress = %u ", &num[i] ) ;
        printf ( "element = %d %d ", num[i], *( num + i ) ) ;
        printf ( "%d %d", *( i + num ), i[num] ) ;
    }
}
```

The output of this program will be:

```
address = 65512 element = 24 24 24 24
address = 65514 element = 34 34 34 34
address = 65516 element = 12 12 12 12
address = 65518 element = 44 44 44 44
address = 65520 element = 56 56 56 56
address = 65522 element = 17 17 17 17
```

TWO-DIMENSIONAL ARRAYS

So far, we have explored arrays with only one dimension. It is also possible for arrays to have two or more dimensions. The two-dimensional array is also called a matrix.

Here is a sample program that stores roll number and marks obtained by a student, side by side in a matrix.

```
# include <stdio.h>
void main( )
```

```
{
    int stud[4][2] ;
    int i, j ;
    for ( i = 0 ; i <= 3 ; i++ )
    {
        printf ( "\n Enter roll no. and marks" ) ;
        scanf ( "%d %d", &stud[i][0], &stud[i][1] ) ;
    }
    for ( i = 0 ; i <= 3 ; i++ )
        printf ( "\n%d %d", stud[i][0], stud[i][1] ) ;
}
```

There are two parts to the program—in the first part, through a **for** loop, we read in the values of roll no. and marks, whereas in the second part, through another **for** loop, we print out these values.

Look at the **scanf( )** statement used in the first **for** loop:

```
scanf ( "%d %d", &stud[i][0], &stud[i][1] ) ;
```

In **stud[i][0]** and **stud[i][1]**, the first subscript of the variable **stud**, is the row number, which changes for every student. The second subscript tells which of the two columns we are talking about—the zeroth column, which contains the roll no., or the first column, which contains the marks. Remember the counting of rows and columns begins with zero. The complete array arrangement is shown in Figure 8.4.

Thus, 1234 is stored in **stud[0][0]**, 56 is stored in **stud[0][1]**, and so on. This arrangement highlights the fact that a two-dimensional array is nothing but a collection of one-dimensional arrays placed one below the other.

In our sample program, the array elements have been stored rowwise and accessed rowwise. However, you can access the array elements columnwise as well. Traditionally, the array elements are being stored and accessed rowwise; therefore we would also stick to the same strategy.

	col. no. 0	col. no. 1
row no. 0	1234	56
row no. 1	1212	33
row no. 2	1434	80
row no. 3	1312	78

FIGURE 8.4

Initializing a Two-Dimensional Array

How do we initialize a two-dimensional array? As simple as this:

```
int stud[4][2] = {
                    { 1234, 56 },
                    { 1212, 33 },
                    { 1434, 80 },
                    { 1312, 78 }
                } ;
```

or even this would work:

```
int stud[4][2] = { 1234, 56, 1212, 33, 1434, 80, 1312, 78 } ;
```

of course, with a corresponding loss in readability.

It is important to remember that, while initializing a 2D array, it is necessary to mention the second (column) dimension, whereas the first dimension (row) is optional.

Thus the declarations,

```
int arr[2][3] = { 12, 34, 23, 45, 56, 45 } ;
int arr[ ][3] = { 12, 34, 23, 45, 56, 45 } ;
```

are perfectly acceptable,

whereas,

```
int arr[2][ ] = { 12, 34, 23, 45, 56, 45 } ;
int arr[ ][ ] = { 12, 34, 23, 45, 56, 45 } ;
```

would never work.

Memory Map of a Two-Dimensional Array

Let us reiterate the arrangement of array elements in a two-dimensional array of students, which contains roll nos. in one column and the marks in the other.

The array arrangement shown in Figure 8.4 is only conceptually true. This is because memory doesn't contain rows and columns. In memory, whether it is a one-dimensional or a two-dimensional array, the array elements are stored in one continuous chain. The arrangement of array elements of a two-dimensional array in memory is shown below in Figure 8.5:

We can easily refer to the marks obtained by the third student using the subscript notation as shown here:

```
printf ( "Marks of third student = %d", stud[2][1] ) ;
```

s[0][0]	s[0][1]	s[1][0]	s[1][1]	s[2][0]	s[2][1]	s[3][0]	s[3][1]
1234	56	1212	33	1434	80	1312	78
65508	65510	65512	65514	65516	65518	65520	65522

FIGURE 8.5

Can we not refer to the same element using pointer notation, the way we did in one-dimensional arrays? The answer is yes. Only the procedure is slightly difficult to understand. So, read on...

Pointers and Two-Dimensional Arrays

The C language embodies an unusual but powerful capability—it can treat parts of arrays as arrays. More specifically, each row of a two-dimensional array can be thought of as a one-dimensional array. This is a very important fact if we wish to access array elements of a two-dimensional array using pointers.

Thus, the declaration,

```
int s[5][2] ;
```

can be thought of as setting up an array of 5 elements, each of which is a one-dimensional array containing 2 integers. We refer to an element of a one-dimensional array using a single subscript. Similarly, if we can imagine **s** to be a one-dimensional array, then we can refer to its zeroth element as **s[0]**, the next element as **s[1]**, and so on. More specifically, **s[0]** gives the address of the zeroth one-dimensional array, **s[1]** gives the address of the first one-dimensional array, and so on. This fact can be demonstrated by the following program.

```
/* Demo: 2-D array is an array of arrays */
# include <stdio.h>
void main( )
{
    int s[4][2] = {
                    { 1234, 56 },
                    { 1212, 33 },
                    { 1434, 80 },
                    { 1312, 78 }
                } ;
    int i ;
    for ( i = 0 ; i <= 3 ; i++ )
        printf ( "\nAddress of %d th 1-D array = %u", i, s[i] ) ;
}
```

s[0][0]	s[0][1]	s[1][0]	s[1][1]	s[2][0]	s[2][1]	s[3][0]	s[3][1]
1234	56	1212	33	1434	80	1312	78
65508	65510	65512	65514	65516	65518	65520	65522

FIGURE 8.6

And here is the output:

```
Address of 0 th 1-D array = 65508
Address of 1 th 1-D array = 65512
Address of 2 th 1-D array = 65516
Address of 3 th 1-D array = 65520
```

Let's figure out how the program works. The compiler knows that **s** is an array containing 4 one-dimensional arrays, each containing 2 integers. Each one-dimensional array occupies 4 bytes (two bytes for each integer). These one-dimensional arrays are placed linearly (zeroth 1D array followed by the first 1D array, etc.). Hence, each one-dimensional array starts 4 bytes further along than the last one, as can be seen in the memory map of the array shown in Figure 8.6.

We know that the expressions **s[0]** and **s[1]** will yield the addresses of the zeroth and first one-dimensional array respectively. From Figure 8.6, these addresses turn out to be 65508 and 65512.

Now, we have been able to reach each one-dimensional array. What remains is to be able to refer to individual elements of a one-dimensional array. Suppose we want to refer to the element **s[2][1]** using pointers. We know (from the earlier program) that **s[2]** will give the address 65516, the address of the second one-dimensional array. Obviously, (65516 + 1) will give the address 65518. (**s[2]** + **1**) will give the address 65518. And the value at this address can be obtained by using the value at the address operator, saying *(**s[2]** + **1**). But, we have already studied while learning one-dimensional arrays that **num[i]** is the same as *(**num** + **i**). Similarly, *(**s[2]** + **1**) is the same as, *(*(**s** + **2**) + **1**). Thus, all the following expressions refer to the same element,

```
s[2][1]
* ( s[2] + 1 )
* ( * ( s + 2 ) + 1 )
```

Using these concepts, the following program prints out each element of a two-dimensional array using pointer notation.

```
/* Pointer notation to access 2-D array elements */
# include <stdio.h>
```

```
void main( )
{
    int s[4][2] = {
                        { 1234, 56 },
                        { 1212, 33 },
                        { 1434, 80 },
                        { 1312, 78 }
                } ;
    int i, j ;

    for ( i = 0 ; i <= 3 ; i++ )
    {
        printf ( "\n" ) ;
        for ( j = 0 ; j <= 1 ; j++ )
            printf ( "%d ", *( *( s + i ) + j ) ) ;
    }
}
```

And here is the output:

```
1234 56
1212 33
1434 80
1312 78
```

Pointer to an Array

If we can have a pointer to an integer, a pointer to a float, and a pointer to a char, then can we not have a pointer to an array? We certainly can. The following program shows how to build and use it.

```
/* Usage of pointer to an array */
# include <stdio.h>
void main( )
{
    int s[4][2] = {
                        { 1234, 56 },
                        { 1212, 33 },
                        { 1434, 80 },
                        { 1312, 78 }
                } ;
    int ( *p )[2] ;
    int i, j, *pint ;
    for ( i = 0 ; i <= 3 ; i++ )
    {
        p = &s[i] ;
        pint = ( int * ) p ;
```

```
            printf ( "\n" ) ;
            for ( j = 0 ; j <= 1 ; j++ )
                printf ( "%d ", *( pint + j ) ) ;
        }
    }
```

And here is the output:

```
1234 56
1212 33
1434 80
1312 78
```

Here, **p** is a pointer to an array of two integers. Note that the parentheses in the declaration of **p** are necessary. Absence of them would make **p** an array of 2 integer pointers. An array of pointers is covered in a later section in this chapter. In the outer **for** loop, we store the address of a new one-dimensional array each time through. Thus, the first time through this loop, **p** would contain the address of the zeroth 1D array. This address is then assigned to an integer pointer **pint**. Lastly, in the inner **for** loop using the pointer **pint**, we have printed the individual elements of the 1D array to which **p** is pointing.

But why should we use a pointer to an array to print elements of a 2D array? Is there any situation where we can appreciate its usage better? The entity pointer to an array is immensely useful when we need to pass a 2D array to a function. This is discussed in the next section.

Passing a 2D Array to a Function

There are three ways in which we can pass a 2D array to a function. These are illustrated in the following program.

```
/* Three ways of accessing a 2-D array */
# include <stdio.h>
void display ( int *q, int , int ) ;
void show ( int ( *q )[4], int, int ) ;
void print ( int q[ ][4], int , int ) ;
void main( )
{
    int a[3][4] = {
                        1, 2, 3, 4,
                        5, 6, 7, 8,
                        9, 0, 1, 6
                } ;
```

```
        display ( a, 3, 4 ) ;
        show ( a, 3, 4 ) ;
        print ( a, 3, 4 ) ;
}
void display ( int *q, int row, int col )
{
        int i, j ;
        for ( i = 0 ; i < row ; i++ )
        {
                for ( j = 0 ; j < col ; j++ )
                        printf ( "%d ", * ( q + i * col + j ) ) ;
                        printf ( "\n" ) ;
        }
        printf ("\n" ) ;
}

void show ( int ( *q )[4], int row, int col )
{
        int i, j ;
        int *p ;

        for ( i = 0 ; i < row ; i++ )
        {
                p = q + i ;
                for ( j = 0 ; j < col ; j++ )
                        printf ( "%d ", * ( p + j ) ) ;

                printf ( "\n" ) ;
        }
        printf ( "\n" ) ;
}

void print ( int q[ ][4], int row, int col )
{
        int i, j ;

        for ( i = 0 ; i < row ; i++ )
        {
                for ( j = 0 ; j < col ; j++ )
                        printf ( "%d ", q[i][j] ) ;
                printf ( "\n" ) ;
        }
        printf ( "\n" ) ;
}
```

And here is the output:

```
1 2 3 4
5 6 7 8
9 0 1 6

1 2 3 4
5 6 7 8
9 0 1 6

1 2 3 4
5 6 7 8
9 0 1 6
```

In the **display( )** function, we have collected the base address of the 2D array being passed to it in an ordinary **int** pointer. Then, through the two **for** loops using the expression *($q + i*col + j$), we have reached the appropriate element in the array. Suppose **i** is equal to 2 and **j** is equal to 3, then we wish to reach the element **a[2][3]**. Let us see whether the expression *($q + i*col + j$) gives this element or not. Refer to Figure 8.7 to understand this.

The expression *($q + i*col + j$) becomes *($65502 + 2*4 + 3$). This turns out to be *($65502 + 11$). Since **65502** is the address of an integer, *($65502 + 11$) turns out to be *(**65524**). Value at this address is 6. This is indeed the same as **a[2][3]**. A more general formula for accessing each array element would be:

```
* ( base address + row no. * no. of columns + column no. )
```

In the **show( )** function, we have defined **q** to be a pointer to an array of 4 integers through the declaration:

```
int ( *q )[4] ;
```

To begin with, **q** holds the base address of the zeroth 1D array, i.e., 4001 (refer to Figure 8.7). This address is then assigned to **p**, an **int** pointer, and then using this pointer, all elements of the zeroth 1D array are accessed. Next time through the loop, when **i** takes a value 1, the expression **q + i** fetches

1	2	3	4	5	6	7	8	9	0	1	6
65502	...04	...06	...08	...10	...12	...14	...16	...18	...20	...22	...24

FIGURE 8.7

the address of the first 1D array. This is because **q** is a pointer to a zeroth 1D array and adding 1 to it would give us the address of the next 1D array. This address is once again assigned to **p**, and in using it, all elements of the next 1D array are accessed.

In the third function, **print( )**, the declaration of **q** looks like this:

```
int q[ ][4] ;
```

This is the same as **int (*q)[4]**, where **q** is pointer to an array of 4 integers. The only advantage is that we can now use the more familiar expression **q[i][j]** to access array elements. We could have used the same expression in **show( )** as well.

ARRAY OF POINTERS

The way there can be an array of **int**s or an array of **float**s, similarly, there can be an array of pointers. Since a pointer variable always contains an address, an array of pointers would be nothing but a collection of addresses. The addresses present in the array of pointers can be addresses of isolated variables or addresses of array elements or any other addresses. All rules that apply to an ordinary array apply to the array of pointers as well. The following program will help clarify the concept.

```
# include <stdio.h>
void main( )
{
    int *arr[4] ; /* array of integer pointers */
    int i = 31, j = 5, k = 19, l = 71, m ;

    arr[0] = &i ;
    arr[1] = &j ;
    arr[2] = &k ;
    arr[3] = &l ;

    for ( m = 0 ; m <= 3 ; m++ )
        printf ( "%d ", * ( arr[m] ) ) ;
}
```

Figure 8.8 shows the contents and the arrangement of the array of pointers in memory. As you can see, **arr** contains addresses of isolated **int** variables **i, j, k,** and **l**. The **for** loop in the program picks up the addresses present in **arr** and prints the values present at these addresses.

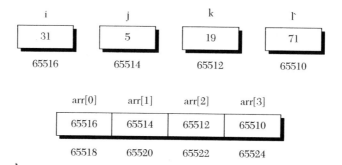

FIGURE 8.8

An array of pointers can even contain the addresses of other arrays. The following program justifies this.

```c
# include <stdio.h>
void main( )
{
    static int a[ ] = { 0, 1, 2, 3, 4 } ;
    int *p[ ] = { a, a + 1, a + 2, a + 3, a + 4 } ;

    printf ( "\n%u %u %d", p, *p, * ( *p ) ) ;
}
```

The output of this program is left for you to figure out.

THREE-DIMENSIONAL ARRAY

We aren't going to show a programming example that uses a three-dimensional array. This is because, in practice, one rarely uses this array. However, an example of initializing a three-dimensional array will consolidate your understanding of subscripts:

```c
int arr[3][4][2] = {
                     {
                       { 2, 4 },
                       { 7, 8 },
                       { 3, 4 },
                       { 5, 6 }
                     },
```

```
            {
                { 7, 6 },
                { 3, 4 },
                { 5, 3 },
                { 2, 3 }
            },
            {
                { 8, 9 },
                { 7, 2 },
                { 3, 4 },
                { 5, 1 },
            }
        } ;
```

A three-dimensional array can be thought of as an array of arrays of arrays. The outer array has three elements, each of which is a two-dimensional array of four one-dimensional arrays, each of which contains two integers. In other words, a one-dimensional array of two elements is constructed first. Then four such one-dimensional arrays are placed one below the other to give a two-dimensional array containing four rows. Then, three such two-dimensional arrays are placed one behind the other to yield a three-dimensional array containing three two-dimensional arrays. In the array declaration, note how the commas have been given. Figure 8.9 should help you in visualising the situation better.

Again, remember that the arrangement shown in Figure 8.9 is only conceptually true. In memory, the same array elements are stored linearly, as shown in Figure 8.10.

How would you refer to the array element 1 in the array in Figure 8.10? The first subscript should be [2], since the element is in the third two-dimensional array; the second subscript should be [3] since the element is in

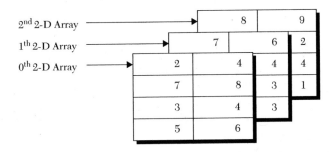

FIGURE 8.9

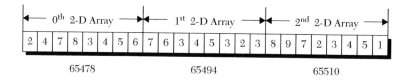

FIGURE 8.10

the fourth row of the two-dimensional array; and the third subscript should be [1] since the element is in second position in the one-dimensional array. We can, therefore, say that the element 1 can be referred to as **arr[2][3][1]**. It should be noted here that the counting of array elements, even for a 3D array, begins with zero. Can we not refer to this element using pointer notation? Of course, yes. For example, the following two expressions refer to the same element in the 3D array:

```
arr[2][3][1]
*( *( *( arr + 2 ) + 3 ) + 1 )
```

SUMMARY

(a) An array is similar to an ordinary variable except that it can store multiple elements of similar type.
(b) Compiler doesn't perform bounds checking on an array.
(c) The array variable acts as a pointer to the zeroth element of the array. In a 1D array, zeroth element is a single value, whereas, in a 2D array this element is a 1D array.
(d) On incrementing a pointer it points to the next location of its type.
(e) Array elements are stored in contiguous memory locations so they can be accessed using pointers.
(f) Only limited arithmetic can be done on pointers.

EXERCISES

Simple arrays

[A] What will be the output of the following programs:

(a)
```
# include <stdio.h>
void main( )
```

```
    {
        int num[26], temp ;
        num[0] = 100 ;
        num[25] = 200 ;
        temp = num[25] ;
        num[25] = num[0] ;
        num[0] = temp ;
        printf ( "\n%d %d", num[0], num[25] ) ;
    }
```

(b)
```
# include <stdio.h>
void main( )
{
    int array[26], i ;
    for ( i = 0 ; i <= 25 ; i++ )
    {
        array[i] = 'A' + i ;
        printf ( "\n%d %c", array[i], array[i] ) ;
    }
}
```

(c)
```
# include <stdio.h>
void main( )
{
    int sub[50], i ;
    for ( i = 0 ; i <= 48 ; i++ ) ;
    {
        sub[i] = i ;
        printf ( "\n%d", sub[i] ) ;
    }
}
```

[B] Point out the errors, if any, in the following program segments:

(a)
```
/* mixed has some char and some int values */
# include <stdio.h>
int char mixed[100] ;
void main( )
{
    int a[10], i ;
    for ( i = 1 ; i <= 10 ; i++ )
    {
        scanf ( "%d", a[i] ) ;
```

```
                    printf ( "% d", a[i] ) ;
            }
    }
(b)  # include <stdio.h>
     void main( )
     {
         int size ;
         scanf ( "%d", & size ) ;
         int arr[size] ;
         for ( i = 1 ; i <= size ; i++ )
         {
                 scanf ( "%d", arr[i] ) ;
                 printf ( "%d", arr[i] ) ;
         }
     }
(c)  # include <stdio.h>
     void main( )
     {
         int i, a = 2, b = 3 ;
         int arr[ 2 + 3 ] ;
         for ( i = 0 ; i < a+b ; i++ )
         {
                 scanf ( "%d", &arr[i] ) ;
                 printf ( "\n%d", arr[i] ) ;
         }
     }
```

[C] Answer the following:

(a) An array is a collection of
   1.   different data types scattered throughout memory
   2.   the same data type scattered throughout memory
   3.   the same data type placed next to each other in memory
   4.   different data types placed next to each other in memory
(b) Are the following array declarations correct?

```
int a (25) ;
int size = 10, b[size] ;
int c = {0,1,2} ;
```

(c) Which element of the array does this expression reference?

```
num[4]
```

(d) What is the difference between the 5s in these two expressions? (Select the correct answer.)

```
int num[5] ;
num[5] = 11 ;
```

1. first is particular element, second is type
2. first is array size, second is particular element
3. first is particular element, second is array size
4. both specify array size

(e) State whether the following statements are True or False:
1. The array **int num[26]** has twenty-six elements.
2. The expression **num[1]** designates the first element in the array
3. It is necessary to initialize the array at the time of declaration.
4. The expression **num[27]** designates the twenty-eighth element in the array.

[D] Attempt the following:

(a) Twenty-five numbers are entered from the keyboard into an array. The number to be searched is entered through the keyboard by the user. Write a program to find if the number to be searched is present in the array, and if it is present, display the number of times it appears in the array.

(b) Implement the Selection Sort, Bubble Sort, and Insertion sort algorithms on a set of 25 numbers. (Refer to Figure 8.11 for the logic of the algorithms)
  – Selection sort
  – Bubble Sort
  – Insertion Sort

(c) Implement the following procedure to generate prime numbers from 1 to 100 into a program. This procedure is called the sieve of Eratosthenes.

step 1 Fill an array **num[100]** with numbers from 1 to 100.

step 2 Starting with the second entry in the array, set all its multiples to zero.

step 3 Proceed to the next nonzero element and set all its multiples to zero.

step 4 Repeat step 3 until you have set up the multiples of all the nonzero elements to zero.

step 5 At the conclusion of step 4, all the nonzero entries left in the array will be prime numbers, so print out these numbers.

Selection Sort

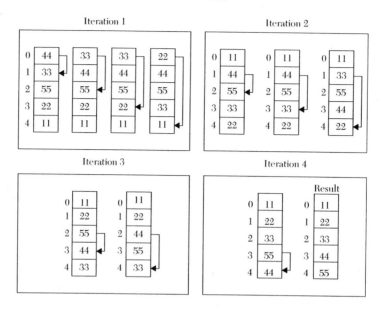

FIGURE 8.11(a)

Bubble Sort

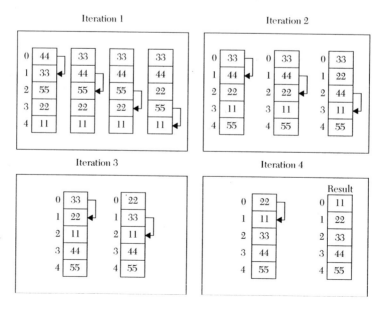

FIGURE 8.11(b)

Insertion Sort

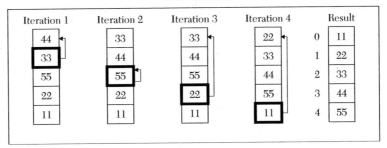

FIGURE 8.11(c)

(d) Twenty-five numbers are entered from the keyboard into an array. Write a program to find out how many of them are positive, how many are negative, how many are even, and how many odd.

(e) Write a program that interchanges the odd and even elements of an array.

More on arrays, arrays and pointers

[E] What will be the output of the following programs:

(a)
```c
# include <stdio.h>
void main( )
{
    int b[ ] = { 10, 20, 30, 40, 50 } ;
    int i ;
    for ( i = 0 ; i <= 4 ; i++ )
        printf ( "\n% d" *( b + i ) ) ;
}
```

(b)
```c
# include <stdio.h>
void main( )
{
    int b[ ] = { 0, 20, 0, 40, 5 } ;
    int i, *k ;
    k = b ;
    for ( i = 0 ; i <= 4 ; i++ )
    {
        printf ( "\n%d" *k ) ;
        k++ ;
    }
}
```

(c)
```c
# include <stdio.h>
void change ( int *, int ) ;
void main( )
{
    int a[ ] = { 2, 4, 6, 8, 10 } ;
    int i ;
    change ( a, 5 ) ;
    for ( i = 0 ; i <= 4 ; i++ )
        printf( "\n%d", a[i] ) ;
}
void change ( int *b, int n )
{
    int i ;
    for ( i = 0 ; i < n ; i++ )
        *( b + i ) = *( b + i ) + 5;
}
```

(d)
```c
# include <stdio.h>
void f ( int *, int ) ;
void main( )
{
    int a[5], i, b = 16 ;
    for ( i = 0 ; i < 5 ; i++ )
        a[i] = 2 * i ;
    f ( a, b ) ;
    for ( i = 0 ; i < 5 ; i++ )
        printf ( "\n%d", a[i] ) ;
    printf( "\n% d", b ) ;
}
void f ( int *x, int y )
{
    int i ;
    for ( i = 0 ; i < 5 ; i++ )
        *( x + i ) += 2 ;
    y += 2 ;
}
```

(e)
```c
# include <stdio.h>
void main( )
{
    static int a[5] ;
    int i ;
    for ( i = 0 ; i <= 4 ; i++ )
        printf ( "\n%d", a[i] ) ;
}
```

(f)
```
# include <stdio.h>
void main( )
{
    int a[5] = { 5, 1, 15, 20, 25 } ;
    int i, j, k = 1, m ;
    i = ++a[1] ;
    j = a[1]++ ;
    m = a[i++] ;
    printf ( "\n%d %d %d", i, j, m ) ;
}
```

[F] Point out the errors, if any, in the following programs:

(a)
```
# include <stdio.h>
void main( )
{
    int array[6] = { 1, 2, 3, 4, 5, 6 } ;
    int i ;
    for ( i = 0 ; i <= 25 ; i++ )
        printf ( "\n%d", array[i] ) ;
}
```

(b)
```
# include <stdio.h>
void main( )
{
    int sub[50], i ;
    for ( i = 1 ; i <= 50 ; i++ )
    {
        sub[i] = i ;
        printf ( "\n%d" , sub[i] ) ;
    }
}
```

(c)
```
# include <stdio.h>
void main( )
{
    int a[ ] = { 10, 20, 30, 40, 50 } ;
    int j ;
    j = a ; /* store the address of zeroth element */
    j = j + 3 ;
    printf ( "\n%d" *j ) ;
}
```

(d)
```
# include <stdio.h>
void main( )
{
    float a[ ] = { 13.24, 1.5, 1.5, 5.4, 3.5 } ;
    float *j ;
    j = a ;
    j = j + 4 ;
    printf ( "\n%d %d %d", j, *j, a[4] ) ;
}
```

(e)
```
# include <stdio.h>
void main( )
{
    float a[ ] = { 13.24, 1.5, 1.5, 5.4, 3.5 } ;
    float *j, *k ;
    j = a ;
    k = a + 4 ;
    j = j * 2 ;
    k = k / 2 ;
    printf ( "\n%d %d", *j, *k ) ;
}
```

(f)
```
# include <stdio.h>
void main( )
{
    int max = 5 ;
    float arr[max] ;
    for ( i = 0 ; i < max ; i++ )
    scanf ( "%f", &arr[i] ) ;
}
```

[G] Answer the following:

(a) What will happen if you try to put so many values into an array when you initialize it that the size of the array is exceeded?
1. nothing
2. possible system malfunction
3. error message from the compiler
4. other data may be overwritten

(b) In an array **int arr[12]**, the word **arr** represents the a_____ of the array.

(c) What will happen if you put too few elements in an array when you initialize it?
1. nothing
2. possible system malfunction

3. error message from the compiler
4. unused elements will be filled with 0s or garbage

(d) What will happen if you assign a value to an element of an array whose subscript exceeds the size of the array?
1. the element will be set to 0
2. nothing, it's done all the time
3. other data may be overwritten
4. error message from the compiler

(e) When you pass an array as an argument to a function, what actually gets passed?
1. address of the array
2. values of the elements of the array
3. address of the first element of the array
4. number of elements of the array

(f) Which of these are reasons for using pointers?
1. To manipulate parts of an array
2. To refer to keywords such as **for** and **if**
3. To return more than one value from a function
4. To refer to particular programs more conveniently

(g) If you don't initialize a static array, What will the elements be set to?
1. 0
2. an undetermined value
3. a floating point number
4. the character constant '\0'

[H] State True or False:

(a) The address of a floating-point variable is always a whole number.
(b) Which of the following is the correct way of declaring a float pointer:
1. float ptr ;
2. float *ptr ;
3. *float ptr ;
4. None of the above

(c) Add the missing statement for the following program to print 35.

```
# include <stdio.h>
void main( )
{
    int j, *ptr ;
    *ptr = 35 ;
    printf ( "\n%d", j ) ;
}
```

(d) If **int s[5]** is a one-dimensional array of integers, which of the following refers to the third element in the array?
1. *(s + 2)
2. *(s + 3)
3. s + 3
4. s + 2

[I] Attempt the following:

(a) Write a program to copy the contents of one array into another in the reverse order.
(b) If array **arr** contains **n** elements, then write a program to check if **arr[0] = arr[n − 1]**, **arr[1] = arr[n − 2]**, and so on.
(c) Find the smallest number in an array using pointers.
(d) Write a program that performs the following tasks:
   – initialize an integer array of 10 elements in **main( )**
   – pass the entire array to a function **modify( )**
   – in **modify( )**, multiply each element of an array by 3
   – return the control to **main( )** and print the new array elements in **main( )**

More than one dimension

[J] What will be the output of the following programs:

(a)
```c
# include <stdio.h>
void main( )
{
    int n[3][3] = {
                        2, 4, 3,
                        6, 8, 5,
                        3, 5, 1
                } ;
    printf ( "\n%d %d %d", *n, n[3][3], n[2][2] ) ;
}
```

(b)
```c
# include <stdio.h>
void main( )
{
    int n[3][3] = {
                        2, 4, 3,
                        6, 8, 5,
                        3, 5, 1
                } ;
```

```
        int i, *ptr ;
        ptr = n ;
        for ( i = 0 ; i <= 8 ; i++ )
                printf ( "\n%d", *( ptr + i ) ) ;
    }
```

(c)
```
    # include <stdio.h>
    void main( )
    {
        int n[3][3] = {
                        2, 4, 3,
                        6, 8, 5,
                        3, 5, 1
                    } ;
        int i, j ;
        for ( i = 0 ; i <= 2 ; i++ )
            for ( j = 0 ; j <= 2 ; j++ )
                printf ( "\n%d %d", n[i][j],
                            *( *( n + i ) + j ) ) ;

    }
```

[K] Point out the errors, if any, in the following programs:

(a)
```
    # include <stdio.h>
    void main( )
    {
        int twod[ ][ ] = {
                            2, 4,
                            6, 8
                        } ;
        printf ( "\n%d", twod ) ;
    }
```

(b)
```
    # include <stdio.h>
    void main( )
    {
        int three[3][ ] = {
                            2, 4, 3,
                            6, 8, 2,
                            2, 3 ,1
                        } ;
        printf ( "\n%d", three[1][1] ) ;

    }
```

[L] Attempt the following:

(a) How will you initialize a three-dimensional array **threed[3][2][3]**?
     How will you refer to the first and last element in this array?

(b) Write a program to pick up the largest number from any 5 row by 5 column matrix.

(c) Write a program to obtain the transpose of a 4 x 4 matrix. The transpose of a matrix is obtained by exchanging the elements of each row with the elements of the corresponding column.

(d) Very often in fairs we come across a puzzle that contains 15 numbered square pieces mounted on a frame. These pieces can be moved horizontally or vertically. A possible arrangement of these pieces is shown in Figure 8.12:

As you can see there is a blank at the bottom right corner. Implement the following procedure through a program:

Draw the boxes as shown in Figure 8.12. Display the numbers in the same order. Allow the user to hit any of the arrow keys (up, down, left, or right).

If the user hits, say, the right arrow key, then the piece with a number 5 should move to the right and a blank should replace the original position of 5. Similarly, if the down arrow key is hit, then 13 should move down and a blank should replace the original position of 13. If the left arrow key or up arrow key is hit, then no action should be taken.

The user would continue hitting the arrow keys until the numbers aren't arranged in ascending order.

Keep track of the number of moves in which the user manages to arrange the numbers in ascending order. The user who manages it in the least number of moves is the one who wins.

How do we tackle the arrow keys? We cannot receive them using the **scanf( )** function. Arrow keys are special keys that are identified by their 'scan codes.' Use the following function in your program. It will return the scan code of the arrow key being hit. Don't worry

1	4	15	7
8	10	2	11
14	3	6	13
12	9	5	

FIGURE 8.12

about how this function is written. We are going to deal with it later. The scan codes for the arrow keys are:

up arrow key – 72 down arrow key – 80
left arrow key – 75 right arrow key – 77

```
/* Returns scan code of the key that has been hit */
# include "dos.h"
getkey( )
{
    union REGS i, o ;
    while ( !kbhit( ) )
            ;
    i.h.ah = 0 ;
    int86 ( 22, & i, & o ) ;
    return ( o.h.ah ) ;
}
```

(e) Match the following with reference to the following program segment:

```
int i, j, = 25;
int *pi, *pj = & j;
.......
....... /* more lines of program */
.......
*pj = j + 5;
j = *pj + 5 ;
pj = pj ;
*pi = i + j
```

Each integer quantity occupies 2 bytes of memory. The value assigned to **i** begin at (hexadecimal) address F9C and the value assigned to j begins at address F9E. Match the value represented by the left-hand side quantities with the right.

1.	&i	a.	30
2.	&j	b.	F9E
3.	pj	c.	35
4.	*pj	d.	FA2
5.	i	e.	F9C
6.	pi	f.	67
7.	*pi	g.	unspecified
8.	(pi + 2)	h.	65

9.	(*pi + 2)	i.	F9E
10.	*(pi + 2)	j.	F9E
		k.	FAO
		l.	F9D

(f) Match the following with reference to the following program segment:

```
int x[3][5] = {
                { 1, 2, 3, 4, 5 },
                { 6, 7, 8, 9, 10 },
                { 11, 12, 13, 14, 15 }
              }, *n = &x ;
```

1.	*(*(x + 2) + 1)	a.	9
2.	*(*x + 2) + 5	b.	13
3.	*(*(x + 1))	c.	4
4.	*(*(x) + 2) + 1	d.	3
5.	*(*(x + 1) + 3)	e.	2
6.	*n	f.	12
7.	*(n + 2)	g.	14
8.	(*(n + 3) + 1	h.	7
9.	*(n + 5) + 1	i.	1
10.	++*n	j.	8
		k.	5
		l.	10
		m.	6

(g) Match the following with reference to the following program segment:

```
struct
{
    int x, y;
} s[ ] = { 10, 20, 15, 25, 8, 75, 6, 2 };
int *i ;
i = s ;
```

1.	*(i + 3)	a.	85
2.	s[i[7]].x	b.	2
3.	s[(s + 2)->y / 3[I]].y	c.	6
4.	i[i[1]-i[2]]	d.	7
5.	i[s[3].y]	e.	16
6.	(s + 1)->x + 5	f.	15
7.	*(1 + i)**(i + 4)/*i	g.	25

8.	s[i[0] − i[4]].y + 10	h.	8
9.	(*(s +* (i + 1)/*i)).x + 2	i.	1
10.	++i[i[6]]	j.	100
		k.	10
		l.	20

(h) Match the following with reference to the following program segment:

```
unsigned int arr[3][3] = {
                            2, 4, 6,
                            9, 1, 10,
                            16, 64, 5
                          } ;
```

1.	**arr	a.	64
2.	**arr <* (*arr + 2)	b.	18
3.	*(arr + 2)/(*(*arr + 1) >** arr)	c.	6
4.	*(arr[1] + 1)| arr[1][2]	d.	3
5.	*(arr[0])	*(arr[2])	e.	0
6.	arr[1][1] < arr[0][1]	f.	16
7.	arr[2][[1] & arr[2][0]	g.	1
8.	arr[2][2]	arr[0][1]	h.	11
9.	arr[0][1] ^ arr[0][2]	i.	20
10.	++**arr + −arr[1][1]	j.	2
		k.	5
		l.	4

(i) Write a program to find if a square matrix is symmetric.

(j) Write a program to add two 6 × 6 matrices.

(k) Write a program to multiply any two 3 × 3 matrices.

(l) Given an array **p[5]**, write a function to shift it circularly left by two positions. Thus, if p[0] = 15, p[1] = 30, p[2] = 28, p[3] = 19, and p[4] = 61, then after the shift p[0] = 28, p[1] = 19, p[2] = 61, p[3] = 15, and p[4] = 30. Call this function for a (4 × 5) matrix and get its rows left-shifted.

(m) A 6 × 6 matrix is entered through the keyboard. Write a program to obtain the determinant value of this matrix.

(n) For the following set of sample data, compute the standard deviation and the mean.

```
-6, -12, 8, 13, 11, 6, 7, 2, -6, -9, -10, 11, 10, 9, 2
```

The formula for standard deviation is

$$\sqrt{\frac{(x_i - \bar{x})^2}{n}}$$

where x_i is the data item and $\bar{x}$ is the mean.

(o) The area of a triangle can be computed by the sine law when 2 sides of the triangle and the angle between them are known.

```
Area = ( 1 / 2 ) ab sin ( angle )
```

Given the following 6 triangular pieces of land, write a program to find their area and determine which is largest.

Plot No.	a	b	angle
1	137.4	80.9	0.78
2	155.2	92.62	0.89
3	149.3	97.93	1.35
4	160.0	100.25	9.00
5	155.6	68.95	1.25
6	149.7	120.0	1.75

(p) For the following set of n data points (x, y), compute the correlation coefficient r, given by

$$r = \frac{\sum xy - \sum x \sum y}{\sqrt{[n \sum x^2 - (\sum x)^2][n \sum y^2 - (\sum y)^2]}}$$

x	y
34.22	102.43
39.87	100.93
41.85	97.43
43.23	97.81
40.06	98.32
53.29	98.32
53.29	100.07
54.14	97.08
49.12	91.59
40.71	94.85
55.15	94.65

(q) For the following set of points given by **(x, y)** fit a straight line given by

```
y = a + bx
```

where,

$$a = y - bx \quad \text{and}$$

$$b = \frac{n \sum yx - \sum x \sum y}{[n \sum x^2 - (\sum x)^2]}$$

X	Y
3.0	1.5
4.5	2.0
5.5	3.5
6.5	5.0
7.5	6.0
8.5	7.5
8.0	9.0
9.0	10.5
9.5	12.0
10.0	14.0

(r) The **X** and **Y** coordinates of 10 different points are entered through the keyboard. Write a program to find the distance of last point from the first point (sum of distances between consecutive points).

(s) A dequeue is an ordered set of elements in which elements may be inserted or retrieved from either end. Using an array, simulate a dequeue of characters and the operations retrieve left, retrieve right, insert left, and insert right. Exceptional conditions, such as dequeue full or empty, should be indicated. Two pointers (namely, left and right) are needed in this simulation.

Chapter 9

PUPPETTING ON STRINGS

In the last chapter, you learned how to define arrays of various sizes and dimensions, how to initialize arrays, how to pass arrays to a function, etc. With this knowledge under your belt, you should be ready to handle strings, which are, simply put, a special kind of array. And strings, the ways to manipulate them, and how pointers are related to strings are the topics of discussion in this chapter.

WHAT ARE STRINGS?

The way a group of integers can be stored in an integer array, similarly, a group of characters can be stored in a character array. Character arrays are also called strings. Many languages internally treat strings as character arrays, but somehow conceal this fact from the programmer. Character arrays, or strings, are used by programming languages to manipulate text, such as words and sentences.

A string constant is a one-dimensional array of characters terminated by a null ('\0'). For example,

```
char name[ ] = \{ 'H', 'A', 'E', 'S', 'L', 'E', 'R', '\0' \} ;
```

Each character in the array occupies one byte of memory and the last character is always '\0'. What character is this? It looks like two characters, but it is actually only one character, with the \ indicating that what follows it is something special. '\0' is called a null character. Note that '\0' and '0' are not same. The ASCII value of '\0' is 0, whereas the ASCII value of '0' is 48. Figure 9.1 shows the way a character array is stored in memory. Note that the elements of the character array are stored in contiguous memory locations.

The terminating null ('\0') is important, because it is the only way the functions that work with a string can know where the string ends. In fact, a string not terminated by a '\0' is not really a string, but merely a collection of characters.

H	A	E	S	L	E	R	\0
65518	65519	65520	65521	65522	65523	65524	65525

FIGURE 9.1

C concedes the fact that you will use strings often and therefore provides a shortcut for initializing strings. For example, the string used in Figure 9.1 can also be initialized as,

```
char name[ ] = "HAESLER" ;
```

Note that, in this declaration '\0' is not necessary. C inserts the null character automatically.

MORE ABOUT STRINGS

In what way are character arrays different from numeric arrays? Can elements in a character array be accessed in the same way as the elements of a numeric array? Do you need to take any special care of '\0'? Why don't numeric arrays end with a '\0'? Declaring strings is okay, but how do you manipulate them? Questions galore! Well, let us settle some of these issues right away with the help of some sample programs.

```
/* Program to demonstrate printing of a string */
# include <stdio.h>
void main( )
{
    char name[ ] = "Klinsman" ;
    int i = 0 ;

    while ( i <= 7 )
    {
        printf ( "%c", name[i] ) ;
        i++ ;
    }
}
```

And here is the output:

```
Klinsman
```

No big deal. We have initialized a character array, and then printed out the elements of this array within a **while** loop. Can we write the **while** loop without using the final value 7? We can; because we know that each character array always ends with a '\0'. The following program illustrates this.

```
# include <stdio.h>
void main( )
{
    char name[ ] = "Klinsman" ;
    int i = 0 ;
```

```
while ( name[i] != '\0' )
{
    printf ( "%c", name[i] ) ;
    i++ ;
}
}
```

And here is the output:

```
Klinsman
```

This program doesn't rely on the length of the string (number of characters in it) to print out its contents and hence is definitely more general than the earlier one. Here is another version of the same program; this one uses a pointer to access the array elements.

```
# include <stdio.h>
void main( )
{
    char name[ ] = "Klinsman" ;
    char *ptr ;
    ptr = name ; /* store base address of string */
    while ( *ptr != `\0' )
    {
        printf ( "%c", *ptr ) ;
        ptr++ ;
    }
}
```

As with the integer array, by mentioning the name of the array, we get the base address (address of the zeroth element) of the array. This base address is stored in the variable **ptr** using,

```
ptr = name ;
```

Once the base address is obtained in **ptr**, *ptr will yield the value at this address, which gets printed promptly through,

```
printf ( "%c", *ptr ) ;
```

Then, **ptr** is incremented to point to the next character in the string. This derives from two facts: array elements are stored in contiguous memory locations and on incrementing a pointer, it points to the immediately next location of its type. This process is carried out until **ptr** points to the last character in the string, that is, '\0'.

In fact, the character array elements can be accessed in exactly the same way as the elements of an integer array. Thus, all the following notations refer to the same element:

```
name[i]
*( name + i )
*( i + name )
i[name]
```

Even though there are so many ways to refer to the elements of a character array, rarely is any one of them used. This is because the **printf( )** function has got a sweet and simple way of doing it, as shown in the following. Note that **printf( )** doesn't print the '\0'.

```
# include <stdio.h>
void main( )
{
    char name[ ] = "Klinsman" ;
    printf ( "%s", name ) ;
}
```

The **% s** used in **printf( )** is a format specification for printing out a string. The same specification can be used to receive a string from the keyboard, as shown here:

```
# include <stdio.h>
void main( )
{
    char name[25] ;

    printf ( "Enter your name " ) ;
    scanf ( "%s", name ) ;
    printf ( "Hello %s!", name ) ;
}
```

And here is a sample run of the program:

```
Enter your name Debashish
Hello Debashish!
```

Note that the declaration **char name[25]** sets aside 25 bytes under the array **name[ ]**, whereas the **scanf( )** function fills in the characters typed at the keyboard into this array until the enter key is pressed. Once enter is pressed, **scanf( )** places a '\0' in the array. Naturally, we should pass the base address of the array to the **scanf( )** function.

While entering the string using **scanf( )**, we must be cautious about two things:

(a) The length of the string should not exceed the dimension of the character array. This is because the C compiler doesn't perform bounds checking on character arrays. Hence, if you carelessly exceed the bounds, there is always a danger of overwriting something important, and in that event, you would have nobody to blame but yourself.

(b) **scanf( )** is not capable of receiving multiword strings. Therefore, names such as 'Debashish Roy' would be unacceptable. The way to get around this limitation is by using the function **gets( )gets( )**. The usage of the functions **gets( )**, and its counterpart, **puts ( )**, is shown below.

```
# include <stdio.h>
void main( )
{
    char name[25] ;
    printf ( "Enter your full name: " ) ;
    gets ( name ) ;
    puts ( "Hello!" ) ;
    puts ( name ) ;
}
```

And here is the output:

```
Enter your full name: Debashish Roy
Hello!
Debashish Roy
```

The program and the output are self-explanatory except for the fact that **puts( )** can display only one string at a time (hence the use of two **puts( )** in the previous program). Also, on displaying a string, unlike **printf( )**, **puts( )** places the cursor on the next line. Though **gets( )** is capable of receiving only one string at a time, the plus point with **gets( )** is that it can receive a multiword string.

If we are prepared to take the trouble, we can make **scanf( )** accept multiword strings by writing it in this manner:

```
char name[25] ;
printf ( "Enter your full name " ) ;
scanf ( "%[^\n]s", name ) ;
```

Here, [^**\n**] indicates that **scanf( )** will keep receiving characters into **name[ ]** until a \n is encountered. Though workable, this is not the best of the ways to call a function.

POINTERS AND STRINGS

Suppose we wish to store "Hello." We may either store it in a string or we may ask the C compiler to store it at some location in memory and assign the address of the string in a **char** pointer. This is shown below:

```
char str[ ] = "Hello" ;
char *p = "Hello" ;
```

There is a subtle difference in usage of these two forms. For example, we cannot assign a string to another, whereas we can assign a **char** pointer to another **char** pointer. This is shown in the following program.

```
void main( )
{
    char str1[ ] = "Hello" ;
    char str2[10] ;

    char *s = "Good Morning" ;
    char *q ;

    str2 = str1 ; /* error */
    q = s ; /* works */
}
```

Also, once a string has been defined, it cannot be initialized to another set of characters. Unlike strings, such an operation is perfectly valid with **char** pointers.

```
void main( )
{
    char str1[ ] = "Hello" ;
    char *p = "Hello" ;
    str1 = "Bye" ; /* error */
    p = "Bye" ; /* works */
}
```

STANDARD LIBRARY STRING FUNCTIONS

With every C compiler, a large set of useful string handling library functions are provided. Figure 9.2 lists the more commonly used functions along with their purpose.

Out of the list in Figure 9.2, we shall discuss the functions **strlen( )**, **strcpy( ) strcat( )**, and **strcmp( )**, since these are the most commonly used

Function	Use
strlen	Finds length of a string
strlwr	Converts a string to lowercase
strupr	Converts a string to uppercase
strcat	Appends one string at the end of another
strncat	Appends first n characters of a string at the end of another
strcpy	Copies a string into another
strncpy	Copies first n characters of one string into another
strcmp	Compares two strings
strncmp	Compares first n characters of two strings
strcmpi	Compares two strings without regard to case ("i" denotes that this function ignores case)
stricmp	Compares two strings without regard to case (identical to strcmpi)
strnicmp	Compares first n characters of two strings without regard to case
strdup	Duplicates a string
strchr	Finds first occurrence of a given character in a string
strrchr	Finds last occurrence of a given character in a string
strstr	Finds first occurrence of a given string in another string
strset	Sets all characters of string to a given character
strnset	Sets first n characters of a string to a given character
strrev	Reverses string

FIGURE 9.2

functions. This will also illustrate how the library functions in general handle strings. Let us study these functions one by one.

strlen( )

This function counts the number of characters present in a string. Its usage is illustrated in the following program.

```
# include <stdio.h>
# include <string.h>
void main( )
{
    char arr[ ] = "Bamboozled" ;
    int len1, len2 ;

    len1 = strlen ( arr ) ;
    len2 = strlen ( "Humpty Dumpty" ) ;
```

```
    printf ( "\nstring = %s length = %d", arr, len1 ) ;
    printf ( "\nstring = %s length = %d", "Humpty Dumpty", len2 ) ;
}
```

The output will be:

```
string = Bamboozled length = 10
string = Humpty Dumpty length = 13
```

Note that, in the first call to the function **strlen( )**, we are passing the base address of the string, and the function, in turn, returns the length of the string. While calculating the length it doesn't count '\0'. Even in the second call,

```
len2 = strlen ( "Humpty Dumpty" ) ;
```

what gets passed to **strlen( )** is the address of the string and not the string itself. Can we not write a function **xstrlen( )**, which imitates the standard library function **strlen( )**? Let us give it a try...

```
/* A look-alike of the function strlen( ) */
# include <stdio.h>
int xstrlen ( char * ) ;
void main( )
{
    char arr[ ] = "Bamboozled" ;
    int len1, len2 ;

    len1 = xstrlen ( arr ) ;
    len2 = xstrlen ( "Humpty Dumpty" ) ;

    printf ( "\nstring = %s length = %d", arr, len1 ) ;
    printf ( "\nstring = %s length = %d", "Humpty Dumpty", len2 ) ;
}

int xstrlen ( char *s )
{
    int length = 0 ;

    while ( *s != '\0' )
    {
        length++ ;
        s++ ;
    }

    return ( length ) ;
}
```

The output will be:

```
string = Bamboozled length = 10
string = Humpty Dumpty length = 13
```

The function **xstrlen( )** is fairly simple. All that it does is keep counting the characters until the end of string is met. Or, in other words, keep counting characters until the pointer **s** points to '\0'.

strcpy( )

This function copies the contents of one string into another. The base addresses of the source and target strings should be supplied to this function. Here is an example of **strcpy( )** in action:

```
# include <stdio.h>
# include <string.h>
void main( )
{
    char source[ ] = "Sayonara" ;
    char target[20] ;
    strcpy ( target, source ) ;
    printf ( "\nsource string = %s", source ) ;
    printf ( "\ntarget string = %s", target ) ;
}
```

And here is the output:

```
source string = Sayonara
target string = Sayonara
```

On supplying the base addresses, **strcpy( )** goes on copying the characters in the source string into the target string until it encounters the end of the source string ('\0'). It is our responsibility to see to it that the target string's dimension is big enough to hold the string being copied into it. Thus, a string gets copied into another, piece-meal, character by character. There is no shortcut for this. Let us now attempt to mimic **strcpy( )**, via our own string copy function, which we will call **xstrcpy( )**.

```
# include <stdio.h>
void xstrcpy ( char *, char * ) ;
void main( )
{
    char source[ ] = "Sayonara" ;
    char target[20] ;
```

```
    xstrcpy ( target, source ) ;
    printf ( "\nsource string = %s", source ) ;
    printf ( "\ntarget string = %s", target ) ;
}
void xstrcpy ( char *t, char *s )
{
    while ( *s != '\0' )
    {
        *t = *s ;
        s++ ;
        t++ ;
    }
    *t = '\0' ;
}
```

The output of the program will be:

```
source string = Sayonara
target string = Sayonara
```

Note that having copied the entire source string into the target string, it is necessary to place a '\0' into the target string, to mark its end.

If you look at the prototype of the **strcpy( )** standard library function, it looks like this:

```
strcpy ( char *t, const char *s ) ;
```

We didn't use the keyword **const** in our version of **xstrcpy( )** and still our function worked correctly. So what is the need of the **const** qualifier?

What would happen if we add the following lines beyond the last statement of **xstrcpy( )**?

```
s = s - 8 ;
*s = 'K' ;
```

This would change the source string to "Kayonara." Can we ensure that the source string doesn't change, even accidentally, in **xstrcpy( )**? We can, by changing the definition as follows:

```
void xstrcpy ( char *t, const char *s )
{
    while ( *s != '\0' )
    {
        *t = *s ;
        s++ ;
```

```
        t++ ;
    }
    *t = '\0' ;
}
```

By declaring **char *s** as **const**, we are declaring that the source string should remain constant (should not change). Thus, the **const** qualifier ensures that your program does not inadvertently alter a variable that you intended to be a constant. It also reminds anybody reading the program listing that the variable is not intended to change.

We can use **const** in several situations. The following code fragment will help you in learning **const**.

```
char *p = "Hello" ; /* pointer is variable, so is string */
*p = 'M' ; /* works */
p = "Bye" ; /* works */

const char *q = "Hello" ; /* string is fixed, pointer is not */
*q = 'M' ; /* error */
q = "Bye" ; /* works */

char const *s = "Hello" ; /* string is fixed, pointer is not */
*s = 'M' ; /* error */
s = "Bye" ; /* works */

char * const t = "Hello" ; /* pointer is fixed, string is not */
*t = 'M' ; /* works */
t = "Bye" ; /* error */

const char * const u = "Hello" ; /* string is fixed, so is pointer */
*u = 'M' ; /* error */
u = "Bye" ; /* error */
```

The keyword **const** can also be used in context of ordinary variables like **int**, **float**, etc. The following program shows how this can be done.

```
# include <stdio.h>
void main( )
{
    float r, a ;
    const float pi = 3.14 ;
    printf ( "\nEnter radius of circle " ) ;
    scanf ( "%f", & r ) ;
    a = pi * r * r ;
    printf ( "\nArea of circle = %f", a ) ;
}
```

strcat( )

This function concatenates the source string at the end of the target string. For example, "Bombay" and "Nagpur" on concatenation would result into a string "BombayNagpur." Here is an example of **strcat( )** at work.

```
# include <stdio.h>
# include <string.h>
void main( )
{
    char source[ ] = "Folks!" ;
    char target[30] = "Hello" ;
    strcat ( target, source ) ;
    printf ( "\nsource string = %s", source ) ;
    printf ( "\ntarget string = %s", target ) ;
}
```

And here is the output:

```
source string = Folks!
target string = HelloFolks!
```

Note that the target string has been made big enough to hold the final string. It is up to you to develop your own **xstrcat( )** on lines of **xstrlen( )** and **xstrcpy( )**.

strcmp( )

This is a function that compares two strings to find out whether they are the same or different. The two strings are compared character by character until there is a mismatch or the end of one of the strings is reached, whichever occurs first. If the two strings are identical, **strcmp( )** returns a value zero. If they're not, it returns the numeric difference between the ASCII values of the first non-matching pair of characters. Here is a program which puts **strcmp( )** in action.

```
# include <stdio.h>
# include <string.h>
void main( )
{
    char string1[ ] = "Jerry" ;
    char string2[ ] = "Ferry" ;
    int i, j, k ;
    i = strcmp ( string1, "Jerry" ) ;
    j = strcmp ( string1, string2 ) ;
    k = strcmp ( string1, "Jerry boy" ) ;
```

```
    printf ( "\n%d %d %d", i, j, k ) ;
}
```

And here is the output:

```
0 4 -32
```

In the first call to **strcmp( )**, the two strings are identical—"Jerry" and "Jerry"—and the value returned by **strcmp( )** is zero. In the second call, the first character of "Jerry" doesn't match with the first character of "Ferry" and the result is 4, which is the numeric difference between ASCII value of 'J' and ASCII value of 'F'. In the third call to **strcmp( )**, "Jerry" doesn't match with "Jerry boy," because the null character at the end of "Jerry" doesn't match the blank in "Jerry boy." The value returned is -32, which is the value of null character minus the ASCII value of space, i.e., '\0' minus ' ', which is equal to -32.

The exact value of mismatch will rarely concern us. All we usually want to know is whether or not the first string is alphabetically before the second string. If it is, a negative value is returned; if it isn't, a positive value is returned. Any nonzero value means there is a mismatch. Try to implement this procedure into a function **xstrcmp( )**.

TWO-DIMENSIONAL ARRAY OF CHARACTERS

In the last chapter, we saw several examples of two-dimensional integer arrays. Let's now look at a similar entity, but one dealing with characters. Our example program asks you to type your name. When you do so, it checks your name against a master list to see if you are worthy of entry to the palace. Here's the program:

```
# include <stdio.h>
# include <string.h>
# define FOUND 1
# define NOTFOUND 0
void main( )
{
    char masterlist[6][10] = {
                                "akshay",
                                "parag",
                                "raman",
                                "srinivas",
                                "gopal",
                                "rajesh"
                            } ;
```

```
    int i, flag, a ;
    char yourname[10] ;

    printf ( "\nEnter your name " ) ;
    scanf ( "%s", yourname ) ;
    flag = NOTFOUND ;
    for ( i = 0 ; i <= 5 ; i++ )
    {
        a = strcmp ( & masterlist[i][0], yourname ) ;
        if ( a == 0 )
        {
            printf ( "Welcome, you can enter the palace" ) ;
            flag = FOUND ;
            break ;
        }
    }
    if ( flag == NOTFOUND )
        printf ( "Sorry, you are a trespasser" ) ;
}
```

And here is the output for two sample runs of this program:

```
Enter your name dinesh
Sorry, you are a trespasser
Enter your name raman
Welcome, you can enter the palace
```

Notice how the two-dimensional character array has been initialized. The order of the subscripts in the array declaration is important. The first subscript gives the number of names in the array, while the second subscript gives the length of each item in the array.

Instead of initializing names, had these names been supplied from the keyboard, the program segment would have looked like this:

```
for ( i = 0 ; i <= 5 ; i++ )
    scanf ( "%s", & masterlist[i][0] ) ;
```

While comparing the strings through **strcmp( )**, note that the addresses of the strings are being passed to **strcmp( )**. As seen in the last section, if the two strings match, **strcmp( )** would return a value 0, otherwise it will return a nonzero value.

The variable **flag** is used to keep a record of whether the control did reach inside the **if** or not. To begin with, we set **flag** to NOTFOUND. Later through the loop, if the names match, **flag** is set to FOUND. When the control reaches beyond the **for** loop, if **flag** is still set to NOTFOUND,

65454	a	k	s	h	a	y	\0		
65464	p	a	r	a	g	\0			
65474	r	a	m	a	n	\0			
65484	s	r	i	n	i	v	a	·s	\0
65494	g	o	p	a	l	\0			
65504	r	a	j	e	s	h	\0		

65513
(last location)

FIGURE 9.3

it means none of the names in the **masterlist[ ][ ]** matched with the one supplied from the keyboard.

The names will be stored in the memory as shown in Figure 9.3. Note that each string ends with a '\0'. The arrangement, as you can appreciate, is similar to that of a two-dimensional numeric array.

Here, 65454, 65464, 65474, etc., are the base addresses of successive names. As seen from the pattern, some of the names do not occupy all the bytes reserved for them. For example, even though 10 bytes are reserved for storing the name "akshay," it occupies only 7 bytes. Thus, 3 bytes go to waste. Similarly, for each name, there is some amount of waste. In fact, the more names, more will be wasted. Can this be avoided? Yes, it can,—by using what is called an 'array of pointers,' which is our next topic of discussion.

ARRAY OF POINTERS TO STRINGS

As we know, a pointer variable always contains an address. Therefore, if we construct an array of pointers, it would contain a number of addresses. Let us see how the names in the earlier example can be stored in an array of pointers.

```
char *names[ ] = {
                "akshay",
                "parag",
                "raman",
                "srinivas",
                "gopal",
                "rajesh"
            } ;
```

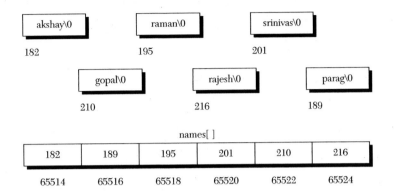

FIGURE 9.4

In this declaration, **names[ ]** is an array of pointers. It contains base addresses of respective names. That is, the base address of "akshay" is stored in **names[0]**, the base address of "parag" is stored in **names[1]**, and so on. This is depicted in Figure 9.4.

In the two-dimensional array of characters, the strings occupied 60 bytes. Compared to an array of pointers, the strings occupy only 41 bytes—a net saving of 19 bytes. A substantial saving, you would agree. But realize that 19 bytes are not actually saved, since 12 bytes are sacrificed for storing the addresses in the array **names[ ]**. Thus, one reason to store strings in an array of pointers is to make a more efficient use of available memory.

Another reason to use an array of pointers to store strings is to obtain greater ease in the manipulation of the strings. This is shown by the following programs. The first one uses a two-dimensional array of characters to store the names, whereas the second uses an array of pointers to strings. The purpose of both the programs is very simple. We want to exchange the position of the names "roman" and "stephany."

```
/* Exchange names using 2D array of characters */
# include <stdio.h>
void main( )
{
    char names[ ][10] = {
                        "arthur",
                        "patty",
                        "roman",
                        "stephany",
                        "gerry",
                        "rajeev"
                      } ;
```

```
    int i ;
    char t ;

    printf ( "\nOriginal: %s %s", & names[2][0], & names[3][0] ) ;

    for ( i = 0 ; i <= 9 ; i++ )
    {
        t = names[2][i] ;
        names[2][i] = names[3][i] ;
        names[3][i] = t ;
    }

    printf ( "\nNew: %s %s", & names[2][0], & names[3][0] ) ;
    }
```

And here is the output:

```
Original: roman stephany
New: stephany roman
```

Note that in this program, to exchange the names we are required to exchange corresponding characters of the two names. In effect, 10 exchanges are needed to interchange two names.

Let us see, if the number of exchanges can be reduced by using an array of pointers to strings. Here is the program:

```
# include <stdio.h>
void main( )
{
    char *names[ ] = {
                        "arthur",
                        "patty",
                        "roman",
                        "stephany",
                        "gerry",
                        "rajeev"
                     } ;
    char *temp ;
    printf ( "Original: %s %s", names[2], names[3] ) ;
    temp = names[2] ;
    names[2] = names[3] ;
    names[3] = temp ;
    printf ( "nNew: %s %s", names[2], names[3] ) ;
}
```

And here is the output:

```
Original: roman stephany
New: stephany roman
```

The output is the same as the earlier program. In this program, all that we are required to do is to exchange the addresses (of the names) stored in the array of pointers, rather than the names themselves. Thus, by effecting just one exchange, we are able to interchange names. This makes handling strings very convenient.

Thus, from the point of view of efficient memory usage and ease of programming, an array of pointers to strings definitely scores over a two-dimensional character array. That is why, even though, in principle, strings can be stored and handled through a two-dimensional array of characters, in actual practice, it is the array of pointers to strings, which is more commonly used.

LIMITATIONS OF ARRAY OF POINTERS TO STRINGS

When we are using a two-dimensional array of characters, we are at liberty to either initialize the strings where we are declaring the array, or receive the strings using the **scanf( )** function. However, when we are using an array of pointers to strings, we can initialize the strings at the place where we are declaring the array, but we cannot receive the strings from the keyboard using **scanf( )**. Thus, the following program would never work out.

```
# include <stdio.h>
void main( )
{
    char *names[6] ;
    int i ;
    for ( i = 0 ; i <= 5 ; i++ )
    {
        printf ( "\nEnter name " ) ;
        scanf ( "%s", names[i] ) ;
    }
}
```

The program doesn't work because; when we are declaring the array, it contains garbage values. And it would be definitely wrong to send these garbage values to **scanf( )** as the addresses where it should keep the strings received from the keyboard.

Solution

If we are bent upon receiving the strings from the keyboard using **scanf( )**, and then storing their addresses in an array of pointers to strings, we can do it in a slightly roundabout manner as shown below.

```
# include <stdio.h>
# include <stdlib.h>
# include <string.h>
void main( )
{
    char *names[6] ;
    char n[50] ;
    int len, i ;
    char *p ;
    for ( i = 0 ; i <= 5 ; i++ )
    {
        printf ( "\nEnter name " ) ;
        scanf ( "%s", n ) ;
        len = strlen ( n ) ;
        p = ( char * ) malloc ( len + 1 ) ; /* +1 for accommodating \0 */
        strcpy ( p, n ) ;
        names[i] = p ;
    }
    for ( i = 0 ; i <= 5 ; i++ )
        printf ( "\n%s", names[i] ) ;
}
```

Here we have first received a name using **scanf( )** in a string **n[ ]**. Then we have found out its length using **strlen( )** and allocated space for making a copy of this name. This memory allocation has been done using a standard library function called **malloc( )**. This function requires the number of bytes to be allocated and returns the base address of the chunk of memory that it allocates. The address returned by this function is always of the type **void** *. This is because **malloc( )** doesn't know what we did to allocate the memory. A **void** * means a pointer that is a legal address, but it is not the address of a **char**, or the address of an **int**, or the address of any other datatype. Hence it has been converted into **char** * using a C language feature called typecasting. Typecasting is discussed in detail in Chapter 15. The prototype of this function has been declared in the file 'stdlib.h.' Hence, we have **#includ**ed this file.

But why didn't we use array to allocate memory? This is because, with arrays, we have to commit to the size of the array at the time of writing the program. Moreover, there is no way to increase or decrease the array size during execution of the program. In other words, when we use arrays, static memory allocation takes place. Unlike this, using **malloc( )**, we can allocate memory dynamically, during execution. The argument that we pass to **malloc( )** can be a variable whose value can change during execution.

Once we have allocated the memory using **malloc( )**, we have copied the name received through the keyboard into this allocated space and finally stored the address of the allocated chunk in the appropriate element of **names[ ]**, the array of pointers to strings.

This solution suffers in performance because we need to allocate memory and then do the copying of string for each name received through the keyboard.

SUMMARY

(a) A string is nothing but an array of characters terminated by '\0'.

(b) Being an array, all the characters of a string are stored in contiguous memory locations.

(c) Though **scanf( )** can be used to receive multiword strings, **gets( )** can do the same job in a cleaner way.

(d) Both **printf( )** and **puts( )** can handle multiword strings.

(e) Strings can be operated upon using several standard library functions like **strlen( )**, **strcpy( )**, **strcat( )**, and **strcmp( )**, which can manipulate strings. More importantly, we imitated some of these functions to learn how these standard library functions are written.

(f) Though in principle a 2D array can be used to handle several strings, in practice an array of pointers to strings is preferred since it takes less space and is efficient in processing strings.

(g) The **malloc( )** function can be used to allocate space in memory on the fly during execution of the program.

EXERCISES

Simple Strings

[A] What will be the output of the following programs:

(a)
```c
# include <stdio.h>
void main( )
```

```
    {
        char c[2] = "A" ;
        printf ( "\n%c", c[0] ) ;
        printf ( "\n%s", c ) ;
    }
```

(b)
```
# include <stdio.h>
void main( )
{
    char s[ ] = "Get organised! learn C!!" ;
    printf ( "\n%s", &s[2] ) ;
    printf ( "\n%s", s ) ;
    printf ( "\n%s", &s ) ;
    printf ( "\n%c", s[2] ) ;
}
```

(c)
```
# include <stdio.h>
void main( )
{
    char s[ ] = "No two viruses work similarly" ;
    int i = 0 ;
    while ( s[i] != 0 )
    {
        printf ( "\n%c %c", s[i], *( s + i ) ) ;
        printf ( "\n%c %c", i[s], *( i + s ) ) ;
        i++ ;
    }
}
```

(d)
```
# include <stdio.h>
void main( )
{
    char s[ ] = "Churchgate: no church no gate" ;
    char t[25] ;
    char *ss, *tt ;
    ss = s ;
    while ( *ss != '\0' )
        *ss++ = *tt++ ;
    printf ( "\n%s", t ) ;
}
```

(e)
```
# include <stdio.h>
void main( )
```

```
    {
        char str1[ ] = { 'H', 'e', 'l', 'l', 'o', 0 } ;
        char str2[ ] = "Hello" ;

        printf ( "\n%s", str1 ) ;
        printf ( "\n%s", str2 ) ;
    }
```

(f)
```
    # include <stdio.h>
    void main( )
    {
        printf ( 5 + "Good Morning " ) ;
    }
```

(g)
```
    void main( )
    {
        printf ( "%c", "abcdefgh"[4] ) ;
    }
```

(h)
```
    # include <stdio.h>
    void main( )
    {
        printf ( "\n%d%d %d", sizeof ( '3' ),
                    sizeof ( "3" ), sizeof ( 3 ) ) ;
    }
```

[B] Point out the errors, if any, in the following programs:

(a)
```
    # include <stdio.h>
    # include <string.h>
    void main( )
    {
        char *str1 = "United" ;
        char *str2 = "Front" ;
        char *str3 ;
        str3 = strcat ( str1, str2 ) ;
        printf ( "\n%s", str3 ) ;
    }
```

(b)
```
    # include <stdio.h>
    void main( )
    {
        int arr[ ] = { 'A', 'B', 'C', 'D' } ;
        int i ;
        for ( i = 0 ; i <= 3 ; i++ )
            printf ( "\n%d", arr[i] ) ;
    }
```

(c)
```
# include <stdio.h>
void main( )
{
    char arr[8] = "Rhombus" ;
    int i ;
    for ( i = 0 ; i <= 7 ; i++ )
        printf ( "\n%d", *arr ) ;
        arr++ ;
}
```

[C] Fill in the blanks:

(a) "A" is a _____ whereas 'A' is a _____.

(b) A string is terminated by a _____ character, which is written as
_____.

(c) The array **char name[10]** can consist of a maximum of _____
characters.

(d) The array elements are always stored in _____ memory locations.

[D] Attempt the following:

(a) Which is more appropriate for reading in a multiword string?
gets( )   printf( )   scanf( )   puts( )

(b) If the string "Alice in Wonderland" is fed to the following **scanf( )**
statement, what will be the contents of the arrays **str1**, **str2**, **str3**,
and **str4**?

```
scanf ( "%s%s%s%s", str1, str2, str3, str4 ) ;
```

(c) Write a program that extracts part of the given string from the specified position. For example, if the sting is "Working with strings is
fun," then from position 4, 4 characters are to be extracted then the
program should return the string as "king." If the number of characters to be extracted is 0, then the program should extract an entire
string from the specified position.

(d) Write a program that converts a string like "124" to an integer 124.

Two-Dimensional Array, Array of Pointers to Strings

[E] Answer the following:

(a) How many bytes in memory would be occupied by the following array
of pointers to strings? How many bytes would be required to store the
same strings if they are stored in a two-dimensional character array?

```
char *mess[ ] = {
                  "Hammer and tongs",
                  "Tooth and nail",
                  "Spit and polish",
                  "You and C"
              } ;
```

(b) Can an array of pointers to strings be used to collect strings from the keyboard? If yes, how? If not, why not?

[F] Attempt the following:

(a) Write a program that uses an array of pointers to strings **str** [ ]. Receive two strings **str1** and **str2** and check if **str1** is embedded in any of the strings in **str**[ ]. If **str1** is found, then replace it with **str2**.

```
char *str[ ] = {
                  "We will teach you how to...",
                  "Move a mountain",
                  "Level a building",
                  "Erase the past",
                  "Make a million",
                  "...all through C!"
              } ;
```

For example, if **str1** contains "mountain" and **str2** contains "car," then the second string in **str** should get changed to "Move a car."

(b) Write a program to sort a set of names stored in an array in alphabetical order.

(c) Write a program to reverse the strings stored in the following array of pointers to strings:

```
char *s[ ] =    {
                  "To err is human...",
                  "But to really mess things up...",
                  "One needs to know C!!"
              } ;
```

(d) Develop a program that receives the month and year from the keyboard as integers and prints the calendar in the following format.

	March 2006					
Mon	Tue	Wed	Thu	Fri	Sat	Sun
		1	2	3	4	5
6	7	8	9	10	11	12
13	14	15	16	17	18	19
20	21	22	23	24	25	26
27	28	29	30	31		

Note that, according to the Gregorian calendar, 01/01/1900 was Monday. With this as the base, the calendar should be generated.

(e) A factory has 3 divisions and stocks 4 categories of products. An inventory table is updated for each division and for each product as they are received. There are three independent suppliers of products to the factory:

(a) Design a data format to represent each transaction.

(b) Write a program to take a transaction and update the inventory.

(c) If the cost per item is also given, write a program to calculate the total inventory values.

(f) Modify the previous program suitably so that once the calendar for a particular month and year has been displayed on the screen, then using arrow keys, the user must be able to change the calendar in the following manner:

Up arrow key   : Next year, same month
Down arrow key   : Previous year, same month
Right arrow key   : Same year, next month
Left arrow key   : Same year, previous month

If the escape key is hit, then the procedure should stop.
Hint: Use the **getkey( )** function discussed in Chapter 8, problem number [L](d).

(g) Write a program to delete all vowels from a sentence. Assume that the sentence is not more than 80 characters long.

(h) Write a program that will read a line and delete from it all occurrences of the word 'the.'

(i) Write a program that takes a set of names of individuals and abbreviates the first, middle, and other names, except the last name, by their first letter.

(j) Write a program to count the number of occurrences of any two vowels in succession in a line of text. For example, in the sentence
    "Please read this application and give me gratuity"
    such occurrences are ea, ea, ui.

Chapter 10

STRUCTURES

289

Which mechanic is good enough who knows how to repair only one type of vehicle? None. The same thing is true about C language. It wouldn't have been so popular had it been able to handle only all **int**s, or all **float**s, or all **char**s at a time. In fact, when we handle real-world data, we don't usually deal with little atoms of information by themselves—things like integers, characters, and such. Instead, we deal with entities that are collections of things, each thing having its own attributes, just as the entity we call a 'book' is a collection of things such as title, author, call number, publisher, number of pages, date of publication, etc. As you can see, all this data is dissimilar, for example, author is a string, whereas number of pages is an integer. For dealing with such collections, C provides a data type called 'structure.' A structure gathers together different atoms of information that comprise a given entity. And structure is the topic of this chapter.

WHY USE STRUCTURES?

We have seen earlier how ordinary variables can hold one piece of information and how arrays can hold a number of pieces of information of the same data type. These two data types can handle a great variety of situations. But quite often we deal with entities that are a collection of dissimilar data types.

For example, suppose you want to store data about a book. You might want to store its name (a string), its price (a float), and number of pages in it (an int). If data about, say, 3 such books is to be stored, then we can follow two approaches:

    (a) Construct individual arrays, one for storing names, another for storing prices, and still another for storing number of pages.
    (b) Use a structure variable.

Let us examine these two approaches one by one. For the sake of programming convenience, assume that the names of books would be a single character long. Let us begin with a program that uses arrays.

```
# include <stdio.h>
void main( )
{
    char name[3] ;
    float price[3] ;
    int pages[3], i ;
```

```
        printf ( "\nEnter names, prices and no. of pages of 3 books\n" ) ;

        for ( i = 0 ; i <= 2 ; i++ )
                scanf ( "%c %f %d", &name[i], &price[i], &pages[i] );

        printf ( "\nAnd this is what you entered\n" ) ;
        for ( i = 0 ; i <= 2 ; i++ )
                printf ( "%c %f %d\n", name[i], price[i], pages[i] );
}
```

And here is the sample run:

```
Enter names, prices and no. of pages of 3 books
A 100.00 354
C 256.50 682
F 233.70 512

And this is what you entered
A 100.000000 354
C 256.500000 682
F 233.700000 512
```

This approach, no doubt, allows you to store names, prices, and number of pages. But as you must have realized, it is an unwieldy approach that obscures the fact that you are dealing with a group of characteristics related to a single entity—the book.

The program becomes more difficult to handle as the number of items relating to the book goes on increasing. For example, we would be required to use a number of arrays if we also decide to store the name of the publisher, date of purchase of the book, etc. To solve this problem, C provides a special data type—the structure.

A structure contains a number of data types grouped together. These data types may or may not be of the same type. The following example illustrates the use of this data type.

```
# include <stdio.h>
void main( )
{
    struct book
    {
        char name ;
        float price ;
        int pages ;
    } ;
    struct book b1, b2, b3 ;
```

```
printf ( "\nEnter names, prices & no. of pages of 3 books\n" ) ;
scanf ( "%c %f %d", &b1.name, &b1.price, &b1.pages ) ;
scanf ( "%c %f %d", &b2.name, &b2.price, &b2.pages ) ;
scanf ( "%c %f %d", &b3.name, &b3.price, &b3.pages ) ;
printf ( "\nAnd this is what you entered" ) ;
printf ( "\n%c %f %d", b1.name, b1.price, b1.pages ) ;
printf ( "\n%c %f %d", b2.name, b2.price, b2.pages ) ;
printf ( "\n%c %f %d", b3.name, b3.price, b3.pages ) ;
}
```

And here is the output:

```
Enter names, prices and no. of pages of 3 books
A 100.00 354
C 256.50 682
F 233.70 512

And this is what you entered
A 100.000000 354
C 256.500000 682
F 233.700000 512
```

This program demonstrates two fundamental aspects of structures:

(a) declaration of a structure
(b) accessing of structure elements

Let us now look at these concepts one by one.

Declaring a Structure

In our example program, the following statement declares the structure type:

```
struct book
{
    char name ;
    float price ;
    int pages ;
} ;
```

This statement defines a new data type called **struct book**. Each variable of this data type will consist of a character variable called **name**, a float variable called **price**, and an integer variable called **pages**. The general form of a structure declaration statement is given below:

```
struct <structure name>
{
    structure element 1 ;
    structure element 2 ;
    structure element 3 ;
    ......
    ......
} ;
```

Once the new structure data type has been defined, one or more variables can be declared to be of that type. For example, the variables **b1**, **b2**, **b3** can be declared to be of the type **struct book**, as,

```
struct book b1, b2, b3 ;
```

This statement sets aside space in memory. It makes space available to hold all the elements in the structure—in this case, 7 bytes—one for **name**, four for **price**, and two for **pages**. These bytes are always in adjacent memory locations.

If we so desire, we can combine the declaration of the structure type and the structure variables in one statement.

For example,

```
struct book
{
    char name ;
    float price ;
    int pages ;
} ;
struct book b1, b2, b3 ;
```

is same as...

```
struct book
{
    char name ;
    float price ;
    int pages ;
} b1, b2, b3 ;
```

or even...

```
struct
{
    char name ;
    float price ;
```

```
      int pages ;
} b1, b2, b3 ;
```

Like primary variables and arrays, structure variables can also be initialized where they are declared. The format used is quite similar to that used to initialize arrays.

```
struct book
{
    char name[10] ;
    float price ;
    int pages ;
} ;
struct book b1 = { "Basic", 130.00, 550 } ;
struct book b2 = { "Physics", 150.80, 800 } ;
struct book b3 = { 0 } ;
```

Note the following points while declaring a structure type:

(a) The closing brace in the structure type declaration must be followed by a semicolon.

(b) It is important to understand that a structure type declaration does not tell the compiler to reserve any space in memory. All a structure declaration does is define the 'form' of the structure.

(c) Usually, structure type declaration appears at the top of the source code file, before any variables or functions are defined. In very large programs they are usually put in a separate header file, and the file is included (using the preprocessor directive # include) in whichever program we want to use this structure type.

(d) If a structure variable is initiated to a value {0}, then all its elements are set to value 0, as shown in **b3**. This is a handy way of initializing structure variables. In absence of this, we would have been required to initialize each individual element to a value 0.

Accessing Structure Elements

Having declared the structure type and the structure variables, let us see how the elements of the structure can be accessed.

In arrays, we can access individual elements of an array using a subscript. Structures use a different scheme. They use a dot (.) operator. So to refer to **pages** of the structure defined in our sample program, we have to use,

```
b1.pages
```

Similarly, to refer to **price**, we would use,

```
b1.price
```

Note that before the dot, there must always be a structure variable, and after the dot, there must always be a structure element.

How Structure Elements are Stored

Whatever the elements of a structure, they are always stored in contiguous memory locations. The following program illustrates this:

```
/* Memory map of structure elements */
# include <stdio.h>
void main( )
{
    struct book
    {
        char name ;
        float price ;
        int pages ;
    } ;
    struct book b1 = { 'B', 130.00, 550 } ;

    printf ( "\nAddress of name = %u", &b1.name ) ;
    printf ( "\nAddress of price = %u", &b1.price ) ;
    printf ( "\nAddress of pages = %u", &b1.pages ) ;
}
```

Here is the output of the program:

```
Address of name = 65518
Address of price = 65519
Address of pages = 65523
```

Actually, the structure elements are stored in memory as shown in the Figure 10.1.

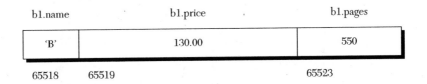

FIGURE 10.1

ARRAY OF STRUCTURES

Our sample program showing usage of structure is rather simple minded. All it does is receive values into various structure elements and outputs these values. But that's all we intended to do anyway—show how structure types are created, how structure variables are declared, and how individual elements of a structure variable are referenced.

In our sample program, to store data of 100 books, we would be required to use 100 different structure variables from **b1** to **b100**, which is definitely not very convenient. A better approach would be to use an array of structures. The following program shows how to use an array of structures.

```
/* Usage of an array of structures */
# include <stdio.h>
void main( )
{
    struct book
    {
        char name ;
        float price ;
        int pages ;
    } ;
    struct book b[100] ;
    int i ;

    for ( i = 0 ; i <= 99 ; i++ )
    {
        printf ( "\nEnter name, price and pages " ) ;
        scanf ( "%c %f %d", &b[i].name, &b[i].price, &b[i].pages ) ;
    }

    for ( i = 0 ; i <= 99 ; i++ )
        printf ( "\n%c %f %d", b[i].name, b[i].price, b[i].pages ) ;
}

linkfloat( )
{
    float a = 0, *b ;
    b = & a ; /* cause emulator to be linked */
    a = *b ; /* suppress the warning - variable not used */
}
```

Now a few comments about the program:

(a) Notice how the array of structures is declared:

```
struct book b[100] ;
```

This provides space in memory for 100 structures of the type **struct book**.

(b) The syntax we use to reference each element of the array **b** is similar to the syntax used for arrays of **int**s and **char**s. For example, we refer to the zeroth book's price as **b[0].price**. Similarly, we refer to the first book's pages as **b[1].pages**.

(c) It should be appreciated what careful thought Dennis Ritchie has put into C language. He first defined array as a collection of similar elements; then realized that dissimilar data types that are often found in real life cannot be handled using arrays, therefore he created a new data type called structure. But even using structures, programming convenience could not be achieved, because a lot of variables (**b1** to **b100** for storing data about hundred books) needed to be handled. Therefore, he allowed us to create an array of structures; an array of similar data types which themselves are a collection of dissimilar data types. Hats off to the genius!

(d) In an array of structures, all elements of the array are stored in adjacent memory locations. Since each element of this array is a structure, and since all structure elements are always stored in adjacent locations, you can very well visualize the arrangement of an array of structures in memory. In our example, **b[0]**'s **name**, **price**, and **pages** in memory would be immediately followed by **b[1]**'s **name**, **price**, and **pages**, and so on.

(e) What is the function **linkfloat( )** doing here? If you don't define it, you are bound to get the error "Floating Point Formats Not Linked" from the majority of C compilers. What causes this error to occur? When parsing our source file, if the compiler encounters a reference to the address of a float, it sets a flag to have the linker link in the floating-point emulator. A floating-point emulator is used to manipulate floating-point numbers in runtime library functions like **scanf( )** and **atof( )**. There are some cases in which the reference to the **float** is a bit obscure and the compiler does not detect the need for the emulator. The most common is using **scanf( )** to read a **float** in an array of structures as shown in our program.

How can we force the formats to be linked? That's where the **link-float( )** function comes in. It forces the linking of the floating-point emulator into an application. There is no need to call this function, just define it anywhere in your program.

ADDITIONAL FEATURES OF STRUCTURES

Let us now explore the intricacies of structures with a view of programming convenience. We will highlight these intricacies with suitable examples:

(a) The values of a structure variable can be assigned to another structure variable of the same type using the assignment operator. It is not necessary to copy the structure elements piecemeal. Obviously, programmers prefer assignment to piecemeal copying. This is shown in the following example.

```c
# include <stdio.h>
# include <string.h>
void main( )
{
    struct employee
    {
        char name[10] ;
        int age ;
        float salary ;
    } ;
    struct employee e1 = { "Sanjay", 30, 5500.50 } ;
    struct employee e2, e3 ;

    /* piece-meal copying */
    strcpy ( e2.name, e1.name ) ; /* e2.name = e1. name is wrong */
    e2.age = e1.age ;
    e2.salary = e1.salary ;

    /* copying all elements at one go */
    e3 = e2 ;

    printf ( "\n%s %d %f", e1.name, e1.age, e1.salary ) ;
    printf ( "\n%s %d %f", e2.name, e2.age, e2.salary ) ;
    printf ( "\n%s %d %f", e3.name, e3.age, e3.salary ) ;
}
```

The output of the program will be:

```
Sanjay 30 5500.500000
Sanjay 30 5500.500000
Sanjay 30 5500.500000
```

The ability to copy the contents of all structure elements of one variable into the corresponding elements of another structure variable is rather surprising, since C does not allow assigning the contents of one array to another just by equating the two. As we saw earlier, for copying arrays, we have to copy the contents of the array element by element.

This copying of all structure elements at one go has been possible only because the structure elements are stored in contiguous memory locations. Had this not been so, we would have been required to copy structure variables element by element. And who knows, had this been so, structures would not have become popular at all.

(b) One structure can be nested within another structure. Using this facility, complex data types can be created. The following program shows nested structures at work.

```c
# include <stdio.h>
void main( )
{
    struct address
    {
        char phone[15] ;
        char city[25] ;
        int pin ;
    } ;

    struct emp
    {
        char name[25] ;
        struct address a ;
    } ;
    struct emp e = { "jeru", "531046", "nagpur", 10 };

    printf ( "\nname = %s phone = %s", e.name, e.a.phone ) ;
    printf ( "\ncity = %s pin = %d", e.a.city, e.a.pin ) ;
}
```

And here is the output:

```
name = jeru phone = 531046
city = nagpur pin = 10
```

Notice the method used to access the element of a structure that is part of another structure. For this, the dot operator is used twice, as in the expression,

```
e.a.pin or e.a.city
```

Of course, the nesting process need not stop at this level. We can nest a structure within a structure, within another structure, which is in still another structure and so on until the time we can comprehend the structure ourselves. Such a construction, however, gives rise to variable names that can be surprisingly self-descriptive, for example:

```
maruti.engine.bolt.large.qty
```

This clearly signifies that we are referring to the quantity of large-sized bolts that fit on an engine of a maruti car.

(c) Like an ordinary variable, a structure variable can also be passed to a function. We may either pass individual structure elements or the entire structure variable at one go. Let us examine both the approaches one by one using suitable programs.

```
/* Passing individual structure elements */
# include <stdio.h>
void display ( char *, char *, int ) ;
void main( )
{
    struct book
    {
        char name[25] ;
        char author[25] ;
        int callno ;
    } ;
    struct book b1 = { "Let us C", "YPK", 101 } ;

    display ( b1.name, b1.author, b1.callno ) ;
}

void display ( char *s, char *t, int n )
{
    printf ( "\n%s %s %d", s, t, n ) ;
}
```

And here is the output:

```
Let us C YPK 101
```

Observe that in the declaration of the structure, **name** and **author** have been declared as arrays. Therefore, when we call the function **display( )** using,

```
display ( b1.name, b1.author, b1.callno ) ;
```

we are passing the base addresses of the arrays **name** and **author**, but the value stored in **callno**. Thus, this is a mixed call—a call by reference as well as a call by value.

It can be immediately realized that to pass individual elements would become more tedious as the number of structure elements goes on increasing. A better way would be to pass the entire structure variable at a time. This method is shown in the following program.

```
# include <stdio.h>
struct book
{
    char name[25] ;
    char author[25] ;
    int callno ;
} ;
void display ( struct book ) ;

void main( )
{
    struct book b1 = { "Let us C", "YPK", 101 } ;
    display ( b1 ) ;
}
void display ( struct book b )
{
    printf ( "\n%s %s %d", b.name, b.author, b.callno ) ;
}
```

And here is the output:

```
Let us C YPK 101
```

Note that here, the calling of the function **display( )** becomes quite compact,

```
display ( b1 ) ;
```

Having collected what is being passed to the **display( )** function, the question becomes, how do we define the formal arguments in the function? We cannot say,

```
struct book b1 ;
```

because the data type, **struct book**, is not known to the function **display( )**. Therefore, it becomes necessary to declare the structure type **struct book** outside **main( )**, so that it becomes known to all functions in the program.

(d) The way we can have a pointer pointing to an **int**, or a pointer pointing to a **char**, we can have a pointer pointing to a **struct**. Such pointers are known as 'structure pointers.'

Let us look at a program that demonstrates the usage of a structure pointer.

```
# include <stdio.h>
void main( )
{
    struct book
    {
        char name[25] ;
        char author[25] ;
        int callno ;
    } ;
    struct book b1 = { "Let us C", "YPK", 101 } ;
    struct book *ptr ;
    ptr = &b1 ;
    printf ( "\n%s %s %d", b1.name, b1.author, b1.callno ) ;
    printf ( "\n%s %s %d", ptr->name, ptr->author, ptr->callno ) ;
}
```

The first **printf( )** is as usual. The second **printf( )**, however, is peculiar. We can't use **ptr.name** or **ptr.callno** because **ptr** is not a structure variable but a pointer to a structure, and the dot operator requires a structure variable on its left. In such cases C provides an operator **->**, called an arrow operator, to refer to the structure elements. Remember that on the left-hand side of the '.' structure operator, there must always be a structure variable, whereas on the left-hand side of the '->' operator, there must always be a pointer to a structure. The arrangement of the structure variable and the pointer to structure in memory is shown in the Figure 10.2.

Can we pass the address of a structure variable to a function? We can. The following program demonstrates this.

```
/* Passing address of a structure variable */
# include <stdio.h>
struct book
```

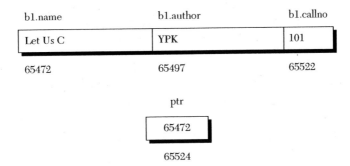

FIGURE 10.2

```
{
    char name[25] ;
    char author[25] ;
    int callno ;
} ;
void display ( struct book * ) ;

void main( )
{
    struct book b1 = { "Let us C", "YPK", 101 } ;
    display ( &b1 ) ;
}

void display ( struct book *b )
{
    printf ( "\n%s %s %d", b->name, b->author, b->callno ) ;
}
```

And here is the output:

```
Let us C YPK 101
```

Again, note that to access the structure elements using a pointer to a structure, we have to use the '->' operator.

Also, the structure **struct book** should be declared outside **main( )** such that this data type is available to **display( )** while declaring a pointer to the structure.

(e) Consider the following code snippet:

```
struct emp
{
    int a ;
```

```
        char ch ;
        float s ;
} ;
struct emp e ;
printf ( "%u %u %u", &e.a, &e.ch, &e.s ) ;
```

If we execute this program using a TC/TC++ compiler, we get the addresses as:

```
65518 65520 65521
```

As expected, in memory the **char** begins immediately after the **int** and **float** begins immediately after the **char**.

However, if we run the same program using a VC++ compiler, then the output turns out to be:

```
1245044 1245048 1245052
```

It can be observed from this output that the **float** doesn't get stored immediately after the **char**. In fact, there is a hole of three bytes after the **char**. Let us understand the reason for this. VC++ is a 32-bit compiler targeted to generate code for a 32-bit microprocessor. The architecture of this microprocessor is such that it is able to fetch the data that is present at an address, which is a multiple of four, much faster than the data present at any other address. Hence the VC++ compiler aligns every element of a structure at an address that is a multiple of four. That's the reason why there were three holes created between the **char** and the **float**.

However, some programs need to exercise precise control over the memory areas where data is placed. For example, suppose we wish to read the contents of the boot sector (first sector on the floppy/hard disk) into a structure. For this the byte arrangement of the structure elements must match the arrangement of various fields in the boot sector of the disk. The **#pragma pack** directive offers a way to fulfill this requirement. This directive specifies packing alignment for structure members. The pragma takes effect at the first structure declaration after the pragma is seen. Turbo C/C++ compiler doesn't support this feature, VC++ compiler does. The following code shows how to use this directive.

```
#pragma pack(1)
struct emp
```

```
{
    int a ;
    char ch ;
    float s ;
} ;
#pragma pack( )

struct emp e ;
printf ( "%u %u %u", &e.a, &e.ch, &e.s ) ;
```

Here, **#pragma pack (1)** lets each structure element begin on a 1-bit boundary as justified by the output of the program given here:

1245044 1245048 1245049

USES OF STRUCTURES

Where are structures useful? The immediate application that comes to the mind is database management. That is, to maintain data about employees in an organization, books in a library, items in a store, financial accounting transactions in a company, etc. But mind you, use of structures stretches far beyond database management. They can be used for a variety of purposes, such as:

(a) Changing the size of the cursor
(b) Clearing the contents of the screen
(c) Placing the cursor at an appropriate position on screen
(d) Drawing any graphics shape on the screen
(e) Receiving a key from the keyboard
(f) Checking the memory size of the computer
(g) Finding out the list of equipment attached to the computer
(h) Formatting a floppy
(i) Hiding a file from the directory
(j) Displaying the directory of a disk
(k) Sending the output to printer
(l) Interacting with the mouse

And that is certainly a very impressive list! At least impressive enough to make you realize how important a data type a structure is and to be thorough with it if you intend to program any of the earlier applications. Some of these applications will be discussed in Chapters 16 to 19.

SUMMARY

(a) A structure is usually used when we wish to store dissimilar data together.

(b) Structure elements can be accessed through a structure variable using a dot (.) operator.

(c) Structure elements can be accessed through a pointer to a structure using the arrow (->) operator.

(d) All elements of one structure variable can be assigned to another structure variable using the assignment (=) operator.

(e) It is possible to pass a structure variable to a function either by value or by address.

(f) It is possible to create an array of structures.

EXERCISES

[A] What will be the output of the following programs:

(a)
```c
# include <stdio.h>
# include <string.h>
void main( )
{
    struct gospel
    {
        int num ;
        char mess1[50] ;
        char mess2[50] ;
    } m ;

    m.num = 1 ;
    strcpy ( m.mess1, "If all that you have is hammer" ) ;
    strcpy ( m.mess2, "Everything looks like a nail" ) ;

    /* assume that the strucure is located at address 1004 */
    printf ( "\n%u %u %u", &m.num, m.mess1, m.mess2 ) ;

}
```

(b)
```c
# include <stdio.h>
struct gospel
```

```
    {
        int num ;
        char mess1[50] ;
        char mess2[50] ;
    } m1 = { 2, "If you are driven by success",
                "make sure that it is a quality drive"
            } ;
    void main( )
    {
        struct gospel m2, m3 ;
        m2 = m1 ;
        m3 = m2 ;
        printf ( "\n%d %s %s", m1.num, m2.mess1, m3.mess2 ) ;
    }
```

[B] Point out the errors, if any, in the following programs:

(a)
```
    # include <stdio.h>
    # include <string.h>
    void main( )
    {
        struct employee
        {
            char name[25] ;
            int age ;
            float bs ;
        } ;
        struct employee e ;
        strcpy ( e.name, "Hacker" ) ;
        age = 25 ;
        printf ( "\n%s %d", e.name, age ) ;
    }
```

(b)
```
    # include <stdio.h>
    void main( )
    {
        struct
        {
            char name[25] ;
            char language[10] ;
        } ;
        struct employee e = { "Hacker", "C" } ;
        printf ( "\n%s %d", e.name, e.language ) ;
    }
```

(c)
```
# include <stdio.h>
struct virus
{

    char signature[25] ;
    char status[20] ;
    int size ;
} v[2] = {
                "Yankee Doodle", "Deadly", 1813,
                "Dark Avenger", "Killer", 1795
        } ;
void main( )
{
    int i ;
    for ( i = 0 ; i <=1 ; i++ )
        printf ( "\n%s %s", v.signature, v.status ) ;
}
```

(d)
```
# include <stdio.h>
struct s
{
    char ch ;
    int i ;
    float a ;
} ;
void f ( struct s ) ;
void g ( struct s * ) ;

void main( )
{
    struct s var = { 'C', 100, 12.55 } ;
    f ( var ) ;
    g ( &var ) ;
}
void f ( struct s v )
{
    printf ( "\n%c %d %f", v -> ch, v -> i, v -> a ) ;
}
void g ( struct s *v )
{
    printf ( "\n%c %d %f", v.ch, v.i, v.a ) ;
}
```

(e)
```
# include <stdio.h>
struct s
{
    int i ;
    struct s *p ;
} ;
void main( )
{
    struct s var1, var2 ;

    var1.i = 100 ;
    var2.i = 200 ;
    var1.p = &var2 ;
    var2.p = &var1 ;
    printf ( "\n%d %d", var1.p -> i, var2.p -> i ) ;

}
```

[C] Answer the following:

(a) Ten floats are to be stored in memory. What would you prefer, an array or a structure?

(b) Given the statement,

```
maruti.engine.bolts = 25 ;
```

which of the following is True?
1. structure bolts is nested within structure engine
2. structure engine is nested within structure maruti
3. structure maruti is nested within structure engine
4. structure maruti is nested within structure bolts

(c) State True or False:
1. All structure elements are stored in contiguous memory locations.
2. An array should be used to store dissimilar elements, and a structure to store similar elements.
3. In an array of structures, not only are all structures stored in contiguous memory locations, but the elements of individual structures are also stored in contiguous locations.

(d)
```
struct time
{
    int hours ;
    int minutes ;
    int seconds ;
} t ;
```

```
struct time *tt ;
tt = &t ;
```

With reference to the previous declarations, which of the following refers to **seconds** correctly:
1. tt.seconds
2. (*tt).seconds
3. time.t
4. tt -> seconds

[D] Attempt the following:

(a) Create a structure to specify data on students given here: roll number, name, department, course, year of joining
 Assume that there are not more than 450 students in the college.
 (a) Write a function to print the names of all students who joined in a particular year.
 (b) Write a function to print the data of a student whose roll number is given.

(b) Create a structure to specify data of customers in a bank. The data to be stored is: account number, name, balance in account. assume a maximum of 200 customers in the bank.
 (a) Write a function to print the account number and name of each customer with a balance below $100.
 (b) If a customer requests a withdrawal or deposit, it is given in the form:
 Acct. no, amount, code (1 for deposit, 0 for withdrawal)
 Write a program to give the message, "The balance is insufficient for the specified withdrawal."

(c) An automobile company has serial numbers for engine parts starting from AA0 to FF9. The other characteristics of parts to be specified in a structure are: year of manufacture, material, and quantity manufactured.
 (a) Specify a structure to store information corresponding to a part.
 (b) Write a program to retrieve information on parts with serial numbers between BB1 and CC6.

(d) A record contains the name of a cricketer, his age, number of test matches that he has played, and the average runs that he has scored in each test match. Create an array of structures to hold records of 20 such cricketers and then write a program to read these records and arrange them in ascending order by average runs. Use the **qsort( )** standard library function.

(e) There is a structure called **employee** that holds information like employee codes, names, and date of joining. Write a program to create an array of structures and enter some data into it. Then ask the user to enter the current date. Display the names of those employees whose tenure is 3 or more years according to the current date.

(f) Write a menu-driven program that depicts the workings of a library. The menu options should be:

1. Add book information
2. Display book information
3. List all books of given author
4. List the title of a specified book
5. List the count of books in the library
6. List the books in the order of catalog number
7. Exit

Create a structure called **library** to hold the catalog number, title of the book, author name, price of the book, and flag indicating whether the book is issued or not.

(g) Write a program that compares two given dates. To store a date, use a structure that contains three members, namely date, month, and year. If the dates are equal, then display a message as "Equal," otherwise "Unequal."

(h) Linked list is a very common data structure often used to store similar data in memory. While the elements of an array occupy contiguous memory locations, those of a linked list are not constrained to be stored in adjacent locations. The individual elements are stored "somewhere" in memory, rather like a dispersed family, but still bound together. The order of the elements is maintained by explicit links between them. Thus, a linked list is a collection of elements called nodes, each of which stores two items of information—an element of the list, and a link, i.e., a pointer or an address that indicates explicitly the location of the node containing the successor of this list element.

Write a program to build a linked list by adding new nodes at the beginning, at the end, or in the middle of the linked list. Also, write a function **display( )** that displays all the nodes present in the linked list.

(i) A stack is a data structure in which the addition of new element or deletion of existing element always takes place at the same end. This end is often known as the 'top' of stack. This situation can be compared to a stack of plates in a cafeteria where every new plate is added to or taken off from the 'top' of the stack. There are several applications where a stack can be put to use. For example, recursion, keeping track of function calls, evaluation of expressions, etc. Write a program to implement a stack using a linked list.

(j)   Unlike a stack, in a queue the addition of a new element takes place at the end (called the 'rear' of queue) whereas deletion takes place at the other end (called 'front' of queue). Write a program to implement a queue using a linked list.

11 CONSOLE INPUT/OUTPUT

As mentioned in the first chapter, Dennis Ritchie wanted C to remain compact. In keeping with this intention, he deliberately omitted everything related to Input/Output (I/O) from his definition of the language. Thus, C simply has no provision for receiving data from any of the input devices (keyboard, disk, etc.), or for sending data to the output devices (VDU, disk, etc.). Then how do we manage I/O, and how is it that we were able to use **printf( )** and **scanf( )** if C has nothing to offer for I/O? This is what we intend to explore in this chapter.

TYPES OF I/O

Though C has no provision for I/O, it, of course, has to be dealt with at some point or another. There is not much use writing a program that spends all its time telling itself a secret. Each operating system has its own facility for inputting and outputting data to and from the files and devices. It's a simple matter for a system programmer to write a few small programs that can link the C compiler to a particular operating system's I/O facilities.

The developers of C compilers do just that. They write several standard I/O functions and put them in libraries. These libraries are available with all C compilers. Whichever C compiler you are using, it's almost certain that you have access to a library of I/O functions.

Do understand that the I/O facilities with different operating systems will be different. Thus, the way one OS displays output on screen may be different than the way another OS does it. For example, the standard library function **printf( )** for a DOS-based C compiler has been written keeping in mind the way DOS outputs characters to the screen. Similarly, the **printf( )** function for a Unix-based compiler has been written keeping in mind the way Unix outputs characters to the screen. We, as programmers, do not have to bother with which **printf( )** has been written in what manner. We should just use **printf( )** and it will take care of the rest of the details that are OS dependent. The same is true about all other standard library functions available for I/O.

There are numerous library functions available for I/O. These can be classified into two broad categories:

(a) Console I/O functions -   Functions to receive input from the keyboard and write output to VDU.

(b) File I/O functions -   Functions to perform I/O operations on a floppy disk or a hard disk.

In this chapter we will discuss only console I/O functions. File I/O functions will be discussed in Chapter 12.

CONSOLE I/O FUNCTIONS

The screen and keyboard together are called a console. Console I/O functions can be further classified into two categories—formatted and unformatted console I/O functions. The basic difference between them is that the formatted functions allow the input read from the keyboard or the output displayed on the VDU to be formatted as per our requirements. For example, if values of average marks and percentage marks are to be displayed on the screen, then the details, like where this output will appear on the screen, how many spaces will be present between the two values, the number of places after the decimal points, etc., can be controlled using formatted functions. The functions available under each of these two categories are shown in Figure 11.1. Now let us discuss these console I/O functions in detail.

Formatted Console I/O Functions

As can be seen from Figure 11.1, the functions **printf( )**, and **scanf( )** fall under the category of formatted console I/O functions. These functions allow us to supply the input in a fixed format and let us obtain the output in the specified form. Let us discuss these functions one by one.

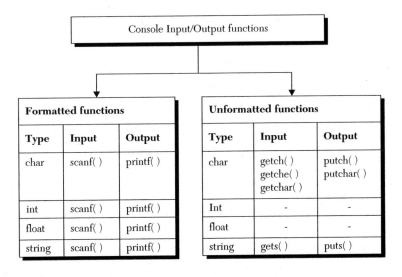

FIGURE 11.1

We have talked a lot about **printf( )**, used it regularly, but without having introduced it formally. Well, better late than never. Its general form looks like this:

```
printf ( "format string", list of variables ) ;
```

The format string can contain:

(a) Characters that are simply printed as they are
(b) Conversion specifications that begin with a % sign
(c) Escape sequences that begin with a \ sign

For example, look at the following program:

```
# include <stdio.h>
void main( )
{
    int avg = 346 ;
    float per = 69.2 ;
    printf ( "Average = %d\nPercentage = %f", avg, per ) ;
}
```

The output of the program will be:

```
Average = 346
Percentage = 69.200000
```

How does the **printf( )** function interpret the contents of the format string? For this, it examines the format string from left to right. So long as it doesn't come across either a % or a \, it continues to dump the characters that it encounters on to the screen. In this example, **Average =** is dumped on the screen. The moment it comes across a conversion specification in the format string, it picks up the first variable in the list of variables and prints its value in the specified format. In this example, the moment %d is met, the variable **avg** is picked up and its value is printed. Similarly, when an escape sequence is met, it takes the appropriate action. In this example, the moment \n is met, it places the cursor at the beginning of the next line. This process continues until the end of the format string is reached.

Format Specifications

The %d and %f used in the **printf( )** are called format specifiers. They tell **printf( )** to print the value of **avg** as a decimal integer and the value of **per** as a float. The following (Figure 11.2) is the list of format specifiers that can be used with the **printf( )** function.

Data type		Format specifier
Integer	short signed	%d or %I
	short unsigned	%u
	long singed	%ld
	long unsigned	%lu
	unsigned hexadecimal	%x
	unsigned octal	%o
Real	float	%f
	double	%lf
Character	signed character	%c
	unsigned character	%c
String		%s

FIGURE 11.2

We can provide the following optional specifiers in the format specifications as shown in Figure 11.3.

Now a short explanation about these optional format specifiers. The field-width specifier tells **printf( )** how many columns on screen should be used while printing a value. For example, **%10d** says, "print the variable as a decimal integer in a field of 10 columns." If the value to be printed happens to not fill up the entire field, the value is right justified and is padded with blanks on the left. If we include the minus sign in the format specifier (as

Specifier	Description
dd	Digits specifying field width
.	Decimal point separating field width from precision (precision stands for the number of places after the decimal point)
dd	Digits specifying precision
-	Minus sign for left justifying the output in the specified field width

FIGURE 11.3

in **%-10d**), this means the left justification is desired and the value will be padded with blanks on the right. If the field-width used turns out to be less than what is required to print the number, the field-width is ignored and the complete number is printed. Here is an example that illustrates all this.

```
# include <stdio.h>
void main( )
{
    int weight = 63 ;
    printf ( "\nweight is %d kg", weight ) ;
    printf ( "\nweight is %2d kg", weight ) ;
    printf ( "\nweight is %4d kg", weight ) ;
    printf ( "\nweight is %6d kg", weight ) ;
    printf ( "\nweight is %-6d kg", weight ) ;
    printf ( "\nweight is %1d kg", weight ) ;
}
```

The output of the program will look like this:

```
Columns 012345678901234567890123 4567890
        weight is 63 kg
        weight is 63 kg
        weight is   63 kg
        weight is     63 kg
        weight is 63 kg
        weight is 63 kg
```

Specifying the field width can be useful in creating tables of numeric values, as the following program demonstrates.

```
# include <stdio.h>
void main( )
{
    printf ( "\n%f %f %f", 5.0, 13.5, 133.9 ) ;
    printf ( "\n%f %f %f", 305.0, 1200.9, 3005.3 ) ;
}
```

And here is the output:

```
5.000000 13.500000 133.900000
305.000000 1200.900000 3005.300000
```

Even though the numbers have been printed, the numbers have not been lined up properly and hence are hard to read. A better way would be something like this:

```
# include <stdio.h>
void main( )
```

```
{
    printf ( "\n% 10.1f %10.1f %10.1f", 5.0, 13.5, 133.9 ) ;
    printf ( "\n% 10.1f %10.1f %10.1f", 305.0, 1200.9, 3005.3 );
}
```

This results into a much better output:

```
01234567890123456789012345678901
        5.0      13.5     133.9
      305.0    1200.9    3005.3
```

The format specifiers can be used even while displaying a string of characters. The following program will clarify this point:

```
/* Formatting strings with printf( ) */
# include <stdio.h>
void main( )
{
    char firstname1[ ] = "Sandy" ;
    char surname1[ ] = "Malya" ;
    char firstname2[ ] = "AjayKumar" ;
    char surname2[ ] = "Gurubaxani" ;

    printf ( "\n%20s%20s", firstname1, surname1 ) ;
    printf ( "\n%20s%20s", firstname2, surname2 ) ;
}
```

And here's the output:

```
012345678901234567890123456789012345678901234567890
               Sandy               Malya
           AjayKumar          Gurubaxani
```

The format specifier **%20s** reserves 20 columns for printing a string and then prints the string in these 20 columns with right justification. This helps lining up names of different lengths properly. Obviously, the format **%-20s** would have left justified the string.

Escape Sequences

We saw earlier how the newline character, **\n**, when inserted in a **printf( )**'s format string, takes the cursor to the beginning of the next line. The newline character is an 'escape sequence,' so called because the backslash symbol (\) is considered as an 'escape' character—it causes an escape from the normal interpretation of a string so that the next character is recognized as one having a special meaning.

The following example shows usage of \n and a new escape sequence \t, called 'tab.' A \t moves the cursor to the next tab stop. An 80-column screen usually has 10 tab stops. In other words, the screen is divided into 10 zones of 8 columns each. Printing a tab takes the cursor to the beginning of the next printing zone. For example, if the cursor is positioned in column 5, then printing a tab takes it to column 8.

```
# include <stdio.h>
void main( )
{
    printf ( "You\tmust\tbe\tcrazy\nto\thate\tthis\tbook" ) ;
}
```

And here's the output:

```
              1         2         3         4
01234567890123456789012345678901234567890
You      must    be      crazy
to       hate    this    book
```

The \n character causes a new line to begin following 'crazy.' The tab and newline are probably the most commonly used escape sequences, but there are others as well. Figure 11.4 shows a complete list of these escape sequences.

The first few of these escape sequences are more or less self-explanatory. \b moves the cursor one position to the left of its current position. \r takes the cursor to the beginning of the line in which it is currently placed. \a alerts the user by sounding the speaker inside the computer. Form feed advances the computer stationery attached to the printer to the top of the next page. Characters that are ordinarily used as delimiters—the single quote, double quote, and the backslash—can be printed by preceding them with the

Esc. Seq.	Purpose	Esc. Seq.	Purpose
\n	New line	\t	Tab
\b	Backspace	\r	Carriage return
\f	Form feed	\a	Alert
\'	Single quote	\"	Double quote
\\	Backslash		

FIGURE 11.4

backslash. Thus, the statement,

```
printf ( "He said, \"Let's do it!\"" ) ;
```

will print:

```
He said, "Let's do it!"
```

So far, we have been describing **printf( )**'s specification as if we are forced to use only **%d** for an integer, only **%c** for a char, only **%s** for a string, and so on. This is not true at all. In fact, **printf( )** uses the specification that we mention and attempts to perform the specified conversion, and does its best to produce a proper result. Sometimes the result is nonsensical, as in the case when we ask it to print a string using **%d**. Sometimes the result is useful, as in the case we ask **printf( )** to print the ASCII value of a character using **%d**. Sometimes the result is disastrous and the entire program blows up.

The following program shows a few of these conversions, some sensible, some weird.

```
# include <stdio.h>
void main( )
{
    char ch = 'z' ;
    int i = 125 ;
    float a = 12.55 ;
    char s[ ] = "hello there !" ;

    printf ( "\n%c %d %f", ch, ch, ch ) ;
    printf ( "\n%s %d %f", s, s, s ) ;
    printf ( "\n%c %d %f",i ,i, i ) ;
    printf ( "\n%f %d\n", a, a ) ;
}
```

And here's the output:

```
z 122 -936283178250178300000000000000000000000000.000000
hello there ! 3280 -
936283178250178300000000000000000000000000.000000
} 125 -936283178250178300000000000000000000000000.000000
12.550000 0
```

It is left to you to analyze the results. Some of the conversions you will find are quite sensible.

Let us now turn our attention to **scanf( )**. **scanf( )** allows us to enter data from keyboard that will be formatted a certain way.

The general form of a **scanf( )** statement is as follows:

```
scanf ( "format string", list of addresses of variables ) ;
```

For example:

```
scanf ( "%d %f %c", &c, &a, &ch ) ;
```

Note that we are sending addresses of variables (addresses are obtained by using '**&**,' the 'address of' operator) to the **scanf( )** function. This is necessary because the values received from the keyboard must be dropped into variables corresponding to these addresses. The values that are supplied through the keyboard must be separated by either blank(s), tab(s), or newline(s). Do not include these escape sequences in the format string.

All the format specifications that we learned in the **printf( )** function are applicable to the **scanf( )** function as well.

sprintf( ) and sscanf( ) Functions

The **sprintf( )** function works similar to the **printf( )** function except for one small difference. Instead of sending the output to the screen as **printf( )** does, this function writes the output to an array of characters. The following program illustrates this.

```
# include <stdio.h>
void main( )
{
    int i = 10 ;
    char ch = 'A' ;
    float a = 3.14 ;
    char str[20] ;

    printf ( "\n%d %c %f", i, ch, a ) ;
    sprintf ( str, "%d %c %f", i, ch, a ) ;
    printf ( "\n%s", str ) ;
}
```

In this program, the **printf( )** prints out the values of **i**, **ch**, and **a** on the screen, whereas **sprintf( )** stores these values in the character array **str**. Since the string **str** is present in memory, what is written into **str** using **sprintf( )** doesn't get displayed on the screen. Once **str** has been built, its contents can be displayed on the screen. This was achieved by the second **printf( )** statement in the program.

The counterpart of **sprintf( )** is the **sscanf( )** function. It allows us to read characters from a string and to convert and store them in C variables according to specified formats. The **sscanf( )** function comes in handy for in-memory conversion of characters to values. You may find it convenient to read in strings from a file and then extract values from a string by using **sscanf( )**. The usage of **sscanf( )** is the same as **scanf( )**, except that the first argument is the string from which reading is to take place.

Unformatted Console I/O Functions

There are several standard library functions available under this category—those that can deal with a single character and those that can deal with a string of characters. For openers, let us look at those that handle one character at a time.

So far, for input we have consistently used the **scanf( )** function. However, for some situations, the **scanf( )** function has one glaring weakness—you need to press the Enter key before the function can digest what you have typed. However, we often want a function that will read a single character the instant it is typed without waiting for the Enter key to be pressed. **getch( )** and **getche( )** are two functions that serve this purpose. These functions return the character that has been most recently typed. The 'e' in the **getche( )** function means it echoes (displays) the character that you typed to the screen. As against this, **getch( )** just returns the character that you typed without echoing it on the screen. **getchar( )** works similarly and echoes the character that you typed on the screen, but unfortunately requires the Enter key to be pressed following the character that you typed. The difference between **getchar( )** and **fgetchar( )** is that the former is a macro whereas the latter is a function.

The prototypes of **getch( )** and **getche( )** are present in the header file **conio.h**. The macro **getchar( )** and the prototype of **fgetchar( )** are present in **stdio.h**. Here is a sample program that illustrates the use of these functions and macro.

```c
# include <stdio.h>
# include <conio.h>
void main( )
{
    char ch ;

    printf ( "\nPress any key to continue" ) ;

    getch( ) ; /* will not echo the character */

    printf ( "\nType any character" ) ;
    ch = getche( ) ; /* will echo the character typed */

    printf ( "\nType any character" ) ;
    getchar( ) ; /* will echo character, must be followed by enter key */
```

```
        printf ( "\nContinue Y/N" ) ;
        fgetchar( ) ; /* will echo character, must be followed by enter key */
}
```

And here is a sample run of this program:

```
Press any key to continue
Type any character B
Type any character W
Continue Y/N Y
```

putch( ) and **putchar( )** form the other side of the coin. They print a character on the screen. As far as the working of **putch( )**, **putchar( )**, and **fputchar( )** is concerned, it's exactly the same. The following program illustrates this.

```
# include <stdio.h>
# include <conio.h>
void main( )
{
    char ch = 'A' ;

    putch ( ch ) ;
    putchar ( ch ) ;
    fputchar ( ch ) ;
    putch ( 'Z' ) ;
    putchar ( 'Z' ) ;
    fputchar ( 'Z' ) ;
}
```

And here is the output:

```
AAAZZZ
```

The limitation of **putch( )**, **putchar( )**, and **fputchar( )** is that they can output only one character at a time.

gets( ) and puts( )

gets( ) receives a string from the keyboard. Why is it needed? Because the **scanf( )** function has some limitations while receiving a string of characters, as the following example illustrates:

```
# include <stdio.h>
void main( )
{
    char name[50] ;

    printf ( "\nEnter name " ) ;
```

```
    scanf ( "%s", name ) ;
    printf ( "%s", name ) ;
}
```

And here is the output:

```
Enter name Jonty Rhodes
Jonty
```

Surprised? Where did "Rhodes" go? It never got stored in the array **name[ ]**, because the moment the blank was typed after "Jonty," **scanf( )** assumed that the name being entered has ended. The result is that there is no way (at least not without a lot of trouble on the programmer's part) to enter a multiword string into a single variable (**name** in this case) using **scanf( )**. The solution to this problem is to use the **gets( )** function. As we said earlier, it gets a string from the keyboard. It is terminated when an Enter key is pressed. Thus, spaces and tabs are perfectly acceptable as part of the input string. More specifically, **gets( )** gets a newline (**\n**) terminated string of characters from the keyboard and replaces the **\n** with a **\0**.

    The **puts( )** function works exactly the opposite to the **gets( )** function. It outputs a string to the screen.

    Here is a program that illustrates the usage of these functions:

```
# include <stdio.h>
void main( )
{
    char footballer[40] ;

    puts ( "Enter name" ) ;
    gets ( footballer ) ; /* sends base address of array */
    puts ( "Happy footballing!" ) ;
    puts ( footballer ) ;
}
```

Here is the sample output:

```
Enter name
Jonty Rhodes
Happy footballing!
Jonty Rhodes
```

Why did we use two **puts( )** functions to print "Happy footballing!" and "Jonty Rhodes"? Because, unlike **printf( )**, **puts( )** can output only one string at a time. If we attempt to print two strings using **puts( )**, only the first one gets printed. Similarly, unlike **scanf( )**, **gets( )** can be used to read only one string at a time.

SUMMARY

(a) There is no keyword available in C for doing input/output.
(b) All I/O in C is done using standard library functions.
(c) There are several functions available for performing console input/output.
(d) The formatted console I/O functions can force the user to receive the input in a fixed format and display the output in a fixed format.
(e) There are several format specifiers and escape sequences available to format input and output.
(f) Unformatted console I/O functions work faster since they do not have the overheads of formatting the input or output.

EXERCISES

[A] What will be the output of the following programs:

(a)
```
# include <stdio.h>
# include <ctype.h>
void main( )
{
     char ch ;
     ch = getchar( ) ;
     if ( islower ( ch ) )
          putchar ( toupper ( ch ) ) ;
     else
          putchar ( tolower ( ch ) ) ;
}
```

(b)
```
# include <stdio.h>
void main( )
{
     int i = 2 ;
     float f = 2.5367 ;
     char str[ ] = "Life is like that" ;

     printf ( "\n%4d\t%3.3f\t%4s", i, f, str ) ;
}
```

(c)
```c
# include <stdio.h>
void main( )
{
        printf ( "More often than \b\b not \rthe person who \
                        wins is the one who thinks he can!" ) ;
}
```

(d)
```c
# include <conio.h>
char p[ ] = "The sixth sick sheikh's sixth ship is sick" ;
void main( )
{
        int i = 0 ;
        while ( p[i] != '\0' )
        {
                putch ( p[i] ) ;
                i++ ;
        }
}
```

[B] Point out the errors, if any, in the following programs:

(a)
```c
# include <stdio.h>
void main( )
{
        int i ;
        char a[ ] = "Hello" ;
        while ( a != '\0' )
        {
            printf ( "%c", *a ) ;
            a++ ;
        }
}
```

(b)
```c
# include <stdio.h>
void main( )
{
        double dval ;
        scanf ( "%f", &dval ) ;
        printf ( "\nDouble Value = %lf", dval ) ;
}
```

(c)
```c
# include <stdio.h>
void main( )
```

```
    {
        int ival ;
        scanf ( "%d\n", &n ) ;
        printf ( "\nInteger Value = %d", ival ) ;
    }
```

(d)
```
    # include <stdio.h>
    void main( )
    {
        char *mess[5] ;
        for ( i = 0 ; i < 5 ; i++ )
            scanf ( "%s", mess[i] ) ;
    }
```

(e)
```
    # include <stdio.h>
    void main( )
    {
        int dd, mm, yy ;
        printf ( "\nEnter day, month and year\n" ) ;
        scanf ( "%d%*c%d%*c%d", &dd, &mm, &yy ) ;
        printf ( "The date is: %d - %d - %d", dd, mm, yy ) ;
    }
```

(f)
```
    # include <stdio.h>
    void main( )
    {
        char text ;
        sprintf ( text, "%4d\t%2.2f\n%s", 12, 3.452,
                    "Merry Go Round" ) ;
        printf ( "\n%s", text ) ;
    }
```

(g)
```
    # include <stdio.h>
    void main( )
    {
        char buffer[50] ;
        int no = 97;
        double val = 2.34174 ;
        char name[10] = "Shweta" ;
        sprintf ( buffer, "%d %lf %s", no, val, name ) ;
        printf ( "\n%s", buffer ) ;
        sscanf ( buffer, "%4d %2.2lf %s", &no, &val, name ) ;
        printf ( "\n%s", buffer ) ;
        printf ( "\n%d %lf %s", no, val, name ) ;
    }
```

[C] Answer the following:

(a) To receive the string "We have got the guts, you get the glory!!" in an array **char str[100]**, which of the following functions would you use?
1. scanf ("%s", str) ;
2. gets (str) ;
3. getche (str) ;
4. fgetchar (str) ;

(b) Which function would you use if a single key were to be received through the keyboard?
1. scanf( )
2. gets( )
3. getche( )
4. getchar( )

(c) If an integer is to be entered through the keyboard, which function would you use?
1. scanf( )
2. gets( )
3. getche( )
4. getchar( )

(d) If a character string is to be received through the keyboard which function would work faster?
1. scanf( )
2. gets( )

(e) What is the difference between **getchar( )**, **fgetchar( )**, **getch( )**, and **getche( )**?

(f) The format string of a **printf( )** function can contain:
1. Characters, format specifications, and escape sequences
2. Character, integers, and floats
3. Strings, integers, and escape sequences
4. Inverted commas, percentage sign, and backslash character

(g) A field-width specifier in a **printf( )** function:
1. Controls the margins of the program listing
2. Specifies the maximum value of a number
3. Controls the size of font used to print numbers
4. Specifies how many columns would be used to print the number

[D] Answer the following:

(a) Write down two functions, **xgets( )** and **xputs( )**, which work similar to the standard library functions **gets( )** and **puts( )**.

(b) Write down a function **getint( )**, which would receive a numeric string from the keyboard, convert it to an integer number, and return the integer to the calling function. A sample usage of **getint( )** is shown here:

```
# include <stdio.h>
void main( )
{
    int a ;
    a = getint( ) ;
    printf ( "you entered %d", a )
}
```

Chapter

12

FILE
INPUT/OUTPUT

Often, it is not enough to just display the data on the screen. This is because if the data is large, only a limited amount of it can be stored in memory and only a limited amount of it can be displayed on the screen. It would be inappropriate to store this data in memory for one more reason. Memory is volatile and its contents would be lost once the program is terminated. So if we need the same data again it would have to be either entered through the keyboard again or would have to be regenerated programmatically. Obviously, both of these operations would be tedious. At such times, it becomes necessary to store the data in a manner that can be later retrieved and displayed either in part or in whole. This medium is usually a 'file' on the disk. This chapter discusses how file I/O operations can be performed.

DATA ORGANIZATION

Before we start doing file input/output let us first find out how data is organized on the disk. All data stored on the disk is in binary form. How this binary data is stored on the disk varies from one OS to another. However, this does not affect the C programmer since he has to use only the library functions written for the particular OS to be able to perform input/output. It is the compiler vendor's responsibility to correctly implement these library functions by taking the help of OS. This is illustrated in Figure 12.1.

FILE OPERATIONS

There are different operations that can be carried out on a file. These are:

(a)　Creation of a new file
(b)　Opening an existing file
(c)　Reading from a file

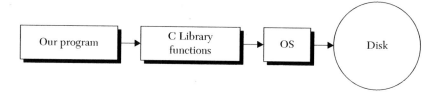

FIGURE 12.1

(d) Writing to a file

(e) Moving to a specific location in a file (seeking)

(f) Closing a file

Let us now write a program to read a file and display its contents on the screen. We will first list the program and show what it does, and then dissect it line by line. Here is the listing:

```
/* Display contents of a file on screen. */
# include <stdio.h>
void main( )
{
    FILE *fp ;
    char ch ;

    fp = fopen ( "PR1.C", "r" ) ;
    while ( 1 )
    {
        ch = fgetc ( fp ) ;
        if ( ch == EOF )
                break ;

        printf ( "%c", ch ) ;
    }
    fclose ( fp ) ;
}
```

On execution of this program, it displays the contents of the file 'PR1.C' on the screen. Let us now examine how it does this.

Opening a File

Before we can read (or write) information from (to) a file on a disk, we must open the file. To open the file we have called the function **fopen( )**. It will open the file "PR1.C" in 'read' mode, which tells the C compiler that we will be reading the contents of the file. Note that "r" is a string and not a character; hence the double quotes and not single quotes. In fact, **fopen( )** performs three important tasks when you open the file in "r" mode:

(a) First, it searches on the disk the file to be opened.

(b) Then it loads the file from the disk into a place in memory called a buffer.

(c) It sets up a character pointer that points to the first character of the buffer.

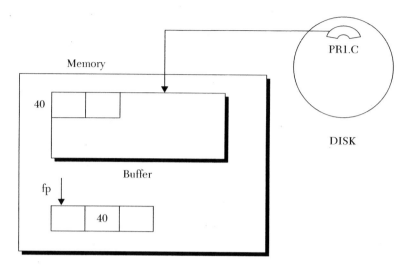

FIGURE 12.2

Why do we need a buffer at all? Imagine how inefficient it would be to actually access the disk every time we want to read a character from it. Every time we read something from a disk, it takes some time for the disk drive to position the read/write head correctly. On a floppy disk system, the drive motor has to actually start rotating the disk from a standstill position every time the disk is accessed. If this were to be done for every character we read from the disk, it would take a long time to complete the reading operation. This is where a buffer comes in. It would be more sensible to read the contents of the file into the buffer while opening the file and then read the file character by character from the buffer rather than from the disk. This is shown in Figure 12.2.

The same argument also applies to writing information in a file. Instead of writing characters in the file on the disk one character at a time, it would be more efficient to write characters in a buffer and then transfer the contents from the buffer to the disk.

To be able to successfully read information from a file such as mode of opening, size of file, place in the file from where the next read operation will be performed, etc., has to be maintained. Since all this information is interrelated, all of it is gathered together by **fopen( )** in a structure called **FILE. fopen( )** returns the address of this structure, which we have collected in the structure pointer called **fp**. We have declared **fp** as

```
FILE *fp ;
```

The **FILE** structure has been defined in the header file "stdio.h" (standing for standard input/output header file). Therefore, it is necessary to # **include** this file.

Reading from a File

Once the file has been opened for reading using **fopen( )**, as we have seen, the file's contents are brought into the buffer (partly or wholly) and a pointer is set up that points to the first character in the buffer. This pointer is one of the elements of the structure to which **fp** is pointing (refer to Figure 12.2).

To read the file's contents from memory, there exists a function called **fgetc( )**. This has been used in our program as,

```
ch = fgetc ( fp ) ;
```

fgetc( ) reads the character from the current pointer position, advances the pointer position so that it now points to the next character, and returns the character that is read, which we collect in the variable **ch**. Note that once the file has been opened, we no longer refer to the file by its name, but through the file pointer **fp**.

We have used the function **fgetc( )** within an indefinite **while** loop. There has to be a way to break out of this **while**. When shall we break out: The moment we reach the end of file. But what is the end of the file? A special character, whose ASCII value is 26, signifies the end of the file. This character is inserted beyond the last character in the file, when it is created.

While reading from the file, when **fgetc( )** encounters this special character, instead of returning the character that it has read, it returns the macro EOF. The EOF macro has been defined in the file "stdio.h." In place of the function **fgetc( )**, we could have used the macro **getc( )** with the same effect.

In our program, we go on reading each character from the file until the end of the file is met. As each character is read, we display it on the screen. Once out of the loop, we close the file.

Trouble Opening a File

There is a possibility that when we try to open a file using the function **fopen( )**, the file may not open. While opening the file in "r" mode, this may happen because the file being opened may not be present on the disk at all. And you obviously cannot read a file that doesn't exist. Similarly, while opening the file for writing, **fopen( )** may fail due to a number of reasons, such as, disk space may be insufficient to create a new file, the disk may be write protected, or the disk is damaged, and so on.

The crux of the matter is that it is important for any program that accesses disk files to check whether a file has been opened successfully before trying to read or write to the file. If the file opening fails due to any of the several reasons mentioned above, the **fopen( )** function returns a value NULL (defined in "stdio.h" as **#define NULL 0**). Here is how this can be handled in a program:

```
# include <stdio.h>
# include <stdlib.h>
void main( )
{
    FILE *fp ;
    fp = fopen ( "PR1.C", "r" ) ;
    if ( fp == NULL )
    {
            puts ( "cannot open file" ) ;
            exit ( 1 ) ;
    }
}
```

The call to the function **exit( )** terminates the execution of the program. Usually, a value of 0 is passed to **exit( )** if the program termination is normal. A nonzero value indicates an abnormal termination of the program. If there are multiple exit points in the program, then the value passed to **exit( )** can be used to find out from where the execution of the program got terminated. There are different ways of examining this value in different programming environments. For example, in the Turbo C++ environment, this value can be seen through the Compile | Information menu item. The prototype of the **exit( )** function is declared in the header file **stdlib.h**.

Closing the File

When we have finished reading from the file, we need to close it. This is done using the function **fclose( )** through the statement,

```
fclose ( fp ) ;
```

Once we close the file, we can no longer read from it using **getc( )** unless we reopen the file. Note that to close the file, we don't use the filename but the file pointer **fp**. On closing the file, the buffer associated with the file is removed from memory.

In this program, we have opened the file for reading. Suppose we open a file with an intention to write characters into it. This time also a buffer would be associated with it. When we attempt to write characters into this file using

fputc( ), the characters will get written to the buffer. When we close this file using **fclose( )**, three operations will be performed:

(a) The characters in the buffer will be written to the file on the disk.
(b) At the end of the file a character with ASCII value 26 will get written.
(c) The buffer will be eliminated from memory.

You can imagine a possibility when the buffer may become full before we close the file. In such a case, the buffer's contents would be written to the disk the moment it becomes full. All this buffer management is done for us by the library functions.

COUNTING CHARACTERS, TABS, SPACES, . . .

Having understood the first file I/O program in detail, let us now try our hand at one more. Let us write a program that will read a file and count how many characters, spaces, tabs, and newlines are present in it. Here is the program:

```c
/* Count chars, spaces, tabs and newlines in a file */
# include <stdio.h>
void main( )
{
    FILE *fp ;
    char ch ;
    int nol = 0, not = 0, nob = 0, noc = 0 ;
    fp = fopen ( "PR1.C", "r" ) ;
    while ( 1 )
    {
        ch = fgetc ( fp ) ;
        if ( ch == EOF )
                break ;
        noc++ ;
        if ( ch == ' ' )
                nob++ ;
        if ( ch == '\n' )
                nol++ ;
        if ( ch == '\t' )
                not++ ;
    }
    fclose ( fp ) ;
    printf ( "\nNumber of characters = %d", noc ) ;
```

```
    printf ( "\nNumber of blanks = %d", nob ) ;
    printf ( "\nNumber of tabs = %d", not ) ;
    printf ( "\nNumber of lines = %d", nol ) ;
}
```

Here is a sample run:

```
Number of characters = 125
Number of blanks = 25
Number of tabs = 13
Number of lines = 22
```

These statistics are true for the file "PR1.C." You may give any other filename and obtain different results. The program is self-explanatory.

In this program too, we have opened the file for reading and then read it character by character. Let us now try a program that needs to open a file for writing.

A FILE-COPY PROGRAM

We have already used the function **fgetc( )**, which reads characters from a file. Its counterpart is a function called **fputc( )**, which writes characters to a file. As a practical use of these character I/O functions, we can copy the contents of one file into another, as demonstrated in the following program. This program takes the contents of a file and copies them into another file, character by character.

```
# include <stdio.h>
# include <stdlib.h>
void main( )
{
    FILE *fs, *ft ;
    char ch ;

    fs = fopen ( "pr1.c", "r" ) ;
    if ( fs == NULL )
    {
        puts ( "Cannot open source file" ) ;
        exit ( 1 ) ;
    }
    ft = fopen ( "pr2.c", "w" ) ;
    if ( ft == NULL )
```

```
    {
        puts ( "Cannot open target file" ) ;
        fclose ( fs ) ;
        exit ( 2 ) ;
    }
    while ( 1 )
    {
        ch = fgetc ( fs ) ;

        if ( ch == EOF )
            break ;
        else
            fputc ( ch, ft ) ;
    }
    fclose ( fs ) ;
    fclose ( ft ) ;
}
```

Hopefully most of the stuff in the program can be easily understood, since it has already been dealt with in the earlier section. Only the function **fputc( )** is new. Let us see how it works.

Writing to a File

The **fputc( )** function is similar to the **putch( )** function, in the sense that both output characters. However, the **putch( )** function always writes to the VDU, whereas, **fputc( )** writes to the file. Which file? The file signified by **ft**. The writing process continues until all characters from the source file have been written to the target file, following which the **while** loop terminates.

Note that our sample file-copy program is capable of copying only text files. To copy files with extension .EXE or .COM, we need to open the files in binary mode, a topic that would be dealt with in sufficient detail in a later section.

FILE OPENING MODES

In our first program on disk I/O, we have opened the file in read ("r") mode. However, "r" is but one of several modes in which we can open a file. The following is a list of all possible modes in which a file can be opened. The tasks performed by **fopen( )**, when a file is opened in each of these modes, are also mentioned.

"r"   Searches the file. If the file is opened successfully, **fopen( )** loads it into memory and sets up a pointer, which points to the first character in it. If the file cannot be opened, **fopen( )** returns NULL.

Operations possible—reading from the file.

"w"   Searches the file. If the file exists, its contents are overwritten. If the file doesn't exist, a new file is created. Returns NULL, if unable to open file.

Operations possible—writing to the file.

"a"   Searches the file. If the file is opened successfully, **fopen( )** loads it into memory and sets up a pointer that points to the last character in it. If the file doesn't exist, a new file is created. Returns NULL, if unable to open file.

Operations possible—adding new contents at the end of the file.

"r+"   Searches the file. If it is opened successfully, **fopen( )** loads it into memory and sets up a pointer, which points to the first character in it. Returns NULL, if unable to open the file.

Operations possible—reading existing contents, writing new contents, modifying existing contents of the file.

"w+"   Searches the file. If the file exists, its contents are overwritten. If the file doesn't exist, a new file is created. Returns NULL, if unable to open file.

Operations possible—writing new contents, reading them back, and modifying existing contents of the file.

"a+"   Searches the file. If the file is opened successfully, **fopen( )** loads it into memory and sets up a pointer, which points to the first character in it. If the file doesn't exist, a new file is created. Returns NULL, if unable to open the file.

Operations possible—reading existing contents, appending new contents to end of the file. Cannot modify existing contents.

STRING (LINE) I/O IN FILES

For many purposes, character I/O is just what is needed. However, in some situations, the usage of functions that read or write entire strings might turn out to be more efficient.

Reading or writing strings of characters to and from files is as easy as reading and writing individual characters. Here is a program that writes strings to a file using the function **fputs( )**.

```
/* Receives strings from keyboard and writes them to file */
# include <stdio.h>
# include <stdlib.h>
# include <string.h>
void main( )
{
    FILE *fp ;
    char s[80] ;
    fp = fopen ( "POEM.TXT", "w" ) ;
    if ( fp == NULL )
    {
        puts ( "Cannot open file" ) ;
        exit ( 1 ) ;
    }
    printf ( "\nEnter a few lines of text:\n" ) ;
    while ( strlen ( gets ( s ) ) > 0 )
    {
        fputs ( s, fp ) ;
        fputs ( "\n", fp ) ;
    }
    fclose ( fp ) ;
}
```

And here is a sample run of the program:

```
Enter a few lines of text:
Shining and bright, they are forever,
so true about diamonds,
more so of memories,
especially yours !
```

Note that each string is terminated by pressing Enter. To terminate the execution of the program, press Enter at the beginning of a line. This creates a string of zero length, which the program recognizes as the signal to close the file and exit.

We have set up a character array to receive the string; the **fputs( )** function then writes the contents of the array to the disk. Since **fputs( )** does not automatically add a newline character to the end of the string, we must do this explicitly to make it easier to read the string back from the file.

Here is a program that reads strings from a disk file.

```
/* Reads strings from the file and displays them on screen */
# include <stdio.h>
# include <stdlib.h>
void main( )
{
    FILE *fp ;
    char s[80] ;
    fp = fopen ( "POEM.TXT", "r" ) ;
    if ( fp == NULL )
    {
        puts ( "Cannot open file" ) ;
        exit ( 1 ) ;
    }
    while ( fgets ( s, 79, fp ) != NULL )
        printf ( "%s" , s ) ;
    fclose ( fp ) ;
}
```

And here is the output:

```
Shining and bright, they are forever,
so true about diamonds,
more so of memories,
especially yours !
```

The function **fgets( )** takes three arguments. The first is the address where the string is stored, and the second is the maximum length of the string. This argument prevents **fgets( )** from reading too long of a string and overflowing the array. The third argument, as usual, is the pointer to the structure **FILE**. On reading a line from the file, the string **s** would contain the line contents '\n' followed by a '\0'. Thus, the string is terminated by **fgets( )** and we do not have to terminate it specifically. When all the lines from the file have been read, we attempt to read one more line, in which case **fgets( )** returns a **NULL**.

The Awkward Newline

We wrote a program earlier that counts the total number of characters present in a file. If we use that program to count the number of characters present in the earlier poem (stored in the file "POEM.TXT"), it would give us the character count as 101. The same file, if seen in the directory, would be reported to contain 105 characters.

This discrepancy occurs because when we attempt to write a "\n" to the file using **fputs( )**, **fputs( )** converts the **\n** to a **\r\n** combination. Here, **\r** stands for carriage return and **\n** for linefeed. If we read the same line back using **fgets( )**, the reverse conversion happens. Thus, when we write the first line of the poem and a "\n" using two calls to **fputs( )**, what gets written to the file is

```
Shining and bright, they are forever,\r\n
```

When the same line is read back into the array **s[ ]** using **fgets( )**, the array contains

```
Shining and bright, they are forever,\n\0
```

Thus, conversion of **\n** to **\r\n** during writing and **\r\n** conversion to **\n** during reading is a feature of the standard library functions and not that of the OS. Hence, the OS counts **\r** and **\n** as separate characters. In our poem there are four lines, therefore there is a discrepancy of four characters (105–101).

RECORD I/O IN FILES

So far, we have dealt with reading and writing only characters and strings. What if we want to read or write numbers from/to a file? Furthermore, what if we desire to read/write a combination of characters, strings, and numbers? For this we would first organize this dissimilar data together in a structure and then use **fprintf( )** and **fscanf( )** library functions to read/write data from/to file. The following program illustrates the use of structures for writing records of employees.

```
/* Writes records to a file using structure */
# include <stdio.h>
# include <conio.h>
void main( )
{
    FILE *fp ;
    char another = 'Y' ;
    struct emp
    {
        char name[40] ;
        int age ;
        float bs ;
    } ;
```

```
        struct emp e ;

        fp = fopen ( "EMPLOYEE.DAT", "w" ) ;

        if ( fp == NULL )
        {
            puts ( "Cannot open file" ) ;
            exit ( 1 ) ;
        }

        while ( another == 'Y' )
        {
            printf ( "\nEnter name, age and basic salary: " ) ;
            scanf ( "%s %d %f", e.name, &e.age, &e.bs ) ;
            fprintf ( fp, "%s %d %f\n", e.name, e.age, e.bs ) ;

            printf ( "Add another record (Y/N) " ) ;
            fflush ( stdin ) ;
            another = getche( ) ;
        }

        fclose ( fp ) ;
}
```

And here is the output of the program:

```
Enter name, age and basic salary: Steve 34 1250.50
Add another record (Y/N) Y
Enter name, age and basic salary: Samuel 21 1300.50
Add another record (Y/N) Y
Enter name, age and basic salary: Roger 34 1400.55
Add another record (Y/N) N
```

In this program, we are just reading the data into a structure variable using **scanf( )**, and then dumping it into a disk file using **fprintf( )**. The user can input as many records as he desires. The procedure ends when the user supplies 'N' for the question 'Add another record (Y/N).'

The key to this program is the function **fprintf( )**, which writes the values in the structure variable to the file. This function is similar to **printf( )**, except that a **FILE** pointer is included as the first argument. As in **printf( )**, we can format the data in a variety of ways by using **fprintf( )**. In fact, all the format conventions of **printf( )** function work with **fprintf( )** as well.

Perhaps you are wondering what we used the function **fflush( )** for. The reason is to get rid of a peculiarity of **scanf( )**. After supplying data for one employee, we would press the Enter key. What **scanf( )** does is it assigns name, age, and salary to appropriate variables and keeps the Enter key unread in the keyboard buffer. So when it's time to supply Y or N for the question 'Another employee (Y/N),' **getch( )** will read the Enter key from the buffer thinking that user has pressed the Enter key. To avoid this problem, we use the function **fflush( )**. It is designed to remove or 'flush out' any data remaining in the buffer. The argument to **fflush( )** must be the buffer that we want to flush out. Here we have used 'stdin,' which means buffer related to a standard input device—a keyboard.

Let us now write a program that reads the employee records created by the previous program. Here is how it can be done:

```
/* Read records from a file using structure */
# include <stdio.h>
# include <stdlib.h>
void main( )
{
    FILE *fp ;
    struct emp
    {
        char name[40] ;
        int age ;
        float bs ;
    } ;
    struct emp e ;

    fp = fopen ( "EMPLOYEE.DAT", "r" ) ;

    if ( fp == NULL )
    {
        puts ( "Cannot open file" ) ;
        exit ( 1 ) ;
    }

    while ( fscanf ( fp, "%s %d %f", e.name, &e.age, &e.bs ) != EOF )
        printf ( "\n%s %d %f", e.name, e.age, e.bs ) ;

    fclose ( fp ) ;
}
```

And here is the output of the program:

```
Steve 34 1250.500000
Samuel 21 1300.500000
Roger 34 1400.500000
```

TEXT FILES AND BINARY FILES

All the programs that we wrote in this chapter so far worked on text files. Some of them would not work correctly on binary files. A text file contains only textual information like letters, digits, and special symbols. In actuality, the ASCII codes of these characters are stored in text files. A good example of a text file is any C program, such as PR1.C.

Compared to this, a binary file is merely a collection of bytes. This collection might be a compiled version of a C program (say PR1.EXE), or music data stored in a wave file, or a picture stored in a graphic file. A very easy way to find out whether a file is a text file or a binary file is to open that file in Turbo C/C++. If on opening the file you can make out what is displayed, then it is a text file, otherwise it is a binary file.

As mentioned while explaining the file-copy program, the program cannot copy binary files successfully. We can improve the same program to make it capable of copying text as well as binary files as shown here:

```c
# include <stdio.h>
# include <stdlib.h>
void main( )
{
    FILE *fs, *ft ;
    int ch ;

    fs = fopen ( "pr1.exe", "rb" ) ;
    if ( fs == NULL )
    {
        puts ( "Cannot open source file" ) ;
        exit ( 1 ) ;
    }

    ft = fopen ( "newpr1.exe", "wb" ) ;

    if ( ft == NULL )
    {
        puts ( "Cannot open target file" ) ;
        fclose ( fs ) ;
        exit ( 2 ) ;
    }

    while ( 1 )
    {
        ch = fgetc ( fs ) ;
```

```
        if ( ch == EOF )
                break ;
        else
                fputc ( ch, ft ) ;
    }
    fclose ( fs ) ;
    fclose ( ft ) ;
}
```

Using this program, we can comfortably copy text as well as binary files. Note that here we have opened the source and target files in the "rb" and "wb" modes respectively. While opening the file in text mode we can use either "r" or "rt," but since text mode is the default mode we usually drop the 't.'

From the programming angle there are three main areas where text and binary mode files are different. These are:

(a) Handling of newlines
(b) Representation of end of file
(c) Storage of numbers

Let us explore these three differences.

Text versus Binary Mode: Newlines

We have already seen that, in text mode, a newline character is converted into the carriage return–linefeed combination before being written to the disk. Likewise, the carriage return–linefeed combination on the disk is converted back into a newline when the file is read by a C program. However, if a file is opened in binary mode, as opposed to text mode, these conversions will not take place.

Text versus Binary Mode: End of File

The second difference between text and binary modes is in the way the end-of-file is detected. In text mode, a special character, whose ASCII value is 26, is inserted after the last character in the file to mark the end of the file. If this character is detected at any point in the file, the read function would return the EOF signal to the program.

Compared to this, there is no such special character present in the binary mode files to mark the end of the file. The binary mode files keep track of the end of the file from the number of characters present in the directory entry of the file.

There is a moral to be derived from the end-of-file marker of text mode files. If a file stores numbers in binary mode, it is important that binary mode only be used for reading the numbers back, since one of the numbers we store might well be the number 26 (hexadecimal 1A). If this number is detected while we are reading the file by opening it in text mode, reading would be terminated prematurely at that point.

Thus, the two modes are not compatible. See to it that the file that has been written in text mode is read back only in text mode. Similarly, the file that has been written in binary mode must be read back only in binary mode.

Text versus Binary Mode: Storage of Numbers

The only function that is available for storing numbers in a disk file is the **fprintf( )** function. It is important to understand how numerical data is stored on the disk by **fprintf( )**. Text and characters are stored one character per byte, as we would expect. Are numbers stored as they are in memory, two bytes for an integer, four bytes for a float, and so on? No.

Numbers are stored as strings of characters. Thus, 1234, even though it occupies two bytes in memory, when transferred to the disk using **fprintf( )**, would occupy four bytes, one byte per character. Similarly, the floating-point number 1234.56 would occupy 7 bytes on disk. Thus, numbers with more digits would require more disk space.

Therefore, if a large amount of numerical data is to be stored in a disk file, using text mode may turn out to be inefficient. The solution is to open the file in binary mode and use those functions (**fread( )** and **fwrite( )**, which are discussed later) that store the numbers in binary format. It means each number would occupy the same number of bytes on disk as it occupies in memory.

RECORD I/O REVISITED

The record I/O program that we did in an earlier section has two disadvantages:

(a) The numbers (basic salary) would occupy more number of bytes, since the file has been opened in text mode. This is because when the file is opened in text mode, each number is stored as a character string.
(b) If the number of fields in the structure increases (say, by adding address, house rent allowance, etc.), writing structures using **fprintf( )**, or reading them using **fscanf( ),** becomes quite clumsy.

Let us now see a more efficient way of reading/writing records (structures). This makes use of two functions **fread( )** and **fwrite( )**. We will write two programs, the first one will write records to the file and the second will read these records from the file and display them on the screen.

```
/* Receives records from keyboard and writes them to a file in binary mode */
# include <stdio.h>
# include <stdlib.h>
void main( )
{
    FILE *fp ;
    char another = 'Y' ;
    struct emp
    {
        char name[40] ;
        int age ;
        float bs ;
    } ;
    struct emp e ;

    fp = fopen ( "EMP.DAT", "wb" ) ;

    if ( fp == NULL )
    {
        puts ( "Cannot open file" ) ;
        exit ( 1 ) ;
    }

    while ( another == 'Y' )
    {
        printf ( "\nEnter name, age and basic salary: " ) ;
        scanf ( "%s %d %f", e.name, &e.age, &e.bs ) ;
        fwrite ( &e, sizeof ( e ), 1, fp ) ;

        printf ( "Add another record (Y/N) " ) ;
        fflush ( stdin ) ;
        another = getche( ) ;
    }
    fclose ( fp ) ;
}
```

And here is the output:

```
Enter name, age and basic salary: Steven 24 1250.50
Add another record (Y/N) Y
Enter name, age and basic salary: Sandra 21 1300.60
Add another record (Y/N) Y
Enter name, age and basic salary: Harmon 28 1400.70
Add another record (Y/N) N
```

Most of this program is similar to the one that we wrote earlier, which used **fprintf( )** instead of **fwrite( )**. Note, however, that the file "EMP.DAT" has now been opened in binary mode.

The information obtained from the keyboard about the employee is placed in the structure variable **e**. Then, the following statement writes the structure to the file:

```
fwrite ( &e, sizeof ( e ), 1, fp ) ;
```

Here, the first argument is the address of the structure to be written to the disk.

The second argument is the size of the structure in bytes. Instead of counting the bytes occupied by the structure ourselves, we let the program do it for us by using the **sizeof( )** operator. The **sizeof( )** operator gives the size of the variable in bytes. This keeps the program unchanged in the event of change in the elements of the structure.

The third argument is the number of such structures that we want to write at one time. In this case, we want to write only one structure at a time. Had we had an array of structures, for example, we might have wanted to write the entire array at once.

The last argument is the pointer to the file we want to write to.

Now, let us write a program to read back the records written to the disk by the previous program.

```
/* Reads records from binary file and displays them on VDU */
# include <stdio.h>
# include <stdlib.h>
void main( )
{
    FILE *fp ;
    struct emp
    {
        char name[40] ;
        int age ;
        float bs ;
    } ;
    struct emp e ;

    fp = fopen ( "EMP.DAT", "rb" ) ;

    if ( fp == NULL )
    {
        puts ( "Cannot open file" ) ;
        exit ( 1 ) ;
    }
```

```
while ( fread ( &e, sizeof ( e ), 1, fp ) == 1 )
    printf ( "\n%s %d %f", e.name, e.age, e.bs ) ;

fclose ( fp ) ;
}
```

Here, the **fread( )** function causes the data read from the disk to be placed in the structure variable **e**. The format of **fread( )** is the same as that of **fwrite( )**. The function **fread( )** returns the number of records read. Ordinarily, this should correspond to the third argument, the number of records we asked for—1 in this case. If we have reached the end of the file, since **fread( )** cannot read anything, it returns a 0. By testing for this situation, we know when to stop reading.

As you can now see, any database management application in C must make use of **fread( )** and **fwrite( )** functions, since they store numbers more efficiently, and make writing/reading of structures quite easy. Note that even if the number of elements belonging to the structure increases, the format of **fread( )** and **fwrite( )** remains the same.

DATABASE MANAGEMENT

So far we have learned to record I/O in bits and pieces. However, in any serious database management application, we will have to combine all that we have learned in a proper manner to make sense. We have attempted to do this in the following menu, driven program. There is a provision to Add, Modify, List, and Delete records, the operations that are imperative in any database management. The following comments will help you in understanding the program:

- The addition of records must always take place at the end of existing records in the file, much in the same way you would add new records in a register manually.
- Listing records means displaying the existing records on the screen. Naturally, records should be listed from first record to last record.
- While modifying records, we must first ask the user which record he intends to modify. Instead of asking the record number to be modified, it would be more meaningful to ask for the name of the employee whose record is to be modified. On modifying the record, the existing record gets overwritten by the new record.
- In deleting records, except for the record to be deleted, the rest of the records must first be written to a temporary file, then the original file must be deleted, and the temporary file must be renamed back to the original.

— Observe carefully the way the file has been opened, first for reading and writing, and if this fails (the first time you run this program it would certainly fail, because the file does not exist), for writing and reading. It is imperative that the file be opened in binary mode.
— Note that the file is being opened only once and closed only once, which is quite logical.
— The **clrscr( )** function clears the contents of the screen and **gotoxy( )** places the cursor at the appropriate position on the screen. The parameters passed to **gotoxy( )** are column number followed by row number.

Given below is the complete listing of the program.

```
/* A menu-driven program for elementary database management */
# include <stdio.h>
# include <stdlib.h>
# include <conio.h>
# include <string.h>
void main( )
{
    FILE *fp, *ft ;
    char another, choice ;
    struct emp
    {
        char name[40] ;
        int age ;
        float bs ;
    } ;
    struct emp e ;
    char empname[40] ;
    long int recsize ;

    fp = fopen ( "EMP.DAT", "rb+" ) ;

    if ( fp == NULL )
    {
    fp = fopen ( "EMP.DAT", "wb+" ) ;

    if ( fp == NULL )
    {
        puts ( "Cannot open file" ) ;
        exit ( 1 ) ;
    }
}

recsize = sizeof ( e ) ;
```

```
while ( 1 )
{
    clrscr( ) ;

    gotoxy ( 30, 10 ) ;
    printf ( "1. Add Records" ) ;
    gotoxy ( 30, 12 ) ;
    printf ( "2. List Records" ) ;
    gotoxy ( 30, 14 ) ;
    printf ( "3. Modify Records" ) ;
    gotoxy ( 30, 16 ) ;
    printf ( "4. Delete Records" ) ;
    gotoxy ( 30, 18 ) ;
    printf ( "0. Exit" ) ;
    gotoxy ( 30, 20 ) ;
    printf ( "Your choice" ) ;

    fflush ( stdin ) ;
    choice = getche( ) ;
    switch ( choice )
    {
        case '1' :

            fseek ( fp, 0 , SEEK_END ) ;
            another = 'Y' ;
            while ( another == 'Y' )
            {
                printf ( "\nEnter name, age and basic sal. " ) ;
                scanf ( "%s %d %f", e.name, &e.age, &e.bs ) ;
                fwrite ( &e, recsize, 1, fp ) ;
                printf ( "\nAdd another Record (Y/N) " ) ;
                fflush ( stdin ) ;
                another = getche( ) ;
            }

            break ;

        case '2' :

            rewind ( fp ) ;

            while ( fread ( &e, recsize, 1, fp ) == 1 )
                printf ( "\n%s %d %f", e.name, e.age, e.bs ) ;

            break ;
```

```
            case '3' :

                another = 'Y' ;
                while ( another == 'Y' )
                {
                    printf ( "\nEnter name of employee to modify " ) ;
                    scanf ( "%s", empname ) ;

                    rewind ( fp ) ;
                    while ( fread ( &e, recsize, 1, fp ) == 1 )
                    {
                        if ( strcmp ( e.name, empname ) == 0 )
                        {
                            printf ( "\nEnter new name, age & bs" ) ;
                            scanf ( "%s %d %f", e.name, &e.age,
                                    &e.bs ) ;
                            fseek ( fp, - recsize, SEEK_CUR ) ;
                            fwrite ( &e, recsize, 1, fp ) ;
                            break ;
                        }
                    }

                    printf ( "\nModify another Record (Y/N) " ) ;
                    fflush ( stdin ) ;
                    another = getche( ) ;
                }

                break ;

            case '4' :

                another = 'Y' ;
                while ( another == 'Y' )
                {
                    printf ( "\nEnter name of employee to delete " ) ;
                    scanf ( "%s", empname ) ;

                    ft = fopen ( "TEMP.DAT", "wb" ) ;

                    rewind ( fp ) ;
                    while ( fread ( &e, recsize, 1, fp ) == 1 )
                    {
                        if ( strcmp ( e.name, empname ) != 0 )
                            fwrite ( &e, recsize, 1, ft ) ;
                    }
```

```
                fclose ( fp ) ;
                fclose ( ft ) ;
                remove ( "EMP.DAT" ) ;
                rename ( "TEMP.DAT", "EMP.DAT" ) ;

                fp = fopen ( "EMP.DAT", "rb+" ) ;

                printf ( "Delete another Record (Y/N) " ) ;
                fflush ( stdin ) ;
                another = getche( ) ;
            }
            break ;

        case '0' :
            fclose ( fp ) ;
            exit ( 0 ) ;
        }
    }
}
```

To understand how this program works, you need to be familiar with the concept of pointers. A pointer is initiated whenever we open a file. On opening a file, a pointer is set up which points to the first record in the file. To be precise, this pointer is present in the structure to which the file pointer returned by **fopen( )** points to. On using the functions **fread( )** or **fwrite( )**, the pointer moves to the beginning of the next record. On closing a file the pointer is deactivated. Note that the pointer movement is of utmost importance since **fread( )** always reads that record where the pointer is currently placed. Similarly, **fwrite( )** always writes the record where the pointer is currently placed.

The **rewind( )** function places the pointer to the beginning of the file, regardless of where it is present right now.

The **fseek( )** function lets us move the pointer from one record to another. In the previous program, to move the pointer to the previous record from its current position, we used the function,

```
fseek ( fp, -recsize, SEEK_CUR ) ;
```

Here, **-recsize** moves the pointer back by **recsize** bytes from the current position. **SEEK_CUR** is a macro defined in "stdio.h."

Similarly, the following **fseek( )** would place the pointer beyond the last record in the file.

```
fseek ( fp, 0, SEEK_END ) ;
```

In fact, **-recsize** or **0** are just the offsets that tell the compiler by how many bytes the pointer should be moved from a particular position. The third argument could be **SEEK_END**, **SEEK_CUR** or **SEEK_SET**. All these act as a reference from which the pointer should be offset. **SEEK_END** means move the pointer from the end of the file, **SEEK_CUR** means move the pointer with reference to its current position, and **SEEK_SET** means move the pointer with reference to the beginning of the file.

If we wish to know where the pointer is positioned right now, we can use the function **ftell( )**. It returns this position as a **long int**, which is an offset from the beginning of the file. The value returned by **ftell( )** can be used in subsequent calls to **fseek( )**. A sample call to **ftell( )** is shown below:

```
position = ftell ( fp ) ;
```

where **position** is a long int.

LOW-LEVEL DISK I/O

In low-level disk I/O, data cannot be written as individual characters, or as strings, or as formatted data. There is only one way data can be written or read in low-level disk I/O functions—as a buffer full of bytes.

Writing a buffer full of data resembles the **fwrite( )** function. However, unlike **fwrite( )**, the programmer must set up the buffer for the data, place the appropriate values in it before writing, and take them out after writing. Thus, the buffer in the low-level I/O functions is very much a part of the program, rather than being invisible as in high-level disk I/O functions.

Low-level disk I/O functions offer the following advantages:

(a) Since these functions parallel the methods that the OS uses to write to the disk, they are more efficient than the high-level disk I/O functions.

(b) Since there are fewer layers of routines to go through, low-level I/O functions operate faster than their high-level counterparts.

Let us now write a program that uses low-level disk input/output functions.

A Low-Level File-Copy Program

Earlier we wrote a program to copy the contents of one file to another. In that program, we had read the file character by character using **fgetc( )**. Each character that was read was written into the target file using **fputc( )**. Instead of performing the I/O on a character-by-character basis, we can read a chunk of bytes from the source file and then write this chunk into the target file. While doing so, the chunk will be read into the buffer and written to the file from the buffer. While doing so, we will manage the buffer ourselves, rather than relying on the library functions to do so. This is what is low-level about this program. Here is a program that shows how this can be done.

```c
/* File-copy program which copies text, .com and .exe files */
# include <fcntl.h>
# include <types.h> /* if present in sys directory use
                        "c:tc\\include\\sys\\types.h" */
# include <stat.h> /* if present in sys directory use
                       "c:\\tc\\include\\sys\\stat.h" */
# include <stdlib.h>
# include <stdio.h>
void main ( int argc, char *argv[ ] )
{
     char buffer[ 512 ], source [ 128 ], target [ 128 ] ;
     int inhandle, outhandle, bytes ;
     printf ( "\nEnter source file name" ) ;
     gets ( source ) ;

     inhandle = open ( source, O_RDONLY | O_BINARY ) ;
     if ( inhandle == -1 )
     {
          puts ( "Cannot open file" ) ;
          exit ( 1 ) ;
     }

     printf ( "\nEnter target file name" ) ;
     gets ( target ) ;

     outhandle = open ( target, O_CREAT | O_BINARY | O_WRONLY,
                    S_IWRITE ) ;
     if ( outhandle == -1 )
     {
          puts ( "Cannot open file" ) ;
          close ( inhandle ) ;
          exit ( 2 ) ;
     }

     while ( 1 )
     {
          bytes = read ( inhandle, buffer, 512 ) ;
```

```
              if ( bytes > 0 )
                    write ( outhandle, buffer, bytes ) ;
              else
                    break ;
      }

    close ( inhandle ) ;
    close ( outhandle ) ;
}
```

Declaring the Buffer

The first difference that you will notice in this program is that we declare a character buffer,

```
char buffer[512] ;
```

This is the buffer in which the data read from the disk will be placed. The size of this buffer is important for efficient operation. Depending on the operating system, buffers of certain sizes are handled more efficiently than others.

Opening a File

We have opened two files in our program, one is the source file from which we read the information, and the other is the target file into which we write the information read from the source file.

As in high-level disk I/O, the file must be opened before we can access it. This is done using the statement,

```
inhandle = open ( source, O_RDONLY | O_BINARY ) ;
```

We open the file for the same reason as we did earlier—to establish communication with the operating system about the file. As usual, we have to supply to **open( )**, the filename and the mode in which we want to open the file. The possible file opening modes are given here:

O_APPEND — Opens a file for appending
O_CREAT   — Creates a new file for writing (has no effect if file already exists)
O_RDONLY — Opens a new file for reading only
O_RDWR   — Creates a file for both reading and writing
O_WRONLY — Creates a file for writing only
O_BINARY — Opens a file in binary mode
O_TEXT   — Opens a file in text mode

These 'O-flags' are defined in the file "fcntl.h." So this file must be included in the program while usng low-level disk I/O. Note that the file "stdio.h" is not necessary for low-level disk I/O. When two or more O-flags are used together, they are combined using the bitwise OR operator (|). Chapter 14 discusses bitwise operators in detail.

The other statement used in our program to open the file is,

```
outhandle = open ( target, O_CREAT | O_BINARY | O_WRONLY,
                    S_IWRITE ) ;
```

Note that since the target file doesn't exist when it is being opened, we have used the O_CREAT flag, and since we want to write to the file and not read from it, we have to use O_WRONLY. And finally, since we want to open the file in binary mode, we have to use O_BINARY.

Whenever the O_CREAT flag is used, another argument must be added to the **open( )** function to indicate the read/write status of the file to be created. This argument is called a 'permission argument.' Permission arguments could be either of the following:

S_IWRITE   —   Writing to the file permitted
S_IREAD   —   Reading from the file permitted

To use these permissions, both the files "types.h" and "stat.h" must be **# include**d in the program along with "fcntl.h."

File Handles

Instead of returning a FILE pointer as **fopen( )** did, in low-level disk I/O, **open( )** returns an integer value called 'file handle.' This is a number assigned to a particular file, which is used thereafter to refer to the file. If **open( )** returns a value of -1, it means that the file couldn't be successfully opened.

Interaction between Buffer and File

The following statement reads the file or as much of it as will fit into the buffer:

```
bytes = read ( inhandle, buffer, 512 ) ;
```

The **read( )** function takes three arguments. The first argument is the file handle, the second is the address of the buffer, and the third is the maximum number of bytes we want to read.

The **read( )** function returns the number of bytes actually read. This is an important number, since it may very well be less than the buffer size

(512 bytes), and we will need to know just how full the buffer is before we can do anything with its contents. In our program we have assigned this number to the variable **bytes**.

For copying the file, we must use both the **read( )** and the **write( )** functions in a **while** loop. The **read( )** function returns the number of bytes actually read. This is assigned to the variable **bytes**. This value will be equal to the buffer size (512 bytes) until the end of the file, when the buffer may only be partially full. The variable **bytes**, therefore, is used to tell **write( )** many bytes to write from the buffer to the target file.

Note that the buffers are created in the stack, which is of limited size. Hence, when large buffers are used, they must be made as global variables, otherwise stack overflow will occur.

I/O UNDER WINDOWS

As said earlier, I/O in C is carried out using functions present in the library that comes with the C compiler targeted for a specific OS. Windows permits several applications to use the same screen simultaneously. Hence, there is a possibility that what is written by one application to the console may get overwritten by the output sent by another application to the console. To avoid such situations, Windows has completely abandoned console I/O functions. It uses a separate mechanism to send output to a window representing an application. The details of this mechanism are discussed in Chapter 17.

Though under Windows, console I/O functions are not used. Still, functions like **fprintf( )**, **fscanf( )**, **fread( )**, **fwrite( )**, **sprintf( )**, and **sscanf( )** work exactly the same under Windows as well.

SUMMARY

(a) File I/O can be performed on a character-by-character basis, a line-by-line basis, a record-by-record basis, or a chunk-by-chunk basis.

(b) Different operations that can be performed on a file are—creation of a new file, opening an existing file, reading from a file, writing to a file, moving to a specific location in a file (seeking), and closing a file.

(c) File I/O is done using a buffer to improve the efficiency.

(d) A file can be a text file or a binary file depending upon its contents.

(e) Library functions convert **\n** to **\r\n** or vice versa while writing/reading to/from a file.

(f) Many library functions convert a number to a numeric string before writing it to a file, thereby using more space on a disk. This can be avoided using the functions **fread( )** and **fwrite( )**.

(g) In low-level file I/O we can do the buffer management ourselves.

EXERCISES

[A] Point out the errors, if any, in the following programs:

(a)
```c
# include <stdio.h>
void openfile ( char *, FILE ** ) ;
void main( )
{
    FILE *fp ;
    openfile ( "Myfile.txt", fp ) ;
    if ( fp == NULL )
            printf ( "Unable to open file... " ) ;
}

void openfile ( char *fn, FILE **f )
{
    *f = fopen ( fn, "r" ) ;
}
```

(b)
```c
# include <stdio.h>
# include <stdlib.h>
void main( )
{
    FILE *fp ;
    char c ;
    fp = fopen ( "TRY.C" ,"r") ;
    if ( fp == null )
    {
            puts ( "Cannot open file" ) ;
            exit( ) ;
    }
    while ( ( c = getc ( fp ) ) != EOF )
            putch ( c ) ;
    fclose ( fp ) ;
}
```

(c)
```c
# include <stdio.h>
void main( )
{
    char fname[ ] = "c:\\students.dat" ;
    FILE *fp ;
    fp = fopen ( fname, "tr" ) ;
    if ( fp == NULL )
            printf ( "\nUnable to open file..." ) ;
}
```

(d)
```c
# include <stdio.h>
void main( )
{
    FILE *fp ;
    char str[80] ;
    fp = fopen ( "TRY.C", "r" ) ;
    while ( fgets ( str, 80, fp ) != EOF )
        fputs ( str ) ;
    fclose ( fp ) ;
}
```

(e)
```c
# include <stdio.h>
void main( )
{
    unsigned char ;
    FILE *fp ;

    fp = fopen ( "trial", `r' ) ;
    while ( ( ch = getc ( fp ) ) != EOF )
        printf ( "%c", ch ) ;

    fclose ( *fp ) ;
}
```

(f)
```c
# include <stdio.h>
void main( )
{
    FILE *fp ;
    char name[25] ;
    int age ;

    fp = fopen ( "YOURS", "r" ) ;
    while ( fscanf ( fp, "%s %d", name, &age ) != NULL )
    fclose ( fp ) ;
}
```

(g)
```c
# include <stdio.h>
void main( )
{
    FILE *fp ;
    char names[20] ;
    int i ;
    fp = fopen ( "students.dat", "wb" ) ;
    for ( i = 0 ; i <= 10 ; i++ )
    {
        puts ( "\nEnter name " ) ;
        gets ( name ) ;
        fwrite ( name, size of ( name ), 1, fp ) ;
    }
    close ( fp ) ;
}
```

(h)
```c
# include <stdio.h>
void main( )
{
    FILE *fp ;
    char name[20] = "Ajay" ;
    int i ;
    fp = fopen ( "students.dat", "r" ) ;
    for ( i = 0 ; i <= 10 ; i++ )
        fwrite ( name, sizeof ( name ), 1, fp ) ;
    close ( fp ) ;
}
```

(i)
```c
# include <fcntl.h>
# include <stdio.h>
void main( )
{
    int fp ;
    fp = open ( "pr22.c" , "r" ) ;
    if ( fp == -1 )
        puts ( "cannot open file" ) ;
    else
        close ( fp ) ;
}
```

(j)
```c
# include <stdio.h>
void main( )
{
    int fp ;
    fp = fopen ( "students.dat", READ | BINARY ) ;
```

```
                    if ( fp == -1 )
                            puts ( "cannot open file" ) ;
                    else
                            close ( fp ) ;
            }
```

[B] Answer the following:

(a) The FILE structure is defined in which of the following files:
   1. stdlib.h
   2. stdio.c
   3. io.h
   4. stdio.h

(b) If a file contains the line "I am a boy\r\n," then on reading this line into the array **str[ ]** using **fgets( )**, what would **str[ ]** contain?
   1. I am a boy\r\n\0
   2. I am a boy\r\0
   3. I am a boy\n\0
   4. I am a boy

(c) State True or False:
   1. The disadvantage of high-level disk I/O functions is that the programmer has to manage the buffers.
   2. If a file is opened for reading it is necessary that the file must exist.
   3. If a file opened for writing already exists, its contents would be overwritten.
   4. For opening a file in append mode, it is necessary that the file should exist.

(d) On opening a file for reading, which of the following activities are performed:
   1. The disk is searched for existence of the file.
   2. The file is brought into memory.
   3. A pointer is set up which points to the first character in the file.
   4. All the above.

(e) Is it necessary that a file created in text mode must always be opened in text mode for subsequent operations?

(f) While using the statement,

```
fp = fopen ( "myfile.c", "r" ) ;
```

what happens if,
   − 'myfile.c' does not exist on the disk
   − 'myfile.c' exists on the disk

(g) What is the purpose of the library function **fflush( )**?

(h) While using the statement,

```
fp = fopen ( "myfile.c", "wb" ) ;
```

what happens if,
- 'myfile.c' does not exist on the disk.
- 'myfile.c' exists on the disk

(i) A floating-point array contains percentage marks obtained by students in an examination. To store these marks in a file 'marks.dat,' in which mode would you open the file and why?

[C] Attempt the following:

(a) Write a program to read a file and display its contents along with line numbers before each line.

(b) Write a program to find the size of a text file without traversing it character by character.

(c) Write a program to apped the contents of one file at the end of another.

(d) Suppose a file contains students' records with each record containing the name and age of a student. Write a program to read these records and display them in sorted order by name.

(e) Write a program to copy one file to another. While doing so, replace all lowercase characters to their equivalent uppercase characters.

(f) Write a program that merges lines alternately from two files and writes the results to a new file. If one file has a less number of lines than the other, the remaining lines from the larger file should be simply copied into the target file.

(g) Write a program to display the contents of a text file on the screen. Make the following provisions:

Display the contents inside a box drawn with opposite corner co-ordinates being (0, 1) and (79, 23). Display the name of the file whose contents are being displayed, and the page numbers in the zeroth row. The moment one screenful of file has been displayed, flash a message 'Press any key...' in the 24th row. When a key is pressed, the next page's contents should be displayed, and so on until the end of the file.

(h) Write a program to encrypt/decrypt a file using:

(1) An offset cipher: In an offset cipher, each character from the source file is offset with a fixed value and then written to the target file.

For example, if a character read from the source file is 'A,' then convert this into a new character by offsetting 'A' by a fixed value, say 128, and then writing the new character to the target file.

(2) A substitution cipher: In this, each character read from the source file is substituted by a corresponding predetermined character and this character is written to the target file.

For example, if character 'A' is read from the source file, and if we have decided that every 'A' is to be substituted by '!,' then a '!' would be written to the target file in place of every 'A.' Similarly, every 'B' would be substituted by '5' and so on.

(i) In the file 'CUSTOMER.DAT' there are 100 records with the following structure:

```
struct customer
{
    int accno ;
    char name[30] ;
    float balance ;
} ;
```

In another file, 'TRANSACTIONS.DAT,' there are several records with the following structure:

```
struct trans
{
    int accno ,
    char trans_type ;
    float amount ;
} ;
```

The element **trans_type** contains D/W indicating deposit or withdrawal of an amount. Write a program to update the 'CUSTOMER.DAT' file, i.e., if the **trans_type** is 'D,' then update the **balance** of 'CUSTOMER.DAT' by adding **amount** to balance for the corresponding **accno**. Similarly, if **trans_type** is 'W,' then subtract the **amount** from **balance**. However, while subtracting the amount make sure that the amount does not get overdrawn, i.e., at least $ 100 should remain in the account.

(j) There are 100 records present in a file with the following structure:

```
struct date
{
    int d, m, y ;
} ;
```

```
struct employee
{
    int empcode[6] ;
    char empname[20] ;
    struct date join_date ;
    float salary ;
} ;
```

Write a program to read these records, arrange them in ascending order by **join_date**, and write them in to a target file.

(k) A hospital keeps a file of blood donors in which each record has the format:

Name: 20 Columns
Address: 40 Columns
Age: 2 Columns
Blood Type: 1 Column (Type 1, 2, 3 or 4)

Write a program to read the file and print a list of all blood donors whose age is below 25 and blood is type 2.

(l) Given a list of names of students in a class, write a program to store the names in a file on disk. Make a provision to display the **n**th name in the list (**n** is data to be read) and to display all names starting with S.

(m) Assume that a Master file contains two fields, Roll no. and name of the student. At the end of the year, a set of students join the class and another set leaves. A transaction file contains the roll numbers and an appropriate code to add or delete a student.

Write a program to create another file that contains the updated list of names and roll numbers. Assume that the master file and the transaction file are arranged in ascending order by roll numbers. The updated file should also be in ascending order by roll numbers.

(n) In a small firm, employee numbers are given in serial numerical order, that is 1, 2, 3, etc.

- Create a file of employee data with the following information: employee number, name, sex, gross salary.
- If more employees join, append their data to the file.
- If an employee with serial number 25 (say) leaves, delete the record by making gross salary 0.
- If some employee's gross salary increases, retrieve the record and update the salary.

Write a program to implement these operations.

(o) Given a text file, write a program to create another text file deleting the words "a," "the," and "an," replacing each one of them with a blank space.

(p) You are given a data file EMPLOYEE.DAT with the following record structure:

```
struct employee {
                int empno ;
                char name[30] ;
                int basic, grade ;
        } ;
```

Every employee has a unique **empno** and there are supposed to be no gaps between employee numbers. Records are entered into the data file in ascending order of employee number. It is intended to check whether there are missing employee numbers. Write a program to read the data file records sequentially and display the list of missing employee numbers.

(q) Write a program to carry out the following:
   – To read a text file "TRIAL.TXT" consisting of a maximum of 50 lines of text, each line with a maximum of 80 characters.
   – Count and display the number of words contained in the file.
   – Display the total number of four-letter words in the text file.
   Assume that the end of a word may be a space, comma, or a full-stop followed by one or more spaces or a newline character.

(r) Write a program to read a list of words, sort the words in alphabetical order, and display them one word per line. Also, give the total number of words in the list. The output format should be:
   Total number of words in the list is _____
   Alphabetical listing of words is:

   Assume the end of the list is indicated by **ZZZZZZ** and there are a maximum of 25 words in the Text file.

(s) Write a program to carry out the following:
   (a) Read a text file 'INPUT.TXT'
   (b) Print each word in reverse order

   Example:

```
Input: INDIA IS MY COUNTRY
Output: AIDNI SI YM YRTNUOC
```

Assume that each word length is a maximum of 10 characters and each word is separated by newline/blank characters.

(t) Write a C program to read a large text file, 'NOTES.TXT,' and print it on the printer in cut-sheets, introducing page breaks at the end of every 50 lines and a pause message on the screen at the end of every page for the user to change the paper.

Chapter 13

MORE ISSUES IN INPUT/OUTPUT

In Chapters 11 and 12 we saw how Console I/O and File I/O are done in C. There are still some more issues related with input/output that remain to be understood. These issues help in making the I/O operations more elegant.

USING *argc* AND *argv*

To execute the file-copy programs that we saw in Chapter 12, we are required to first type the program, compile it, and then execute it. This program can be improved in two ways:

(a) There should be no need to compile the program every time to use the file-copy utility. It means the program must be executable at the command prompt (A > , or C > if you are using MS-DOS, Start | Run dialog if you are using Windows, and $ prompt if you are using Unix).

(b) Instead of the program prompting us to enter the source and target filenames, we must be able to supply them at the command prompt, in the form:

```
filecopy PR1.C PR2.C
```

where, PR1.C is the source filename and PR2.C is the target filename.

The first improvement is simple. In MS-DOS, the executable file (the one that can be executed at the command prompt and has an extension .EXE) can be created in Turbo C/C++ by using the F9 key to compile the program. In the VC++ compiler under Windows, the same can be done by using F7 to compile the program. Under Unix this is not required, since in Unix, every time we compile a program, we always get an executable file.

The second improvement is possible by passing the source filename and target filename to the function **main( )**. This is illustrated here:

```
# include <stdio.h>
# include <stdlib.h>
void main ( int argc, char *argv[ ] )
{
    FILE *fs, *ft;
    char ch ;

    if ( argc != 3 )
    {
        puts ( "Improper number of arguments" ) ;
```

```
            exit ( ) ;
      }

fs = fopen ( argv[1], "r" ) ;
if ( fs == NULL )
      {
            puts ( "Cannot open source file" ) ;
            exit ( ) ;
      }

ft = fopen ( argv[2], "w" ) ;
if ( ft == NULL )
      {
            puts ( "Cannot open target file" ) ;
            fclose ( fs ) ;
            exit( ) ;
      }

while ( 1 )
      {
            ch = fgetc ( fs ) ;

            if ( ch == EOF )
                  break ;
            else
                  fputc ( ch, ft ) ;

      }
            fclose ( fs ) ;
            fclose ( ft ) ;
      }
```

The arguments that we pass on to **main( )** at the command prompt are called command line arguments. The function **main( )** can have two arguments, traditionally named **argc** and **argv**. Out of these, **argv** is an array of pointers to strings and **argc** is an **int** whose value is equal to the number of strings to which **argv** points. When the program is executed, the strings on the command line are passed to **main( )**. More precisely, the strings at the command line are stored in memory and the address of the first string is stored in **argv[0]**, the address of the second string is stored in **argv[1]**, and so on. The argument **argc** is set to the number of strings given on the command line. For example, in our sample program, if at the command prompt we give,

```
filecopy PR1.C PR2.C
```

then,

```
argc would contain 3
argv[0] would contain base address of the string "filecopy"
argv[1] would contain base address of the string "PR1.C"
argv[2] would contain base address of the string "PR2.C"
```

Whenever we pass arguments to **main( )**, it is a good habit to check whether the correct number of arguments have been passed on to **main( )** or not. In our program, this has been done through,

```
if ( argc != 3 )
{
    printf ( "Improper number of arguments" ) ;
    exit( ) ;
}
```

The rest of the program is the same as the earlier file-copy program. This program is better than the earlier file-copy program on two counts:

(a) There is no need to recompile the program every time we want to use this utility. It can be executed at the command prompt.
(b) We are able to pass the source file name and target file name to **main( )**, and utilize them in **main( )**.

One final comment— the **while** loop that we have used in our program can be written in a more compact form, as shown here:

```
while ( ( ch = fgetc ( fs ) ) != EOF )
    fputc ( ch, ft ) ;
```

This avoids the usage of an indefinite loop and a **break** statement to come out of this loop. Here, first **fgetc (fs)** gets the character from the file, assigns it to the variable **ch**, and then **ch** is compared against **EOF**. Remember that it is necessary to put the expression

```
ch = fgetc ( fs )
```

within a pair of parentheses, so that first the character read is assigned to variable **ch** and then it is compared with **EOF**.

There is one more way of writing the **while** loop. It is shown here:

```
while ( !feof ( fs ) )
{
    ch = fgetc ( fs ) ;
    fputc ( ch, ft ) ;
}
```

Here, **feof( )** is a macro that returns a 0 if the end of the file is not reached. Hence we use the **!** operator to negate this 0 to the truth value. When the end of the file is reached, **feof( )** returns a nonzero value, **!** makes it 0, and since now the condition evaluates to false, the **while** loop gets terminated.

Note that in each one of them, the following three methods for opening a file are the same, since in each one of them, essentially a base address of the string (pointer to a string) is being passed to **fopen( )**.

```
fs = fopen ( "PR1.C" , "r" ) ;
fs = fopen ( filename, "r" ) ;
fs = fopen ( argv[1] , "r" ) ;
```

DETECTING ERRORS IN READING/WRITING

When we perform a read or write operation on a file, we are not always successful in doing so. Naturally, there must be a provision to test whether our attempt to read/write was successful or not.

The standard library function **ferror( )** reports any error that might have occurred during a read/write operation on a file. It returns a zero if the read/write is successful and a nonzero value in case of a failure. The following program illustrates the usage of **ferror( )**.

```
# include <stdio.h>
void main( )
{
    FILE *fp ;
    char ch ;

    fp = fopen ( "TRIAL", "w" ) ;

    while ( !feof ( fp ) )
    {
        ch = fgetc ( fp ) ;
        if ( ferror( ) )
        {
            printf ( "Error in reading file" ) ;
            break ;
        }
        else
            printf ( "% c", ch ) ;
    }
```

```
        fclose ( fp ) ;
}
```

In this program, the **fgetc( )** function would obviously fail the first time around since the file has been opened for writing, whereas **fgetc( )** is attempting to read from the file. The moment the error occurs, **ferror( )** returns a nonzero value and the **if** block gets executed. Instead of printing the error message using **printf( )**, we can use the standard library function **perror( )**, which prints the error message specified by the compiler. Thus, in the previous program, the **perror( )** function can be used as shown here:

```
if ( ferror( ) )
{
      perror ( "TRIAL" ) ;
      break ;
}
```

Note that when the error occurs, the error message that is displayed is:

```
TRIAL: Permission denied
```

This means we can precede the system error message with any message of our choosing. In our program, we have just displayed the filename in place of the error message.

STANDARD I/O DEVICES

To perform reading or writing operations on a file, we need to use the function **fopen( )**, which sets up a file pointer to refer to this file. Most OSs also predefine pointers for three standard files. To access these pointers, we need not use **fopen( )**. These standard file pointers are shown in Figure 13.1

Thus, the statement **ch = fgetc(stdin)** would read a character from the keyboard rather than from a file. We can use this statement without any need to use the **fopen( )** or **fclose( )** function calls.

Standard File pointer	Description
Stdin	standard input device (Keyboard)
Stdout	standard output device (VDU)
Stderr	standard error device (VDU)

FIGURE 13.1

Note that under MS-DOS two more standard file pointers are available—
stdprn and **stdaux**. They stand for standard printing device and standard
auxiliary device (serial port). The following program shows how to use the
standard file pointers. It reads a file from the disk and prints it on the printer.

```
/* Prints file contents on printer*/
# include <stdio.h>
# include <stdlib.h>
void main( )
{
    FILE *fp ;
    char ch ;
    fp = fopen ( "poem.txt", "r" ) ;

    if ( fp == NULL )
    {
        printf ( "Cannot open file" ) ;
        exit( ) ;
    }

    while ( ( ch = fgetc ( fp ) ) != EOF )
        fputc ( ch, stdprn ) ;

    fclose ( fp ) ;
}
```

The statement **fputc (ch, stdprn)** writes a character read from the file to
the printer. Note that although we opened the file on the disk, we didn't open
stdprn, the printer. Standard files and their use in redirection will be dealt
with in more detail in the next section.

Note that these standard file pointers have been defined in the file
"stdio.h." Therefore, it is necessary to include this file in the program that
uses these standard file pointers.

I/O REDIRECTION

Most operating systems incorporate a powerful feature that allows a program
to read and write files, even when such a capability has not been incorporated
in the program. This is done through a process called 'redirection.'

Normally, a C program receives its input from the standard input device,
which is assumed to be the keyboard, and sends its output to the standard
output device, which is assumed to be the VDU. In other words, the OS makes

certain assumptions about where input should come from and where output should go. Redirection permits us to change these assumptions.

For example, using redirection, the output of the program that normally goes to the VDU can be sent to the disk or the printer without really making a provision for it in the program. This is often a more convenient and flexible approach than providing a separate function in the program to write to the disk or printer. Similarly, redirection can be used to read information from a disk file directly into a program, instead of receiving the input from the keyboard.

To use a redirection facility is to execute the program from the command prompt, inserting the redirection symbols at appropriate places. Let us understand this process with the help of a program.

Redirecting the Output

Let's see how we can redirect the output of a program, from the screen to a file. We'll start by considering the simple program shown below:

```
/* File name: util.c */
# include <stdio.h>
void main( )
{
    char ch ;
    while ( ( ch = getc ( stdin ) ) != EOF )
        putc ( ch, stdout ) ;
}
```

On compiling this program, we would get an executable file UTIL.EXE. Normally, when we execute this file, the **putc( )** function will cause whatever we type to be printed on screen, until we type Ctrl-Z, at which point the program will terminate, as shown in the following sample run. The Ctrl-Z character is often called an end-of-file character.

```
C>UTIL.EXE
perhaps I had a wicked childhood,
perhaps I had a miserable youth,
but somewhere in my wicked miserable past,
there must have been a moment of truth ^Z
C>
```

Now let's see what happens when we invoke this program in a different way, using redirection:

```
C>UTIL.EXE > POEM.TXT
C>
```

Here we are causing the output to be redirected to the file POEM.TXT. Can we prove that this output has indeed gone to the file POEM.TXT? Yes, by using the TYPE command as follows:

```
C>TYPE POEM.TXT
perhaps I had a wicked childhood,
perhaps I had a miserable youth,
but somewhere in my wicked miserable past,
there must have been a moment of truth
C>
```

There's the result of our typing sitting in the file. The redirection operator, '>,' causes any output intended for the screen to be written to the file whose name follows the operator.

Note that the data to be redirected to a file doesn't need to be typed by a user at the keyboard; the program itself can generate it. Any output normally sent to the screen can be redirected to a disk file. As an example, consider the following program for generating the ASCII table on screen:

```
/* File name: ascii.c*/
# include <stdio.h>
void main( )
{
    int ch ;

    for ( ch = 0 ; ch <= 255 ; ch++ )
        printf ( "\n% d % c", ch, ch ) ;
}
```

When this program is compiled and then executed at the command prompt using the redirection operator,

```
C>ASCII.EXE > TABLE.TXT
```

the output is written to the file. This can be a useful capability any time you want to capture the output in a file, rather than displaying it on the screen.

DOS predefines a number of filenames for its own use. One of these names is PRN, which stands for the printer. Output can be redirected to the printer by using this filename. For example, if you invoke the "ascii.exe" program this way:

```
C>ASCII.EXE > PRN
```

the ASCII table will be printed on the printer.

Redirecting the Input

We can also redirect input to a program so that, instead of reading a character from the keyboard, a program reads it from a file. Let us now see how this can be done.

To redirect the input, we need to have a file containing something to be displayed. Suppose we use a file called NEWPOEM.TXT containing the following lines:

```
Let's start at the very beginning,
A very good place to start!
```

We'll assume that by using some text editor, these lines have been placed in the file NEWPOEM.TXT. Now, we use the input redirection operator '<' before the file, as shown here:

```
C>UTIL.EXE < NEWPOEM.TXT
Let's start at the very beginning,
A very good place to start!
C>
```

The lines are printed on the screen with no further effort on our part. Using redirection, we've made our program UTIL.C perform the work of the TYPE command.

Both Ways at Once

Redirection of input and output can be used together; the input for a program can come from a file via redirection, at the same time its output can be redirected to a file. Such a program is called a filter. The following command demonstrates this process.

```
C>UTIL.EXE < NEWPOEM.TXT > POETRY.TXT
```

In this case, our program receives the redirected input from the file NEW-POEM.TXT and instead of sending the output to the screen; it would redirect it to the file POETRY.TXT.

Similarly, to send the contents of the file NEWPOEM.TXT to the printer, we can use the following command:

```
C>UTIL.EXE < NEWPOEM.TXT > PRN
```

While using such multiple redirections, don't try to send output to the same file from which you are receiving input. This is because the output file is erased before it's written to. So by the time we manage to receive the input from a file, it is already erased.

Redirection can be a powerful tool for developing utility programs to examine or alter data in files. Thus, redirection is used to establish a relationship between a program and a file. Another OS operator can be used to relate two programs directly, so that the output of one is fed directly into another, with no files involved. This is called 'piping,' and is done using the operator '|,' called pipe. We won't pursue this topic, but you can read about it in the OS help/manual.

SUMMARY

(a) We can pass parameters to a program at the command line using the concept of 'command line arguments.'

(b) The command line argument **argv** contains values passed to the program, whereas **argc** contains a number of arguments.

(c) We can use the standard file pointer **stdin** to take input from standard input devices, such as keyboard.

(d) We can use the standard file pointer **stdout** to send output to a standard output device, such as a monitor.

(e) We can use the standard file pointers **stdprn** and **stdaux** to interact with printer and auxiliary devices respectively.

(f) Redirection allows a program to read from or write to files at the command prompt.

(g) The operators < and > are called redirection operators.

EXERCISES

[A] Answer the following:

(a) How will you use the following program to
  - Copy the contents of one file into another.
  - Print a file on the printer.
  - Create a new file and add some text to it.
  - Display the contents of an existing file.

```
# include <stdio.h>
void main( )
{
    char ch, str[10] ;
```

```
        while ( ( ch = getc ( stdin ) ) != -1 )
            putc ( ch, stdout ) ;
    }
```

(b) State True or False:
1. We can send arguments at the command line even if we define the **main( )** function without parameters.
2. To use standard file pointers we don't need to open the file using **fopen( )**.
3. Using **stdaux**, we can send output to the printer if the printer is attached to the serial port.
4. The zeroth element of the **argv** array is always the name of the executable file.

(c) Point out the errors, if any, in the following program:

```
# include <stdio.h>
void main ( int ac, char ( * ) av[ ] )
{
    printf ( "\n% d", ac ) ;
    printf ( "\n% s", av[0] ) ;
}
```

[B] Attempt the following:

(a) Write a program using command line arguments to search for a word in a file and replace it with the specified word. The usage of the program is shown as follows.

```
C> change <old word> <new word> <filename>
```

(b) Write a program that can be used at the command prompt as a calculating utility. The usage of the program is shown as follows.

```
C> calc <switch> <n> <m>
```

Where **n** and **m** are two integer operands. **switch** can be any one of the arithmetic or comparison operators. If an arithmetic operator is supplied, the output should be the result of the operation. If a comparison operator is supplied, then the output should be **True** or **False**.

Chapter 14

OPERATIONS ON BITS

So far, we have dealt with characters, integers, floats, and their variations. The smallest element in memory on which we are able to operate as yet is a byte; and we operated on it by making use of the data type **char**. However, we haven't attempted to look within these data types to see how they are constructed out of individual bits, and how these bits can be manipulated. Being able to operate on a bit level can be very important in programming, especially when a program must interact directly with the hardware. This is because the programming languages are byte oriented, whereas hardware tends to be bit oriented. Let us now delve inside the byte and see how it is constructed and how it can be manipulated effectively. So let us take apart the byte—bit by bit.

BITWISE OPERATORS

One of C's powerful features is a set of bit manipulation operators. These permit the programmer to access and manipulate individual bits within a piece of data. The various bitwise operators available in C are shown in Figure 14.1.

These operators can operate upon **int**s and **char**s, but not on **float**s and **double**s. Before moving on to the details of the operators, let us first take a look at the bit numbering scheme in integers and characters. Bits are numbered from zero onward, increasing from right to left as shown in Figure 14.2:

Throughout this discussion of bitwise operators, we are going to use a function called **showbits( )**, but we are not going to show you the details of the function immediately. The task of **showbits( )** is to display the binary representation of any integer or character value.

Operator	Meaning
~	One's complement
>>	Right shift
<<	Left shift
&	Bitwise AND
|	Bitwise OR
^	Bitwise XOR(Exclusive OR)

FIGURE 14.1

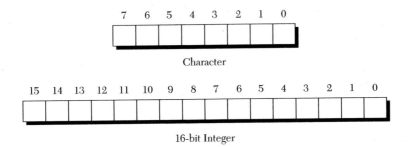

FIGURE 14.2

We begin with a plain-jane example of **showbits( )** in action.

```
/* Print binary equivalent of integers using  showbits( ) function */
# include <stdio.h>
void showbits ( int ) ;
void main( )
{
    int j ;

    for ( j = 0 ; j <= 5 ; j++ )
    {
        printf ( "\nDecimal %d is same as binary ", j ) ;
        showbits ( j ) ;
    }
}
```

And here is the output:

```
Decimal 0 is same as binary 0000000000000000
Decimal 1 is same as binary 0000000000000001
Decimal 2 is same as binary 0000000000000010
Decimal 3 is same as binary 0000000000000011
Decimal 4 is same as binary 0000000000000100
Decimal 5 is same as binary 0000000000000101
```

Let us now explore the various bitwise operators one by one.

One's Complement Operator

On taking one's complement of a number, all 1s present in the number are changed to 0s and all 0s are changed to 1s. For example, one's complement of 1010 is 0101. Similarly, one's complement of 1111 is 0000. Note that, here when we talk of a number, we are talking of the binary equivalent of the number. Thus, one's complement of 65 means one's complement of

0000 0000 0100 0001, which is the binary equivalent of 65. One's complement of 65, therefore, would be, 1111 1111 1011 1110. One's complement operator is represented by the symbol ~ (tilde). The following program shows one's complement operator in action.

```
# include <stdio.h>
void main( )
{
    int j, k ;

    for ( j = 0 ; j <= 3 ; j++ )
    {
        printf ( "\nDecimal %d is same as binary ", j ) ;
        showbits ( j ) ;
        k = ~j ;
        printf ( "\nOne's complement of %d is ", j ) ;
        showbits ( k ) ;
    }
}
```

And here is the output of the program:

```
Decimal 0 is same as binary 0000000000000000
One's complement of 0 is 1111111111111111
Decimal 1 is same as binary 0000000000000001
One's complement of 1 is 1111111111111110
Decimal 2 is same as binary 0000000000000010
One's complement of 2 is 1111111111111101
Decimal 3 is same as binary 0000000000000011
One's complement of 3 is 1111111111111100
```

In real-world situations, where could the one's complement operator be useful? Since it changes the original number beyond recognition, one potential place where it can be effectively used is in development of a file encryption utility as shown here:

```
/* File encryption utility */
# include <stdio.h>
void encrypt( ) ;
void main( )
{
    encrypt( ) ;
}

void encrypt( )
```

```
{
    FILE *fs, *ft ;
    char ch ;

    fs = fopen ( "SOURCE.C", "r" ) ; /* normal file */
    ft = fopen ( "TARGET.C", "w" ) ; /* encrypted file */

    if ( fs == NULL || ft == NULL )
    {
        printf ( "\nFile opening error!" ) ;
        exit ( 1 ) ;
    }

    while ( ( ch = getc ( fs ) ) != EOF )
        putc ( ~ch, ft ) ;

    fclose ( fs ) ;
    fclose ( ft ) ;
}
```

How would you write the corresponding decrypt function? Would there be any problem in tackling the end of file marker? It may be recalled here that the end of the file in text files is indicated by a character whose ASCII value is 26.

Right-Shift Operator

The right-shift operator is represented by >>. It needs two operands. It shifts each bit in its left operand to the right. The number of places the bits are shifted depends on the number following the operator (i.e., its right operand).

Thus, **ch >> 3** would shift all bits in **ch** three places to the right. Similarly, **ch >> 5** would shift all bits 5 places to the right.

For example, if the variable **ch** contains the bit pattern 11010111, then, **ch >> 1** would give 01101011 and **ch >> 2** would give 00110101.

Note that as the bits are shifted to the right, blanks are created on the left. These blanks must be filled somehow. They are always filled with zeros. The following program demonstrates the effect of the right-shift operator.

```
# include <stdio.h>
void showbits ( int ) ;
void main( )
{
    int i = 5225, j, k ;
```

```
printf ( "\nDecimal %d is same as binary ", i ) ;
showbits ( i ) ;

for ( j = 0 ; j <= 5 ; j++ )
{
    k = i >>j ;
    printf ( "\n%d right shift %d gives ", i, j ) ;
    showbits ( k ) ;

}
}
```

The output of the program will be:

```
Decimal 5225 is same as binary 0001010001101001
5225 right shift 0 gives 0001010001101001
5225 right shift 1 gives 0000101000110100
5225 right shift 2 gives 0000010100011010
5225 right shift 3 gives 0000001010001101
5225 right shift 4 gives 0000000101000110
5225 right shift 5 gives 0000000010100011
```

Note that if the operand is a multiple of 2, then shifting the operand one bit to the right is the same as dividing it by 2 and ignoring the remainder. Thus,

```
64 >> 1 gives 32
64 >> 2 gives 16
128 >> 2 gives 32
```

but,

```
27 >> 1 is 13
49 >> 1 is 24 .
```

A Word of Caution

In the expression **a >> b**, if **b** is negative, then the result is unpredictable. If **a** is negative, then its left-most bit (sign bit) would be 1. On some computers, right shifting **a** would result in extending the sign bit. For example, if **a** contains -1, its binary representation would be 1111111111111111. Without sign extension, the operation **a >> 4** would be 0000111111111111. However, on the machine this expression was executed the result turns out to be 1111111111111111. Thus, the sign bit 1 continues to get extended.

Left-Shift Operator

This is similar to the right-shift operator, the only difference being that the bits are shifted to the left, and for each bit shifted, a 0 is added to the right of the number. The following program should clarify this.

```
# include <stdio.h>
void showbits ( int ) ;
void main( )
{
    int i = 5225, j, k ;

    printf ( "\nDecimal %d is same as binary ", i ) ;
    showbits ( i ) ;

    for ( j = 0 ; j <= 4 ; j++ )
    {
        k = i << j ;
        printf ( "\n%d left shift %d gives ", i, j ) ;
        showbits ( k ) ;
    }
}
```

The output of the program will be:

```
Decimal 5225 is same as binary 0001010001101001
5225 left shift 0 gives 0001010001101001
5225 left shift 1 gives 0010100011010010
5225 left shift 2 gives 0101000110100100
5225 left shift 3 gives 1010001101001000
5225 left shift 4 gives 0100011010010000
```

Having acquainted ourselves with the left-shift and right-shift operators, let us now find out the practical utility of these operators.

In DOS/Windows, the date on which a file is created (or modified) is stored as a 2-byte entry in the 32-byte directory entry of that file. Similarly, a 2-byte entry is made of the time of creation or modification of the file. Remember that DOS/Windows doesn't store the date (day, month, and year) of file creation as an 8-byte string, but as a codified 2-byte entry, thereby saving 6 bytes for each file entry in the directory. The bitwise distribution of year, month, and date in the 2-byte entry is shown in Figure 14.3.

DOS/Windows converts the actual date into a 2-byte value using the following formula:

```
date = 512 * ( year - 1980 ) + 32 * month + day
```

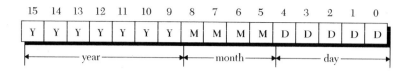

FIGURE 14.3

Suppose 09/03/1990 is the date, then on conversion the date will be,

```
date = 512 * ( 1990 - 1980 ) + 32 * 3 + 9 = 5225
```

The binary equivalent of 5225 is 0001 0100 0110 1001. This binary value is placed in the date field in the directory entry of the file as shown in Figure 14.4.

Just to verify this bit distribution, let us take the bits representing the month,

```
month = 0011
      = 1 * 2 + 1 * 1
      = 3
```

Similarly, the year and the day can also be verified.

When we issue the command DIR or use Windows Explorer to list the files, the file's date is again presented on the screen in the usual date format of mm/dd/yy. How does this integer-to-date conversion take place? Obviously, using left-shift and right-shift operators.

When we take a look at Figure 14.4 depicting the bit pattern of the 2-byte date field, we see that the year, month, and day exist as a bunch of bits in contiguous locations. Separating each of them is a matter of applying the bitwise operators.

For example, to get year as a separate entity from the 2-byte entry, we right-shift the entry by 9 (see Figure 14.5).

On similar lines, left-shifting by 7, followed by right-shifting by 12, yields the month (see Figure 14.6).

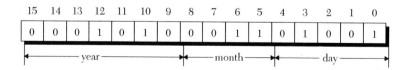

FIGURE 14.4

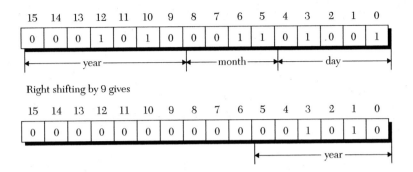

FIGURE 14.5

Finally, for obtaining the day, left-shift date by 11 and then right-shift the result by 11. Left-shifting by 11 gives 0100100000000000. Right-shifting by 11 gives 0000000000001001.

This entire logic can be put into a program as shown here:

```
/* Decoding date field in directory entry using bitwise operators */
# include <stdio.h>
void main( )
{
    unsigned int d = 9, m = 3, y = 1990, year, month, day, date ;
```

15	14	13	12	11	10	9	8	7	6	5	4	3	2	1	0
0	0							0	1	1	0	1	0	0	1

|←————— year —————→|←— month —→|←— day —→|

Left shifting by 7 gives,

15	14	13	12	11	10	9	8	7	6	5	4	3	2	1	0
0	0	1	1	0	1	0	0	1	0	0	0	1	0	1	0

|←—— month ——→|←—— day ——→|

Right shifting by 12 gives,

15	14	13	12	11	10	9	8	7	6	5	4	3	2	1	0
0	0	0	0	0	0	0	0	0	0	0	0	0	0	1	1

|←—— month —→|

FIGURE 14.6

First bit	Second bit	First bit & Second bit
0	0	0
0	1	0
1	0	0
1	1	1

FIGURE 14.7

```
date = ( y - 1980 ) * 512 + m * 32 + d ;
printf ( "\nDate = %u", date ) ;
year = 1980 + ( date >> 9 ) ;
month = ( (date << 7 ) >> 12 ) ;
day = ( (date << 11 ) >> 11 ) ;
printf ( "\nYear = %u ", year ) ;
printf ( "Month = %u ", month ) ;
printf ( "Day = %u", day ) ;
}
```

And here is the output:

```
Date = 5225
Year = 1990 Month = 3 Day = 9
```

Bitwise AND Operator

This operator is represented as **&**. Remember, it is different than **&&**, the logical AND operator. The **&** operator operates on two operands. While operating upon these two operands they are compared on a bit-by-bit basis. Hence both the operands must be of the same type (either **char** or **int**). The second operand is often called an AND mask. The **&** operator operates on a pair of bits to yield a resultant bit. The rules that decide the value of the resultant bit are shown in Figure 14.7:

This can be represented in a more understandable form as a 'truth table' shown in Figure 14.8.

&	0	1
0	0	0
1	0	1

FIGURE 14.8

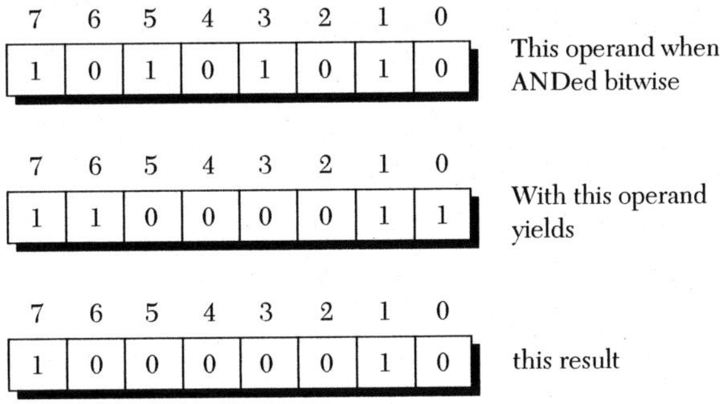

7	6	5	4	3	2	1	0
1	0	1	0	1	0	1	0

This operand when ANDed bitwise

7	6	5	4	3	2	1	0
1	1	0	0	0	0	1	1

With this operand yields

7	6	5	4	3	2	1	0
1	0	0	0	0	0	1	0

this result

FIGURE 14.9

The example given in Figure 14.9 shows more clearly what happens while ANDing one operand with another. The rules given in Figure 14.8 are applied to each pair of bits one by one.

Work through the truth table and confirm that the result obtained is really correct.

Thus, it must be clear that the operation is being performed on individual bits, and the operation performed on one pair of bits is completely independent of the operation performed on the other pairs.

Probably, the best use of the AND operator is to check whether a particular bit of an operand is ON or OFF. This is explained in the following example.

Suppose, from the bit pattern 10101101 of an operand, we want to check whether bit number 3 is ON (1) or OFF (0). Since we want to check the bit number 3, the second operand for the AND operation should be $1 * 2^3$, which is equal to 8. This operand can be represented bitwise as 00001000.

Then the ANDing operation would be,

```
10101101    Original bit pattern
00001000    AND mask
--------
00001000    Resulting bit pattern
```

The resulting value we get in this case is 8, i.e, the value of the second operand. The result turned out to be 8 since the third bit of the first operand was ON. Had it been OFF, the bit number 3 in the resulting bit pattern would have evaluated to 0 and the complete bit pattern would have been 00000000.

Thus, depending upon the bit number to be checked in the first operand, we decide the second operand, and on ANDing these two operands the result decides whether the bit was ON or OFF. If the bit is ON (1), the resulting value turns out to be a nonzero value, which is equal to the value of second operand. If the bit is OFF (0), the result is zero, as seen earlier. The following program puts this logic into action.

```
/* To test whether a bit in a number is ON or OFF */
# include <stdio.h>
void main( )
{
    int i = 65, j ;

    printf ( "\nvalue of i = %d", i ) ;
    j = i & 32 ;

    if ( j == 0 )
            printf ( "\nand its fifth bit is off" ) ;
    else
            printf ( "\nand its fifth bit is on" ) ;

    j = i & 64 ;

    if ( j == 0 )
            printf ( "\nwhereas its sixth bit is off" ) ;
    else
            printf ( "\nwhereas its sixth bit is on" ) ;
}
```

And here is the output:

```
Value of i = 65
and its fifth bit is off
whereas its sixth bit is on
```

In every file entry present in the directory, there is an attribute byte. The status of a file is governed by the value of individual bits in this attribute byte. The AND operator can be used to check the status of the bits of this attribute byte. The meaning of each bit in the attribute byte is shown in Figure 14.10.

Now, suppose we want to check whether a file is a hidden file or not. A hidden file is one that is never shown in the directory, even though it exists on the disk. From the bit classification of attribute byte in Figure 14.10, we only need to check whether bit number 1 is ON or OFF.

So, our first operand in this case becomes the attribute byte of the file in question, whereas the second operand is the $1*2^1 = 2$, as discussed earlier. Similarly, it can be checked whether the file is a system file or not, whether the file is a read-only file or not, and so on.

Bit numbers								Meaning
7	6	5	4	3	2	1	0	
.	.	.	.	.	.	.	1	Read only
.	.	.	.	.	.	1	.	Hidden
.	.	.	.	.	1	.	.	System
.	.	.	.	1	.	.	.	Volume label entry
.	.	.	1	.	.	.	.	Subdirectory entry
.	.	1	.	.	.	.	.	Archive bit
.	1	.	.	.	.	.	.	Unused
1	.	.	.	.	.	.	.	Unused

FIGURE 14.10

The second, and equally important use of the AND operator is in changing the status of the bit, or more precisely, to switch OFF a particular bit.

If the first operand happens to be 00000111, then to switch OFF bit number 1, our AND mask bit pattern should be 11111101. On applying this mask, we get,

```
00000111   Original bit pattern
11111101   AND mask
--------
00000101   Resulting bit pattern
```

Here, in the AND mask, we keep the value of all other bits as 1 except the one that is to be switched OFF (which is purposefully kept as 0). Therefore, regardless of whether the first bit is ON or OFF previously, it is switched OFF. At the same time, the value 1 provided in all the other bits of the AND mask (second operand) keeps the bit values of the other bits in the first operand unaltered.

Let's summarize the uses of the bitwise AND operator:

(a) It is used to check whether a particular bit in a number is ON or OFF.
(b) It is used to turn OFF a particular bit in a number.

Bitwise OR Operator

Another important bitwise operator is the OR operator, which is represented as |. The rules that govern the value of the resulting bit obtained after the ORing of two bits is shown in the truth table in Figure 14.11.

	0	1
0	0	1
1	1	1

FIGURE 14.11

Using the truth table, confirm the result obtained on ORing the two operands as shown here:

```
11010000    Original bit pattern
00000111    OR mask
--------
11010111    Resulting bit pattern
```

The bitwise OR operator is usually used to put ON a particular bit in a number.

Let us consider the bit pattern 11000011. If we want to put ON bit number 3, then the OR mask to be used would be 00001000. Note that all the other bits in the mask are set to 0 and only the bit, which we want to set ON in the resulting value, is set to 1.

Bitwise XOR Operator

The XOR operator is represented as $\wedge$ and is also called an Exclusive OR Operator. The OR operator returns 1, when any one of the two bits or both the bits are 1, whereas XOR returns 1 only if one of the two bits is 1. The truth table for the XOR operator is given in Figure 14.12.

The XOR operator is used to toggle a bit ON or OFF. A number XORed with another number twice gives the original number. This is shown in the following program.

```
# include <stdio.h>
void main( )
{
    int b = 50 ;
```

$\wedge$	0	1
0	0	1
1	1	0

FIGURE 14.12

```
    b = b ^ 12 ;
    printf ( "\n%d", b ) ; /* this will print 62 */

    b = b ^ 12 ;
    printf ( "\n%d", b ) ; /* this will print 50 */
}
```

THE *showbits( )* FUNCTION

We have used this function quite often in this chapter. Now we have sufficient knowledge of bitwise operators and hence are in a position to understand it. The function is given here, followed by a brief explanation.

```
showbits ( int n )
{
    int i, k, andmask ;

    for ( i = 15 ; i >= 0 ; i-- )
    {
        andmask = 1 << i ;
        k = n & andmask ;

        k == 0 ? printf ( "0" ) : printf ( "1" ) ;
    }
}
```

All that is being done in this function is using an AND operator and a variable **andmask**, to check the status of individual bits. If the bit is OFF we print a 0, otherwise we print a 1.

The first time through the loop, the variable **andmask** will contain the value 1000000000000000, which is obtained by left-shifting 1, fifteen places. If the variable **n**'s most significant bit is 0, then **k** would contain a value 0, otherwise it would contain a nonzero value. If **k** contains 0, then **printf( )** will print out 0, otherwise it will print out 1.

On the second go-around of the loop, the value of **i** is decremented and hence the value of **andmask** changes, which will now be 0100000000000000. This checks whether the next most significant bit is 1 or 0, and prints it out accordingly. The same operation is repeated for all bits in the number.

When working with computers, we are often required to use hexadecimal numbers. The reason for this is—everything a computer does is based on binary numbers, and hexadecimal notation is a convenient way of expressing binary numbers. Before justifying this statement let us first discuss what numbering systems are, why computers use binary numbering system, how binary and hexadecimal numbering systems are related, and how to use hexadecimal numbering systems in everyday life.

HEXADECIMAL NUMBERING SYSTEM

When we talk about different numbering systems we are really talking about the base of the numbering system. For example, the binary numbering system has base 2 and hexadecimal numbering system has base 16, just the way the decimal numbering system has base 10. The base represents the number of digits you can use before you run out of digits. For example, in the decimal numbering system, when we have used digits from 0 to 9, we run out of digits. That's the time we put a 1 in the column to the left—the tens column—and start constructing numbers again. This results into numbers from 10 to 99. Once we reach 99, we again run out of digits. That's when we go one column to the left—the hundreds column—and again start constructing numbers like 100, 101, 102, ..., etc., up to 999.

Since the decimal numbering system is a base 10 numbering system, any number in it is constructed using some combination of digits 0 to 9. This seems perfectly natural. However, the choice of 10 as a base is quite arbitrary, having its origin possibly in the fact that man has 10 fingers. It is very easy to use other bases as well. For example, if we wanted to use base 8, or octal numbering system, which uses only eight digits (0 to 7), here's how the counting would look:

```
0, 1, 2, 3, 4, 5, 6, 7, 10, 11,
12, .., .., 77, 100, 101, 102, .., .., 777, 1000, ..
```

Similarly, a hexadecimal numbering system has a base 16. In hex notation, the ten digits 0 through 9 are used to represent the values zero through nine, and the remaining six values, ten through fifteen, are represented by symbols A to F. The hex digits A to F are usually written in capitals, but lowercase letters are also perfectly acceptable. Here is how the counting in hex would look:

```
0, 1, 2, 3, 4, 5, 6, 7, 8, 9, A, B, C, D, E, F,
10, 11, 12, .., .., FF, 100, .., .., FFF
```

The hex numbers are built out of hex digits in much the same way the decimal numbers are built out of decimal digits. For example, when we write the decimal number 342, we mean,

```
  3 times 100 (square of 10)
+ 4 times 10
+ 2 times 1
```

Similarly, if we use number 342 as a hex number, we mean,

```
  3 times 256 (square of 16)
+ 4 times 16
+ 2 times 1
```

RELATION BETWEEN BINARY AND HEX

In the binary numbering system, there are only two digits—0 and 1. Here is how the counting in binary would look:

```
0, 1, 10, 11, 100, 101, 110, 111, 1000, 1001, 1010, .., .., 1111, 10000, ..
```

The binary numbering system is a natural system for computers because each of the thousands of electronic circuits in the computer are in one of two states—on or off. Thus, the binary numbering system corresponds nicely with the circuits in the computer—0 means off, and 1 means on. 0 and 1 are called bits, a short-form of binary digits.

Hex numbers are used primarily as shorthand for binary numbers that the computers work with. Every hex digit represents four bits of binary information as shown in Figure 14.13.

In the binary numbering system, 4 bits taken at a time can give rise to sixteen different numbers, so the only way to represent each of these

Hex	Binary	Hex	Binary
0	0000	8	1000
1	0001	9	1001
2	0010	A	1010
3	0011	B	1011
4	0100	C	1100
5	0101	D	1101
6	0110	E	1110
7	0111	F	1111

FIGURE 14.13

sixteen 4-bit binary numbers in a simple and short way is to use a base sixteen numbering system.

Suppose we want to represent a binary number 11000101 in a short way. One way is to find its decimal equivalent by multiplying each binary digit with an appropriate power of 2 as shown here:

$$1 * 2^7 + 1 * 2^6 + 0 * 2^5 + 0 * 2^4 + 0 * 2^3 + 1 * 2^2 + 0 * 2^1 + 1 * 2^0$$

which is equal to 197.

Another method is much simpler. Just look at Figure 14.13. From it, find out the hex digits for the two four-bit sets (1100 and 0101). These happen to be C and 5. Therefore, the binary number's hex equivalent is C5. You will agree this is an easier way to represent the binary number than to find its decimal equivalent. In this method, neither multiplication nor addition is needed. In fact, since there are only 16 hex digits, it's fairly easy to memorize the binary equivalent of each one. Quick now, what's binary 1100 in hex? That's right C. You are already getting the hang of it. With a little practice it is easy to translate even long numbers into hex. Thus, 1100 0101 0011 1010 binary is C53A hex.

As it happens with many unfamiliar subjects, learning hexadecimal requires a little practice. Try your hand at converting some binary numbers and vice versa. Soon you will be talking hexadecimal as if you had known it all your life.

SUMMARY

(a) To help manipulate hardware-oriented data—individual bits rather than bytes—a set of bitwise operators are used.

(b) The bitwise operators include operators like one's complement, right-shift, left-shift, bitwise AND, OR, and XOR.

(c) The one's complement converts all zeros in its operand to 1s and all 1s to 0s.

(d) The right-shift and left-shift operators are useful in eliminating bits from a number—either from the left or from the right.

(e) The bitwise AND operator is useful in testing whether a bit is on/off and in putting off a particular bit.

(f) The bitwise OR operator is used to turn on a particular bit.

(g) The XOR operator works almost the same as the OR operator except for one minor variation.

(h) It is more convenient to convert binary numbers into their hexadecimal equivalents than converting them to their decimal equivalents.

EXERCISES

[A] Answer the following:

(a) The information about colors is to be stored in bits of a **char** variable called **color**. The bit numbers 0 to 6, each represent 7 colors of a rainbow, i.e., bit 0 represents violet, 1 represents indigo, and so on. Write a program that asks the user to enter a number and based on this number it reports which colors in the rainbow the number represents.

(b) A company planning to launch a new newspaper conducts a survey. The various parameters considered in the survey were, the economic status (upper, middle, and lower class) the languages readers prefer (English, Hindi, Regional language) and category of paper (daily, supplement, tabloid). Write a program that reads the data of 10 respondents through the keyboard and stores the information in an array of integers. The bit-wise information to be stored in an integer is given here:

Bit Number	Information
0	Upper class
1	Middle class
2	Lower class
3	English
4	Hindi
5	Regional Language
6	Daily
7	Supplement
8	Tabloid

At the end, give the statistical data for the number of persons who read English daily, the number of upper class people who read tabloid, and the number of regional language readers.

(c) In an intercollege competition, various sports like cricket, basketball, football, hockey, lawn tennis, table tennis, carom and chess are played between different colleges. The information regarding the games won by a particular college is stored in bit numbers 0, 1, 2, 3, 4, 5, 6, 7, and 8, respectively, of an integer variable called **game**. The college that wins in 5 or more than 5 games is awarded the Champion of Champions trophy. If a number representing the bit pattern is entered through the keyboard, then write a program to find out whether the college won the Champion of the Champions trophy or not, along with the names of the games won by the college.

(d) An animal could be a canine (dog, wolf, fox, etc.), a feline (cat, lynx, jaguar, etc.), a cetacean (whale, narwhal, etc.) or a marsupial (koala, wombat, etc.). The information whether a particular animal is canine, feline, cetacean, or marsupial is stored in bit numbers 0, 1, 2, and 3, respectively, of an integer variable called **type**. Bit number 4 of the variable **type** stores the information about whether the animal is carnivore or herbivore.

For the following animal, complete the program to determine whether the animal is a herbivore or a carnivore. Also, determine whether the animal is a canine, feline, cetacean, or a marsupial.

```
struct animal
{
    char name[30] ;
    int type ;
}
struct animal a = { "OCELOT", 18 } ;
```

(e) The time field in the directory entry is 2 bytes long. Distribution of different bits, which account for hours, minutes, and seconds, is given in Figure 14.14. Write a function that would receive the 2-byte time entry and return to the calling function, the hours, minutes, and seconds.

(f) In order to save disk space, information about a student is stored in an integer variable. If bit number 0 is on, then it indicates Ist year student, bit number 1 to 3 stores IInd year, IIIrd year, and IVth year student, respectively. Bits 4 to 7 store the stream mechanical, chemical, electronics, and IT. The rest of the bits store room number. Based on the given data, write a program that asks for the room number and displays the information about the student, if its data exists in the array. The contents of the array are,

```
int data[ ] = { 273, 548, 786, 1096 } ;
```

15	14	13	12	11	10	9	8	7	6	5	4	3	2	1	0
H	H	H	H	H	M	M	M	M	M	M	S	S	S	S	S

FIGURE 14.14

(g) What will be the output of the following program:

```
# include <stdio.h>
void main( )
{
    int i = 32, j = 65, k, l, m, n, o, p ;
    k = i | 35 ;
    l = ~k ;
    m = i & j ;
    n = j ^ 32 ;
    o = j << 2 ;
    p = i >> 5 ;
    printf ( "\nk = %d l = %d m = %d", k, l, m ) ;
    printf ( "\nn = %d o = %d p = %d", n, o, p ) ;
}
```

Chapter **15**

MISCELLANEOUS FEATURES

The topics discussed in this chapter were either too large or far too removed from the mainstream C programming for inclusion in the earlier chapters. These topics provide certain useful programming features, and could prove to be of immense help in certain programming strategies. In this chapter, we will examine enumerated data types, the **typedef** keyword, typecasting, bit fields, function pointers, functions with a variable number of arguments and unions.

ENUMERATED DATA TYPE

The enumerated data type gives you an opportunity to invent your own data type and define what values the variable of this data type can take. This can help in making the program listings more readable, which can be an advantage when a program gets complicated or when more than one programmer will be working on it. Using enumerated the data type can also help you reduce programming errors.

As an example, one could invent a data type called **mar_status**, which can have four possible values—single, married, divorced, or widowed. Don't confuse these values with variable names; married, for instance, has the same relationship to the variable **mar_status** as the number 15 has with a variable of type **int**.

The format of the **enum** definition is similar to that of a structure. Here's how the previous example can be implemented:

```
enum mar_status
{
    single, married, divorced, widowed
} ;
enum mar_status person1, person2 ;
```

Like structures, this declaration has two parts:

(a) The first part declares the data type and specifies its possible values. These values are called 'enumerators.'
(b) The second part declares variables of this data type.

Now we can give values to these variables:

```
person1 = married ;
person2 = divorced ;
```

Remember, we can't use values that aren't in the original declaration.

Thus, the following expression would cause an error:

```
person1 = unknown ;
```

Internally, the compiler treats the enumerators as integers. Each value on the list of permissible values corresponds to an integer, starting with 0. Thus, in our example, single is stored as 0, married is stored as 1, divorced as 2, and widowed as 3.

This way of assigning numbers can be overridden by the programmer by initializing the enumerators to different integer values as shown here:

```
enum mar_status
{
    single = 100, married = 200, divorced = 300, widowed = 400
} ;
enum mar_status person1, person2 ;
```

Uses of Enumerated Data Type

Enumerated variables are usually used to clarify the operation of a program. For example, if we need to use employee departments in a payroll program, it makes the listing easier to read if we use values like assembly, manufacturing, and accounts rather than the integer values 0, 1, 2, etc. The following program illustrates this point.

```
# include <stdio.h>
# include <string.h>
void main( )
{
    enum emp_dept
    {
        assembly, manufacturing, accounts, stores
    };
    struct employee
    {
        char name[30] ;
        int age ;
        float bs ;
        enum emp_dept department ;
    };
    struct employee e ;

    strcpy ( e.name, "Lothar Mattheus" ) ;
    e.age = 28 ;
    e.bs = 5575.50 ;
    e.department = manufacturing ;
```

```
    printf ( "\nName = %s", e.name ) ;
    printf ( "\nAge = %d", e.age ) ;
    printf ( "\nBasic salary = %f", e.bs ) ;
    printf ( "\nDept = %d", e.department ) ;

    if ( e.department == accounts )
        printf ( "\n%s is an accounant", e.name ) ;
    else
        printf ( "\n%s is not an accounant", e.name ) ;
}
```

And here is the output of the program...

```
Name = Lothar Mattheus
Age = 28
Basic salary = 5575.50
Dept = 1
Lothar Mattheus is not an accountant
```

Let us now dissect the program. We first defined the data type **enum emp_dept** and specified the four possible values, namely, assembly, manufacturing, accounts, and stores. Then we defined a variable **department** of the type **enum emp_dept** in a structure. The structure, **employee**, has three other elements containing employee information.

The program first assigns values to the variables in the structure. The statement,

```
e.department = manufacturing ;
```

assigns the value manufacturing to the **e.department** variable. This is much more informative to anyone reading the program than a statement like,

```
e.department = 1 ;
```

The next part of the program shows an important weakness of using **enum** variables—there is no way to use the enumerated values directly in input/output functions like **printf( )** and **scanf( )**.

The **printf( )** function is not smart enough to perform the translation; the department is printed out as 1 and not manufacturing. Of course, we can write a function to print the correct enumerated values, using a **switch** statement, but that would reduce the clarity of the program. Even with this limitation, however, there are many situations in which enumerated variables are a godsend!

Are Enums Necessary?

Is there a way to achieve what was achieved in the previous program using enums? Yes, using macros as shown here:

```c
# include <string.h>
# define ASSEMBLY 0
# define MANUFACTURING 1
# define ACCCOUNTS 2
# define STORES 3

void main( )
{
    struct employee
    {
        char name[30] ;
        int age ;
        float bs ;
        int department ;
    };
    struct employee e ;
    strcpy ( e.name, "Lothar Mattheus" ) ;
    e.age = 28 ;
    e.bs = 5575.50 ;
    e.department = MANUFACTURING ;
}
```

If the same effect—convenience and readability—can be achieved using macros, then why should we prefer enums? Because, macros have a global scope, whereas the scope of enums can either be global (if declared outside all functions) or local (if declared inside a function).

RENAMING DATA TYPES WITH *typedef*

There is one more technique, which, in some situations, can help to clarify the source code of a C program. This technique is to make use of the **typedef** declaration. Its purpose is to redefine the name of an existing variable type.

For example, consider the following statement in which the type **unsigned long int** is redefined to the type **TWOWORDS**:

```c
typedef unsigned long int TWOWORDS ;
```

Now we can declare variables of the type **unsigned long int** by writing,

```
TWOWORDS var1, var2 ;
```

instead of

```
unsigned long int var1, var2 ;
```

Thus, **typedef** provides a short and meaningful way to call a data type. Usually, uppercase letters are used to make it clear that we are dealing with a renamed data type.

While the increase in readability is probably not great in this example, it can be significant when the name of a particular data type is long and unwieldy, as it often is with structure declarations. For example, consider the following structure declaration:

```
struct employee
{
    char name[30] ;
    int age ;
    float bs ;
};
struct employee e ;
```

This structure declaration can be made more handy to use when renamed using **typedef** as shown here:

```
struct employee
{
    char name[30] ;
    int age ;
    float bs ;
} ;
typedef struct employee EMP ;
EMP e1, e2 ;
```

Thus, by reducing the length and apparent complexity of data types, **typedef** can help to clarify source listing and save time and energy spent in understanding a program.

The previous **typedef** can also be written as:

```
typedef struct employee
{
    char name[30] ;
    int age ;
    float bs ;
} EMP ;
EMP e1, e2 ;
```

typedef can also be used to rename pointer data types as shown here:

```
struct employee
{
    char name[30] ;
    int age ;
    float bs ;
}
typedef struct employee * PEMP ;
PEMP p ;
p -> age = 32 ;
```

TYPECASTING

Sometimes we are required to force the compiler to explicitly convert the value of an expression to a particular data type. This will be clear from the following example:

```
# include <stdio.h>
void main( )
{
    float a ;
    int x = 6, y = 4 ;
    a = x / y ;
    printf ( "\nValue of a = % f", a ) ;
}
```

And here is the output:

```
Value of a = 1.000000
```

The answer turns out to be 1.000000 and not 1.5. This is because 6 and 4 are both integers and hence **6 / 4** yields an integer, 1. This 1, when stored in **a**, is converted to 1.000000. But what if we don't want the quotient to be truncated? One solution is to make either **x** or **y** a **float**. Let us say that other requirements of the program do not permit us to do this. In such a case, what do we do? Use type casting. The following program illustrates this.

```
# include <stdio.h>
void main( )
{
    float a ;
    int x = 6, y = 4 ;
    a = ( float ) x / y ;
    printf ( "\nValue of a = % f", a ) ;
}
```

And here is the output:

```
Value of a = 1.500000
```

This program uses type casting. This consists of putting a pair of parentheses around the name of the data type. In this program we said,

```
a = ( float ) x / y ;
```

The expression (**float**) causes the variable **x** to be converted from type **int** to type **float** before being used in the division operation.

Here is another example of type casting:

```
# include <stdio.h>
void main( )
{
    float a = 6.35 ;

    printf ( "\nValue of a on type casting = % d", ( int ) a ) ;
    printf ( "nValue of a = % f", a ) ;
}
```

And here is the output:

```
Value of a on type casting = 6
Value of a = 6.350000
```

Note that the value of **a** doesn't get permanently changed as a result of typecasting. Rather it is the value of the expression that undergoes type conversion whenever the cast appears.

BIT FIELDS

If, in a program, a variable is to take only two values 1 and 0, we really only need a single bit to store it. Similarly, if a variable is to take values from 0 to 3, then two bits are sufficient to store these values. And if a variable is to take values from 0 through 7, then three bits will be enough, and so on.

Why waste an entire integer when one or two or three bits will do? Well, for one thing, there aren't any one bit or two bit or three bit data types available in C. However, when there are several variables whose maximum values are small enough to pack into a single memory location, we can use 'bit fields' to store several values in a single integer. To demonstrate how bit fields work, let us consider an example. Suppose we want to store the following data about an employee. Each employee can:

(a) be male or female
(b) be single, married, divorced, or widowed
(c) have one of eight different hobbies
(d) can choose from any of the fifteen different schemes proposed by the company to pursue his/her hobby.

This means we need one bit to store gender, two to store marital status, three for hobby, and four for scheme (with one value used for those who are not desirous of availing any of the schemes). We need ten bits altogether, which means we can pack all this information into a single integer, since an integer is 16 bits long.

To do this using bit fields, we declare the following structure:

```
struct employee
{
     unsigned gender : 1 ;
     unsigned mar_stat : 2 ;
     unsigned hobby : 3 ;
     unsigned scheme : 4 ;
} ;
```

The colon in this declaration tells the compiler that we are talking about bit fields and the number after it tells how many bits to allot for the field.

Once we have established a bit field, we can reference it just like any other structure element, as shown in the program given here:

```
# include <stdio.h>
# define MALE 0 ;
# define FEMALE 1 ;
# define SINGLE 0 ;
# define MARRIED 1 ;
# define DIVORCED 2 ;
# define WIDOWED 3 ;

void main( )
{
     struct employee
     {
          unsigned gender : 1 ;
          unsigned mar_stat : 2 ;
          unsigned hobby : 3 ;
          unsigned scheme : 4 ;
     } ;
```

```
        struct employee e ;

        e.gender = MALE ;
        e.mar_status = DIVORCED ;
        e.hobby = 5 ;
        e.scheme = 9 ;

        printf ( "\nGender = %d", e.gender ) ;
        printf ( "\nMarital status = %d", e.mar_status ) ;
        printf ( "nBytes occupied by e = %d", sizeof ( e ) ) ;
}
```

And here is the output:

```
Gender = 0
Marital status = 2
Bytes occupied by e = 2
```

POINTERS TO FUNCTIONS

Every type of variable that we have discussed so far, with the exception of register, has an address. We have seen how we can reference variables of the type **char**, **int**, **float**, etc., through their addresses—that is by using pointers. Pointers can also point to C functions. And why not? C functions have addresses. If we know the function's address, we can point to it, which provides another way to invoke it. Let us see how this can be done.

```
# include <stdio.h>
void display( ) ;
void main( )
{
    printf ( "\nAddress of function display is % u", display ) ;
    display( ) ; /* usual way of invoking a function */
}

void display( )
{
    puts ( "\nLong live viruses!!" ) ;
}
```

The output of the program will be:

```
Address of function display is 1125
Long live viruses!!
```

Note that, to obtain the address of a function, all that we have to do is mention the name of the function, as has been done in the previous **printf( )** statement. This is similar to mentioning the name of the array to get its base address.

Now let us see how using the address of a function, we can manage to invoke it. This is shown in the program given here:

```
/* Invoking a function using a pointer to a function */
# include <stdio.h>
void display( ) ;
void main( )
{
    void ( *func_ptr )( ) ;

    func_ptr = display ; /* assign address of function */
    printf ( "\nAddress of function display is %u", func_ptr ) ;
    ( *func_ptr )( ) ; /* invokes the function display( ) */
}
void display( )
{
    puts ( "\nLong live viruses!!" ) ;
}
```

The output of the program will be:

```
Address of function display is 1125
Long live viruses!!
```

In **main( )**, we declare the function **display( )** as a function returning nothing. But what are we to make of the declaration,

```
void ( *func_ptr )( ) ;
```

that comes in the next line? We are obviously declaring something that, like **display( )**, will return nothing, but what is it? And why is ***func_ptr** enclosed in parentheses?

If we glance down a few lines in our program, we see the statement,

```
func_ptr = display ;
```

so we know that **func_ptr** is being assigned the address of **display( )**. Therefore, **func_ptr** must be a pointer to the function **display( )**. Thus, all that the declaration

```
void ( *func_ptr )( ) ;
```

means is, that **func_ptr** is a pointer to a function, which returns nothing. And to invoke the function, we are just required to write the statement,

```
( *func_ptr )( ) ; /* or simply, func_ptr( ) ; */
```

Pointers to functions are certainly awkward and off-putting. And why use them at all when we can invoke a function in a much simpler manner? What is the possible gain of using this esoteric feature of C? There are two possible uses:

(a) in implementing callback mechanisms used popularly in Windows programming
(b) in binding functions dynamically at runtime in C++ programming

The first of these topics is discussed briefly in Chapter 17. The second topic is beyond the scope of this book. If you want to explore it further, you can refer the book *Let Us C++* or *Test Your C++ Skills* by Yashavant Kanetkar.

FUNCTIONS RETURNING POINTERS

The way functions return an **int**, a **float**, a **double**, or any other data type, it can even return a pointer. However, to make a function return a pointer, it has to be explicitly mentioned in the calling function as well as in the function definition. The following program illustrates this.

```
int *fun( ) ;
void main( )
{
    int *p ;
    p = fun ( ) ;
}

int *fun( )
{
    static int i = 20 ;
    return ( &i ) ;
}
```

This program just indicates how an integer pointer can be returned from a function. Beyond that, it doesn't serve any useful purpose. This concept can be put to use while handling strings. For example, look at the following program, which copies one string into another and returns the pointer to the target string.

```c
char *copy ( char *, char * ) ;
void main( )
{
    char *str ;
    char *copy ( char *, char * ) ;
    char source[ ] = "Jaded" ;
    char target[10] ;

    str = copy ( target, source ) ;
    printf ( "\n%s", str ) ;
}

char *copy ( char *t, char *s )
{
    char *r ;

    r = t ;

    while ( *s != '\0' )
    {
        *t = *s ;
        t++ ;
        s++ ;
    }

    *t = '\0' ;
    return ( r ) ;
}
```

Here we have sent the base addresses of **source** and **target** strings to **copy( )**. In the **copy( )** function, the **while** loop copies the characters in the source string into the target string. Since during copying **t** is continuously incremented, before entering into the loop, the initial value of **t** is safely stored in the character pointer **r**. Once copying is over, this character pointer **r** is returned to **main( )**.

FUNCTIONS WITH A VARIABLE NUMBER OF ARGUMENTS

We have used **printf( )** so often without realizing how it works properly regardless of how many arguments we pass to it. How do we go about writing such routines that can take a variable number of arguments? And what have pointers got to do with it? There are three macros available in the file "stdarg.h" called **va_start**, **va_arg**, and **va_list** that allow us to handle this situation. These macros provide a method for accessing the arguments of the function when a function takes a fixed number of arguments followed by a variable number of arguments. The fixed number of arguments are accessed in the normal way, whereas the optional arguments are accessed using the macros **va_start** and **va_arg**. Out of these macros, **va_start** is used to initialize a pointer to the beginning of the list of optional arguments. On the other hand, the macro **va_arg** is used to advance the pointer to the next argument.

Let us put these concepts into action using a program. Suppose we wish to write a function **findmax( )**, which would find out the maximum value from a set of values, regardless of the number of values passed to it. Here is how we can do it:

```c
# include <stdarg.h>
int findmax ( int, ...) ;
void main( )
{
    int max ;

    max = findmax ( 5, 23, 15, 1, 92, 50 ) ;
    printf ( "\nmaximum = %d", max ) ;

    max = findmax ( 3, 100, 300, 29 ) ;
    printf ( "\nmaximum = %d", max ) ;
}

int findmax ( int tot_num, ...)
{
    int max, count, num ;

    va_list ptr ;

    va_start ( ptr, tot_num ) ;
    max = va_arg ( ptr, int ) ;

    for ( count = 1 ; count < tot_num ; count++ )
    {
        num = va_arg ( ptr, int ) ;
        if ( num > max )
            max = num ;
    }
```

```
        return ( max ) ;
}
```

Note how the **findmax( )** function has been declared. The ellipses (. . .) indicate that the number of arguments after the first argument will be variable.

Here we are making two calls to **findmax( )**, first to find the maximum out of 5 values and the second to find the maximum out of 3 values. Note that for each call the first argument is the count of arguments that follow the first argument. The value of the first argument passed to **findmax( )** is collected in the variable **tot_num**. **findmax( )** begins with a declaration of a pointer **ptr** of the type **va_list**. Observe the next statement carefully:

```
va_start ( ptr, tot_num ) ;
```

This statement sets up **ptr** such that it points to the first variable argument in the list. If we are considering the first call to **finndmax( )**, **ptr** would now point to 23. The statement **max = va_arg (ptr, int)** would assign the integer being pointed to by **ptr** to **max**. Thus 23 would be assigned to **max**, and **ptr** would now start pointing to the next argument, i.e., 15. The rest of the program is fairly straightforward. We just keep picking up successive numbers in the list and keep comparing them with the latest value in **max** until all the arguments in the list have been scanned. The final value in **max** is then returned to **main( )**.

How about another program to help you understand? This one calls a function **display( )**, which is capable of printing any number of arguments of any type.

```
# include <stdio.h>
# include <stdarg.h>
void display ( int, int, ...) ;
void main( )
{
    display ( 1, 2, 5, 6 ) ;
    display ( 2, 4, 'A', 'a', 'b', 'c' ) ;
    display ( 3, 3, 2.5, 299.3, -1.0 ) ;
}

void display ( int type, int num, ...)
{
    int i, j ;
    char c ;
    float f ;
    va_list ptr ;
```

```
va_start ( ptr, num ) ;
printf ( "\n" ) ;
switch ( type )
{
    case 1 :
        for ( j = 1 ; j <= num ; j++ )
        {
            i = va_arg ( ptr, int ) ;
            printf ( "%d ", i ) ;
        }
        break ;

    case 2 :
        for ( j = 1 ; j <= num ; j++ )
        {
            c = va_arg ( ptr, char ) ;
            printf ( "%c ", c ) ;
        }
        break ;

    case 3 :
        for ( j = 1 ; j <= num ; j++ )
        {
            f = ( float ) va_arg ( ptr, double ) ;
            printf ( "%f ", f ) ;
        }
}
}
```

Here we pass two fixed arguments to the function **display( )**. The first one indicates the data type of the arguments to be printed and the second indicates the number of such arguments to be printed. Once again, through the statement **va_start (ptr, num)** we set up **ptr** such that it points to the first argument in the variable list of arguments. Then, depending upon whether the value of type is 1, 2, or 3, we print out the arguments as **ints**, **chars**, or **floats**.

In all calls to **display( )**, the second argument indicated how many values we are trying to print. Contrast this with **printf( )**. To it we never pass an argument indicating how many values we are trying to print. Then how does **printf( )** figure this out? Simple. It scans the format string and counts the number of format specifiers that we have used in it to decide how many values are being printed.

UNIONS

Unions are derived data types, the way structures are. But unions have the same relationship to structures that you might have with a distant cousin who resembled you, but turned out to be smuggling contraband in Mexico. That is, unions and structures look alike, but are engaged in totally different enterprises.

Both structures and unions are used to group a number of different variables together. But while a structure enables us to treat a number of different variables stored at different places in memory, a union enables us to treat the same space in memory as a number of different variables. That is, a union offers a way for a section of memory to be treated as a variable of one type on one occasion, and as a different variable of a different type on another occasion.

You might wonder why it would be necessary to do such a thing, but we will see several practical applications of unions soon. First, let us take a look at a simple example:

```
/* Demo of union at work */
# include <stdio.h>
void main( )
{
    union a
    {
        int i ;
        char ch[2] ;
    };
    union a key ;

    key.i = 512 ;
    printf ( "\nkey.i = %d", key.i ) ;
    printf ( "\nkey.ch[0] = %d", key.ch[0] ) ;
    printf ( "\nkey.ch[1] = %d", key.ch[1] ) ;
}
```

And here is the output:

```
key.i = 512
key.ch[0] = 0
key.ch[1] = 2
```

As you can see, first we declared a data type of the type **union a**, and then a variable **key** to be of the type **union a**. This is similar to the way we first

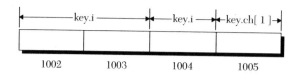

FIGURE 15.1

declare the structure type and then the structure variables. Also, the union elements are accessed exactly the same way in which the structure elements are accessed, using a '.' operator. However, the similarity ends here. To illustrate this, let us compare the following data types:

```
struct a
{
    int i ;
    char ch[2] ;
} ;
struct a key ;
```

This data type would occupy 4 bytes in memory, 2 for **key.i** and one each for **key.ch[0]** and **key.ch[1]**, as shown in Figure 15.1.

Now we declare a similar data type, but instead of using a structure we use a union.

```
union a
{
    int i ;
    char ch[2] ;
} ;
union a key ;
```

Representation of this data type in memory is shown in Figure 15.2.

As shown in Figure 15.2, the union occupies only 2 bytes in memory. Note that the same memory locations that are used for **key.i** are also being used by **key.ch[0]** and **key.ch[1]**. It means that the memory locations used by **key.i** can also be accessed using **key.ch[0]** and **key.ch[1]**. What purpose does this

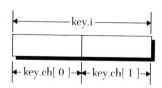

FIGURE 15.2

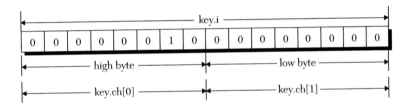

FIGURE 15.3

serve? Well, now we can access the two bytes simultaneously (by using **key.i**) or the same two bytes individually (using **key.ch[0]** and **key.ch[1]**).

This is a frequent requirement while interacting with the hardware, i.e., sometimes we are required to access two bytes simultaneously and sometimes each byte individually. Faced with such a situation, using a union is usually the answer.

Perhaps you would be able to understand the union data type more thoroughly if we take a fresh look at the output of the earlier program. Here it is:

```
key.i = 512
key.ch[0] = 0
key.ch[1] = 2
```

Let us understand this output in detail. 512 is an integer, a 2-byte number. Its binary equivalent will be 0000 0010 0000 0000. We would expect that this binary number, when stored in memory, would look as shown in Figure 15.3.

If the number is stored in this manner, then the output of **key.ch[0]** and **key.ch[1]** should have been 2 and 0. But, if you look at the output of the program, it is exactly the opposite. Why is it so? Because, in CPUs that follow little-endian architecture (Intel CPUs, for example), when a 2-byte number is stored in memory, the low byte is stored before the high byte. It means, actually, 512 would be stored in memory as shown in Figure 15.4. In CPUs with big-endian architecture this reversal of bytes does not happen.

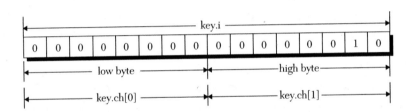

FIGURE 15.4

Now we can see why the value of **key.ch[0]** is printed as 0 and the value of **key.ch[1]** is printed as 2.

One last thing. We can't assign different values to the different union elements at the same time. That is, if we assign a value to **key.i**, it gets automatically assigned to **key.ch[0]** and **key.ch[1]**. Vice versa, if we assign a value to **key.ch[0]** or **key.ch[1]**, it is bound to get assigned to **key.i**. Here is a program that illustrates this fact.

```
# include <stdio.h>
void main( )
{
    union a
    {
        int i ;
        char ch[2] ;
    };
    union a key ;
    key.i = 512 ;
    printf ( "\nkey.i = %d", key.i ) ;
    printf ( "\nkey.ch[0] = %d", key.ch[0] ) ;
    printf ( "\nkey.ch[1] = %d", key.ch[1] ) ;

    key.ch[0] = 50 ; /* assign a new value to key.ch[0] */
    printf ( "\nkey.i = %d", key.i ) ;
    printf ( "\nkey.ch[0] = %d", key.ch[0] ) ;
    printf ( "\nkey.ch[1] = %d", key.ch[1] ) ;
}
```

And here is the output:

```
key.i = 512
key.ch[0] = 0
key.ch[1] = 2
key.i= 562
key.ch[0] = 50
key.ch[1] = 2
```

Before we move on to the next section, let us reiterate that a union provides a way to look at the same data in several different ways. For example, there can exist a union as shown here:

```
union b
{
    double d ;
    float f[2] ;
    int i[4] ;
```

```
    char ch[8] ;
};
union b data ;
```

In what different ways can the data be accessed from it? Sometimes, as a complete set of eight bytes (**data.d**), sometimes as two sets of 4 bytes each (**data.f[0]** and **data.f[1]**), sometimes as four sets of 2 bytes each (**data.i[0]**, **data.i[1]**, **data.i[2]**, and **data.[3]**) and sometimes as eight individual bytes (**data.ch[0]**, **data.ch[1]** ... **data.ch[7]**).

Also note that, there can exist a union, where each of its elements is of different size. In such a case, the size of the union variable will be equal to the size of the longest element in the union.

Union of Structures

Just as one structure can be nested within another, a union can also be nested in another union. Not only that, there can be a union in a structure, or a structure in a union. Here is an example of stuctures nested in a union.

```
# include <stdio.h>
void main( )
{
    struct a
    {
        int i ;
        char c[2] ;
    };
    struct b
    {
        int j ;
        char d[2] ;
    };
    union z
    {
        struct a key ;
        struct b data ;
    };
    union z strange ;

    strange.key.i = 512 ;
    strange.data.d[0] = 0 ;
    strange.data.d[1] = 32 ;

    printf ( "\n%d", strange.key.i ) ;
    printf ( "\n%d", strange.data.j ) ;
```

```
        printf ( "\n%d", strange.key.c[0] ) ;
        printf ( "\n%d", strange.data.d[0] ) ;
        printf ( "\n%d", strange.key.c[1] ) ;
        printf ( "\n%d", strange.data.d[1] ) ;
}
```

And here is the output:

```
512
512
0
0
32
32
```

Just as we do with nested structures, we access the elements of the union in this program using the '.' operator twice. Thus,

```
strange.key.i
```

refers to the variable **i** in the structure **key** in the union **strange**. Analysis of the output of the this program is left to the reader.

UTILITY OF UNIONS

Suppose we wish to store information about employees in an organization. The items of information are as shown here:

```
Name
Grade
Age
If Grade = HSK (Highly Skilled)
    hobbie name
    credit card no.
If Grade = SSK (Semi Skilled)
    Vehicle no.
    Distance from Co.
```

Since this is dissimilar information, we can gather it together using a structure as shown here:

```
struct employee
{
    char n[ 20 ] ;
    char grade[ 4 ] ;
    int age ;
    char hobby[10] ;
```

```
    int crcardno ;
    char vehno[10] ;
    int dist ;
} ;
struct employee e ;
```

Though grammatically there is nothing wrong with this structure, it suffers from a disadvantage. For any employee, depending upon his grade, either the fields hobby and credit card no. or the fields vehicle number and distance would get used. Both sets of fields would never get used. This would lead to a waste of memory with every structure variable that we create, since every structure variable would have all four fields apart from name, grade, and age. This can be avoided by creating a **union** between these sets of fields. This is shown here:

```
sruct info1
{
    char hobby[10] ;
    int crcardno ;
} ;
sruct info2
{
    char vehno[10] ;
    int dist ;
} ;
union info
{
    struct info1 a ;
    struct info2 b ;
} ;
struct emp
{
    char n[ 20 ] ;
    char grade[ 4 ] ;
    int age ;
    union info f ;
} ;
struct employee e ;
```

THE *volatile* QUALIFIER

When we define variables in a function, the compiler may optimize the code that uses the variable. That is, the compiler may compile the code in a manner that will run in the most efficient way possible. The compiler achieves this by using a CPU register to store the variable's value rather than storing it in a stack.

However, if we declare the variable as volatile, then it serves as a warning to the compiler that it should not *optimize* the code containing this variable. In such a case, whenever we use the variable, its value would be loaded from memory into register, operations would be performed on it, and the result would be written back to the memory location allocated for the variable.

We can declare a volatile variable as:

```
volatile int j ;
```

Another place where we may want to declare a variable as volatile is when the variable is not within the control of the program and is likely to get altered from outside the program. For example, the variable

```
volatile float temperature ;
```

might get modified through the digital thermometer attached to the computer.

SUMMARY

(a) The enumerated data type and the **typedef** declaration add to the clarity of the program.

(b) Typecasting makes the data type conversions for specific operations.

(c) When the information to be stored can be represented using a few bits of a byte we can use bit fields to pack more information in a byte.

(d) Every C function has an address that can be stored in a pointer to a function. Pointers to functions provide one more way to call functions.

(e) We can write a function that receives a variable number of arguments.

(f) Unions permit access to the same memory locations in multiple ways.

EXERCISES

[A] What will be the output of the following programs:

```
(a) # include <stdio.h>
    void main( )
```

```
{
    enum status { pass, fail, atkt } ;
    enum status stud1, stud2, stud3 ;
    stud1 = pass ;
    stud2 = fail ;
    stud3 = atkt ;
    printf ( "\n%d %d %d", stud1, stud2, stud3 ) ;
}
```

(b)
```
# include <stdio.h>
void main( )
{
    printf ( "%f", ( float ) ( ( int ) 3.5 / 2 ) ) ;
}
```

(c)
```
# include <stdio.h>
void main( )
{
    float i, j ;
    i = ( float ) 3 / 2 ;
    j = i * 3 ;
    printf ( "\n%d", ( int ) j ) ;
}
```

[B] Point out the error, if any, in the following programs:

(a)
```
# include <stdio.h>
void main( )
{
    typedef struct patient
    {
        char name[20] ;
        int age ;
        int systolic_bp ;
        int diastolic_bp ;
    } ptt ;
    ptt p1 = { "anil", 23, 110, 220 } ;
    printf ( "\n%s %d", p1.name, p1.age ) ;
    printf ( "\n%d %d", p1.systolic_bp, p1.diastolic_bp );
}
```

(b)
```
# include <stdio.h>
void show( ) ;
```

```
void main( )
{
    void ( *s )( ) ;
    s = show ;
    ( *s )( ) ;
}
void show( )
{
    printf ( "\ndon't show off. It won't pay in the long run" ) ;
}
```

(c)
```
\# include <stdio.h>
int show( ) ;
void main( )
{
    int ( *s )( ) ;
    s = show( ) ;
    ( *s )( ) ;
}
float show( )
{
    printf ( "\nControl did reach here" ) ;
    return ( 3.33 ) ;
}
```

(d)
```
# include <stdio.h>
void show ( int, float ) ;
void main( )
{
    void ( *s )( int, float ) ;
    s = show ;
    ( *s )( 10, 3.14 ) ;
}
void show ( int i, float f )
{
    printf ( "\n%d %f", i, f ) ;
}
```

[C] Attempt the following:

(a) Create an array of four function pointers. Each pointer should point to a different function. Each of these functions should receive two integers and return a float. Using a loop, call each of these functions using the addresses present in the array.

(b) Write a function that receives a variable number of arguments, where the arguments are the coordinates of a point. Based on the number of arguments received, the function should display a type of shape, like a point, line, triangle, etc., that can be drawn.

(c) Write a program that stores information about a date in a structure containing three members—day, month, and year. Using bit fields, the day number should get stored in the first 5 bits of day, the month number in 4 bits of month, and year in 12 bits of year. Write a program to read the date of joining of 10 employees and display them in ascending order of year.

(d) Write a program to read and store information about an insurance policy holder. The information contains details like gender, whether the holder is minor/major, policy name, and duration of the policy. Make use of bit-fields to store this information.

16

C Under Windows

S o far, we have learned every single keyword, operator, and instruction available in C. Thus, we are through with the language elements that were there to learn. We did all this learning by compiling our programs using a 16-bit compiler like Turbo C/C++. Now it is time to move on to more serious stuff. To make a beginning one has to take a very important decision—should we attempt to build programs that are targeted toward 16-bit environments, like MS-DOS, or 32-bit environments, like Windows/Linux. Obviously, we should choose the 32-bit platform because that is what is in commercial use today and will remain so until the 64-bit environment takes over in the future. That raises a very important question—is it futile to learn C programming using 16-bit compilers like Turbo C/C++? Absolutely not! The typical 32-bit environment offers so many features that the beginner is likely to feel lost. Contrasted with this, 16-bit compilers offer a very simple learning environment that a novice can master quickly.

Now that the C fundamentals are out of the way and you are confident about the language features, it is time for us to delve into the modern 32-bit operating environments. In today's commercial world, 16-bit operating environments, like DOS, are more or less dead. More and more software is being created for 32-bit environments like Windows and Linux. In this chapter, we will explore how C programming is done under Windows. Chapters 20 and 21 are devoted to exploring C under Linux.

WHICH WINDOWS...

To a common user, the differences amongst the various versions of Windows such as Windows 95, 98, ME, NT, 2000, XP, Server 2003, etc., is limited to only visual appearances—things like color of the title bar, shape of the buttons, desktop, task bar, menu, etc. But, the truth is much farther than that. Architecturally, there are huge differences amongst them. So many that Microsoft categorizes the different versions under two major heads— Consumer Windows and the Windows NT Family. Windows 95, 98, and ME fall under the Consumer Windows, whereas Windows NT, 2000, XP, and Vista fall under the Windows NT Family. Consumer Windows was targeted toward the home or small office users, whereas NT family was targeted toward business users. Microsoft no longer provides support for Consumer Windows. Hence, in this book, we will concentrate only on NT Family Windows. So, in the rest of this book, whenever we refer to Windows, we mean Windows NT family, unless explicitly specified.

SALIENT FEATURES OF WINDOWS PROGRAMMING

Windows OS offers a Graphical User Interface (GUI) to interact with it. Secondly, Windows OS permits a user to execute several programs simultaneously, switching effortlessly from one to another by pointing at windows and clicking them with the mouse. Mastering the GUI environment and getting comfortable with the multitasking feature is, at most, a matter of a week or so. However, from the programmer's point of view, programming for Windows is a whole new ball game!

Before we start writing C programs under Windows, let us first understand the important features of programming under the Windows environment. These are as follows:

(a) Powerful API functions
(b) Sharing of functions
(c) Consistent look and feel for all applications
(d) Hardware-independent programming
(e) Event-driven programming model

Let us discuss them one by one.

Powerful API Functions

Windows provides functions within itself that can be called the way we call any other user-defined function or library function. These functions are called API (Application Programming Interface) functions. There are literally hundreds of very rich API functions available. They help an application perform not only the simple tasks, like creating a window, drawing a line, performing file input/output, etc., but also complicated tasks, like connecting to a network, interacting with the serial port, modifying a bitmap, playing a MP3 file, etc. The key to Windows programming is to understand these API functions and use them effectively to create rich applications with effortless ease.

Sharing of Functions

A C under Windows program calls several API functions during the course of its execution. Imagine how much disk space would have been wasted had each of these functions become part of the .EXE file of each program. To avoid this, the API functions are defined in special files that have the extension .DLL. DLL stands for Dynamic Link Libraries and are binary files. The functions present in DLLs can be linked during execution. These functions can also be shared between several applications running in Windows. Since linking is done dynamically (during execution) the functions do not become part of the executable file. As a result, the size of .EXE files does not get out of hand. It is also possible to create your own DLLs. You would like to do this for two reasons:

(a) Sharing common code between different executable files.
(b) Breaking an application into component parts to provide a way to easily upgrade an application's components.

Consistent Look and Feel

Consistent look and feel means that each program offers a consistent and similar user interface. As a result, a user doesn't have to spend long periods of time mastering a new program. Every program occupies a window—a rectangular area on the screen. A window is identified by a title bar. Most program functions are initiated through the program's menu. The display of information too large to fit on a single screen can be viewed using scroll bars. Some menu items invoke dialog boxes, into which the user enters additional information. One dialog box is found in almost every Windows program. It opens a file. This dialog box looks the same (or very similar) in many different Windows programs, and it is almost always invoked from the same menu option.

Once you know how to use one Windows program, you're in a good position to easily learn another. The menus and dialog boxes allow users to experiment with a new program and explore its features. Most Windows programs have a keyboard interface, as well as a mouse interface. Although most functions of Windows programs can be controlled through the keyboard, using the mouse is often easier for many chores.

From the programmer's perspective, the consistent user interface results from using the Windows API functions for constructing menus and dialog boxes. All menus have the same keyboard and mouse interfaces because Windows—rather than the application program—handles this job.

Hardware-Independent Programming

As we saw earlier, a Windows program can always call Windows API functions. Thus, an application can easily communicate with OS. What is new in Windows is that the OS can also communicate with an application. Let us understand, with the help of an example, why it does so.

Suppose we have written a program that contains a menu item, which on selection is supposed to display a string "Hello World" in the window. The menu item can be selected either using the keyboard or using the mouse. On executing this program, it will perform the initializations and then wait for the user input. Sooner or later the user would press the key or click the mouse to select the menu-item. This key-press or mouse-click is known as an 'event.' The occurrence of this event is sensed by the keyboard or mouse device driver. The device driver would now inform Windows about it. Windows would in turn notify the application about the occurrence of this event. This notification is known as a 'message.' Thus, the OS has communicated with the application. When the application receives the message, it communicates back with the OS by calling a Windows API function to display the string "Hello World" in the window. This API function in turn communicates with the device driver of the graphics card (that drives the screen) to display the string. Thus, there is a two-way communication between the OS and the application. This is shown in Figure 16.1.

Suppose the keyboard and the mouse are now replaced with a new keyboard and mouse. Doing so would not affect the application at all. This is because at no time does the application carry out any direct communication with the devices. Any differences that may be there in the new set of mouse and keyboard would be handled by the device driver and not by the application program. Similarly, if the screen or the graphics card is replaced, no change would be required in the program. In short, hardware independence at work! At times a change of device may necessitate a change in the device driver program, but never a change in the application.

Event-Driven Programming Model

When a user interacts with a Windows program a lot of events occur. For each event, a message is sent to the program and the program reacts to it. Since the order in which the user would interact with the user-interface elements of the program cannot be predicted, the order of occurrence of events, and

FIGURE 16.1

hence the order of messages, also becomes unpredictable. As a result, the order of calling the functions in the program (that react to different messages) is dictated by the order of occurrence of events. Hence, this programming model is called the 'Event-driven Programming Model.'

There can be hundreds of ways in which the user may interact with an application. In addition to this, some events may occur without any user interaction. For example, events occur when we create a window, when the window's contents are to be drawn, etc. Thus, literally hundreds of messages may be sent to an application thereby creating chaos. Naturally, a question comes—in which order would these messages get processed by the application. Order is brought to this chaos by putting all the messages that reach the application into a 'queue.' The messages in the queue are processed in First In First Out (FIFO) order.

In fact, the OS maintains several such queues. There is one queue that is common to all applications. This queue is known as the 'System Message Queue.' In addition, there is one queue per application. Such queues are called 'Application Message Queues.' Let us understand the need for maintaining so many queues.

When we click a mouse and an event occurs, the device driver posts a message into the System Message Queue. The OS retrieves this message, then finds out to which application the message has been sent. Next, it posts a message into the Application Message Queue of the application in which the mouse was clicked. Figure 16.2 shows this complete mechanism.

That's really all there is to event-driven programming. Your job is to anticipate what users are likely to do with your application's user interface objects and have a function waiting, ready to execute at the appropriate time. Just when that time is, no one except the user can really say.

OBVIOUS PROGRAMMING DIFFERENCES

Now that we understand the Windows programming model at a macro level, let us dig further and see some obvious issues that you would be required to deal with while developing programs for the Windows environment. These include:

(a) Size of integers
(b) Heavy use of **typedef**
(c) Size of pointers

Let us discuss them one by one.

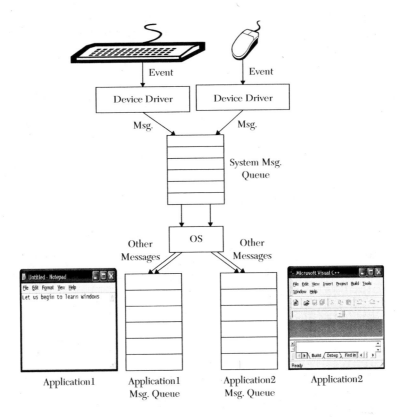

FIGURE 16.2

Integers

Under a 16-bit environment, the size of an integer is 2 bytes. Under a 32-bit environment, an integer has 4 bytes. Hence, its range is −2147483648 to +2147483647. Thus, there is no difference between an **int** and a **long int**. But what if we wish to store the age of a person in an integer? It would be improper to sacrifice a 4-byte integer for storing age when we know that age is hardly going to exceed hundred. In such a case it would be more sensible to use a **short int** since it is only 2 bytes long.

Heavy Use of *typedef*

Take a look at the following declarations:

```
COLORREF color ;
HANDLE h ;
WPARAM w ;
LPARAM l ;
```

Are COLORREF, HANDLE, etc., new datatypes? Not at all. They are merely **typedef**s of the normal integer datatype. A typical C under Windows program would contain several such **typedef**s. There are two reasons why Windows-based C programs make heavy use of **typedef**s. These are:

(a) A typical Windows program is required to perform several complex tasks. For example, a program may print documents, send emails, perform file I/O, manage multiple threads of execution, draw in a window, play sound files, or perform operations over the network, all apart from normal data processing tasks. All of these operations need to use integers. In a program that carries out such tasks, if we start using the normal integer data type to represent variables that hold different entities, we would soon lose track of what that integer value actually represents. This can be overcome by suitably using **typedef** to redefine the integer datatype as shown earlier.

(b) At several places in Windows programming we are required to gather and work with dissimilar but interrelated data. This can be done using a structure. But when we define any structure variable we are required to precede it with the keyword **struct**. This can be avoided by using **typedef** as shown here:

```
struct rect
{
    int top, left, bottom, right ;
} ;
typedef struct rect RECT ;
typedef struct rect* PRECT ;
RECT r ;
PRECT pr ;
```

What have we achieved with this? It makes user-defined data types, like structures, look, act, and behave similar to standard data types like integers, floats, etc. You would agree that the following declarations

```
RECT r ;
int i ;
```

are more logical than

```
struct RECT r ;
int i ;
```

Imagine a situation where each programmer **typedef**s the integer to represent a color in different ways. Some of these could be as follows:

```
typedef int COL ;
typedef int COLOR ;
typedef int COLOUR ;
typedef int COLORREF ;
```

To avoid this chaos, Microsoft has done several **typedef**s for commonly required entities in Windows programming. All these have been stored in header files. These header files are provided as part of 32-bit compilers like Visual C++.

Size of Pointers

Since Windows permits multiple programs to co-exist in memory, it needs powerful 32-bit microprocessor to execute these programs and ample memory to house them. Whenever we store a value at a memory location, the address of this memory location has to be stored in the CPU register at some point in time. Hence, the amount of memory that a microprocessor can access depends on the size of the CPU registers. A 32-bit microprocessor has 32-bit CPU registers. This means that we can store 2^{32} unique addresses in the CPU registers at different times. As a result, we can access 4 GB of memory locations using 32-bit registers. In our programs the 32-bit addresses have to be stored in pointers. Hence every pointer under a 32-bit environment is a 4-byte entity.

We have now covered enough ground to be able to actually start C under Windows programming. We will be using Visual C++ 6.0 to compile our C under Windows programs. Here we go. . .

THE FIRST WINDOWS PROGRAM

To keep things simple, we will begin with a program that merely displays a "Hello" message in a message box. Here is the program:

```
# include <windows.h>
int _stdcall WinMain ( HINSTANCE hInstance, HINSTANCE hPrevInstance,
                       LPSTR lpszCmdline, int nCmdShow )
{
    MessageBox ( 0, "Hello!", "Title", 0 ) ;
    return ( 0 ) ;
}
```

FIGURE 16.3

Naturally, a question should come to your mind—how do I create and run this program and what output does it produce? First, take a look at the output that it produces. Here it is in Figure 16.3.

Let us now look at the steps that one needs to carry out to create and execute this program:

(a) Start VC++ from 'Start | Programs | Microsoft Visual C++ 6.0.' The VC++ IDE window will get displayed.

(b) From the File | New menu, select 'Win32 Application,' and give a project name, say, 'sample1.' Click on OK.

(c) From the File | New menu, select 'C++ Source File,' and give a suitable file name, say, 'sample1.' Click on OK.

(d) The 'Win32 Application-Step 1 of 1' window will appear. Select the 'An empty project' option and click the 'Finish' button.

(e) A 'New Project Information' dialog will appear. Close it by clicking on OK.

(f) Again, select 'File | New | C++ Source File.' Give the file name as 'sample1.c.' Click on OK.

(g) Type the program in the 'sample1.c' file that gets opened in the VC++ IDE.

(h) Save this file using the 'Save' option from the File menu.

To execute the program, follow the steps mentioned here:

(a) From the Build menu, select 'Build sample1.exe.'

(b) Assuming that no errors were reported in the program, select 'Execute sample1.exe' from the Build menu.

Let us now try to understand the program. The way every C under DOS program begins its execution with **main( )**, every C under Windows program begins its execution with **WinMain( )**. Thus, **WinMain( )** becomes the entry point for a Windows program. A typical **WinMain( )** looks like this:

```
int __stdcall WinMain ( HINSTANCE hInstance, HINSTANCE hPrevInstance,
                        LPSTR lpszCmdLine, int nCmdShow )
```

Note the **__stdcall** before **WinMain( )**. It indicates the calling convention used by the **WinMain( )** function. Calling conventions indicate two things:

(a) The order (left to right or right to left) in which the arguments are pushed onto the stack when a function call is made.

(b) Whether the caller function or called function removes the arguments from the stack at the end of the call.

Out of the different calling conventions available, the most commonly used conventions are **__cdecl** and **__stdcall**. Both of these calling conventions pass arguments to functions from right to left. In **__cdecl**, the stack is cleaned up by the calling function, whereas, in the case of **__stdcall**, the stack is cleaned up by the called function. All API functions use **__stdcall** calling convention. If not mentioned, the **__cdecl** calling convention is assumed by the compiler.

HINSTANCE and LPSTR are nothing but **typedef**s. The first is an **unsigned int** and the second is a **pointer** to a **char**. These **typedef**s are defined in 'windows.h.' This header file must always be included while writing a C program under Windows. **hInstance**, **hPrevInstance**, **lpszCmdLine**, and **nCmdShow** are variable names. In place of these we can use simple variable names like **i**, **j**, **k**, and **l** respectively. Let us now understand the meaning of these parameters as well as the rest of the program.

—   **WinMain( )** receives four parameters, which are:

hInstance: This is the 'instance handle' for the running application. Windows creates this ID number when the application starts. We will use this value in many Windows functions to identify an application's data.

A handle is simply a 32-bit number that refers to an entity. The entity could be an application, a window, an icon, a brush, a cursor, a bitmap, a file, a device, or any such entity. The actual value of the handle is unimportant to your programs, but the Windows module that gives your program the handle knows how to use it to refer to an entity. What is important is that there is a unique handle for each entity and we can refer and reach the entity only using its handle.

hPrevInstance: This parameter is a remnant of earlier versions of Windows and is no longer significant. Now it always contains a value 0. It is being persisted with only to ensure backward compatibility.

lpszCmdLine: This is a pointer to a character string containing the command-line arguments passed to the program. This is similar to the **argv**, **argc** parameters passed to **main( )** in a DOS program.

nCmdShow: This is an integer value that is passed to the function. This integer tells the program how the window should appear when it is displayed for the first time—as a minimized window, as an icon, as a normal-sized window, or as a maximized window.

- The **MessageBox( )** function pops up a message box whose title is 'Title' and which contains a 'Hello!' message.
- Returning **0** from **WinMain( )** indicates success, whereas returning a nonzero value indicates failure.
- Instead of printing 'Hello!' in the message box we can print the command-line arguments that the user may supply while executing the program. The command-line arguments can be supplied to the program by executing it from the Start | Run menu as shown in Figure 16.4.

Note from Figure 16.4 that 'myapp.exe' is the name of our application, whereas, 'abc ijk xyz' represents command-line arguments. The parameter **lpszCmdline** points to the string "abc ijk xyz." This string can be printed using the following statement:

```
MessageBox ( 0, lpszCmdline, "Title", 0 ) ;
```

If the entire command-line, including the filename, is to be retrieved we can use the **GetCommandLine( )** function.

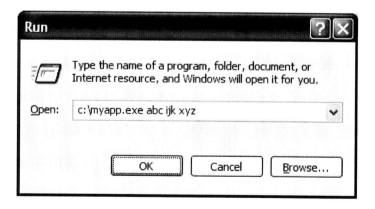

FIGURE 16.4

HUNGARIAN NOTATION

You must have observed from the program that a specific convention is being used for constructing variable names and function names. This convention is called Hungarian Notation. This variable-naming convention is so called in honor of the legendary Microsoft programmer Charles Simonyi. According to this convention, the variable name begins with a lowercase letter or letters that denotes the data type of the variable. For example, the **sz** prefix in **szCmdLine** stands for 'string terminated by zero'; the prefix **h** in **hInstance** stands for 'handle'; the prefix **n** in **nCmdShow** stands for **int**. Prefixes are often combined to form other prefixes, as **lpsz** in **lpszCmdLine** stands for 'long pointer to a zero terminated string.'

THE ROLE OF THE MESSAGE BOX

Often, during the course of execution of a program, we are required to display certain results on the screen. We do this to ascertain whether we are getting the results as per our expectations. In a sequential DOS-based program we can easily achieve this using **printf( )** statements. Under Windows, the screen is a shared resource. So you can imagine what chaos it would create if all running applications are permitted to write to the screen. You would not be able to make out which output is from which application. Hence, no Windows program is permitted to write anything directly to the screen. That's where a message box enters the scene. Using it, we can display intermediate results during the course of execution of a program. It can be dismissed either by clicking the 'close' button in its title bar or by clicking the 'OK' button present in it. There are numerous variations that you can try with the **MessageBox( )**. Some of these are given below:

```
MessageBox ( 0, "Are you sure", "Caption", MB_YESNO ) ;
MessageBox ( 0, "Print to the Printer", "Caption", MB_YESNO CANCEL) ;
MessageBox ( 0, "icon is all about style", "Caption", MB_OK |
             MB_ICONINFORMATION ) ;
```

You can put these statements within **WinMain( )** and see the results for yourself. Though the message boxes give you flexibility in displaying results, buttons, and icons, there is a limit to which you can stretch them. What if we want to draw a free hand drawing or display an image in the message box. This would not be possible. To achieve this we need to create a full-fledged window. The next section discusses how this can be done.

HERE COMES THE WINDOW...

Before we proceed with the actual creation of a window, it would be a good idea to identify the various elements of it. These elements are shown in Figure 16.5.

Note that every window drawn on the screen need not necessarily have every element shown in Figure 16.5. For example, a window may not contain the minimize box, the maximize box, the scroll bars, and the menu.

Let us now create a simple program that creates a window on the screen. Here is the program:

```
# include <windows.h>
int _stdcall WinMain ( HINSTANCE hInstance, HINSTANCE hPrevInstance,
                  LPSTR lpszCmdLine, int nCmdShow )
{
    HWND h ;

    h = CreateWindow ( "BUTTON", "Press Me",
            WS_OVERLAPPEDWINDOW, 10, 10, 150, 100, 0, 0, h, 0 ) ;
    ShowWindow ( h, nCmdShow ) ;
    MessageBox ( 0, "Hi!", "Waiting", MB_OK ) ;
    return 0 ;
}
```

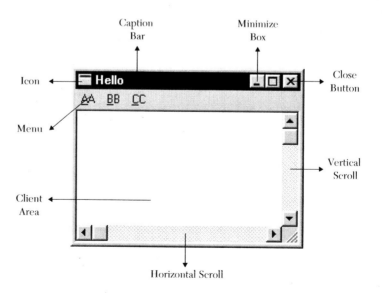

FIGURE 16.5

FIGURE 16.6

Here is the output of the program in Figure 16.6.

Let us now understand the program. Every window enjoys certain properties—background color, shape of cursor, shape of icon, etc. All these properties taken together are known as 'window class.' The meaning of 'class' here is 'type.' Windows insists that a window class should be registered with it before we attempt to create windows of that type. Once a window class is registered, we can create several windows of that type. Each of these windows would enjoy the same properties that have been registered through the window class. There are several predefined window classes. Some of these are BUTTON, EDIT, LISTBOX, etc. Our program has created a window using the predefined BUTTON class.

To actually create a window we need to call the API function **CreateWindow( )**. This function requires several parameters starting with the window class. The second parameter indicates the text that is going to appear on the button surface. The third parameter specifies the window style. The style WS_OVERLA-PPEDWINDOW is a collection of the following styles:

```
WS_OVERLAPPED | WS_CAPTION | WS_SYSMENU | WS_THICKFRAME |
WS_MINIMIZEBOX | WS_MAXIMIZEBOX
```

As you can make out from these macros, they essentially control the look and feel of the window being created. All these macros are **#define**d in the 'Windows.h' header file.

The next four parameters specify the window's initial position and size—the x and y screen coordinates of the window's top left corner and the window's width and height in pixels. The next three parameters specify the handles to the parent window, the menu, and the application instance respectively. The last parameter is a pointer to the window-creation data.

We can easily devote a section of this book to **CreateWindow( )** and its parameters. But don't get scared of it. Nobody is supposed to remember all the parameters, their meaning, and their order. You can always use MSDN (Microsoft Developer Network) to help you understand the minute details of each parameter. This help is available as part of the VC++ 6.0 product. It is also available on the net at *http://www.msdn.microsoft.com/library*.

Note that **CreateWindow( )** merely creates the window in memory. We still have to display it on the screen. This can be done using the **ShowWindow( )** API function. **CreateWindow( )** returns the handle of the created window. Our program uses this handle to refer to the window while calling **ShowWindow( )**. The second parameter passed to **ShowWindow( )** signifies whether the window would appear minimized, maximized, or normal. If the value of this parameter is **SW_SHOWNORMAL** we get a normal-sized window, if it is **SW_SHOWMINIMIZED** we get a minimized window, and if it is **SW_SHOWMINIMIZED** we get a maximized window. We have passed **nCmdShow** as the second parameter. This variable contains **SW_SHOWNORMAL** by default. Hence our program displays a normal-sized window.

On executing this program a window and a message box appears on the screen as shown in Figure 16.7. The window and the message box disappear as soon as we click on OK. This is because on doing so, control returns from **MessageBox( )** and then execution of **WinMain( )** comes to an end.

You can try to remove the call to **MessageBox( )** and see the result. You would observe that no sooner does the window appear it disappears. Thus, a

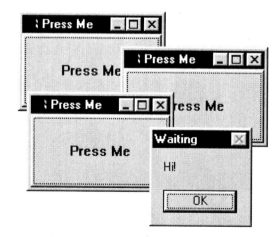

FIGURE 16.7

call to **MessageBox( )** serves a similar purpose as **getch( )** does in sequential programming.

MORE WINDOWS

Now that we know how to create a window, let us create several windows on the screen. The program to do this is given below.

```
# include <windows.h>

int _stdcall WinMain ( HINSTANCE hInstance, HINSTANCE hPrevInstance,
                       LPSTR lpszCmdLine, int nCmdShow )
{
    HWND h[10] ;
    int x ;

    for ( x = 0 ; x <= 9 ; x++ )
    {
        h[x] = CreateWindow ( "BUTTON", "Press Me",
                          WS_OVERLAPPEDWINDOW, x * 20,
                          x * 20, 150, 100, 0, 0, i, 0 ) ;
        ShowWindow ( h[x], ncmdShow ) ;
    }

    MessageBox ( 0, "Hi!", "Waiting", 0 ) ;
    return 0 ;
}
```

On execution of this program, several windows and a message box are displayed on the screen as shown in Figure 16.7

Note that each window created in this program is assigned a different handle. You may experiment a bit with this program by changing the name of the window class to EDIT and watch the result.

A REAL-WORLD WINDOW

Suppose we wish to create a window and draw a few shapes in it. For creating such a window there is no standard window class available. Hence, we would have to create our own window class, register it with Windows OS, and then create a window on the basis of it. Instead of straightway jumping to a program that draws shapes in a window, let us first write a program that creates a window using our window class and lets us interact with it. Here is the program:

```
# include <windows.h>
# include "helper.h"

void OnDestroy ( HWND ) ;

int __stdcall WinMain ( HINSTANCE hInstance, HINSTANCE hPrevInstance,
                        LPSTR lpszCmdline, int nCmdShow )
{
    MSG m ;

    /* perform application initialization */
    InitInstance ( hInstance, nCmdShow, "title" ) ;

    /* message loop */
    while ( GetMessage ( &m, 0, 0, 0 ) )
        DispatchMessage ( &m ) ;

    return 0 ;
}


LRESULT CALLBACK WndProc ( HWND hWnd, UINT message,
                           WPARAM wParam, LPARAM lParam )
{
    switch ( message )
    {
        case WM_DESTROY :
            OnDestroy ( hWnd ) ;
            break ;
        default :
            return DefWindowProc ( hWnd, message, wParam, lParam ) ;
    }
    return 0 ;
}
void OnDestroy ( HWND hWnd )
{
    PostQuitMessage ( 0 ) ;
}
```

On execution of this program the window shown in Figure 16.8 appears on the screen. We can use the minimize and the maximize button in its title bar to minimize and maximize the window. We can stretch its size by dragging its

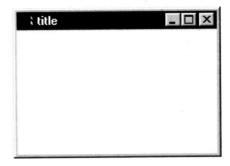

FIGURE 16.8

boundaries. Finally, we can close the window by clicking on the close window button in the title bar.

Let us now try to understand this program step by step.

Creation and Displaying of a Window

Creating and displaying a window on the screen is a 4-step process. These steps are:

(a) Creation of a window class.
(b) Registering the window class with the OS.
(c) Creation of a window based on the registered class.
(d) Displaying the window on the screen.

Creation of a window class involves the setting up of elements of a structure called **WNDCLASSEX**. These elements govern the properties of the window. Registration of a window class, creation of a window, and displaying of a window involves calling the API functions **RegisterClassEx( )**, **CreateWindow( )**, and **ShowWindow( )** respectively. Since all the 4 steps mentioned earlier would be required in almost every program in this chapter, you can write this code in a user-defined function called **InitInstance( )** in the file 'helper.h.'

Though writing code in a header file goes against the convention, you can still do so to achieve simplicity. The complete listing of the 'helper.h' file is available in Appendix E. Alternately, you can download it from the following link:

www.kicit.com/books/letusc/sourcecode/helper.h

On execution of this program, as expected, **WinMain( )** starts off by calling the function **InitInstance( )** present in the 'helper.h' file. This file has been **#include**d at the beginning of the program. Remember to copy this file to your project directory—the directory in which you are going to create this program. Once the window has been created and displayed, let us see how we can interact with it.

Interaction with Windows

As and when the user interacts with the window—by stretching its boundaries or clicking the buttons in the title bar, etc., a suitable message is posted into the message queue of our application. Our application should now pick the messages from the message queue and process them.

A message contains a message ID and some other additional information about the message. For example, for a mouse-click message, the additional information would be a handle to the window with which the user has interacted, the coordinates of the mouse cursor, and the status of, mouse buttons. Since it is difficult to memorize the message IDs, they have been suitably **#define**d in 'windows.h.' The message ID and the additional information are stored in a structure called MSG.

In **WinMain( )**, this MSG structure is retrieved from the message queue by calling the API function **GetMessage( )**. The first parameter passed to this function is the address of the **MSG** structure variable. **GetMessage( )** would pick the message info from the message queue and place it in the structure variable passed to it. Don't bother about the other parameters right now.

After picking up the message from the message queue, we need to process it. This is done by calling the **DispatchMessage( )** API function. This function does several activities. These are as follows:

(a) From the MSG structure that we pass to it, **DispatchMessage( )** extracts the handle of the window for which this message is meant for.

(b) From the handle it figures out the window class based on which the window has been created.

(c) From the window class structure it obtains the address of a function called **WndProc( )** (short for window procedure). Earlier, in **InitInstance( )**, while filling the **WNDCLASSEX** structure, one of the elements has been set up with the address of a user-defined function called **WndProc( )**.

(d) Using this address it calls the function **WndProc( )**.

Since several messages get posted into the message queue, picking of the message and processing it should be done repeatedly. Hence calls to **GetMesage( )** and **DispatchMessage( )** have been made in a **while** loop in **WinMain( )**. When **GetMessage( )** encounters a message with the

ID **WM_QUIT**, it returns a **0**. Now the control comes out of the loop and **WinMain( )**'s execution comes to an end.

Reacting to Messages

As we saw in the previous section, for every message picked up from the message queue the control is transferred to the **WndProc( )** function. This function is shown here:

```
LRESULT CALLBACK WndProc ( HWND hWnd, UINT message,
                           WPARAM wParam, LPARAM lParam )
```

This function always receives four parameters. The first parameter is the handle to the window for which the message has been received. The second parameter is the message ID, whereas the third and fourth parameters contain additional information about the message.

LRESULT is a **typedef** of a **long int** and represents the return value of this function. **CALLBACK** is a **typedef** of **__stdcall**. This **typedef** has been done in 'windows.h.' **CALLBACK** indicates that the **WndProc** function has been registered with Windows (through **WNDCLASSEX** structure in **InitInstance( )**) with an intention that Windows would call this back (through the **DispatchMessage( )** function).

In the **WndProc( )** function we have checked the message ID using a **switch**. If the ID is **WM_DESTROY**, then we have called the function **OnDestroy( )**. This message is posted to the message queue when the user clicks on the 'Close Window' button in the title bar. In the **OnDestroy( )** function we have called the API function **PostQuitMessage( )**. This function posts a **WM_QUIT** message into the message queue. As we saw earlier, when this message is picked up, the message loop and **WinMain( )** are terminated.

For all messages other than **WM_DESTROY**, the control lands in the **default** clause of **switch**. Here we have simply made a call to the **DefWindowProc( )** API function. This function does the default processing of the message that we have decided not to tackle. The default processing for a different message would be different. For example, on double-clicking the title bar, **DefWindowProc( )** maximizes the window.

Actually, when we close the window a **WM_CLOSE** message is posted into the message queue. Since we have not handled this message, the **DefWindowProc( )** function gets called to tackle this message. The **DefWindowProc( )** function destroys the window and places a **WM_DESTROY** message in the message queue. As discussed earlier, in **WndProc( )** we have made the provision to terminate the application on encountering **WM_DESTROY**.

That brings us to the end of a lonnngggg explanation! You can now heave a sigh of relief. It is recommended that you go through this explanation until you are absolutely sure that you understand every detail of it. A very clear understanding of it will help you make a good Windows programmer. For your convenience there is a flowchart of the entire working application in Figure 16.9.

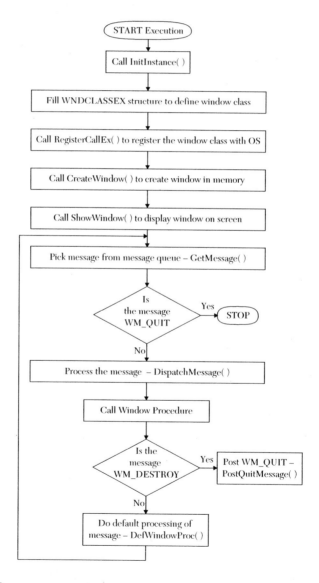

FIGURE 16.9

PROGRAM INSTANCES

Windows allows you to run more than one copy of a program at a time. This is handy for cutting and pasting between two copies of Notepad or when running more than one terminal session with a terminal emulator program. Each running copy of a program is called a 'program instance.'

Windows performs an interesting memory optimization trick. It shares a single copy of the program's code between all running instances. For example, if you get three instances of Notepad running, there will only be one copy of Notepad's code in memory. All three instances share the same code, but will have separate memory areas to hold the text data being edited. The difference between handling of the code and the data is logical, as each instance of Notepad might edit a different file, so the data must be unique to each instance. The program logic to edit the files is the same for every instance, so there is no reason why a single copy of Notepad's code cannot be shared.

SUMMARY

(a) Under Windows, an integer is four bytes long. To use a two-byte integer, prequalify it with **short**.

(b) Under Windows, a pointer is four bytes long.

(c) Windows programming involves a heavy usage of **typedef**s.

(d) DOS uses a Sequential Programming Model, whereas Windows uses an Event-driven Programming Model.

(e) Entry point of every Windows program is a function called **WinMain( )**.

(f) Under Windows, there is two-way communication between the program and the OS.

(g) Windows maintains a system message queue common for all applications.

(h) Windows maintains an application message queue per running application.

(i) Calling conventions decide the order in which the parameters are passed to a function and whether the calling function or the called function clears the stack.

(j) Commonly used calling conventions are __**cdecl** and __**stdcall**.

(k) Message boxes are often used to ascertain the flow of a program.

(l) A 'window class' specifies various properties of the window that we are creating.

(m) The header file 'Windows.h' contains declaration of several macros used in Windows programming.

(n) When the user clicks in a window, or moves the mouse pointer on the window, messages are generated and posted in the application message queue.

(o) A message contains the message ID and additional information about the message.

(p) The **GetMessage( )-DispatchMessage( )** loop breaks when **GetMessage( )** encounters the WM_QUIT message.

(q) If we don't handle a message received by our application, then the **DefWindowProc( )** function is called to do the default processing.

EXERCISES

[A] State True or False:

(a) MS-DOS uses a sequential programming model.

(b) API functions under Windows do not have names.

(c) DOS functions are called using an interrupt mechanism.

(d) One of the parameters of **WinMain( )**, called **hPrevInstance**, is no longer relevant.

(e) **MessageBox( )** is an API function.

(f) Calling the **MessageBox( )** function displays the specified string in console window.

(g) The **CreateWindow( )** function creates and displays the window on the screen.

(h) The **ShowWindow( )** function can display only the maximized window.

(i) Every window has to be created using a preregistered window class.

(j) Window classes are similar to classes in C++.

(k) We can use the predefined window classes but cannot create our own.

(l) The style WS_OVERLAPPED | WS_CAPTION | WS_MINIMIZEBOX will create a window with a caption bar and minimize box only.

(m) To be able to interact with a window it is necessary to implement the message loop.

[B] Answer the following:

(a) Why is the Event-driven Programming Model better than the Sequential Programming Model?

(b) What is the difference between an event and a message?

(c) Why does Windows maintain a different message queue for each application?

(d) In which situations do messages get posted into an application message queue?

(e) Outline the steps that a typical Windows program follows during execution.

(f) Run any Windows-based program and see whether you can identify all the elements of the application window.

(g) How would you minimize a window programmatically?

(h) What would happen if we do not place the WM_QUIT message in the message queue when the user tries to close the window.

(i) Explain the need of the **RegisterClassEx( )** function.

(j) What is the difference between the **GetMessage( )** and **DispatchMessage( )** functions?

[C] Attempt the following:

(a) Write a program that prints the value of hInstance in a message box.

(b) Write a program that displays three buttons 'Yes,' 'No,' and 'Cancel' in the message box.

(c) Write a program that receives a number as a command-line argument and prints its factorial value in a message box.

(d) Write a program that displays command-line arguments, including file name, in a message box.

(e) Write a program that receives an integer as a command-line argument, creates a button window, and, based on the value of the integer, displays a button window as maximized / minimized / normal.

(f) Try to display a window with different combinations of window styles and observe the results.

Chapter 17

GRAPHICS UNDER WINDOWS

- Graphics as of Now
- Device-Independent Drawing
- Hello Windows
- Drawing Shapes
- Types of Pens
- Types of Brushes
    - Code and Resources
- Freehand Drawing, the Paintbrush Style
    - Capturing the Mouse
- Device Context, A Closer Look
- Displaying a Bitmap
- Animation at Work
    - WM_CREATE and *OnCreate( )*
    - WM_TIMER and *OnTimer( )*
    - A Few More Points …
- Windows, the Endless World …
- Summary
- Exercises

459

Since the beginning of time, colors and shapes have fascinated mankind like nothing else. Otherwise, people would have still been using the character-oriented interfaces of MS-DOS or Unix. In fact, the graphical ability of Windows has played a very important role in its success story. Once you get a hang of how to draw inside a window it opens up immense possibilities that you never thought were possible.

GRAPHICS AS OF NOW

The world has progressed far beyond 16 colors and 640 × 480 resolution graphics that Turbo C/C++ compilers offered under the MS-DOS environment. Today, we are living in a world of 1024 × 768 resolution offering 16.7 million colors. Graphical menus, icons, colored cursors, bitmaps, wave files, and animations are the order of the day. So much so that a 16-color graphics program built using Turbo C working on a poor resolution almost hurts the eye. Moreover, with the whole lot of Windows API functions to support graphics activity, there is so much that can be achieved in a graphics program under Windows. This chapter will help you understand and appreciate these new capabilities.

DEVICE-INDEPENDENT DRAWING

Windows allows programmers to write programs to display text or graphics on the screen without concern over the specifics of the video hardware. A Windows program that works on a VGA display will work without modification on an SVGA or on an XGA display that Windows supports.

During the original design of Windows, one of the goals was to provide 'device independence.' Device independence means that the same program should be able to work using different screens, keyboards, and printers without modification to the program. Windows takes care of the differences in hardware, allowing the programmer to concentrate on the program itself. If you have ever had to update the code of an MS-DOS program for the latest printer, plotter, video display, or keyboard, you will appreciate device independence as a huge advantage for the developer.

Windows programs do not send data directly to the screen or printer. A Windows program knows where (screen/printer) its output is being sent. However, it does not know how it will be sent there, neither does it need to bother to know this. This is because Windows uses a standard and consistent way to send the output to screen/printer. This standard way uses an entity called Device Context, or simply a DC. Different DCs are associated with different devices. For example, a screen DC is associated with a screen, a printer DC is associated with a printer, etc. Any drawing that we do using the screen DC is directed to the screen. Similarly, any drawing done using the printer DC is directed to the printer. Thus, the only thing that changes from drawing on screen and drawing on printer is the DC that is used.

A Windows program obtains a handle (ID value) for the screen or printer's DC. The output data is sent to the screen/printer using its DC, and then Windows and the Device Driver for the device takes care of sending it to the real hardware. The advantage of using the DC is that the graphics and text commands that we send using the DC are always the same, regardless of where the physical output is showing up.

The part of Windows that converts the Windows graphics function calls to the actual commands sent to the hardware is the GDI, or Graphics Device Interface. The GDI is a program file called GDI32.DLL and is stored in the Windows System directory. The Windows environment loads GDI32.DLL into memory when it is needed for graphical output. Windows also loads a 'device driver' program if the hardware conversions are not part of GDI32.DLL. Common examples are VGA.SYS for VGA video screen and HPPLC.SYS for the HP LaserJet printer. Drivers are just programs that assist the GDI in converting Windows graphics commands to hardware commands.

Thus, GDI provides all the basic drawing functionality for Windows; the device context represents the device, providing a layer of abstraction that insulates your applications from the trouble of drawing directly to the hardware. The GDI provides this insulation by calling the appropriate device driver function in response to windows graphics function calls.

HELLO WINDOWS

We will begin our tryst with graphics programming under Windows by displaying a message "Hello Windows" in different fonts. Note that, though we are displaying text under Windows, even text gets drawn graphically in the window. First, take a look at the following program before we set out to understand it.

```
# include <windows.h>
# include "helper.h"
```

```
void OnPaint ( HWND ) ;
void OnDestroy ( HWND ) ;

int __stdcall WinMain ( HINSTANCE hInstance, HINSTANCE hPrevInstance,
LPSTR lpszCmdline, int nCmdShow )
{
    MSG m ;

    /* Perform application initialization */
    InitInstance ( hInstance, nCmdShow, "Text" ) ;
    /* Main message loop */
    while ( GetMessage ( &m, NULL, 0, 0 ) )
        DispatchMessage(&m);

    return 0 ;
}
LRESULT CALLBACK WndProc ( HWND hWnd, UINT message,
                           WPARAM wParam, LPARAM lParam )
{
    switch ( message )
    {
        case WM\_DESTROY :
            OnDestroy ( hWnd ) ;
            break ;
        case WM\_PAINT :
            OnPaint ( hWnd ) ;
            break ;
        default :
            return DefWindowProc ( hWnd, message, wParam, lParam ) ;
    }
    return 0 ;
}

void OnDestroy ( HWND hWnd )
{
    PostQuitMessage ( 0 ) ;
}
void OnPaint ( HWND hWnd )
{
    HDC hdc ;
    PAINTSTRUCT ps ;
    HFONT hfont ;
    LOGFONT f = { 0 } ;
    HGDIOBJ holdfont ;
```

```
char *fonts[ ] = { "Arial", "Times New Roman", "Comic Sans MS" } ;
int i ;
hdc = BeginPaint ( hWnd, &ps ) ;

for ( i = 0 ; i < 3 ; i++ )
{
        strcpy ( f.lfFaceName, fonts[ i ] ) ; /* copy font name */
        f.lfHeight = 40 * ( i + 1 ) ; /* font height */
        f.lfItalic = 1 ; /* italic */

        hfont = CreateFontIndirect ( &f ) ;
        holdfont = SelectObject ( hdc, hfont ) ;

        SetTextColor ( hdc, RGB ( 0, 0, 255 ) ) ;

        TextOut ( hdc, 10, 70 * i, "Hello Windows", 13 ) ;

        SelectObject ( hdc, holdfont ) ;
        DeleteObject ( hfont ) ;
}
        EndPaint ( hWnd, &ps ) ;
}
```

On execution of this program the window shown in Figure 17.1 appears.

Drawing to a window involves handling the **WM_PAINT** message. This message is generated whenever the client area of the window needs to be redrawn. This redrawing would be required in the following situations:

(a) When the window is displayed for the first time.
(b) When the window is minimized and then maximized.

FIGURE 17.1

(c) When some portion of the window is overlapped by another window and the overlapped window is dismissed.

(d) When the size of the window changes on stretching its boundaries.

(e) When the window is dragged out of the screen and then brought back into the screen.

Would a **WM_PAINT** message be generated when the cursor is dragged in the window? No. In this case the window saves the area overlapped by the cursor and restores it when the cursor moves to another position.

When the **switch-case** structure inside **WndProc( )** finds that the message ID passed to **WndProc( )** is **WM_PAINT**, it calls the function **OnPaint( )**. Within **OnPaint( )** we have called the API function **Begin-Paint( )**. This function obtains a handle to the device context. Additionally, it also fills the PAINTSTRUCT structure with information about the area of the window that needs to be repainted. Lastly, it removes **WM_PAINT** from the message queue. After obtaining the device context handle, the control enters a loop.

Inside the loop we have displayed "Hello Windows" in three different fonts. Each time through the loop we have setup a **LOGFONT** structure **f**. This structure is used to indicate the font properties like font name, font height, italic or normal, etc. Note that in addition to these there are other font properties that may be set up. The properties that we have not set up in the loop are all initialized to **0**. Once the font properties have been set up we call the **CreateFontIndirect( )** API function to create the font. This function loads the relevant font file. Then, using the information in the font file and the font properties set up in the **LOGFONT** structure, it creates a font in memory. **CreateFontIndirect( )** returns the handle to the font created in memory. This handle is then passed to the **SelectObject( )** API function to get the font into the DC. This function returns the handle to the existing font in the DC, which is preserved in a **holdfont** variable. Next we used the **SetTextColor( )** API function to set the color of the text to be displayed through **TextOut( )**. The **RGB( )** macro uses the red, green, and blue component values to generate a 32-bit color value. Note that each color component can take a value from **0** to **255**. To **TextOut( )** we have to pass the handle to the DC, position where the text is to be displayed, and its length.

With **hfont**, only one font can be associated at a time. Hence, before associating another font with it, we have deleted the existing font using the **DeleteObject( )** API function. Once outside the loop, we have called the **EndPaint( )** API function to release the DC handle. If not released, we would be wasting precious memory, because the device context structure would remain in memory but we would not be able access it.

In place of **TextOut( )** we can also use the **DrawText( )** API function. This function permits finer control over the way the text is displayed. You can explore this function on your own.

DRAWING SHAPES

If text is so near can graphics be far behind? Now that we know how to draw text in a window, let us now create a simple program that displays different shapes in a window. Instead of showing the entire program, the following is the listing of **OnPaint( )**. The rest of the program is same as in the previous section. Here onward, we will only be showing the **OnPaint( )** handler, unless otherwise required.

```
void OnPaint ( HWND hWnd )
{
    HDC hdc ;
    PAINTSTRUCT ps ;
    HBRUSH hbr ;
    HGDIOBJ holdbr ;
    POINT pt[5] = { 250, 150, 250, 300, 300, 350, 400, 300, 320, 190 } ;

    hdc = BeginPaint ( hWnd, &ps ) ;

    hbr = CreateSolidBrush ( RGB ( 255, 0, 0 ) ) ;
    holdbr = SelectObject ( hdc, hbr ) ;

    MoveToEx ( hdc, 10, 10, NULL ) ;
    LineTo ( hdc, 200, 10 ) ;

    Rectangle ( hdc, 10, 20, 200, 100 ) ;

    RoundRect ( hdc, 10, 120, 200, 220, 20, 20 ) ;

    Ellipse ( hdc, 10, 240, 200, 340 ) ;

    Pie ( hdc, 250, 10, 350, 110, 350, 110, 350, 10 ) ;

    Polygon ( hdc, pt, 5 ) ;

    SelectObject ( hdc, holdbr ) ;
    DeleteObject ( hbr ) ;
```

```
        EndPaint ( hWnd, &ps ) ;
}
```

On execution of this program the window shown in Figure 17.2 appears.

For drawing any shape we need a pen to draw its boundary and a brush to paint the area enclosed by it. The DC contains a default pen and brush. The default pen is a solid pen of black color and the default brush is white in color. In this program we have used the default pen and a blue colored solid brush for drawing the shapes.

As before, we begin by obtaining a handle to the DC using the **Begin-Paint( )** function. For creating a solid-colored brush we need to call the **CreateSolidBrush( )** API function. The parameter passed to this function specifies the color of the brush. This color is created as a combination of red, green, and blue components using a macro called **RGB**. Each component can take any value from 0 to 255. The function **CreateSolidBrush( )** returns the handle of the brush, which we have preserved in the **hbr** variable. Next, we have selected this brush in the DC. The handle of the default brush in DC is collected in the **holdbr** variable.

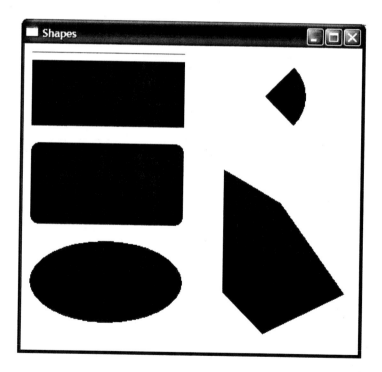

FIGURE 17.2

Once we have selected the brush into the DC, we are ready to draw the shapes. For drawing the line, we have used the **MoveToEx( )** and **LineTo( )** API functions. Similarly, for drawing a rectangle, we have used the **Rectangle( )** function.

The **RoundRect( )** function draws a rectangle with rounded corners. In **RoundRect (x1, y1, x2, y2, x3, y3)**, **x1, y1** represents the *x*- and *y*-coordinates of the upper-left corner of the rectangle. Likewise, **x2, y2** represent coordinates of the bottom right corner of the rectangle. **x3, y3** specify the width and height of the ellipse used to draw the rounded corners.

Note that the rectangle and the rounded rectangle are drawn from **x1, y1** up to **x2-1, y2-1**.

Parameters of **Ellipse( )** specify coordinates of the bounding rectangle of the ellipse.

The **Pie( )** function draws a pie-shaped wedge by drawing an elliptical arc whose center and two endpoints are joined by lines. The center of the arc is the center of the bounding rectangle specified by **x1, y1** and **x2, y2**. In **Pie(x1, y1, x2, y2, x3, y3, x4, y4)**, **x1, y1** and **x2, y2** specify the *x*- and *y*-coordinates of the upper-left corner and bottom right corner respectively, of the bounding rectangle. **x3, y3** and **x4, y4** specify the *x*- and *y*-coordinates of the arc's starting point and ending point respectively.

In **Polygon (hdc, lpPoints, nCount)**, **lpPoints** points to an array of points that specifies the vertices of the polygon. Each point in the array is a **POINT** structure. **nCount** specifies the number of vertices stored in the array. The system closes the polygon automatically, if necessary, by drawing a line from the last vertex to the first.

Once we are through with drawing the shapes, the old brush is selected back in the DC and then the brush created by us is deleted using the **DeleteObject( )** function.

TYPES OF PENS

In the previous program we used the default solid black pen of 1 pixel thickness. We can create pens of different style, color, and thickness to do our drawing. The following **OnPaint( )** handler shows how this can be achieved.

```
void OnPaint ( HWND hWnd )
{
    HDC hdc ;
    PAINTSTRUCT ps ;
    HPEN hpen ;
    HGDIOBJ holdpen ;
```

```
hdc = BeginPaint ( hWnd, &ps ) ;

hpen = CreatePen ( PS_DASH, 1, RGB ( 255, 0, 0 ) ) ;
holdpen = SelectObject ( hdc, hpen ) ;

MoveToEx ( hdc, 10, 10, NULL ) ;
LineTo ( hdc, 500, 10 ) ;

SelectObject ( hdc, holdpen ) ;
DeleteObject ( hpen ) ;

hpen = CreatePen ( PS_DOT, 1, RGB ( 255, 0, 0 ) ) ;
holdpen = SelectObject ( hdc, hpen ) ;

MoveToEx ( hdc, 10, 60, NULL ) ;
LineTo ( hdc, 500, 60 ) ;

SelectObject ( hdc, holdpen ) ;
DeleteObject ( hpen ) ;
hpen = CreatePen ( PS_DASHDOT, 1, RGB ( 255, 0, 0 ) ) ;
holdpen = SelectObject ( hdc, hpen ) ;

MoveToEx ( hdc, 10, 110, NULL ) ;
LineTo ( hdc, 500, 110 ) ;

SelectObject ( hdc, holdpen ) ;
DeleteObject ( hpen ) ;

hpen = CreatePen ( PS_DASHDOTDOT, 1, RGB ( 255, 0, 0 ) ) ;
holdpen = SelectObject ( hdc, hpen ) ;

MoveToEx ( hdc, 10, 160, NULL ) ;
LineTo ( hdc, 500, 160 ) ;

SelectObject ( hdc, holdpen ) ;
DeleteObject ( hpen ) ;

hpen = CreatePen ( PS_SOLID, 10, RGB ( 255, 0, 0 ) ) ;
holdpen = SelectObject ( hdc, hpen ) ;

MoveToEx ( hdc, 10, 210, NULL ) ;
LineTo ( hdc, 500, 210 ) ;
```

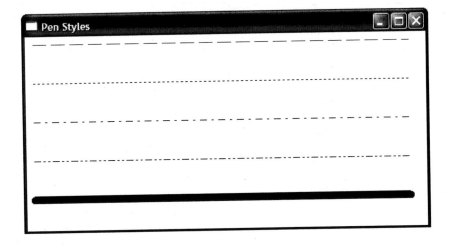

FIGURE 17.3

```
    SelectObject ( hdc, holdpen ) ;
    DeleteObject ( hpen ) ;

    EndPaint ( hWnd, &ps ) ;
}
```

On execution of this program, the window shown in Figure 17.3 appears.

A new pen can be created using the **CreatePen( )** API function. This function needs three parameters—pen style, pen thickness, and pen color. Different macros like PS_SOLID, PS_DOT, etc., have been defined in 'windows.h' to represent different pen styles. Note that, for pen styles other than PS_SOLID, the pen thickness has to be 1 pixel.

TYPES OF BRUSHES

The way we can create different types of pens, we can also create three different types of brushes. These are—solid brush, hatch brush, and pattern brush. Let us now write a program that shows how to build these brushes and then use them to fill rectangles. Here is the **OnPaint( )** handler that achieves this.

```
void OnPaint ( HWND hWnd )
{
    HDC hdc ;
    PAINTSTRUCT ps ;
```

```
            HBRUSH hbr ;
            HGDIOBJ holdbr ;
            HBITMAP hbmp ;

            hdc = BeginPaint ( hWnd, &ps ) ;

            hbr = CreateSolidBrush ( RGB (255, 0, 0 ) ) ;
            holdbr = SelectObject ( hdc, hbr ) ;

            Rectangle ( hdc, 5, 5, 105, 100 ) ;

            SelectObject ( hdc, holdbr ) ;
            DeleteObject ( hbr ) ;

            hbr = CreateHatchBrush ( HS_CROSS, RGB ( 255, 0, 0 ) ) ;
            holdbr = SelectObject ( hdc, hbr ) ;

            Rectangle ( hdc, 125, 5, 225, 100 ) ;

            SelectObject ( hdc, holdbr ) ;
            DeleteObject ( hbr ) ;

            hbmp = LoadBitmap ( hInst, MAKEINTRESOURCE ( IDB_BITMAP1 ) ) ;

            hbr = CreatePatternBrush ( hbmp ) ;
            holdbr = SelectObject ( hdc, hbr ) ;

            Rectangle ( hdc, 245, 5, 345, 100 ) ;

            SelectObject ( hdc, holdbr ) ;
            DeleteObject ( hbr ) ;
            DeleteObject ( hbmp ) ;

            EndPaint ( hWnd, &ps ) ;

            DeleteObject ( hbr ) ;
}
```

On execution of this program, the window shown in Figure 17.4 appears.

In the **OnPaint( )** handler we have drawn three rectangles—first using a solid brush, second using a hatched brush, and third using a pattern brush. Creating and using a solid brush and hatched brush is simple. We simply have to make calls to **CreateSolidBrush( )** and **CreateHatchBrush( )** respectively. For the hatch brush we have used the style HS_CROSS. There are several other styles defined in 'windows.h' that you can experiment with.

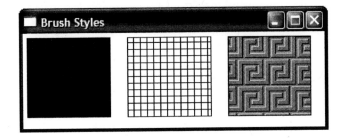

FIGURE 17.4

For creating a pattern brush, we need to first create a bitmap (pattern). Instead of creating this pattern, we have used a ready-made bitmap file. You can use any other bitmap file present on your hard disk.

Bitmaps, menus, icons, and cursors that a Windows program may use are its resources. When we compile such a program we usually want these resources to become a part of our .EXE file. If so done, we do not have to ship these resources separately. To be able to use a resource (a bitmap file in our case) it is not enough to just copy it in the project directory. Instead, we need to carry out the following steps to add a bitmap file to the project.

(a) From the 'Insert' menu option of VC++ 6.0, select the 'Resource' option.
(b) From the dialog that pops up, select 'bitmap' followed by the import button.
(c) Select the suitable .bmp file.
(d) From the 'File' menu, select the save option to save the generated resource script file (Script1.rc). When we select 'Save,' one more file called 'resource.h' also gets created.
(e) Add the 'Script1.rc' file to the project using the Project | Add to Project | Files menu option.

While using the bitmap in the program it is always referred to using an ID. The ID is **#define**d in the file 'resource.h.' Information linking the ID with the actual .bmp file on the disk has to be stored somewhere. This is done in the 'Script1.rc' file. We need to include the 'resource.h' file in the program.

To create the pattern brush we first need to load the bitmap in memory. We have done this using the **LoadBitmap( )** API function. The first parameter passed to this function is the handle to the instance of the program. When the **InitInstance( )** function is called from **WinMain( )** it stores the instance handle in a global variable **hInst**. We have passed this **hInst** to **LoadBitmap( )**. The second parameter passed to it is a string representing the bitmap. This string is created from the resource ID using the **MAKEIN-TRESOURCE** macro. The **LoadBitmap( )** function returns the handle to the bitmap. This handle is then passed to the **CreatePatternBrush( )** function. Next, this brush is selected into the DC and a rectangle is drawn using it.

Note that if the size of the bitmap is bigger than the rectangle being drawn, then the bitmap is suitably clipped. On the other hand, if the bitmap is smaller than the rectangle, it is suitably replicated.

While doing the clean up, first the brush is deleted followed by the bitmap.

Code and Resources

A program consists of both instructions and static data. Static data is that portion of the program that is not executed as machine instructions and which does not change as the program executes. Static data are character strings, data to create fonts, bitmaps, etc. The designers of Windows wisely decided that static data should be handled separately from the program code. The Windows term for static data is 'Resource data,' or simply 'Resources.' By separating static data from the program code, the creators of Windows were able to use a standard C/C++ compiler to create the code portion of the finished Windows program, and they only had to write a 'Resource compiler' to create the resources that Windows programs use. Separating the code from the resource data has other advantages, like reducing memory demands and making programs more portable. It also means that a programmer can work on the program's logic, while a designer works on how the program looks.

FREEHAND DRAWING, THE PAINTBRUSH STYLE

Even if you are knee high in computers you must have used Microsoft Paint-Brush. It provides a facility to draw a freehand drawing using a mouse. Let us see if we too can achieve this. We can indicate where the freehand drawing begins by clicking the left mouse button. Then, as we move the mouse on the table with the left mouse button depressed, the freehand drawing should get drawn in the window. This drawing should continue until we do not release the left mouse button.

The mouse input comes in the form of messages. For freehand drawing we need to tackle three mouse messages—**WM_LBUTTONDOWN** for a left-button click, **WM_MOUSEMOVE** for mouse movement, and **WM_LBUTTONUP** for releasing the left mouse button. Let us now see how these messages are tackled for drawing freehand. The **WndProc( )** function and the message handlers that perform this task are given here:

```
int x1, y1, x2, y2 ;

LRESULT CALLBACK WndProc ( HWND hWnd, UINT message,
                                WPARAM wParam, LPARAM lParam )
{
    switch ( message )
    {
        case WM\_DESTROY :
            OnDestroy ( hWnd ) ;
            break ;

        case WM_LBUTTONDOWN :
            OnLButtonDown ( hWnd, LOWORD ( lParam ),
                                HIWORD ( lParam ) ) ;
            break ;

        case WM_LBUTTONUP :
            OnLButtonUp( ) ;
            break ;

        case WM_MOUSEMOVE :
            OnMouseMove ( hWnd, wParam, LOWORD ( lParam ),
                                    HIWORD ( lParam ) ) ;
            break ;

        default:
            return DefWindowProc ( hWnd, message, wParam, lParam ) ;
    }
    return 0 ;
}

void OnLButtonDown ( HWND hWnd, int x, int y )
{
    SetCapture ( hWnd ) ;
    x1 = x ;
    y1 = y ;
}

void OnMouseMove ( HWND hWnd, int flags, int x, int y )
{
    HDC hdc ;
    RECT r ;
```

```
            if ( flags == MK\_LBUTTON ) /* is left mouse button depressed */
            {
                hdc = GetDC ( hWnd ) ;
                GetClientRect ( hWnd, \& r ) ;
                if ( x >= r.left && x <= r.right && y >= r.top && y <= r.bottom )
                {
                    x2 = x ;
                    y2 = y ;
                    MoveToEx ( hdc, x1, y1, NULL ) ;
                    LineTo ( hdc, x2, y2 ) ;

                    ReleaseDC ( hWnd, hdc ) ;

                    x1 = x2 ;
                    y1 = y2 ;
                }
            }
        }
        void OnLButtonUp( )
        {
            ReleaseCapture( ) ;
        }
```

On execution of this program, the window shown in Figure 17.5 appears. We can now click the left mouse button with the mouse pointer placed anywhere in the window. We can then drag the mouse on the table to draw the freehand. The freehand drawing will continue until we release the left mouse button.

It appears that, for drawing freehand, we should simply receive the mouse coordinates as it is moved and then highlight the pixels at these coordinates using the **SetPixel( )** API function. However, if we do so, the freehand would be broken at several places. This is because, usually, the mouse is dragged pretty fast, whereas the mouse move messages don't arrive so fast. A solution to this problem is to construct the freehand using small little line segments. This is what has been done in our program. These lines are so small is size that you would not even recognize that the freehand has been drawn by connecting these small lines.

Let us now discuss each mouse handler. When the **WM_LBUTTON-DOWN** message arrives, the **WndProc( )** function calls the handler **OnLButtonDown( )**. While doing so, we have passed the mouse coordinates where the click occurred. These coordinates are obtained in **lParam** in **Wnd-Proc( )**. In **lParam** the low-order 16 bits contain the current x-coordinate of the mouse, whereas the high-order 16 bits contain the y-coordinate. The

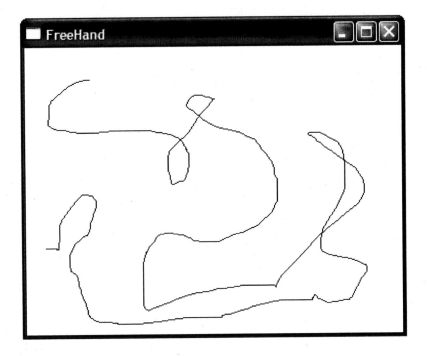

FIGURE 17.5

LOWORD and **HIWORD** macros have been used to separate out these x- and y-coordinates from **lParam**.

In **OnLButtonDown( )** we have preserved the starting point of freehand in global variables **x1** and **y1**.

When **OnMouseMove( )** gets called, it checks whether the left mouse button stands depressed. If it stands depressed, then the **flags** variable contains **MK_LBUTTON**. If it does, then the current mouse coordinates are set up in the global variables **x2, y2**. A line is then drawn between **x1, y1** and **x2, y2** using the functions **MoveToEx( )** and **LineTo( )**. Next time around, **x2, y2** should become the starting point of the next line. Hence the current values of **x2, y2** are stored in **x1, y1**.

Note that, here we have obtained the DC handle using the API function **GetDC( )**. This is because we are carrying out the drawing activity in reaction to a message other than **WM_PAINT**. Also, the handle obtained using **GetDC( )** should be released using a call to the **ReleaseDC( )** function.

You can try using **BeginPaint( ) / EndPaint( )** in mouse handlers and **GetDC( ) / ReleaseDC( )** in **OnPaint( )**. Can you draw any conclusions?

Capturing the Mouse

If, in the process of drawing freehand, the mouse cursor goes outside the client area, then the window below our window would start getting mouse messages. So our window would not receive any messages. If this has to be avoided, then we should ensure that our window continues to receive mouse messages even when the cursor goes out of the client area of our window. The process of doing this is known as mouse capturing.

We have captured the mouse in the **OnLButtonDown( )** handler by calling the API function **SetCapture( )**. As a result, the program continues to respond to mouse events during freehand drawing even if the mouse is moved outside the client area. In the **OnLButtonUp( )** handler we have released the captured mouse by calling the **ReleaseCapture( )** API function.

DEVICE CONTEXT, A CLOSER LOOK

Now that we have written a few programs and are comfortable with the idea of selecting objects like font, pen, and brush into the DC, it is time for us to understand how Windows achieves the device-independent drawing using the concept of DC. In fact, a DC is nothing but a structure that holds handles of various drawing objects like font, pen, brush, etc. A screen DC and its working is shown in Figure 17.6.

You can make following observations from Figure 17.6:

(a) The DC doesn't hold the drawing objects like pen, brush, etc. It merely holds their handles.

(b) With each DC, a default monochrome bitmap of size 1 pixel x 1 pixel is associated.

(c) Default objects like black pen, white brush, etc., are shared by different DCs in the same or different applications.

(d) The drawing objects that an application explicitly creates can be shared within DCs of the same application, but is never shared between different applications.

(e) Two different applications would need two different DCs even though both would be used to draw to the same screen. In other words, with one screen multiple DCs can co-exist.

(f) A common Device Driver would serve the drawing requests coming from different applications. (Truly speaking, the request comes from GDI functions that our application calls).

Screen and printer DC is OK, but what purpose would a memory DC serve? Well, that is what the next program will explain.

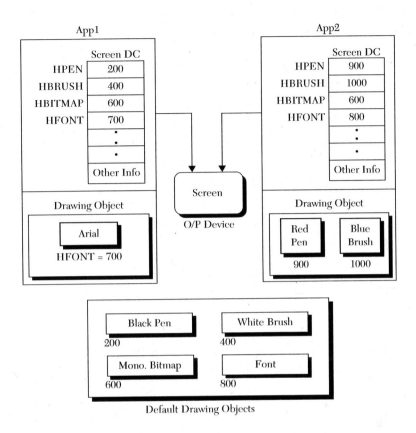

FIGURE 17.6

DISPLAYING A BITMAP

We are familiar with drawing normal shapes on screen using a device context. How about drawing images on the screen? Windows does not permit displaying a bitmap image directly using a screen DC. This is because there might be color variations in the screen on which the bitmap was created and the screen on which it is being displayed. To account for such possibilities while displaying a bitmap Windows uses a different mechanism—a 'Memory DC.'

The way anything drawn using a screen DC goes to screen, anything drawn using a printer DC goes to a printer, similarly, anything drawn using a memory DC goes to memory (RAM). But where in RAM—in the 1 × 1 pixel bitmap whose handle is present in memory DC. (Note that this handle was of little use in the case of screen/printer DC.) Thus, if we attempt to draw a line using a memory DC, it would end up on the 1 × 1 pixel bitmap. You will

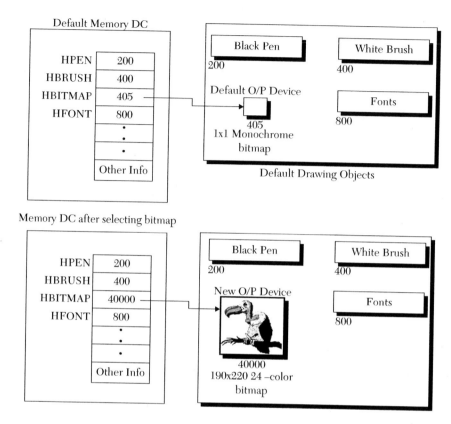

FIGURE 17.7

agree that 1 × 1 is too small a place to draw even a small line. Therefore, we need to expand the size and color capability of this bitmap. How can this be done? Simple, just replace the handle of the 1 × 1 bitmap with the handle of a bigger and colored bitmap object. This is shown in Figure 17.7.

What purpose would just increasing the bitmap size/color serve? Whatever we draw here would get drawn on the bitmap but would still not be visible. We can make it visible by simply copying the bitmap image (including what has been drawn on it) to the screen DC by using the API function **BitBlt( )**.

Before transferring the image to the screen DC we need to make the memory DC compatible with the screen DC. Here 'making compatible' means making certain adjustments in the contents of the memory DC structure. Looking at these values, the screen device driver would suitably adjust the colors when the pixels in the bitmap of memory DC is transferred to screen DC using the **BitBlt( )** function.

Let us now take a look at the program that puts all these concepts in action. The program merely displays the image of a vulture in a window. Here is the code:

```
void OnPaint ( HWND hWnd )
{
    HDC hdc ;
    HBITMAP hbmp ;
    HDC hmemdc ;
    HGDIOBJ holdbmp ;
    PAINTSTRUCT ps ;

    hdc = BeginPaint ( hWnd, &ps ) ;

    hbmp = LoadBitmap ( hInst, MAKEINTRESOURCE ( IDB_BITMAP1 ) ) ;

    hmemdc = CreateCompatibleDC ( hdc ) ;
    holdbmp = SelectObject ( hmemdc, hbmp ) ;

    BitBlt ( hdc, 10, 20, 190, 220, hmemdc, 0, 0, SRCCOPY ) ;

    EndPaint ( hWnd, &ps ) ;

    SelectObject ( hmemdc, holdbmp ) ;
    DeleteObject ( hbmp ) ;
    DeleteDC ( hmemdc ) ;
}
```

On executing the program, we get the window shown in Figure 17.8.

As usual, we begin our drawing activity in **OnPaint( )** by first getting the screen DC using the **BeginPaint( )** function. Next, we loaded the vulture bitmap image in memory by calling the **LoadBitmap( )** function. Its usage is similar to what we saw while creating a pattern brush in an earlier section of this chapter. Then we created a memory device context and made its properties compatible with that of the screen DC. To do this, we called the API function **CreateCompatibleDC( )**. Note that we have passed the handle to the screen DC to this function. The function in turn returns the handle to the memory DC. After this, we have selected the loaded bitmap into the memory DC. Lastly, we have performed a bit block transfer (a bit-by-bit copy) from memory DC to screen DC using the function **BitBlt( )**. As a result of this the vulture now appears in the window.

We have made the call to **BitBlt( )** as shown here:

```
BitBlt ( hdc, 10, 20, 190, 220, hmemdc, 0, 0, SRCCOPY ) ;
```

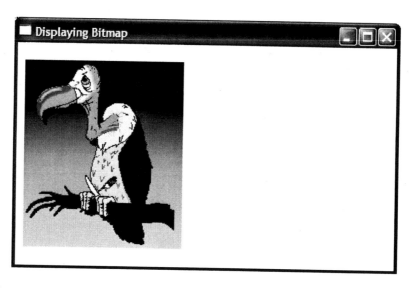

FIGURE 17.8

Let us now understand its parameters. These are as follows:

    hdc—Handle to target DC where the bitmap is to be blitted

    10, 20—Position where the bitmap is to be blitted

    190, 220—Width and height of bitmap being blitted

    0, 0—Top left corner of the source image. If we give 10, 20, then the image from 10, 20 to the bottom right corner of the bitmap would get blitted.

    SRCCOPY—Specifies one of the raster-operation codes. These codes define how the color data for the source rectangle is to be combined with the color data for the destination rectangle to achieve the final color. SRCCOPY means that the pixel color of source should be copied onto the destination pixel of the target.

ANIMATION AT WORK

Speed is the essence of life. So having the ability to display a bitmap in a window is fine, but if we can add movement and sound to it there's nothing like it. So let us now see how to achieve this animation and sound effect.

    If we are to animate an object in the window we need to carry out the following steps:

(a) Create an image that to animate, as a resource.

(b) Prepare the image for later display.

(c) Repeatedly display this prepared image at suitable places in the window, taking care that when the next image is displayed the previous image is erased.

(d) Check for collisions while displaying the prepared image.

Let us now write a program that on execution makes a red-colored ball move in the window. As the ball strikes the walls of the window a noise occurs. Note that the width and height of the red-colored ball is 22 pixels. The following is the **WndProc( )** function and the various message handlers that help achieve animation and sound effects.

```
HBITMAP hbmp ;
int x, y ;
HDC hmemdc ;
HGDIOBJ holdbmp ;

LRESULT CALLBACK WndProc ( HWND hWnd, UINT message,
                           WPARAM wParam, LPARAM lParam )
{
    switch ( message )
    {
        case WM_DESTROY :
            OnDestroy ( hWnd ) ;
            break ;
        case WM_CREATE :
            OnCreate ( hWnd ) ;
            break ;
        case WM_TIMER :
            OnTimer ( hWnd ) ;
            break ;
        default :
            return DefWindowProc ( hWnd, message, wParam, lParam ) ;
    }
    return 0 ;
}

void OnCreate ( HWND hWnd )
{
    RECT r ;
    HDC hdc ;

    hbmp = LoadBitmap ( hInst, MAKEINTRESOURCE ( IDB_BITMAP1 ) ) ;

    hdc = GetDC ( hWnd ) ;
```

```
        hmemdc = CreateCompatibleDC ( hdc ) ;
        holdbmp = SelectObject ( hmemdc, hbmp ) ;

        ReleaseDC ( hWnd, hdc ) ;

        srand ( time ( NULL ) ) ;

        GetClientRect ( hWnd, \& r ) ;

        x = rand( ) % r.right - 22 ;
        y = rand( ) % r.bottom - 22 ;

        SetTimer ( hWnd, 1, 50, NULL ) ;
}
void OnDestroy ( HWND hWnd )
{
        KillTimer ( hWnd, 1 ) ;
        SelectObject ( hmemdc, holdbmp ) ;
        DeleteDC ( hmemdc ) ;
        DeleteObject ( hbmp ) ;
        PostQuitMessage ( 0 ) ;
}

void OnTimer ( HWND hWnd )
{
        HDC hdc ;
        RECT r ;
        const int wd = 22, ht = 22 ;
        static int dx = 10, dy = 10 ;

        hdc = GetDC ( hWnd ) ;
        BitBlt ( hdc, x, y, wd, ht, hmemdc, 0, 0, WHITENESS ) ;
        GetClientRect ( hWnd, &r ) ;

        x += dx ;
        if ( x < 0 )
        {
            x = 0 ;
            dx = 10 ;
            PlaySound ("chord.wav", NULL, SND_FILENAME | SND_ASYNC ) ;
        }
        else if ( x > ( r.right - wd ) )
        {
            x = r.right - wd ;
```

```
        dx = -10 ;
        PlaySound ("chord.wav", NULL, SND_FILENAME | SND_ASYNC ) ;
    }
    y += dy ;
    if ( y < 0 )
    {
        y = 0 ;
        dy = 10 ;
        PlaySound ("chord.wav", NULL, SND_FILENAME | SND_ASYNC ) ;
    }
    else if ( y > ( r.bottom - ht ) )
    {
        y = r.bottom - ht ;
        dy = -10 ;
        PlaySound ( "chord.wav", NULL, SND_FILENAME | SND_ASYNC );
    }

    BitBlt ( hdc, x, y, wd, ht, hmemdc, 0, 0, SRCCOPY ) ;
    ReleaseDC ( hWnd, hdc ) ;
}
```

From the **WndProc( )** function you can observe that we have handled two new messages here—**WM_CREATE** and **WM_TIMER**. For these messages we have called the handlers **OnCreate( )** and **OnTimer( )** respectively. Let us now understand these handlers one by one.

WM_CREATE and *OnCreate( )*

The **WM_CREATE** message arrives whenever a new window is created. Since a window is usually created only once, the one-time activity that is to be carried out in a program is usually done in the **OnCreate( )** handler. In our program, to make the ball move we need to display it at different places at different times. To do this it will be necessary to blit the ball image several times. However, we need to load the image only once. As this is a one-time activity, it has been done in the handler function **OnCreate( )**.

You are already familiar with the steps involved in preparing the image for blitting—loading the bitmap, creating a memory DC, making it compatible with screen DC, and selecting the bitmap in the memory DC.

Apart from preparing the image for blitting, we have also done some intialializations, like setting up values in some variables to indicate the initial position of the ball. We have also called the **SetTimer( )** function. This function tells Windows to post a message, **WM_TIMER**, into the message queue of our application every 50 milliseconds.

WM_TIMER and *OnTimer( )*

If we are to perform an activity at regular intervals we have two choices:

(a) Use a loop and monitor within the loop when is it time to perform that activity.

(b) Use the Windows timer mechanism. This mechanism, when used, posts a WM_TIMER message at regular intervals to our application.

The first method would seriously hamper the responsiveness of the program. If the control is within the loop and a new message arrives, the message would not get processed unless the control goes out of the loop. The second choice is better because it makes the program event driven. That is, whenever **WM_TIMER** arrives its handler does the job that we want to get periodically executed. At other times the application is free to handle other messages that come to its queue.

All that we have done in the **OnTimer( )** handler is erase the ball from a previous position and draw it at a new position. We have also checked if the ball has hit the boundaries of the window. If so, we have played a sound file using the **PlaySound( )** API function and then changed the direction of the ball.

A Few More Points . . .

A few more points worth noting before we close our discussion on animation . . .

(a) One application can set up multiple timers to do different jobs at different intervals. Hence we need to pass the ID of the timer that we want to set up to the **SetTimer( )** function. In our program we have specified the ID as 1.

(b) For multiple timers, Windows will post multiple **WM_TIMER** messages. Each time it will pass the timer ID additional information about the message.

(c) For drawing, as well as erasing, the ball we have used the same function—**BitBlt( )**. While erasing we have used the raster operation code **WHITENESS**. When we use this code the color values of the source pixels get ignored. Thus, red-colored pixels of the ball would get ignored leading to erasure of the ball in the window.

(d) The size of the client area of the window can be obtained using the **GetClientRect( )** API function.

(e) We want that every time we run the application the initial position of the ball should be different. To ensure this we have generated its initial x, y coordinates using the standard library function **rand( )**. However, this function doesn't generate true random numbers. To ensure that we do get true random numbers, somehow we need to tie the random number generation with time, as time of each execution of our program would be different. This has been achieved by making the call

```
srand ( time ( NULL ) ) ;
```

Here, **time( )** is a function that returns the time. We have further passed this time to the **srand( )** function.

(f) To be able to use the **rand( )** and **srand( )** functions include the file 'stdlib.h.' Similarly, for the **time( )** function to work include the file 'time.h.'

(g) In the call to the **PlaySound( )** function, the first parameter is the name of the wave file that is to be played. If the first parameter is filename, then the second has to be NULL. The third parameter is a set of flags. **SND_FILENAME** indicates that the first parameter is the filename, whereas **SND_ASYNC** indicates that the sound should be played in the background.

(h) To be able to use the **PlaySound( )** function we need to link the library 'winmm.lib.' This is done by using the 'Project | Settings' menu item. On selection of this menu item a dialog pops up. In the 'Link' tab of this dialog mention the name 'winmm.lib' in the 'Object / Library modules' edit box.

(i) When the application terminates we have to instruct Windows not to send **WM_TIMER** messages to our application any more. For this we have called the **KillTimer( )** API function, passing to it the ID of the timer.

WINDOWS, THE ENDLESS WORLD . . .

The biggest hurdle in Windows programming is a sound understanding of its programming model. In this chapter and the previous chapter, we have tried to catch the essence of Windows' Event-driven Programming model. Once you understand it thoroughly the rest is just a matter of understanding and calling the suitable API functions to get your job done. Windows API is truly an endless world. It covers areas like Networking, Internet programming, Telephony, Drawing and Printing, Device I/O, Imaging, Messaging, Multimedia, Windowing, Database programming, and Shell programming, to name a few. The programs that we have written have merely scratched the surface. No matter how many programs that we write under Windows, several more still remain to be written. The intention of this chapter was to unveil before you, to give you the first glimpse, of what is possible under Windows. The intention all along was not to catch fish for you, but to show you how to catch fish so that you can go fishing all your life. Having made a sound beginning, the rest is for you to explore.

SUMMARY

(a) In DOS, programmers had to write separate graphics code for every new video adapter. In Windows, the code, once written, works on any video adapter.

(b) A Windows program cannot draw directly on an output device like a screen or printer. Instead, it draws to the logical display surface using device context.

(c) When the window is displayed for the first time, or when it is moved or resized, the **OnPaint( )** handler gets called.

(d) It is necessary to obtain the device context before drawing text or graphics in the client area.

(e) A device context is a structure containing information required to draw on a display surface. The information includes color of pen and brush, screen resolution, color palettes, etc.

(f) To draw using a new pen or brush, it is necessary to select them into the device context.

(g) If we don't select any brush or pen into the device context, then the drawing drawn in the client area would be drawn with the default pen (black pen) and default brush (white brush).

(h) RGB is a macro representing the Red, Green, and Blue elements of a color. RGB (0, 0, 0) gives black color, whereas RGB (255, 255, 255) gives white color.

(i) Animation involves repeatedly drawing the same image at successive positions.

EXERCISES

[A] State True or False:

(a) Device independence means the same program is able to work using different screens, keyboards, and printers without modifications to the program.

(b) The WM_PAINT message is generated whenever the client area of the window needs to be redrawn.

(c) The API function **EndPaint( )** is used to release the DC.

(d) The default pen in the DC is a solid pen of white color.

(e) The pen thickness for the pen style other than PS_SOLID has to be 1 pixel.

(f) **BeginPaint( )** and **GetDC( )** can be used interchangeably.

(g) If we drag the mouse from (10, 10) to (110, 100), 100 WM_MOUSEMOVE messages would be posted into the message queue.

(h) The WM_PAINT message is raised when the window contents are scrolled.

(i) With each DC a default monochrome bitmap of size 1 pixel × 1 pixel is associated.

(j) The WM_CREATE message arrives whenever a window is displayed.

[B] Answer the following:

(a) What is meant by Device-independent Drawing and how it is achieved?

(b) Explain the significance of the WM_PAINT message.

(c) How does Windows manage the code and various resources of a program?

(d) What do you mean by 'capturing' a mouse?

(e) Write down the steps that need to be carried out to animate an object.

[C] Attempt the following:

(a) Write a program that displays "hello" at any place in the window where you click the left mouse button. If you click the right mouse button, the color of subsequent "hello"s should change.

(b) Write a program that would draw a line by joining the new point where you have clicked the left mouse button with the last point where you clicked the left mouse button.

(c) Write a program to gradient fill the entire client area with shades of blue color.

(d) Write a program to create chessboard like boxes (8 × 8) in the client area. If the window is resized the boxes should also get resized so that all 64 boxes are visible at all times.

(e) Write a program that displays only the upper half of a bitmap of size 40 × 40.

(f) Write a program that displays different text in different colors and fonts at different places after every 10 seconds.

Chapter 18   INTERNET PROGRAMMING

All successful people are usually well connected. It has become an important ingredient for the 'success' formula. Computing has taken this connectedness to the next logical step. 'Every device and person will ultimately get connected to every other device and person'—that is where network programming is headed. Therefore, learning and knowing network programming has become more relevant today than ever before.

Often, we need our application to write some data into a file stored on a remote machine connected through the network, display some message on the desktop of a remote machine, or simply exchange messages across the machines connected to the network. Using the Windows Socket Library (commonly known as WinSock) accessing data from another machine or writing data to it has become as simple as doing these jobs on a local machine.

NETWORK COMMUNICATION

Network communication is much like the normal postal communication where the goal is to send/receive letters. There are five players involved in this process:

- The person who will send a letter
- The apartment address to which the letter should be sent
- The apartment mailbox into which the letter will finally land
- The postal network to move the letter from city to city
- The rules, such as writing the address in legible form, stamping the envelope, dropping the envelope in letter box, etc.

In computer networks, there are also five players involved when sending messages from one computer to another:

- The application that will send a message (similar to person)
- The address of the machine to which the message will be sent (similar to an apartment address)
- The port number to which the message will finally be delivered. In a machine there may be several applications that are communicating with applications on other machines. To ensure that message meant for one application is not accidentally delivered to another application, each application uses a specific port number for communication.
- The wired or wireless computer network to make the communication between machines possible.

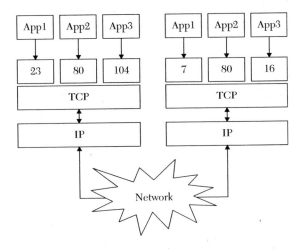

FIGURE 18.1

— The set of rules (commonly called protocols) that the network, computers, and applications agree upon to make the communication meaningful.

The protocols that are commonly used in network communication are TCP (Transmission Control Protocol) and IP (Internet Protocol). Out of these, the IP protocol indicates how to move the data across the network. The TCP protocol is responsible for error detection, retransmission, congestion control, and flow control end-to-end. In a computer network, the machines may be in different cities separated by several thousand miles. As a result, there may be several possible paths along which data can be transmitted from the source machine to the destination machine. To decide which out of the several interconnecting paths is least congested, devices called 'routers' are put in the network. The routers route the data from one machine to another along the least congested path. The network itself (the routers) needs only to support the IP protocol, whereas the endpoints (computers) support the TCP protocol.

Figure 18.1 captures the essence of what we have discussed in the previous paragraphs.

PACKETS AND SOCKETS

Traditional telecommunications links transmit data as a series of bytes, characters, or bits alone. Unlike this, in a computer network data is transmitted in the form of packets. Once the data is formatted into a packet, the network can transmit longer messages more efficiently and reliably.

A packet consists of three elements—header, payload, and trailer. As the names suggest, the header and trailer are used to mark the beginning of the packet and end of the packet, whereas payload contains the actual data that is to be transmitted. The technical word for a packet is a 'datagram.'

Another term that is commonly used in network communication is socket. A socket is one of the endpoints in a communication channel. A socket is used by applications as an interface to the underlying network and protocols. Applications that communicate with one another in a network carry out the communication using sockets. Windows provides a set of API functions for creating sockets and sending/receiving packets through them. This set of functions is commonly known as Winsock API.

BEFORE WE START...

There are a few things to go over before we can actually start socket programming. Unless you know them thoroughly, we cannot begin our first program—so make sure that you understand them clearly.

Protocols

Network communication is very complex. It involves taking decisions about how to create packets, how to detect and correct errors in transmission of data, which path to use for sending packets from one machine to another, how to support multiple OS, how to deal with heterogeneous network cabling, etc. To make this complexity more manageable, the different aspects of network communication is divided into layers. Each layer can use different protocols. The layers, along with the commonly used protocols in each layer, are given here:

Application Layer—HTTP, SMTP, POP3, FTP
Transport Layer—TCP, UDP
Network Layer—IP, ICMP
Physical Layer—Ethernet

There are many more protocols available in each layer than the ones mentioned. All of these protocols are implemented as a protocol stack by the OS (Operating System) and its components.

The Ethernet physical layer indicates how bits will be transmitted through different physical media (network cables, such as CAT5, fiber optic, etc.) at different speeds.

The IP protocol serves two important purposes:

(a) It provides for transmitting blocks of data from the source machine (often called the host) to the destination machine (host). Hosts are identified by a unique address.

(b) IP fragments large blocks at the source and reassembles them at destination. This is necessary to ensure smooth transmission of data through networks that cannot handle a single large block of data.

IP is a best-effort protocol. It doesn't guarantee the correctness of the delivered data. The packets may be lost, may get duplicated, or may be delivered out of order. These aspects of packet delivery are addressed by a transport layer protocol like TCP and UDP.

The protocols used in the application layer are chosen based on what the application intends to do. For example, for browsing the Internet, the HTTP protocol is used, for email the SMTP and POP3 protocols are used.

Most of our programs in this chapter will use the protocols in the application layer.

IP Addresses

To be able to identify the computers in a computer and carry out communication between them using Internet Protocol (IP), each of them has to be assigned a unique address. This address is called an IP address. Regardless of the number of machines in the network, the IP address of each machine is always 4 bytes long. Thus, there can be 2^{32} unique IP addresses. These addresses are commonly written using 4 numbers (one number per byte) in a dotted-decimal notation. In this notation, each byte in the IP address is separated using a dot. One example of this notation is IP address 192.168.100.10.

To avoid miscommunication between machines in a network, their IP addresses must be unique. This uniqueness can be achieved in the case of small networks, especially when these networks are not connected to the outside world. However, to guarantee uniqueness of IP addresses in big networks spanning cities and continents, the IP addresses are created and managed by a central authority called the Internet Assigned Numbers Authority (IANA). IANA allocates superblocks of addresses to Regional Internet Registrars. These, in turn, allocate smaller blocks to Internet Service Providers and enterprises, who in turn further allocate the addresses to individual devices.

Port Numbers

It is common to send emails through your email application at the same time as you download a file from a website. Here, the email application is communicating with an email server program residing on another machine, whereas the web browser is communicating with a web server program running on yet another machine. The IP address of the machine on which the email application and the web browser is running is the same. In such a case, the data sent by the web server should not go to the email application; similarly, the data sent by the email server should not go to the web browser. To avoid such situations the email application and the web browser use different port numbers on the same machine (IP address) for carrying out communication. These ports are not physical ports and should not be confused with serial, parallel, or USB ports. Standard applications use standard port numbers.

Email programs and web browsers are standard applications. Hence they use standard port numbers. After call, you should not be required to make a phone call to the place where the web server is present and ask which port number it is using so that you can send a request to it for downloading a file. IANA is responsible for assigning standard port numbers. Port numbers used by applications that use some common protocols are as follows:

HTTP—80
SMTP—25
POP3—110
FTP—20, 21
Time—37
Telnet—23
Whois—43

There is another important reason why the idea of port numbers was created. The network link speed is usually so high that one application would not be able to use the entire capacity of the connection by itself. For example, when you visit a website and a page is downloaded in your browser, unless you click a link and make a request for another page, the network link is idle. Hence, to meaningfully utilize the capacity of the network link, it becomes important to be able to share the same link for multiple applications. This means multiple applications running on the machine will use the same IP address of the machine, but different port numbers.

Byte Ordering

Different types of machines may use different byte orders. For example, consider a 32-bit hexadecimal number AABBCCDD. Some machines may store this number in the order AABBCCDD, whereas some other may store it in the order DDCCBBAA. The first machine in this case is called big-endian, whereas the other is known as little-endian. As you can see, in a little-endian machine the lower-order byte is stored earlier than the higher-order byte.

When this 32-bit number is transmitted over the IP network, the bytes are always transmitted in a big-endian order.

Suppose the little-endian machine is to send the 32-bit number to the big-endian machine. Now it would be necessary to first convert the number to big-endian order before transmitting it over the network. Vice versa, if the big-endian machine is to transmit a 32-bit number, it has to be converted to a little-endian order when it is received on the little-endian machine.

The byte ordering used on the host is called host byte-ordering, whereas the one-used by the network is called network byte-ordering. Any words sent through the network should be converted to network byte-order prior to transmission and back to host byte-order once received. To facilitate this conversion Windows Socket API defines a set of functions to convert 16-bit and 32-bit integers to and from network byte order. These functions are:

htonl( )—Host-to-Network-long
htons ( )—Host-to-Network-short
ntohl( )—Network-to-Host-long
ntohs ( )—Network-to-Host-short

GETTING STARTED . . .

Having had a reasonable introduction to network communication, let us now write our first socket program. Here it is:

```
# include "stdafx.h"
# include <windows.h>
# include <winsock.h>
# include <stdio.h>

int APIENTRY WinMain ( HINSTANCE hInstance, HINSTANCE
                       hPrevInstance, LPSTR lpCmdLine, int nCmdShow )
{
    WSADATA ws ;
    char buf[ 1000 ], buf1[ 100 ], buf2[ 100 ], buf3[ 100 ], buf4[ 100 ],
        buf5[ 100 ], buf6[ 100 ] ;

    WSAStartup ( 0x0101, &ws ) ;

    buf[ 0 ] = "" ;

    sprintf ( buf1,"\nWinsock Ver Requested : %d.%d",
            HIBYTE ( ws.wVersion ), LOBYTE ( ws.wVersion ) ) ;
```

```
sprintf ( buf2,"\nWinsock Ver Available : %d.%d",
          HIBYTE ( ws.wHighVersion ), LOBYTE ( ws.wHighVersion ) ) ;
sprintf ( buf3,"\nCurrent WinSock Implementation : %s",
          & ws.szDescription ) ;
sprintf ( buf4, "\nSystem Status : %s", &ws.szSystemStatus ) ;
sprintf ( buf5, "\nMaximum Sockets : %u",ws.iMaxSockets ) ;
sprintf ( buf6, "\nMaximum message size : %u",ws.iMaxUdpDg ) ;
strcat ( strcat ( strcat ( strcat ( strcat ( strcat ( buf, buf1 ),
         buf2 ), buf3 ), buf4 ), buf5 ), buf6 ) ;
MessageBox ( 0, buf, "Info", 0 ) ;
WSACleanup( ) ;

return 0 ;
}
```

Here is the output of the program, shown in Figure 18.2:

Let us now try to understand the program. In **WinMain( )** we have called a function **WSAStartUp( )**. This function has to be called in every socket-based program. This function initiates the use of WSOCK32.DLL by our program. Unless **WSAStartup( )** is called, other winsock functions cannot be called.

We have passed two parameters to the **WSAStartup( )** function—a value 0x0101 and address of the structure variable of type **WSADATA**. There are two versions of the winsock library available—version 1.1 and version 2.0. By passing **0x0101** to **WSAStartup( )** we are indicating that we propose to use winsock version 1.1 for our program. The **WSADATA** structure is declared in the file **winsock.h**. Once called, **WSAStartup( )** fills up the structure variable and returns 0 if successful. We have then gathered the contents of

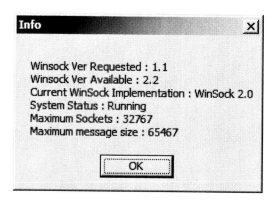

FIGURE 18.2

the structure into a variable **buf** and displayed them on the screen using a call to **MessageBox( )**. The HIBYTE and LOBYTE macros are used to separate the high and the low bytes from a 2-byte integer (word).

Note that you need to create this program as a Win32 application in VC++ 6.0. Once you have typed the program, add 'wsock32.lib' in the 'Link' tab of the 'Project | Settings' menu. If you propose to use winsock version 2.0 in your program, then you need to add the file 'ws2_32.lib' in the 'Link' tab. Note that the wsock32.lib and ws2_32.ib files contain only the list of the winsock functions. The actual definitions of functions belonging to version 1.1 and 2.0 are present in the files 'wsock32.dll' and 'ws2_32.dll' respectively.

At the end we have called the function **WSACleanup( )** to allow the winsock DLL (WSOCK32.DLL or WS2_32.DLL) to free any resources for the application.

WHAT'S THE TIME NOW

There are several time servers available on the Internet that maintain an accurate measure of current time. We can easily write a program to connect to one of these servers and obtain the current date and time. The program given below demonstrates how this can be achieved.

```
# include "stdafx.h"
# include <windows.h>
# include <winsock.h>
# include <stdlib.h>
# include <stdio.h>

# define BUFSIZE 16 // maximum buffer size
# define LINESIZE 99 // maximum line length
# define BASE1900 9435484800

char *timeservers[ ] = {

                        "129.6.15.28",
                        "129.6.15.29",
                        "132.163.4.101",
                        "132.163.4.102",
                        "132.163.4.103",
                        "128.138.140.44",
                        "192.43.244.18",
                        "131.107.1.10",
                        "69.25.96.13",
```

```
                                    "216.200.93.8",
                                    "208.184.49.9",
                                    "207.126.98.204",
                                    "207.200.81.113",
                                    "64.236.96.53"

                    } ;

ULONG BufToUL ( unsigned char * ) ;
void DisplayTime ( ULONG ) ;

int__stdcall WinMain ( HINSTANCE hInstance, HINSTANCE hPrevInstance,
char *lpszCmdline, int nCmdShow )
{
    WSADATA ws ;
    SOCKET hSocket ;
    int ret ;
    SOCKADDR_IN sa ;
    char sendbuffer[ ] = "send anything to get the server's attention" ;
    unsigned char recvbuffer[ BUFSIZE ] = { 0 } ;
    ULONG numsec ;
    char str1[ 50 ], str2[ 50 ] ;

    WSAStartup ( 0x0101, &ws ) ;

    hSocket = socket ( AF_INET, SOCK_DGRAM, 0 ) ;
    if ( hSocket == INVALID_SOCKET )
    {
        MessageBox ( 0, "Could not create socket", "Error", 0 ) ;
        WSACleanup( ) ;
        return 1 ;
    }

    sa.sin_family = AF_INET;
    sa.sin_addr.s_addr = inet_addr ( timeservers[ 4 ] ) ;
    sa.sin_port = htons ( IPPORT_TIMESERVER ) ;
    ret = sendto ( hSocket, sendbuffer, sizeof ( sendbuffer ), 0,
                   ( sockaddr * )&sa, sizeof ( SOCKADDR_IN ) ) ;
    if ( ret == SOCKET_ERROR )
    {
        MessageBox ( 0, "Could not send packet", "Error", 0 ) ;
        WSACleanup( ) ;
        return 1 ;
    }

    int nAddrSize = sizeof ( SOCKADDR_IN ) ;
```

```
        ret = recvfrom ( hSocket, ( char * ) recvbuffer, BUFSIZE, 0,
                        ( sockaddr * )& sa, & nAddrSize ) ;
    if ( ret == SOCKET_ERROR )
    {
          MessageBox ( 0, "Could not receive data", "Error", 0 ) ;
          WSACleanup( ) ;
          return 1 ;
    }

    numsec = BufToUL ( recvbuffer ) ;
    _ultoa ( numsec, str1, 10 ) ;

    sprintf ( str2, "Seconds since Jan 1, 1900 = %s", str1 );
    MessageBox ( 0, str2, "Time Reported", 0 ) ;

    DisplayTime ( numsec ) ;

    WSACleanup( ) ;
    return 0 ;
}


ULONG BufToUL ( unsigned char *pbuf )
{
 return ( ( ULONG ) pbuf[ 0 ] << 24) + ( ( ULONG ) pbuf[ 1 ] << 16 ) +
        ( ( ULONG ) pbuf[ 2 ] << 8 ) + ( ULONG )pbuf[ 3 ] ;
}


void DisplayTime ( ULONG seconds )
{
    char str[ LINESIZE ] ;
    SYSTEMTIME st ;
    FILETIME ft, localft ;
    char *day[ ] = { "Sun", "Mon", "Tue", "Wed", "Thu", "Fri", "Sat" } ;

    _int64 thistime = BASE1900 + seconds ;
    thistime *= 10000000 ;
    ft.dwHighDateTime = ( DWORD ) ( thistime >> 32 ) ;
    ft.dwLowDateTime = ( DWORD ) thistime ;
    FileTimeToLocalFileTime ( &ft, &localft ) ;
    FileTimeToSystemTime ( &localft, &st ) ;
    sprintf ( str, "%s %u-%u-%u %u:%u:%u", day[ st.wDayOfWeek ],
                st.wDay, st.wMonth, st.wYear,
                st.wHour, st.wMinute, st.wSecond ) ;
    MessageBox ( 0,str, "Time", 0 ) ;
}
```

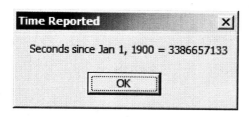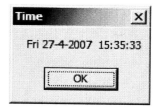

FIGURE 18.3

In Figure 18.3 is the output of the program.

As in the previous program, here, too, we have begun by calling **WSAStartup( )** to initiate the use of WSOCK32.DLL by our program. Once this is done, we need to carry out the following steps:

(a) Create a socket
(b) Send a request to the time server using this socket
(c) Receive the date and time in the response from the time server.

Let us now understand these steps in detail.

Creation of a Socket

Socket is a communication endpoint. When we create a socket we must specify for communication with another machine which protocols it will use in the network layer and transport layer. We should also indicate the style of communication that we intend to carry out using this socket. The prototype of the **socket( )** function is as follows:

```
socket ( address family, style, protocol ) ;
```

In the first parameter we provide the network layer protocol. Since we want to use IP protocol at the network layer, we have specified this using the macro AF_INET.

In the second parameter we need to provide the style of communication. The **socket( )** function supports two communication styles defined by the macros SOCK_STREAM and SOCK_DGRAM. Each communication style has different characteristics. For example, the SOCK_STREAM style is like a pipe. Once this socket establishes a communication (pipe) with a particular remote socket, it can transmit data reliably as a stream of bytes.

The SOCK_DGRAM style is used for sending individually addressed datagrams, unreliably. In this style there is no notion of 'connection.' Hence, while sending the data through such a socket, we need to indicate the destination for each datagram.

While using the SOCK_DGRAM style, the packets are sent on a best-effort basis with no guarantee of delivery of the packets, sequence of packets, or nonduplication of packets. This style of communication is used in situations where it is acceptable to simply resend a packet if no response is seen in a reasonable amount of time.

In the last parameter we provide the transport layer protocol. Since we intend to use the UDP protocol, we have specified this using the macro IPPROTO_UDP. If we want to use the TCP protocol, then we need to use the macro IPPROTO_TCP. Instead of these two macros we can use 0, which means the **socket( )** function should use the appropriate default protocol based on the values of the first two parameters.

All of these macros are defined in the file 'winsock.h.' Once the socket is created, the **socket( )** function returns a number that represents the socket. This number is often called a socket descriptor. If the **socket( )** function fails to create a socket, it returns a value INVALID_SOCKET.

Sending Data to a Time Server

Once we have created the UDP-based socket we need to use it to send data to the time server. This is achieved using the **sendto( )** function. The call to this function is shown here:

```
ret = sendto ( hSocket, sendbuffer, sizeof ( sendbuffer ), 0,
            ( sockaddr * )&sa, sizeof ( SOCKADDR_IN ) ) ;
```

This function transmits the data that is present in the array **sendbuffer[ ]** using the socket specified by **hSocket** to the destination address specified in the structure **sa**. We also need to pass the size of the packet and the size of the destination address. The argument value 0 stands for flags. The flags value can be used to influence the behavior of the function invocation beyond the options specified for the associated socket. To make a request to the time server to send time, any packet can be sent to it, regardless of its contents.

Take a careful look at the way the destination address and the port number is set up in the structure variable **sa**.

```
SOCKADDR_IN sa ;
sa.sin_family = AF_INET;
sa.sin_addr.s_addr = inet_addr ( timeservers[ 4 ] ) ;
sa.sin_port = htons ( IPPORT_TIMESERVER ) ;
```

The structure SOCKADDR_IN consists of address family, port number, and a structure called **sin_addr**, which can hold the IP address. We have set up

AF_INET as the address family, the IP address of one of the time servers in the address structure, and 37 (IPPORT_TIMESERVER) as the port number.

The **inet_addr( )** function converts a string containing a dotted IP address into a proper address for the IN_ADDR structure, which is part of the SOCKADDR structure. Before setting the port number, we have converted it into the network byte-ordering system by calling the **htons( )** function that we have discussed in a previous section of this chapter.

Receiving Date and Time

When the time server returns time we collect it using a call to the socket API function **recvfrom( )** as shown here:

```
ret = recvfrom ( hSocket, ( char * ) recvbuffer, BUFSIZE, 0,
                  ( sockaddr * )&sa, &nAddrSize ) ;
```

The parameters of the **recvfrom( )** function are almost the same as the parameters of **sendto( )**, except the last parameter. This is an in/out parameter. It means when we make the call it acts as an input parameter indicating the size of the socket address when we make the call. When we return from **recvfrom( )** it contains the number of bytes we were able to receive in this call.

The time server returns the number of seconds that have elapsed since Jan. 1, 1900, up to the time when the request for time was sent to it. This time is received in a character buffer. We converted this time into an **unsigned long int** through the function **BigEndianToUL( )**. Next we converted this **unsigned long int numsec** into a string and displayed it on the screen through a call to **MessageBox( )**.

The **DisplayTime( )** function is used to convert the seconds into an appropriate date and time. In this function, we first have to set up the FILETIME structure with a 64-bit value representing the number of 100-nanosecond intervals since January 1, 1601 (Univeral Coordinated Time or UTC). Then we used the functions **FileTimeToLocalFileTime( )** and **File-TimeToSystemTime( )** to obtain the date and the time. We have displayed the date and time in a message box.

COMMUNICATING WITH THE WHOIS SERVER

We commonly obtain information about the owner of a particular site from the 'About Us' link on the site. This information is often inadequate. In such cases we can use the 'Whois' protocol to obtain this information. Whois is a TCP-based query/response protocol which we can obtain information about the owner of a domain name, its IP address, etc. People use this data for good as well as bad purposes. For example, the data obtained can be used by a Certificate Authority to validate the registration for ecommerce sites, or the same data can be used by malicious users to send unsolicited emails.

The following is the program that obtains information about the site 'www.vsnl.com' using the whois protocol.

```c
# include "stdafx.h"
# include <windows.h>
# include <winsock.h>

# define NETWORK_ERROR -1
# define NETWORK_OK 0

int APIENTRY WinMain ( HINSTANCE hInstance, HINSTANCE
                       hPrevInstance, LPSTR lpCmdLine, int nCmdShow )
{
    WSADATA ws ;
    int nret ;

    // Initialize Winsock
    WSAStartup ( 0x0101, &ws ) ;

    // Create the socket
    SOCKET commsocket ;

    commsocket = socket ( AF_INET, SOCK_STREAM, IPPROTO_TCP ) ;
    if ( commsocket == INVALID_SOCKET )
    {
        MessageBox ( 0, "Could not create comm. socket", "Error", 0 ) ;
        WSACleanup( ) ;
        return NETWORK_ERROR ;
    }

    SOCKADDR_IN serverInfo ;
    serverInfo.sin_family = AF_INET ;
    /* whois.networksolutions.com */
    serverInfo.sin_addr.s_addr = inet_addr ( "205.178.188.12" ) ;
    serverInfo.sin_port = htons ( 43 ) ;

    nret = connect ( commsocket, ( LPSOCKADDR ) &serverInfo,
                     sizeof ( struct sockaddr ) ) ;
```

```
if ( nret == SOCKET_ERROR )
{
    MessageBox ( 0, "Could not connect to server", "Error", 0 ) ;
    WSACleanup( ) ;
    return NETWORK_ERROR ;
}

char sendbuffer[ 256 ] = "vsnl.com\r\n" ;
char recvbuffer[ 5000 ] ;

nret = send ( commsocket, sendbuffer, strlen ( sendbuffer ), 0 ) ;
if ( nret == SOCKET_ERROR )
{
    MessageBox ( 0, "Could not send request to server", "Error", 0 ) ;
    WSACleanup( ) ;
    return NETWORK_ERROR ;
}

nret = recv ( commsocket, recvbuffer, sizeof ( recvbuffer ), 0 ) ;
if ( nret != SOCKET_ERROR )
    MessageBox ( 0, recvbuffer, "Contents Received", 0 ) ;

closesocket ( commsocket ) ;
WSACleanup( ) ;
return NETWORK_OK ;
}
```

On execution of this program, the following output shown in Figure 18.4 will get generated. The output shows the registrant, domain name, technical contact, administrative contact, etc.

Most of the program is the same as the time client that we wrote in the last section. However, there are a few noticeable differences. We are using TCP protocol instead of UDP, hence instead of **sendto( )** and **recvfrom( )**, we have used the functions **send( )** and **recv( )**. Also, instead of connecting to the time server we are connecting to the whois server 'whois.networksolutions.com' at port number 43. Note that instead of setting the site name whois.networksolutions.com in the SOCKADDR_IN structure we have set its IP address 205.178.188.12. This IP address can be obtained using the ping command at the command prompt as shown below:

```
C:\> ping whois.networksolutions.com
```

Also, instead of sending any packet to the whois server, we are specifically sending the name of the site (vsnl.com) whose information we intended to

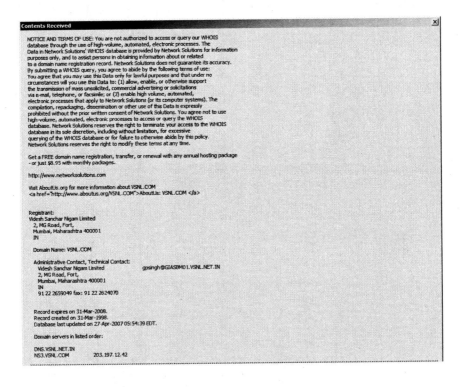

FIGURE 18.4

obtain. You can try this program to obtain information about other sites as well.

GIVE ME THE HOME PAGE

Whenever we type a request in the browse to visit a site our request goes to the web server where the site is hosted. On receiving the request, the web server software responds to that request by sending the home page of that site in the form of HTML. This request is a GET request made using a protocol called HTTP (Hyper Text Transfer Protocol). If we want, we too can make an HTTP GET request from our program. Instead of displaying the HTML response in a web browser we simply display it in a message box. The following program shows how this can be achieved.

```
#include "stdafx.h"
#include <windows.h>
#include <winsock.h>
```

```
#define NETWORK_ERROR -1
#define NETWORK_OK 0

int APIENTRY WinMain ( HINSTANCE hInstance, HINSTANCE
                       hPrevInstance, LPSTR lpCmdLine, int nCmdShow )
{
    WSADATA ws ;
    int nret ;

    // Initialize Winsock
    WSAStartup ( 0x0101, &ws ) ;

    // Create the socket
    SOCKET commsocket ;

    commsocket = socket ( AF_INET, SOCK_STREAM, IPPROTO_TCP ) ;
        if ( commsocket == INVALID_SOCKET )
        {
            MessageBox ( 0, "Could not create comm.. socket", "Error", 0 ) ;
            WSACleanup( ) ;
            return NETWORK_ERROR ;
        }

// Fill a SOCKADDR_IN struct with address information of server
SOCKADDR_IN serverInfo ;
serverInfo.sin_family = AF_INET ;
// www.yahoo.com
serverInfo.sin_addr.s_addr = inet_addr ( "66.94.234.13" ) ;
serverInfo.sin_port = htons ( 80 ) ;

nret = connect ( commsocket, ( LPSOCKADDR ) &serverInfo,
                 sizeof ( struct sockaddr ) ) ;
if ( nret == SOCKET_ERROR )
{
    MessageBox ( 0, "Could not connect to server", "Error", 0 ) ;
    WSACleanup( ) ;
    return NETWORK_ERROR ;
}

char sendbuffer[ 256 ] = "GET / \r\n" ;
char recvbuffer[ 256 ] ;
char str[ 10000 ] = "" ;
nret = send ( commsocket, sendbuffer, strlen ( sendbuffer ), 0 ) ;
```

```
if ( nret == SOCKET_ERROR )
{
     MessageBox ( 0, "Could not send GET request", "Error", 0 ) ;
     WSACleanup( ) ;
     return NETWORK_ERROR ;
}


do
{
     strset ( recvbuffer,' ' ) ;
     nret = recv ( commsocket, recvbuffer, sizeof ( recvbuffer ), 0 ) ;
     strcat ( str, recvbuffer ) ;
} while ( nret != 0 ) ;

MessageBox ( 0, str, "Contents Received", 0 ) ;

closesocket ( commsocket ) ;
WSACleanup( ) ;
return NETWORK_OK ;
}
```

As you can clearly see from this program, most of the code that we have written is repetitive. To begin with, we perform the standard steps—initialize winsock, create socket, fill address, connect to server. Once that is done, we send a HTTP GET request to port number 80 of the server www.yahoo.com. Then in a loop, we have collected the response by calling the function **recv( )** repeatedly. This response is finally displayed in a message box.

SENDING AND RECEIVING EMAILS

The way web sites are governed by HTTP protocol, likewise, for sending emails, a protocol called SMTP (Simple Mail Transfer Protocol) is used, and for receiving emails, the commonly used protocol is POP3 (Post Office Protocol Version 3). The following are programs that demonstrate how to receive and send emails.

```
// POP3 Client
#include "stdafx.h"
#include <windows.h>
#include <stdio.h>
#include<winsock.h>
```

```
#define NETWORK_ERROR -1
#define NETWORK_OK 0

int __stdcall WinMain ( HINSTANCE hInstance, HINSTANCE hPrevInstance,
                        LPSTR lpszCmdline, int nCmdShow )
{
    WSADATA ws ;
    int nret ;

    // initialize Winsock
    WSAStartup ( 0x0101, &ws ) ;

    // create communication socket
    SOCKET commsocket ;
    commsocket = socket ( AF_INET, SOCK_STREAM, IPPROTO_TCP ) ;
    if ( commsocket == INVALID_SOCKET )
    {
        MessageBox ( 0, "Could not create comm. socket", "Error", 0 ) ;
        WSACleanup( ) ;
        return NETWORK_ERROR ;
    }

    // fill a SOCKADDR_IN struct with address information of server
    SOCKADDR_IN serverInfo ;
    HOSTENT *he ;
    serverInfo.sin_family = AF_INET ;
    he = gethostbyname ( "mailbox.kicit.com" ) ;
    serverInfo.sin_addr.s_addr = *( ( unsigned long * ) he -> h_addr ) ;
    serverInfo.sin_port = htons ( 110 ) ;

    nret = connect ( commsocket, ( LPSOCKADDR ) &serverInfo,
                     sizeof ( struct sockaddr ) ) ;
    if ( nret == SOCKET_ERROR )
    {
        MessageBox ( 0, "Could not connect to server", "Error", 0 ) ;
        WSACleanup( ) ;
        return NETWORK_ERROR ;
    }

    char sendbuffer[ 256 ] = "" ;
    char recvbuffer[ 10000 ] = "" ;
    nret = recv ( commsocket, recvbuffer, 10000, 0 ) ;
```

```
if ( nret == SOCKET_ERROR )
{
      MessageBox ( 0, "Could not connect to server", "Error", 0 ) ;
      WSACleanup( ) ;
      return NETWORK_ERROR ;
}
else
      MessageBox ( 0, recvbuffer, "Recd. from server", 0 ) ;

// copy user id
strcpy ( sendbuffer,"USER kanetkar@kicit.com\r\n" ) ;
nret = send ( commsocket, sendbuffer, strlen ( sendbuffer ), 0 ) ;
if ( nret == SOCKET_ERROR )
{
      MessageBox ( 0, "Could not send user id to server", "Error", 0 ) ;
      WSACleanup( ) ;
      return NETWORK_ERROR ;
}

strnset ( recvbuffer, ' ', sizeof ( recvbuffer ) ) ;
nret = recv ( commsocket, recvbuffer, sizeof ( recvbuffer ), 0 ) ;
if ( nret == SOCKET_ERROR )
{
      MessageBox ( 0, "No response for user id from server", "Error", 0 ) ;
      WSACleanup( ) ;
      return NETWORK_ERROR ;
}
else
      MessageBox ( 0, recvbuffer, "Recd. from server", 0 ) ;

// copy password
strcpy ( sendbuffer,"PASS newyear2008\r\n" ) ;
nret = send ( commsocket, sendbuffer, strlen ( sendbuffer ), 0 ) ;
if ( nret == SOCKET_ERROR )
{
      MessageBox ( 0, "Could not send password to server", "Error", 0 ) ;
      WSACleanup( ) ;
      return NETWORK_ERROR ;
}

strnset ( recvbuffer, ' ', sizeof ( recvbuffer ) ) ;
nret = recv ( commsocket, recvbuffer, sizeof ( recvbuffer ), 0 ) ;
```

```
if ( nret == SOCKET_ERROR )
{
     MessageBox ( 0, "No response for password", "Error", 0 ) ;
     WSACleanup( ) ;
     return NETWORK_ERROR ;
}
else
     MessageBox ( 0, recvbuffer, "Recd. from server", 0 ) ;

strcpy ( sendbuffer, "STAT\r\n" ) ;
nret = send ( commsocket, sendbuffer, strlen ( sendbuffer ), 0 ) ;
if ( nret == SOCKET_ERROR )
{
     MessageBox ( 0, "Could not send STAT to server", "Error", 0 ) ;
     WSACleanup( ) ;
     return NETWORK_ERROR ;
}

strnset ( recvbuffer, ' ', sizeof ( recvbuffer ) ) ;
nret = recv ( commsocket, recvbuffer, sizeof ( recvbuffer ), 0 ) ;
if ( nret == SOCKET_ERROR )
{
     MessageBox ( 0, "No response for STAT from server", "Error", 0 ) ;
     WSACleanup( ) ;
     return NETWORK_ERROR ;
}
else
     MessageBox ( 0, recvbuffer, "Recd. from server", 0 ) ;

strcpy ( sendbuffer,"RETR 1 \r\n" ) ;
nret = send ( commsocket, sendbuffer, strlen ( sendbuffer ), 0 ) ;
if ( nret == SOCKET_ERROR )
{
     MessageBox ( 0, "Could not send RETR 1 to server", "Error", 0 ) ;
     WSACleanup( ) ;
     return NETWORK_ERROR ;
}

strnset ( recvbuffer, ' ', sizeof ( recvbuffer ) ) ;
nret = recv ( commsocket, recvbuffer, sizeof ( recvbuffer ), 0 ) ;
if ( nret == SOCKET_ERROR )
{
     MessageBox ( 0, "No response for RETR 1", "Error", 0 ) ;
     WSACleanup( ) ;
     return NETWORK_ERROR ;
}
```

```
    else
            MessageBox ( 0, recvbuffer, "Your mail", 0 ) ;

    closesocket ( commsocket ) ;
    WSACleanup( ) ;
    return NETWORK_OK ;
}
```

Here, once we have initialized winsock through a call to **WSAStartup( )**, we created a socket and connected to the email server called 'mailbox.kicit.com' through a call to the function **connect( )**. Before making this call, we obtained the IP address of the mail server by calling **gethostbyname( )**. This function returns a pointer to a structure called HOSTENT. One of the elements of this structure contains a pointer to the IP address of mail server. We have extracted this IP address through the statement:

```
serverInfo.sin_addr.s_addr = *( ( unsigned long * ) he -> h_addr ) ;
```

Once we are connected to the server we communicate it through predetermined POP3 commands. Each time we send a POP3 command to the email server through a call to **send( )**, it sends a response, which we collect using a call to the **recv( )** function. The following is the list of commands that we have sent to the email server along with their purpose:

USER   — This command is used to send a username to the server.
PASS   — This command is used to send a password to the server.
STAT   — This command is used to obtain the total number of messages in the mailbox and the total size of the emails.
RETR 1 — This command is used to retrieve message number one from mailbox.

In addition to these there exist other POP3 commands like LIST, DELE, NOOP, RSET, and QUIT. In our program we haven't used these commands.

On collecting the response sent by the email server for each of these commands, we have displayed these responses through message boxes. Some of these responses are shown in Figure 18.5.

When you execute this program, you will have to suitably replace the name of the email server, login name, and password that is relevant for you.

Now that we know how to receive mail from a mail server, let us try a program that can send mail to the email server. This program is given here:

```
// SMTP Client

#include "stdafx.h"
#include <windows.h>
```

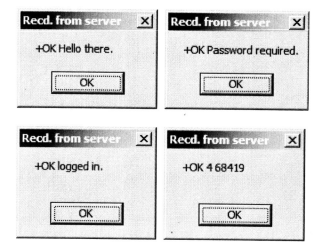

FIGURE 18.5

```
#include <stdio.h>
#include<winsock.h>

#define NETWORK_ERROR -1
#define NETWORK_OK 0

int__stdcall WinMain ( HINSTANCE hInstance, HINSTANCE hPrevInstance,
                       LPSTR lpszCmdline, int nCmdShow )
{
    WSADATA ws ;
    int nret ;

    // initialize Winsock
    WSAStartup ( 0x0101, &ws ) ;

    // create communication socket
    SOCKET commsocket ;
    commsocket = socket ( AF_INET, SOCK_STREAM, IPPROTO_TCP ) ;
    if ( commsocket == INVALID_SOCKET )
    {
        MessageBox ( 0, "Could not create comm. socket", "Error", 0 ) ;
        WSACleanup( ) ;
        return NETWORK_ERROR ;
    }

    // fill a SOCKADDR_IN struct with address information of server
```

```
SOCKADDR_IN serverInfo ;
struct hostent *he ;

serverInfo.sin_family = AF_INET ;
he = gethostbyname ( "mailbox.dcubesoft.com");
serverInfo.sin_addr.s_addr = *( ( unsigned long * ) he -> h_addr ) ;
serverInfo.sin_port = htons ( 25 ) ;

nret = connect ( commsocket, ( LPSOCKADDR ) &serverInfo,
                 sizeof ( struct sockaddr ) ) ;
if ( nret == SOCKET_ERROR )
{
     MessageBox ( 0, "Could not connect to server", "Error", 0 ) ;
     WSACleanup( ) ;
     return NETWORK_ERROR ;
}

char sendbuffer[ 256 ] = "" ;
char recvbuffer[ 10000 ] = "" ;

nret = recv ( commsocket, recvbuffer, 10000, 0 ) ;
if ( nret == SOCKET_ERROR )
{
     MessageBox ( 0, "No response from server", "Error", 0 ) ;
     WSACleanup( ) ;
     return NETWORK_ERROR ;
}
else
     MessageBox ( 0, recvbuffer, "Recd. from server", 0 ) ;

strcpy ( sendbuffer, "HELO aaa.com\r\n" ) ;
nret = send ( commsocket, sendbuffer, strlen ( sendbuffer ), 0 ) ;
if ( nret == SOCKET_ERROR )
{
     MessageBox ( 0, "Could not send HELO to server", "Error", 0 ) ;
     WSACleanup( ) ;
     return NETWORK_ERROR ;
}

strnset ( recvbuffer, ' ', sizeof ( recvbuffer ) ) ;
nret = recv ( commsocket, recvbuffer, 10000, 0 ) ;
if ( nret == SOCKET_ERROR )
{
     MessageBox ( 0, "No response for HELO from server", "Error", 0 ) ;
```

```
        WSACleanup ( ) ;
        return NETWORK_ERROR ;
    }
    else
        MessageBox ( 0, recvbuffer, "Recd. from server", 0 ) ;

    strcpy ( sendbuffer, "MAIL FROM:<kanetkar@dcubesoft.com>\r\n" ) ;
    nret = send ( commsocket, sendbuffer, strlen ( sendbuffer ), 0 ) ;
    if ( nret == SOCKET_ERROR )
    {
        MessageBox ( 0, "Could not send MAIL FROM to ser.", "Error", 0 ) ;
        WSACleanup( ) ;
        return NETWORK_ERROR ;
    }

    strnset ( recvbuffer, ' ', sizeof ( recvbuffer ) ) ;
    nret = recv ( commsocket, recvbuffer, 10000, 0 ) ;
    if ( nret == SOCKET_ERROR )
    {
        MessageBox ( 0, "No response for MAIL FROM", "Error", 0 ) ;
        WSACleanup( ) ;
        return NETWORK_ERROR ;
    }
    else
        MessageBox ( 0, recvbuffer, "Recd. from server", 0 ) ;

    strcpy ( sendbuffer, "RCPT TO:<kanetkar@dcubesoft.com>\r\n" ) ;
    nret = send ( commsocket, sendbuffer, strlen ( sendbuffer ), 0 ) ;
    if ( nret == SOCKET_ERROR )
    {
        MessageBox ( 0, "Could not send RCPT TO to server", "Error", 0 ) ;
        WSACleanup( ) ;
        return NETWORK_ERROR ;
    }

    strnset ( recvbuffer, ' ', sizeof ( recvbuffer ) ) ;
    nret = recv ( commsocket, recvbuffer, 10000, 0 ) ;
    if ( nret == SOCKET_ERROR )
    {
        MessageBox ( 0, "No response for RCPT TO", "Error", 0 ) ;
        WSACleanup( ) ;
        return NETWORK_ERROR ;
    }
```

```
else
      MessageBox ( 0, recvbuffer, "Recd. from server", 0 ) ;

strcpy ( sendbuffer,"DATA\r\n" ) ;
nret = send ( commsocket, sendbuffer, strlen ( sendbuffer ), 0 ) ;

if ( nret == SOCKET_ERROR )
{
      MessageBox ( 0, "Could not send DATA to server", "Error", 0 ) ;
      WSACleanup( ) ;
      return NETWORK_ERROR ;
}

strnset ( recvbuffer, ' ', sizeof ( recvbuffer ) ) ;
nret = recv ( commsocket, recvbuffer, 10000, 0 ) ;
if ( nret == SOCKET_ERROR )
{
      MessageBox ( 0, "No response for DATA from server", "Error", 0 ) ;
      WSACleanup( ) ;
      return NETWORK_ERROR ;
}
else
      MessageBox ( 0, recvbuffer, "Recd. from server", 0 ) ;

strcpy ( sendbuffer,"SUBJECT: Welcome to the electronic world\r\n");
nret = send ( commsocket, sendbuffer, strlen ( sendbuffer ), 0 ) ;

strcpy ( sendbuffer,"FROM: kanetkar@dcubesoft.com\r\n" ) ;
nret = send ( commsocket, sendbuffer, strlen ( sendbuffer ), 0 ) ;

strcpy ( sendbuffer,"TO: ypk\r\n");
nret = send ( commsocket, sendbuffer, strlen ( sendbuffer ), 0 ) ;

strcpy ( sendbuffer,"DATE: 20 Aug 207 13:24 IST\r\n");
nret = send ( commsocket, sendbuffer, strlen ( sendbuffer ), 0 ) ;

strcpy ( sendbuffer,"MESSAGE_ID: <123@e.com>\r\n");
nret = send ( commsocket, sendbuffer, strlen ( sendbuffer ), 0 ) ;

strcpy ( sendbuffer,"Hello\r\n");
nret = send ( commsocket, sendbuffer, strlen ( sendbuffer ), 0 ) ;

strcpy ( sendbuffer,"How are you\r\n");
nret = send ( commsocket, sendbuffer, strlen ( sendbuffer ), 0 ) ;
```

```
strcpy ( sendbuffer,"\r\n.\r\n");
nret = send ( commsocket, sendbuffer, strlen ( sendbuffer ), 0 ) ;

strcpy ( sendbuffer,"QUIT\r\n");
nret = send ( commsocket, sendbuffer, strlen ( sendbuffer ), 0 ) ;

strnset ( recvbuffer, ' ', sizeof ( recvbuffer ) ) ;
nret = recv ( commsocket, recvbuffer, 10000, 0 ) ;
MessageBox ( 0, recvbuffer, "Recd. from server", 0 ) ;

closesocket ( commsocket ) ;
WSACleanup( ) ;
return NETWORK_OK ;
}
```

While sending email to the mail server we have to open the communication by sending a message HELO aaa.com (yes, it is not HELLO). In place of aaa.com you can use anything else, as it doesn't matter. Once the server sends an OK response for this message, we need to send the following messages to it in the order in which they are mentioned:

MAIL FROM
RCPT TO
DATA
SUBJECT
FROM
TO
MESSAGEID
Actual message

The actual message is the body of the email. This must be followed by sending a full-stop (.) on an independent line. This marks the end of the email. Once you have carefully followed the POP3 client, this program will be a natural progression. In Figure 18.6 are some of the messages that the author received from the server when he executed this program.

TWO-WAY COMMUNICATION

So far, we have only written client programs that communicated with already-existing server programs. Let us now try to create a server as well and then see how we can carry out two-way communication between them. Let us begin with the server first. Here is the program for it.

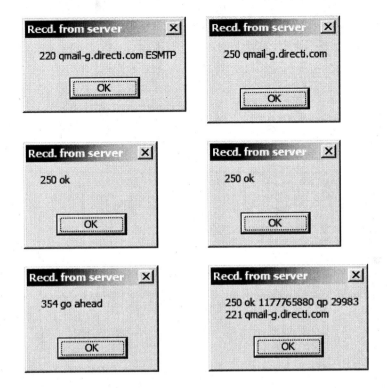

FIGURE 18.6

```
// Server Program

#include <windows.h>
#include <winsock.h>
#include <stdio.h>

#define NETWORK_ERROR -1
#define NETWORK_OK 0

int WINAPI WinMain ( HINSTANCE hInstance, HINSTANCE hPrevInstance,
                     LPSTR lpszCmdline, int nCmdShow )
{
    WSADATA ws ;
    int nret ;

    WSAStartup ( 0x0101, &ws ) ;
```

```
SOCKET listeningSocket ;

listeningSocket = socket ( AF_INET, SOCK_STREAM, IPPROTO_TCP);
if ( listeningSocket == INVALID_SOCKET )
{
        MessageBox ( 0, "Could not create listening socket", "Error", 0. ) ;
        WSACleanup( ) ;
        return NETWORK_ERROR ;
}


// Use a SOCKADDR_IN struct to fill in address information
SOCKADDR_IN serverInfo ;

serverInfo.sin_family = AF_INET ;
serverInfo.sin_addr.s_addr = inet_addr ( "127.0.0.1" ) ;
serverInfo.sin_port = htons ( 10000 ) ;

// Bind the socket to our local server address
nret = bind ( listeningSocket, ( SOCKADDR * ) &serverInfo,
                sizeof ( struct sockaddr ) ) ;
if ( nret == SOCKET_ERROR )
{
        MessageBox ( 0, "Could not bind listening socket", "Error", 0 ) ;
        WSACleanup( ) ;
        return NETWORK_ERROR ;
}


// make the socket listen. Up to 10 connections may wait at any one time
nret = listen ( listeningSocket, 10 ) ;
if ( nret == SOCKET_ERROR )
{
        MessageBox ( 0, "Could not listen", "Error", 0 ) ;
        WSACleanup( ) ;
        return NETWORK_ERROR ;
}


// Wait for a client
SOCKET commsocket ;
commsocket = accept ( listeningSocket, NULL, NULL ) ;
if ( commsocket == INVALID_SOCKET )
{

        MessageBox ( 0, "Couldn't accept connection request", "Error", 0 ) ;
```

```
                WSACleanup( ) ;
                return NETWORK_ERROR ;
        }

        char sendbuffer[ 256 ] = "From Server: Hi there!" ;
        char recvbuffer[ 256 ] ;

        nret = recv ( commsocket, recvbuffer, 255, 0 ) ;
        recvbuffer [ nret ] = 0 ;

        if ( nret == SOCKET_ERROR )
        {
                MessageBox ( 0, "Could not receive msg from client", "Error", 0 ) ;
                WSACleanup( ) ;
                return NETWORK_ERROR ;
        }
        else
        {
                MessageBox ( NULL, recvbuffer, "Message from client", MB_OK ) ;

                nret = send ( commsocket, sendbuffer, 255, 0 ) ;
                if ( nret == SOCKET_ERROR )
                {
                        MessageBox ( 0, "Could not send msg to client", "Error", 0 ) ;
                        WSACleanup( ) ;
                        return NETWORK_ERROR ;
                }
        }

        closesocket ( commsocket ) ;
        closesocket ( listeningSocket ) ;

        WSACleanup( ) ;
        return NETWORK_OK ;
}
```

In all the programs that we have created in this chapter, we created one socket and then used it to connect to a specific server at a specific port. Once connected, through the same socket we communicated with the server. In the server program, there is a major change here. In this program we will have to create two sockets—a listening socket and a communication socket. Using the listening socket, the server will wait for a connection request from the client. Once this request is received, the communication is carried out with the client using the communication socket.

The process of creating a listening socket is similar to the procedure that we have adopted so far in other programs in this chapter. The socket that we have created so far using the **socket( )** function has no address. The clients connecting to the server can find this socket for communication only if we give it an address. This is called *binding* the address to the socket, and it is done by calling the **bind( )** function. Before calling this function we need to set the IP address and port number of the server in the SOCKADDR structure. This is done through the statements given below:

```
serverInfo.sin_family = AF_INET ;
serverInfo.sin_addr.s_addr = inet_addr ( "127.0.0.1" ) ;
serverInfo.sin_port = htons ( 10000 ) ;
```

The IP address 127.0.0.1 is usually called the 'localhost.' This address is used to indicate the "address of the machine on which the program is running." This saves the trouble of finding the actual IP address of the machine on which the server is running. We have chosen the port number as 10000. There is nothing special about this number. You are free to choose any other suitable number.

Once the listening socket is bound to the IP address the **listen( )** function is called, which places the socket in a state in which it can listen for an incoming connection from the client. After this, another winsock function called **accept( )** is called. This function is a blocking function. This means that the control would not return from this function unless a connection request comes from the client. As soon as the client connection request arrives, the **accept( )** function accepts the connection request, creates a new socket for communication, and returns its descriptor, which is collected in **commsocket**. Once the communication socket is created, the communication is carried out with the client using the common **recv( )** and **send( )** functions.

Now that the server program is ready, let us take a look at the client program. This is shown below.

```
// Client Program

#include<windows.h>
#include<winsock.h>
#include<stdio.h>

#define NETWORK_ERROR -1
#define NETWORK_OK 0
```

```
void ReportError ( int, const char * ) ;

int__stdcall WinMain ( HINSTANCE hInstance, HINSTANCE hPrevInstance,
                       LPSTR lpszCmdline, int nCmdShow )
{
    WSADATA ws ;
    int nret ;

    // Initialize Winsock
    WSAStartup ( 0x0101, &ws ) ;

    // Create the socket
    SOCKET commsocket ;

    commsocket = socket ( AF_INET, SOCK_STREAM, IPPROTO_TCP ) ;
    if ( commsocket == INVALID_SOCKET )
    {
        MessageBox ( 0, "Could not create comm.. socket", "Error", 0 ) ;
        WSACleanup( ) ;
        return NETWORK_ERROR ;
    }

    // Fill a SOCKADDR_IN struct with address information of server
    SOCKADDR_IN serverInfo ;
    serverInfo.sin_family = AF_INET ;
    serverInfo.sin_addr.s_addr = inet_addr ( "127.0.0.1" ) ;
    serverInfo.sin_port = htons ( 10000 ) ;

    nret = connect ( commsocket, ( LPSOCKADDR ) &serverInfo,
                     sizeof ( struct sockaddr ) ) ;
    if ( nret == SOCKET_ERROR )
    {
        MessageBox ( 0, "Could not connect to server", "Error", 0 ) ;
        WSACleanup( ) ;
        return NETWORK_ERROR ;
    }

    char sendbuffer[ 256 ] = "From client: Hello how are you" ;
    char recvbuffer[ 256 ] ;

    nret = send ( commsocket, sendbuffer, strlen ( sendbuffer ), 0 ) ;
    if ( nret == SOCKET_ERROR )
```

```
    {
            MessageBox ( 0, "Could not send bytes to server", "Error", 0 ) ;
            WSACleanup( ) ;
            return NETWORK_ERROR ;
    }

    nret = recv ( commsocket, recvbuffer, 32, 0 ) ;
    if ( nret == SOCKET_ERROR )
    {
            MessageBox ( 0, "Could not connect to server", "Error", 0 ) ;
            WSACleanup( ) ;
            return NETWORK_ERROR ;
    }
    else
            MessageBox ( 0, recvbuffer, "Error", 0 ) ;

    closesocket ( commsocket ) ;
    WSACleanup( ) ;
    return NETWORK_OK ;
}
```

You will agree that the client program is pretty straightforward. It connects to the server on the same machine at port number 10000. Once the connection is established, it just sends a message to the server. When the server responds to this message, the client collects it and displays it through the message box. Figure 18.7 summarizes the activities that we are carrying out on the server and client.

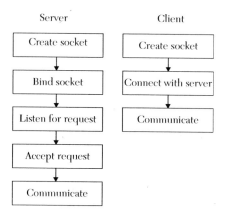

FIGURE 18.7

SUMMARY

(a) Network and Internet programming can be done under Windows using the WinSock socket library.
(b) Complexity of network communication is managed by dividing it into different layers—Application, Transport, Network, Physical.
(c) Different protocols are used at different layers.
(d) Standard protocols use standard port numbers.
(e) IP addresses are mentioned using dotted decimal format.
(f) Socket is a communication endpoint.
(g) Typical activities that are carried out in a network client program are—create socket, connect to server, send and receive messages.
(h) Typical activities that are carried out in a network server program are—create socket, bind socket, listen for connection request, accept connection request, send and receive messages.

EXERCISES

[A] State whether the following statements are True or False:

(a) Internet uses the 7-layer OSI model for network programming.
(b) It is necessary to bind the socket created on the client machine to the client machine's IP address.
(c) **Listen( )** is a blocking function, whereas **accept( )** is a non-blocking function.
(d) SMTP protocol is used for accessing web pages from a site.
(e) Time servers always return the local standard time.
(f) Every working site on the Internet has a corresponding entry in the whois database.
(g) SMTP and POP3 protocols can be used interchangeably for sending/ receiving emails.
(h) If a program creates a socket, then calling of **closesocket( )** and **WSACleanup( )** function before terminating the program is optional.
(i) IP protocol is responsible for reliable delivery of packets, detecting errors in transmission and flow control.

[B] Attempt the following:

(a) Modify the POP3 client program discussed in this chapter to retrieve all the emails in the mailbox one after the other.

(b) Using the following API functions, write a ping utility to check whether you can connect to a particular site or not.

```
IcmpCreateFile( )
IcmpCloseHandle( )
IcmpSendEcho( )
```

Chapter **19**

C Under Linux

Today the programming world is divided into two major camps—the Windows world and the Linux world. Since its humble beginning about a decade ago, Linux has steadily drawn the attention of programmers across the globe and has successfully created a community of its own. How big and committed is this community is one of the hottest debates that is raging in all parts of the world. You can look at the hot discussions and the flame wars on this issue on numerous sites on the Internet. Before you decide to join the Windows or the Linux camp you should first get familiar with both of them. The last 3 chapters concentrated on Windows programming. This and the next one will deal with Linux programming. Without any further discussions, let us now set out on the Linux voyage. Hopefully, you find the journey interesting and exciting.

WHAT IS LINUX?

Linux is a clone of the Unix operating system. Its kernel was written from scratch by Linus Trovalds with assistance from a loosely knit team of programmers across the world on the Internet. It has all the features you would expect in a modern OS. Moreover, unlike Windows or Unix, Linux is available completely free of cost. The kernel of Linux is available in source code form. Anybody is free to change it to suit his requirement, with a precondition that the changed kernel can be distributed only in the source code form. Several programs, frameworks, and utilities have been built around the Linux kernel. A common user may not want the headaches of downloading the kernel, going through the complicated compilation process, then downloading the frameworks, programs, and utilities. Hence, many organizations have come forward to make this job easy. They distribute the precompiled kernel, programs, utilities, and frameworks on a common media. Moreover, they also provide installation scripts for easy installations of the Linux OS and applications. Some of the popular distributions are RedHat, SUSE, Caldera, Debian, Mandrake, Slackware, etc. Each of them contain the same kernel but may contain different application programs, libraries, frameworks, installation scripts, utilities, etc. Which one is better than the other is only a matter of taste.

Linux was first developed for x86-based PCs (386 or higher). These days it also runs on Compaq Alpha AXP, Sun SPARC, Motorola 68000 machines (like Atari ST and Amiga), MIPS, PowerPC, ARM, Intel Itanium, SuperH, etc. Thus, Linux works on literally every conceivable microprocessor architecture.

Under Linux, one is faced with simply too many choices of Linux distributions, graphical shells and managers, editors, compilers, linkers, debuggers, etc. For simplicity (in the author's opinion), we have chosen the following combination for the programs in Chapters 19 and 20:

Linux Distribution — Red Hat Linux 9.0
Console Shell   — BASH
Graphical Shell   — KDE 3.1-10
Editor   — KWrite
Compiler   — GNU C and C++ compiler (gcc)

We will be using and discussing these in the sections to follow.

C PROGRAMMING UNDER LINUX

Is C under Linux any different than C under DOS or C under Windows? Well, it is same as well as different. It is the same to the extent of using language elements like data types, control instructions, and the overall syntax. The usage of standard library functions is also the same even though the implementation of each might be different under a different OS. For example, a **printf( )** would work under all OSs, but the way it is defined is likely to be different for different OSs. However, the programmer doesn't suffer because of this, since, he can continue to call **printf( )** the same way, no matter how it is implemented.

But there the similarity ends. If we are to build programs that utilize the features offered by the OS, then things are bound to be different across OSs. For example, if we were to write a C program that would create a Window and display a message "hello" at the point where the user clicks the left mouse button, the architecture of this program would be very closely tied with the OS under which it is being built. This is because the mechanisms for creating a window, reporting a mouse click, handling a mouse click, displaying the message, closing the window, etc., are very closely tied with the OS for which the program is being built. In short, the programming architecture (better known as programming model) for each OS is different. Hence, naturally, the program that achieves the same task under different OSs would have to be different.

THE 'HELLO LINUX' PROGRAM

As with any new platform, we will begin our journey in the Linux world by creating a simple 'hello world' program. Here is the source code:

```
# include <stdio.h>
void main( )
```

```
{
    printf ( "Hello Linux\n" ) ;
}
```

The program is exactly the same as compared to a console program under DOS/Windows. It begins with **main( )** and uses the **printf( )** standard library function to produce its output. So what is the difference? The difference is in the way programs are typed, compiled, and executed. The steps for typing, compiling, and executing the program are discussed next.

The first hurdle to cross is the typing of this program. Though any editor can be used to do so, we have preferred to use the editor called 'KWrite.' This is because it is a very simple yet elegant editor compared to other editors like 'vi' or 'emacs.' Note that KWrite is a text editor and is a part of the K Desktop environment (KDE). Installation of Linux and KDE is discussed in Appendix F. Once KDE is started, select the following command from the desktop panel to start KWrite:

K Menu | Accessories | More Accessories | KWrite

If you face any difficulty in starting the KWrite editor, please refer Appendix G. Assuming that you have been able to start KWrite successfully, carry out the following steps:

(a) Type the program and save it under the name 'hello.c.'
(b) At the command prompt, switch to the directory containing 'hello.c' using the **cd** command.
(c) Now compile the program using the **gcc** compiler as shown here:

```
# gcc hello.c
```

(d) On successful compilation, **gcc** produces a file named 'a.out.' This file contains the machine code of the program, which can now be executed.
(e) Execute the program using the following command.

```
# ./a.out
```

(f) Now you should be able to see the output 'Hello Linux' on the screen.

Having created a "Hello Linux" program and gone through the edit-compile-execute cycle once, let us now turn our attention to Linux-specific programming. We will begin with processes.

PROCESSES

Gone are the days when only one job (task) could be executed in memory at any time. Today, the modern OSs like Windows and Linux permit execution of several tasks simultaneously. Hence, these OSs are aptly called 'Multitasking' OSs.

In Linux, each running task is known as a 'process.' Even though it may appear that several processes are being executed by the microprocessor simultaneously, in actuality it is not so. What happens is that, the microprocessor divides the execution time equally among all the running processes. Thus, each process gets the microprocessor's attention in a round robin manner. Once the time-slice allocated for a process expires, the operation that it is currently executing is put on hold and the microprocessor now directs its attention to the next process. Thus, at any given moment, if we take the snapshot of memory, we will see that only one process is being executed by the microprocessor. The switching of processes happens so fast that we get a false impression that the processor is executing several processes simultaneously.

The scheduling of processes is done by a program called 'Scheduler,' which is a vital component of the Linux OS. This scheduler program is fairly complex. Before switching over to the next thread it stores the information about the current process. This includes current values of CPU registers, contents of System Stack and Application Stack, etc. When this process again gets the time slot, these values are restored. This process of shifting over from one thread to another is often called a Context Switch. Note that, Linux uses preemptive scheduling, meaning thereby that the context switch is performed as soon as the time slot allocated to the process is over, no matter whether the process has completed its job or not.

Kernel assigns each process running in memory a unique ID to distinguish it from other running processes. This ID is often known as processes ID or simply PID. It is very simple to print the PID of a running process programmatically. Here is the program that achieves this:

```
# include <stdio.h>
void main( )
{
    printf ( "Process ID = %d", getpid( ) ) ;
}
```

Here, **getpid( )** is a library function that returns the process ID of the calling process. When the execution of the program comes to an end, the process stands terminated. Every time we run the program a new process is created.

Hence, the kernel assigns a new ID to the process each time. This can be verified by executing the program several times—each time it will produce a different output.

PARENT AND CHILD PROCESSES

As we know, our running program is a process. From this process we can create another process. There is a parent-child relationship between the two processes. The way to achieve this is by using a library function called **fork( )**. This function splits the running process into two processes, the existing one is known as the parent and the new process is known as the child. Here is a program that demonstrates this:

```
# include <stdio.h>
# include <sys/types.h>
void main( )
{
    printf ( "Before Forking\n" ) ;
    fork( ) ;
    printf ( "After Forking\n" ) ;
}
```

Here is the output of the program:

```
Before Forking
After Forking
After Forking
```

Watch the output of the program. You may notice that all the statements after the **fork( )** are executed twice—once by the parent process and the second time by the child process. In other words, **fork( )** has managed to split our process into two.

But why on earth would we like to do this? At times, we want our program to perform two jobs simultaneously. Since these jobs may be interrelated, we may not want to create two different programs to perform them. Let's try an example. Suppose we want to perform two jobs—copy contents of a source file to a target file and display an animated GIF file indicating that the file copy is in progress. The GIF file should continue to play until file copy is taking place. Once the copying is over, the playing of the GIF file should be stopped. Since both of these jobs are interrelated, they cannot be performed in two different programs. Also, they cannot be performed one after another. Both jobs should be performed simultaneously.

At such times, we would want to use **fork( )** to create a child process and then write the program in such a manner that file copy is done by the parent and displaying of the animated GIF file is done by the child process. The following program shows how this can be achieved. Note that, the issue here is to show how to perform two different but interrelated jobs simultaneously. Hence we have skipped the actual code for file copying and playing the animated GIF file.

```
# include <stdio.h>
# include <sys/types.h>

void main( )
{
    int pid ;
    pid = fork( ) ;
    if ( pid == 0 )
    {
        printf ( "In child process\n" ) ;
        /* code to play animated GIF file */
    }
    else
    {
        printf ( "In parent process\n" ) ;
        /* code to copy file */
    }
}
```

As we know, **fork( )** creates a child process and duplicates the code of the parent process in the child process. There onward, the execution of the **fork( )** function continues in both the processes. Thus, the duplication code inside **fork( )** is executed once, whereas the remaining code inside it is executed in both the parent as well as the child process. Hence, control would come back from **fork( )** twice, even though it is actually called only once. When control returns from **fork( )** of the parent process, it returns the PID of the child process. As against this, when control returns from **fork( )** of the child process, it always returns a 0. This can be exploited by our program to segregate the code that we want to execute in the parent process, from the code that we want to execute in the child process. We have done this in our program using an **if** statement. In the parent process the 'else block' will get executed, whereas in the child process the 'if block' will get executed.

Let us now write one more program. This program will use the **fork( )** call to create a child process. In the child process we will print the PID of the child and its parent, whereas in the parent process we will print the PID of the parent and its child. Here is the program:

```
# include <stdio.h>
# include <sys/types.h>
void main( )
{
    int pid ;
    pid = fork( ) ;

    if ( pid == 0 )
    {
        printf ( "Child : Hello I am the child process\n" ) ;
        printf ( "Child : Child's PID: %d\n", getpid( ) ) ;
        printf ( "Child : Parent's PID: %d\n'', getppid( ) ) ;
    }
    else
    {
        printf ( "Parent : Hello I am the parent process\n" ) ;
        printf ( "Parent : Parent's PID: %d\n'', getpid( ) ) ;
        printf ( "Parent : Child's PID: %d\n", pid ) ;
    }
}
```

The following is the output of the program:

```
Child : Hello I am the child process
Child : Child's PID: 4706
Child : Parent's PID: 4705
Parent : Hello I am the Parent process
Parent : Parent's PID: 4705
Parent : Child's PID: 4706
```

In addition to **getpid( )**, there is another related function that we have used in this program—**getppid( )**. As the name suggests, this function returns the PID of the parent of the calling process.

You can tally the PIDs from the output and convince yourself that you have understood the **fork( )** function well. A lot of things that follow use the **fork( )** function. So make sure that you understand it thoroughly.

Note that, even Linux internally uses **fork( )** to create new child processes. Thus, there is a inverted tree-like structure of all the processes running in memory. The father of all these processes is a process called **init**. If we want to get a list of all the running processes in memory we can do so using the **ps** command as shown here:

```
# ps -A
```

Here, the switch **–A** indicates that we want to list all the running processes.

MORE PROCESSES

Suppose we want to execute a program on the disk as part of a child process. For this, we should first create a child process using **fork( )** and then, from within the child, process we should call an **exec** function to execute the program on the disk as part of a child process. Note that, there is a family of **exec** library functions, each basically does the same job, but with a minor variation. For example, the **execl( )** function permits us to pass a list of command-line arguments to the program to be executed. **execv( )** also does the same job as **execl( )** except that the command-line arguments can be passed to it in the form of an array of pointers to strings. There also exist other variations, like **execle( )** and **execvp( )**.

Let us now view a program that uses **execl( )** to run a new program in the child process.

```
# include <stdio.h>
# include <unistd.h>
void main( )
{
    int pid ;
    pid = fork( ) ;
    if ( pid == 0 )
    {
        execl ( "/bin/ls","-al", "/etc", NULL ) ;
        printf ( "Child: After exec( )\n") ;
    }
    else
        printf ( "Parent process\n" ) ;
}
```

After forking a child process, we have called the **execl( )** function. This function accepts a variable number of arguments. The first parameter to **execl( )** is the absolute path of the program to be executed. The remaining parameters describe the command-line arguments for the program to be executed. The last parameter is an end-of-argument marker, which must always be **NULL**. Thus, in our case, we have called upon the **execl( )** function to execute the **ls** program as shown here:

```
ls -al /etc
```

As a result, all the contents of the **/etc** directory are listed on the screen. Note that the **printf( )** after the call to the **execl( )** function is not executed. This is because the **exec** family functions overwrite the image of the calling process with the code and data of the program that is to be executed. In our case, the child process's memory was overwritten by the code and data of the **ls** program. Hence, the call to **printf( )** did not materialize.

It would make little sense to call **execl( )** before **fork( )**. This is because a child would not get created and **execl( )** would simply overwrite the main process itself. As a result, no statement beyond the call to **execl( )** would ever get executed. Hence **fork( )** and **execl( )** usually go hand in hand.

ZOMBIES AND ORPHANS

We know that the **ps –A** command lists all the running processes. But from where does the **ps** program get this information? Well, Linux maintains a table containing information about all the processes. This table is called the 'Process Table.' Apart from other information, the process table contains an entry of 'exit code' of the process. This integer value indicates the reason why the process was terminated. Even though the process comes to an end, its entry will remain in the process table until such time that the parent of the terminated process queries the exit code. This act of querying deletes the entry of the terminated process from the process table and returns the exit code to the parent that raised the query.

When we fork a new child process and the parent and the child continue to execute, there are two possibilities—either the child process ends first or the parent process ends first. Let us discuss both these possibilities.

(a) Child terminates earlier than the parent

In this case, until the time the parent queries the exit code of the terminated child, the entry of the child process will continue to exist. Such a process in Linux terminology is known as a 'Zombie' process. Zombie means ghost. The moral is, a parent process should query the process table immediately after the child process has terminated. This will prevent a zombie.

What if the parent terminates without querying? In such a case, the zombie child process is treated as an 'Orphan' process. Immediately, the father of all processes—**init**—adopts the orphaned process. Next, as a responsible parent, **init** queries the process table, as a result of which, the child process entry is eliminated from the process table.

(b) Parent terminates earlier than the child

Since every parent process is launched from the Linux shell, the parent of the parent is the **shell** process. When our parent process terminates, the **shell** queries the process table. Thus, a proper cleanup happens for the parent process. However, the child process that is still running is left orphaned. Immediately, the **init** process will adopt it and when its execution is over **init** will query the process table to clean up the entry for the child process. Note that, in this case, the child process does not become a zombie.

Thus, when a zombie or an orphan gets created, the OS takes over and ensures that a proper cleanup of the relevant process table entry happens. However, as a good programming practice, our program should get the exit code of the terminated process and thereby ensure a proper cleanup. Note that, here, cleanup is important (it happens anyway). Why is it important to get the exit code of the terminated process? It is because it is the exit code that will give an indication about whether the job assigned to the process was completed successfully or not. The following program shows how this can be done.

```c
# include <stdio.h>
# include <unistd.h>
# include <sys/types.h>
void main( )
{
    unsigned int i = 0 ;
    int pid, status ;
    pid = fork( ) ;
    if ( pid == 0 )
    {
        while ( i < 4294967295U )
            i++ ;
        printf ( "The child is now terminating\n" ) ;
    }
    else
    {
        waitpid ( pid, &status, 0 ) ;
        if ( WIFEXITED ( status ) )
            printf ( "Parent: Child terminated normally\n" ) ;
        else
            printf ( "Parent: Child terminated abnormally\n" ) ;
    }
    return 0 ;
}
```

In this program we have applied a big loop in the child process. This loop ensures that the child does not terminate immediately. From within the parent process we have made a call to the **waitpid( )** function. This function makes the parent process wait until the time the execution of the child process does not come to an end. This ensures that the child process never becomes orphaned. Once the child process terminates, the **waitpid( )** function queries its exit code and returns back to the parent. As a result of querying, the child process does not become a zombie.

The first parameter of the **waitpid( )** function is the pid of the child process for which the wait has to be performed. The second parameter is the address of an integer variable, which is set up with the exit status code of the child process. The third parameter is used to specify some options to control the behavior of the wait operation. We have not used this parameter and hence we have passed a **0**. Next, we have made use of the **WIFEXITED( )** macro to test if the child process exited normally or not. This macro takes the status value as a parameter and returns a nonzero value if the process terminated normally. Using this macro, the parent suitably prints a message to report the termination status (normal/abnormal) of its child process.

ONE INTERESTING FACT

When we use **fork( )** to create a child process, the child process does not contain the entire data and code of the parent process. Then does it mean that the child process contains the data and code below the **fork( )** call? Even this is not so. In actuality, the code never gets duplicated. Linux internally manages to intelligently share it—although, some data is shared, some is not. Until the time both processes do not change the value of the variables, they keep getting shared. However, if any of the processes (either child or parent) attempt to change the value of a variable it is no longer shared. Instead, a new copy of the variable is made for the process that is attempting to change it. This not only ensures data integrity but also saves precious memory.

SUMMARY

(a) Linux is a free OS whose kernel was built by Linus Trovalds and friends.

(b) A Linux distribution consists of the kernel with source code along with a large collection of applications, libraries, scripts, etc.

(c) C programs under Linux can be compiled using the popular **gcc** compiler.

(d) The basic scheduling unit in Linux is a 'Process.' Processes are scheduled by a special program called 'Scheduler.'

(e) The **fork( )** library function can be used to create child processes.

(f) The **Init** process is the father of all processes.

(g) The **execl( )** library function is used to execute another program from within a running program.

(h) The **execl( )** function overwrites the image (code and data) of the calling process.

(i) **execl( )** and **fork( )** usually go hand in hand.

(j) The **ps** command can be used to get a list of all processes.

(k) The **kill** command can be used to terminate a process.

(l) A 'zombie' is a child process that has terminated, but its parent is running and has not called a function to get the exit code of the child process.

(m) An 'orphan' is a child process whose parent have terminated.

(n) Orphaned processes are adopted by the **init** process automatically.

(o) A parent process can avoid the creation of zombie and orphan processes using **waitpid( )** function.

EXERCISES

[A] State True or False:

(a) We can modify the kernel of Linux OS.

(b) All distributions of Linux contain the same collection of applications, libraries, and installation scripts.

(c) The basic scheduling unit in Linux is a file.

(d) The **execl( )** library function can be used to create a new child process.

(e) The scheduler process is the father of all processes.

(f) A family of **fork( )** and **exec( )** functions are available, each doing basically the same job but with minor variations.

(g) The **fork( )** completely duplicates the code and data of the parent process into the child process.

(h) The **fork( )** overwrites the image (code and data) of the calling process.

(i) The **fork( )** is called twice but returns once.

    (j) Every zombie process is essentially an orphan process.

    (k) Every orphan process is essentially a zombie process.

[B] Answer the following:

    (a) If a program contains four calls to **fork( )** one after the other, how many total processes would get created?

    (b) What is the difference between a zombie process and an orphan process?

    (c) Write a program that prints the command-line arguments that it receives. What would be the output of the program if the command-line argument is * ?

    (d) What purpose do the functions **getpid( )** and **getppid( )** serve?

    (e) Rewrite the program in the section 'Zombies and Orphans' in this chapter by replacing the **while** loop with a call to the **sleep( )** function. Do you observe any change in the output of the program?

    (f) How does **waitpid( )** prevent the creation of zombie or orphan processes?

20

MORE LINUX PROGRAMMING

Communication is the essence of all progress. This is true in real life as well as in programming. In today's world, a program that runs in isolation is of little use. A worthwhile program has to communicate with the outside world in general and with the OS in particular. In Chapters 16 and 17 we saw how a Windows-based program communicates with Windows. In this chapter let us explore how this communication happens under Linux.

COMMUNICATION USING SIGNALS

In the last chapter, we used the **fork( )** and **exec( )** library functions to create a child process and to execute a new program respectively. These library functions got the job done by communicating with the Linux OS. Thus, the direction of communication was from the program to the OS. The reverse communication—from the OS to the program—is achieved using a mechanism called a 'Signal.' Let us now write a simple program that will help you experience the signal mechanism.

```
# include <stdio.h>
void main( )
{
    while ( 1 )
        printf ( "Pogram Running\n" ) ;
}
```

The program is fairly straightforward. All that we have done here is use an infinite **while** loop to print the message "Program Running" on the screen. When the program is running, we can terminate it by pressing the Ctrl + C. When we press Ctrl + C, the keyboard device driver informs the Linux kernel about pressing of this special key combination. The kernel reacts to this by sending a signal to our program. Since we have done nothing to handle this signal, the default signal handler gets called. In this default signal handler there is code to terminate the program. Therefore, on pressing Ctrl + C, the program gets terminated.

But how on earth would the default signal handler get called. Well, it is simple. There are several signals that can be sent to a program. A unique number is associated with each signal. To avoid remembering these numbers, they have been defined as macros like **SIGINT**, **SIGKILL**, **SIGCONT**, etc., in the file 'signal.h.' Every process contains several 'signal ID/function pointer' pairs indicating for which signal which function should be called. If we do not decide to handle a signal, then against that signal ID the address of the default signal handler function is present. It is precisely this default signal handler for **SIGINT** that got called when we pressed Ctrl + C when the previous program was executed. INT in **SIGINT** stands for interrupt.

Let us now see how can we prevent the termination of our program even after hitting Ctrl + C. This is shown in the following program:

```
# include <stdio.h>
# include <signal.h>

void sighandler ( int signum )
{
    printf ( "SIGINT received. Inside sighandler\n" ) ;
}

void main( )
{
    signal ( SIGINT, ( void* ) sighandler ) ;
    while ( 1 )
        printf ( "Program Running\n" ) ;
}
```

In this program we have registered a signal handler for the SIGINT signal by using the **signal( )** library function. The first parameter of this function specifies the ID of the signal that we wish to register. The second parameter is the address of a function that should get called whenever the signal is received by our program. This address has to be typecasted to a **void** * before passing it to the **signal( )** function.

Now, when we press Ctrl + C, the registered handler, namely, **sighandler( )** will get called. This function will display the message 'SIGINT received. Inside sighandler' and return the control back to **main( )**. Note that, unlike the default handler, our handler does not terminate the execution of our program. So the only way to terminate it is to kill the running process from a different terminal. For this we need to open a new instance of command prompt (terminal). Next, do a **ps –a** to obtain the list of processes running at all the command prompts that we have launched. Note the process ID of **a.out**. Finally, kill the 'a.out' process by saying,

```
# kill 3276
```

The terminal on which the author executed **a.out** was **tty1**, and its process ID turned out to be **3276**. In your case the terminal name and the process ID might be a different number.

If we wish, we can abort the execution of the program in the signal handler itself by using the **exit (0)** beyond the **printf( )**.

Note that signals work asynchronously. That is, when a signal is received, no matter what our program is doing, the signal handler would immediately get called. Once the execution of the signal handler is over, the execution of the program is resumed from the point where it left off when the signal was received.

HANDLING MULTIPLE SIGNALS

Now that we know how to handle one signal, let us try to handle multiple signals. Here is the program to do this:

```c
# include <stdio.h>
# include <unistd.h>
# include <sys/types.h>
# include <signal.h>

void inthandler ( int signum )
{
    printf ( "\nSIGINT Received\n" ) ;
}

void termhandler ( int signum )
{
    printf ( "\nSIGTERM Received\n" ) ;
}

void conthandler ( int signum )
{
    printf ( "\nSIGCONT Received\n" ) ;
}

void main( )
{
    signal ( SIGINT, inthandler ) ;
    signal ( SIGTERM, termhandler ) ;
    signal ( SIGCONT, conthandler ) ;

    while ( 1 )
        printf ( "\rProgram Running" ) ;
}
```

In this program, apart from **SIGINT**, we have additionally registered two new signals, namely, **SIGTERM** and **SIGCONT**. The **signal( )** function is called three times to register a different handler for each of the three signals. After registering the signals, we enter an infinite **while** loop to print the 'Program running' message on the screen.

As in the previous program, here too, when we press Ctrl + C, the handler for the SIGINT i.e., **inthandler( )**, is called. However, when we try to kill the program from the second terminal using the **kill** command, the program does not terminate. This is because, when the **kill** command is used, it sends the running program a **SIGTERM** signal. The default handler for the message terminates the program. Since we have handled this signal ourselves, the handler for **SIGTERM** i.e., **termhandler( )** gets called. As a result, the **printf( )** statement in the **termhandler( )** function gets executed and the message 'SIGTERM Received' gets displayed on the screen. Once the execution of the **termhandler( )** function is over, the program resumes its execution and continues to print 'Program Running.' Then how are we supposed to terminate the program? Simple. Use the following command from another terminal:

```
kill -SIGKILL 3276
```

As the command indicates, we are trying to send a **SIGKILL** signal to our program. A **SIGKILL** signal terminates the program.

Most signals may be caught by the process, but there are a few signals that the process cannot catch, and they cause the process to terminate. Such signals are often known as uncatchable signals. The **SIGKILL** signal is an uncatchable signal that forcibly terminates the execution of a process.

Note that, even if a process attempts to handle the **SIGKILL** signal by registering a handler for it, the control would still always land in the default **SIGKILL** handler, which would terminate the program.

The **SIGKILL** signal is used as a last resort to terminate a program that gets out of control. One such process that makes use of this signal is a system shutdown process. It first sends a **SIGTERM** signal to all processes, waits for a while, thus giving a 'grace period' to all the running processes. However, after the grace period is over, it forcibly terminates all the remaining processes using the **SIGKILL** signal.

That leaves only one question—when does a process receive the **SIGCONT** signal? Let's try to answer this question. A process under Linux can be suspended using the Ctrl + Z command. The process is stopped, but is not terminated, i.e., it is suspended. This gives rise to the uncatchable **SIGSTOP** signal. To resume the execution of the suspended process, we can make use of the **fg** (foreground) command. As a result of which, the suspended program resumes its execution and receives the **SIGCONT** signal (CONT means continue execution).

REGISTERING A COMMON HANDLER

Instead of registering a separate handler for each signal, we may decide to handle all signals using a common signal handler. This is shown in the following program:

```
# include <stdio.h>
# include <unistd.h>
# include <sys/types.h>
# include <signal.h>

void sighandler ( int signum )
{
    switch ( signum )
    {
        case SIGINT :
            printf ( "SIGINT Received\n" ) ;
            break ;

        case SIGTERM :
            printf ( "SIGTERM Received\n" ) ;
            break ;

        case SIGCONT :
            printf ( "SIGCONT Received\n" ) ;
            break ;
    }
}

void main( )
{
    signal ( SIGINT, sighandler ) ;
    signal ( SIGTERM, sighandler ) ;
    signal ( SIGCONT, sighandler ) ;

    while ( 1 )
        printf ( "\rProgram running" ) ;
}
```

In this program, during each call to the **signal( )** function, we have specified the address of a common signal handler named **sighandler( )**. Thus, the same signal handler function would get called when one of the three signals are received. This does not lead to a problem since inside the **sighandler( )** we can figure out the signal ID using the first parameter of the function.

In our program, we have made use of the **switch-case** construct to print a different message for each of the three signals.

Note that, we can easily afford to mix the two methods of registering signals in a program. That is, we can register separate signal handlers for some of the signals and a common handler for some other signals. Registering a common handler makes sense if we want to react to different signals in exactly the same way.

BLOCKING SIGNALS

Sometimes, we may want that flow of execution of a critical/time-critical portion of the program be unhampered by the occurrence of one or more signals. In such a case, we may decide to block the signal. Once we are through with the critical/time-critical code, we can unblock the signals(s). Note that, if a signal arrives when it is blocked, it is simply queued into a signal queue. When the signals are unblocked, the process immediately receives all the pending signals one after another. Thus, the blocking of signals defers the delivery of signals to a process until the execution of some critical/time-critical code is over. Instead of completely ignoring the signals or letting the signals interrupt the execution, it is preferable to block the signals for the moment and deliver them some time later. Let us now write a program to understand signal blocking. Here is the program:

```
# include <stdio.h>
# include <unistd.h>
# include <sys/types.h>
# include <signal.h>

void sighandler ( int signum )
{
    switch ( signum )
    {
        case SIGTERM :
            printf ( "SIGTERM Received\n" ) ;
            break ;

        case SIGINT :
            printf ( "SIGINT Received\n" ) ;
            break ;
```

```
                case SIGCONT :
                    printf ( "SIGCONT Received\n" ) ;
                    break ;
            }
    }

    void main( )
    {
        char buffer [ 80 ] = "\0" ;
        sigset_t block ;

        signal ( SIGTERM, sighandler ) ;
        signal ( SIGINT, sighandler ) ;
        signal ( SIGCONT, sighandler ) ;

        sigemptyset ( &block ) ;
        sigaddset ( &block, SIGTERM ) ;
        sigaddset ( &block, SIGINT ) ;

        sigprocmask ( SIG_BLOCK, &block, NULL ) ;

        while ( strcmp ( buffer, "n" ) != 0 )
        {
            printf ( "Enter a String: " ) ;
            gets ( buffer ) ;
            puts ( buffer ) ;
        }

        sigprocmask ( SIG_UNBLOCK, &block, NULL ) ;

        while ( 1 )
            printf ( "\rProgram Running" ) ;
    }
```

In this program we have registered a common handler for the **SIGINT**, **SIGTERM**, and **SIGCONT** signals. Next, we want to repeatedly accept strings in a buffer and display them on the screen until the time the user does not enter an "n" from the keyboard. Additionally, we want that this activity of receiving input should not be interrupted by the **SIGINT** or the **SIGTERM** signals. However, a **SIGCONT** should be permitted. So, before we proceed with the loop, we must block the **SIGINT** and **SIGTERM** signals. Once we are through with the loop, we must unblock these signals. This blocking and unblocking of signals can be achieved using the **sigprocmask( )** library function.

The first parameter of the **sigprocmask( )** function specifies whether we want to block/unblock a set of signals. The next parameter is the address of a structure (**typedef**ed as **sigset_t**) that describes a set of signals that we want to block/unblock. The last parameter can be either NULL or the address of a **sigset_t**-type variable, which would be set up with the existing set of signals before blocking/unblocking signals.

There are library functions that help us to populate the **sigset_t** structure. The **sigemptyset( )** empties a **sigset_t** variable so that it does not refer to any signals. The only parameter that this function accepts is the address of the **sigset_t** variable. We have used this function to quickly initialize the **sigset_t** variable block to a known empty state. To block the **SIGINT** and **SIGTERM** we have to add the signals to the empty set of signals. This can be achieved using the **sigaddset( )** library function. The first parameter of **sigaddset( )** is the address of the **sigset_t** variable and the second parameter is the ID of the signal that we wish to add to the existing set of signals.

After the loop, we have also used an infinite **while** loop to print the 'Program running' message. This is done so that we can easily check that until the time the loop that receives input is over, the program cannot be terminated using Ctrl + C or a **kill** command since the signals are blocked. Once the user enters "n" from the keyboard the control comes out of the **while** loop and unblocks the signals. As a result, pending signals, if any, are immediately delivered to the program. So if we press Ctrl + C or use the **kill** command when the execution of the loop that receives input is not over, these signals would be kept pending. Once we are through with the loop, the signal handlers would be called.

EVENT-DRIVEN PROGRAMMING

Having understood the mechanism of signal processing, let us now see how signaling is used by Linux-based libraries to create event-driven GUI programs. As you know, in a GUI program, events occur typically when we click on the window, type a character, close the window, repaint the window, etc. We have chosen the GTK library version 2.0 to create the GUI applications. Here, GTK stands for Gimp's Tool Kit. The following is the first program that uses this toolkit to create a window on the screen.

```
/* mywindow.c */
# include <gtk/gtk.h>

void main ( int argc, char *argv[ ] )
```

```
{
    GtkWidget *p ;

    gtk_init ( &argc, &argv ) ;
    p = gtk_window_new ( GTK_WINDOW_TOPLEVEL ) ;
    gtk_window_set_title ( p , "Sample Window" ) ;
    g_signal_connect ( p, "destroy", gtk_main_quit, NULL ) ;
    gtk_widget_set_size_request ( p, 300, 300 ) ;
    gtk_widget_show ( p ) ;
    gtk_main( ) ;
}
```

We need to compile this program as follows:

```
gcc mywindow.c `pkg-config gtk+-2.0 --cflags --libs`
```

Here we are compiling the program 'mywindow.c' and then linking it with the necessary libraries from the GTK toolkit. Note the quotes that we have used in the command. Here we are using the program "pkg-config," which can be obtained from *www.freedesktop.org*. This program reads the .pc that comes with GTK to determine what compiler switches are needed to compile programs that use GTK. --cflags will output a list of included directories for the compiler to look in, and --libs will output the list of libraries for the compiler to link with and the directories to find them in.

Here is the output of the program in Figure 20.1.

The GTK library provides a large number of functions that makes it very easy for us to create GUI programs. Every window under GTK is known as a widget. To create a simple window we have to carry out the following steps:

(a) Initialize the GTK library with a call to the **gtk_init( )** function. This function requires the addresses of the command-line arguments received in **main( )**.

(b) Next, call the **gtk_window_new( )** function to create a top-level window. The only parameter this function takes is the type of window to be created. A top-level window can be created by specifying the **GTK_WINDOW_TOPLEVEL** value. This call creates a window in memory and returns a pointer to the widget object. The widget object is a structure (**GtkWidget**) variable that stores lots of information, including the attributes of the window it represents. We have collected this pointer in a **GtkWidget** structure pointer called **p**.

(c) Set the title for the window by making a call to the **gtk_window_ set_title( )** function. The first parameter of this function is a pointer to the **GtkWidget** structure representing the window for which the

FIGURE 20.1

title has to be set. The second parameter is a string describing the text to be displayed in the title of the window.

(d) Register a signal handler for the destroy signal. The **destroy** signal is received whenever we try to close the window. The handler for the **destroy** signal should perform clean-up activities and then shut-down the application. GTK provides a ready-made function called **gtk_main_quit( )** that does this job. We only need to associate this function with the destroy signal. This can be achieved using the **g_signal_connect( )** function. The first parameter of this function is the pointer to the widget for which the destroy signal handler has to be registered. The second parameter is a string that specifies the name of the signal. The third parameter is the address of the signal handler routine. We have not used the fourth parameter.

(e) Resize the window to the desired size using the **gtk_widget_set_size_request( )** function. The second and the third parameters specify the height and the width of the window respectively.

(f) Display the window on the screen using the function **gtk_widget_show( )**.

(g) Wait in a loop to receive events for the window. This can be accomplished using the **gtk_main( )** function.

How about another program that draws a few shapes in the window? Here is the program:

```
/* myshapes.c */
# include <gtk/gtk.h>

int expose_event ( GtkWidget *widget, GdkEventExpose *event )
{
    GdkGC* p ;
    GdkPoint arr [ 5] = { 250, 150, 250, 300, 300, 350, 400, 300, 320, 190 } ;

    p = gdk_gc_new ( widget -> window ) ;
    gdk_draw_line ( widget -> window, p, 10, 10, 200, 10 ) ;
    gdk_draw_rectangle ( widget -> window, p, TRUE, 10, 20, 200, 100 ) ;
    gdk_draw_arc ( widget -> window, p, TRUE, 200, 10, 200, 200,
                   315 * 64, 90 * 64 ) ;
    gdk_draw_polygon ( widget -> window, p, TRUE , arr, 5 ) ; /* True -- fill */
    gdk_gc_unref ( p ) ;

    return TRUE ;
}
void main( int argc, char *argv[ ] )
{
    GtkWidget *p ;

    gtk_init ( &argc, &argv ) ;
    p = gtk_window_new ( GTK_WINDOW_TOPLEVEL ) ;
    gtk_window_set_title ( p, "Sample Window" ) ;
    g_signal_connect ( p, "destroy", gtk_main_quit, NULL ) ;
    g_signal_connect ( p , "expose_event", expose_event, NULL ) ;
    gtk_widget_set_size_request ( p, 500, 500 ) ;
    gtk_widget_show ( p ) ;
    gtk_main( ) ;
}
```

Figure 20.2 shows the output of the program.

This program is similar to the first one. The only difference is that, in addition to the destroy signal, we have registered a signal handler for the **expose_event** using the **g_signal_connect( )** function. This signal is sent to our process whenever the window needs to be redrawn. By writing the

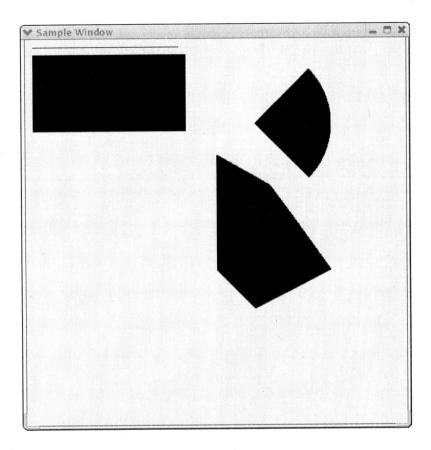

FIGURE 20.2

code for drawing shapes in the handler for this signal we are assured that the drawing will never vanish if the window is dragged outside the screen and then brought back in, or some other window uncovers a portion of our window that was previously overlapped, and so on. This is because an **expose_event** signal would be sent to our application, which would immediately redraw the shapes in our window.

Similar to the way Windows has a device context, under Linux we have a graphics context. In order to draw in the window we need to obtain a graphics context for the window using the **gdk_gc_new( )** function. This function returns a pointer to the graphics context structure. This pointer must be passed to the drawing functions like **gdk_draw_line( )**, **gdk_draw_rectangle()**, **gdk_draw_arc( )**, **gdk_draw_polygon( )**, etc. The arguments passed to most of these functions are self-explanatory. Note that, the last two arguments that are passed to **gdk_draw_arc( )** represent the starting angle and the ending angle of the arc. These angles are always mentioned as a multiple of 64 and the ending angle is measured relative to the starting angle. Once we are through with drawing, we should release the graphics context using the **gdk_gc_unref( )** function.

WHERE DO YOU GO FROM HERE

You have now understood signal processing, the heart of programming under Linux. With that knowledge under your belt you are now capable of exploring the vast world of Linux on your own. Complete Linux programming deserves a book on its own. The idea here was to raise the hood and show you what lies underneath it. If you have taken a good look at it, you can try the rest yourselves. Good luck!

SUMMARY

(a) Programs can communicate with the Linux OS using library functions.

(b) The Linux OS communicates with a program by means of signals.

(c) The interrupt signal (**SIGINT**) is sent by the kernel to our program when we press Ctrl + C.

(d) A term signal (**SIGTERM**) is sent to the program when we use the **kill** command.

(e) A process cannot handle an uncatchable signal.

(f) The **kill –SIGKILL** variation of the **kill** command generates an uncatchable **SIGKILL** signal that terminates a process.

(g) A process can block a signal or a set of signals using the **sigprocmask( )** function.

(h) Blocked signals are delivered to the process when the signals are unblocked.

(i) A **SIGSTOP** signal is generated when we press Ctrl + Z.

(j) A **SIGSTOP** signal is an uncatchable signal.

(k) A suspended process can be resumed using the **fg** command.

(l) A process receives the **SIGCONT** signal when it resumes execution.

(m) In GTK, the **g_signal_connect( )** function can be used to connect a function with an event.

EXERCISES

[A] State True or False:

   (a) All registered signals must have a separate signal handler.
   (b) Blocked signals are ignored by a process.
   (c) Only one signal can be blocked at a time.
   (d) Blocked signals are ignored once the signals are unblocked.
   (e) If our signal handler gets called, the default signal handler still gets called.
   (f) The **gtk_main( )** function makes uses of a loop to prevent the termination of the program.
   (g) Multiple signals can be registered at a time using a single call to the **signal( )** function.
   (h) The **sigprocmask( )** function can block as well as unblock signals.

[B] Answer the following:

   (a) How does the Linux OS know if we have registered a signal or not?
   (b) What happens when we register a handler for a signal?
   (c) Write a program to verify whether **SIGSTOP** and **SIGKILL** signals are uncatchable signals.
   (d) Write a program to handle the **SIGINT** and **SIGTERM** signals. From inside the handler for the **SIGINT** signal, write an infinite loop to print the message 'Processing Signal.' Run the program and make use of Ctrl + C more than once. Run the program once again and press Ctrl + C once. Then use the **kill** command. What are your observations?
   (e) Write a program that blocks the **SIGTERM** signal during execution of the **SIGINT** signal.

Appendix A

PRECEDENCE TABLE

Description	Operator	Associativity
Function expression	( )	Left to right
Array expression	[ ]	Left to right
Structure operator	->	Left to right
Structure operator	.	Left to right
Unary minus	-	Right to left
Increment/Decrement	++ --	Right to left
One's complement	~	Right to left
Negation	!	Right to left
Address of	&	Right to left
Value of address	*	Right to left
Type cast	(type)	Right to left
Size in bytes	sizeof	Right to left
Multiplication	*	Left to right
Division	/	Left to right
Modulus	%	Left to right
Addition	+	Left to right
Subtraction	-	Left to right
Left shift	<<	Left to right
Right shift	>>	Left to right
Less than	<	Left to right
Less than or equal to	<=	Left to right
Greater than	>	Left to right
Greater than or equal to	>=	Left to right
Equal to	==	Left to right
Not equal to	!=	Left to right
Bitwise AND	&	Left to right
Bitwise exclusive OR	^	Left to right
Bitwise inclusive OR	|	Left to right
Logical AND	&&	Left to right
Logical OR	||	Left to right
Conditional	? :	Right to left
Assignment	=	Right to left
	*= /= %=	Right to left
	+= -= &=	Right to left
	^= |=	Right to left
	<<= >>=	Right to left
Comma	,	Right to left

FIGURE A1.1

Appendix B

LIBRARY FUNCTIONS

- ▓ Arithmetic Functions
- ▓ Data Conversion Functions
- ▓ Character Classification Functions
- ▓ String Manipulation Functions
- ▓ Searching and Sorting Functions
- ▓ I/O Functions
- ▓ File Handling Functions
- ▓ Directory Control Functions
- ▓ Buffer Manipulation Functions
- ▓ Memory Allocation Functions
- ▓ Process Control Functions
- ▓ Time-Related Functions
- ▓ Miscellaneous Functions

L et alone discussing each library function in detail, even a complete list of these functions would occupy scores of pages. However, this book would be incomplete if it has nothing to say about library functions. The following is a list of library functions that are important. The functions have been classified into broad categories.

Arithmetic Functions

Function	Use
Abs	Returns the absolute value of an integer
Cos	Calculates cosine
cosh	Calculates hyperbolic cosine
exp	Raises the exponential e to the xth power
fabs	Finds absolute value
floor	Finds largest integer less than or equal to argument
fmod	Finds floating-point remainder
hypot	Calculates hypotenuse of right triangle
log	Calculates natural logarithm
log10	Calculates base 10 logarithm
modf	Breaks down argument into integer and fractional parts
pow	Calculates a value raised to a power
sin	Calculates sine
sinh	Calculates hyperbolic sine
sqrt	Finds square root
tan	Calculates tangent
tanh	Calculates hyperbolic tangent

Data Conversion Functions

Function	Use
atof	Converts string to float
atoi	Converts string to int
atol	Converts string to long
ecvt	Converts double to string
fcvt	Converts double to string
gcvt	Converts double to string
itoa	Converts int to string
ltoa	Converts long to string

Function	Use
strtod	Converts string to double
strtol	Converts string to long integer
strtoul	Converts string to an unsigned long integer
ultoa	Converts unsigned long to string

Character Classification Functions

Function	Use
isalnum	Tests for alphanumeric character
isalpha	Tests for alphabetic character
isdigit	Tests for decimal digit
islower	Tests for lowercase character
isspace	Tests for white space character
isupper	Tests for uppercase character
isxdigit	Tests for hexadecimal digit
tolower	Tests character and converts to lowercase if uppercase
toupper	Tests character and converts to uppercase if lowercase

String Manipulation Functions

Function	Use
strcat	Appends one string to another
strchr	Finds first occurrence of a given character in a string
strcmp	Compares two strings
strcmpi	Compares two strings without regard to case
strcpy	Copies one string to another
strdup	Duplicates a string
stricmp	Compares two strings without regard to case (identical to strcmpi)
strlen	Finds length of a string
strlwr	Converts a string to lowercase
strncat	Appends a portion of one string to another
strncmp	Compares a portion of one string with portion of another string
strncpy	Copies a given number of characters of one string to another
strnicmp	Compares a portion of one string with a portion of another without regard to case

Function	Use
strrchr	Finds last occurrence of a given character in a string
strrev	Reverses a string
strset	Sets all characters in a string to a given character
strstr	Finds first occurrence of a given string in another string
strupr	Converts a string to uppercase

Searching and Sorting Functions

Function	Use
bsearch	Performs binary search
lfind	Performs linear search for a given value
qsort	Performs quick sort

I/O Functions

Function	Use
close	Closes a file
fclose	Closes a file
feof	Detects end-of-file
fgetc	Reads a character from a file
fgetchar	Reads a character from keyboard (function version)
fgets	Reads a string from a file
fopen	Opens a file
fprintf	Writes formatted data to a file
fputc	Writes a character to a file
fputchar	Writes a character to screen (function version)
fputs	Writes a string to a file
fscanf	Reads formatted data from a file
fseek	Repositions file pointer to given location
ftell	Gets current file pointer position
getc	Reads a character from a file (macro version)
getch	Reads a character from the keyboard
getche	Reads a character from keyboard and echoes it
getchar	Reads a character from keyboard (macro version)
gets	Reads a line from keyboard
kbhit	Checks for a keystroke at the keyboard
lseek	Repositions file pointer to a given location
open	Opens a file

Function	Use
printf	Writes formatted data to screen
putc	Writes a character to a file (macro version)
putch	Writes a character to the screen
putchar	Writes a character to screen (macro version)
puts	Writes a line to file
read	Reads data from a file
rewind	Repositions file pointer to beginning of a file
scanf	Reads formatted data from keyboard
sscanf	Reads formatted input from a string
sprintf	Writes formatted output to a string
tell	Gets current file pointer position
write	Writes data to a file

File Handling Functions

Function	Use
remove	Deletes file
rename	Renames file
unlink	Deletes file

Directory Control Functions

Function	Use
chdir	Changes current working directory
getcwd	Gets current working directory
fnsplit	Splits a full path name into its components
findfirst	Searches a disk directory
findnext	Continues *findfirst* search
mkdir	Makes a new directory
rmdir	Removes a directory

Buffer Manipulation Functions

Function	Use
memchr	Returns a pointer to the first occurrence, within a specified number of characters, of a given character in the buffer
memcmp	Compares a specified number of characters from two buffers

Function	Use
memcpy	Copies a specified number of characters from one buffer to another
memicmp	Compares a specified number of characters from two buffers without regard to the case of the characters
memmove	Copies a specified number of characters from one buffer to another
memset	Uses a given character to initialize a specified number of bytes in the buffer

Memory Allocation Functions

Function	Use
calloc	Allocates a block of memory
free	Frees a block allocated with *malloc*
malloc	Allocates a block of memory
realloc	Reallocates a block of memory

Process Control Functions

Function	Use
abort	Aborts a process
atexit	Executes function at program termination
execl	Executes child process with argument list
exit	Terminates the process
spawnl	Executes child process with argument list
spawnlp	Executes child process using PATH variable and argument list
system	Executes an MS-DOS command

Time-related Functions

Function	Use
clock	Returns the elapsed CPU time for a process
difftime	Computes the difference between two times
ftime	Gets current system time as structure
strdate	Returns the current system date as a string
strtime	Returns the current system time as a string

Function	Use
time	Gets current system time as long integer
setdate	Sets DOS date
getdate	Gets system date

Miscellaneous Functions

Function	Use
delay	Suspends execution for an interval (milliseconds)
getenv	Gets value of environment variable
getpsp	Gets the Program Segment Prefix
perror	Prints error message
putenv	Adds or modifies value of environment variable
random	Generates random numbers
randomize	Initializes random number generation with a random value based on time
sound	Turns PC speaker on at specified frequency
nosound	Turns PC speaker off

Appendix C

CHASING THE BUGS

C programmers are great innovators of our times. However, there is no shortage of horror stories about programs that took twenty times longer to 'debug' as they did to 'write.' Many a time programs had to be rewritten all over again because the bugs present in them could not be located. Bugs are C programmer's birthright. But how do we chase them away. No sure-shot way for that. A list of the more common programming mistakes might be of help. They are not arranged in any particular order. But as you will realize, surely a great help!

[1] Omitting the ampersand before the variables used in **scanf( )**. For example,

```
int choice ;
scanf ( "%d", choice ) ;
```

Here, the **&** before the variable choice is missing. Another common mistake with **scanf( )** is to give blanks either just before the format string or immediately after the format string as in,

```
int choice ;
scanf ( " %d ", &choice ) ;
```

Note that this is not a mistake, but until you understand **scanf( )** thoroughly, this is going to cause trouble. Safety is in eliminating the blanks.

[2] Using the operator = instead of the operator = =. For example, the following **while** loop becomes an infinite loop since every time, instead of checking the value of **i** against 10, it assigns the value 10 to **i**. As 10 is a nonzero value, the condition will always be treated as true, forming an infinite loop.

```
int i = 10 ;
while ( i = 10 )
{
    printf ( "got to get out" ) ;
    i++ ;
}
```

[3] Ending a loop with a semicolon. Observe the following program.

```
int j = 1 ;
while ( j <= 100 ) ;
```

```
{
    printf ( "\nCompguard" ) ;
    j++ ;
}
```

Here, inadvertently, we have fallen into an indefinite loop. The cause is the semicolon after **while**. This semicolon is treated as a null statement by the compiler as shown here:

```
while ( j <= 100 )
    ;
```

This is an indefinite loop since the null statement keeps getting executed indefinitely as **j** never gets incremented.

[4] Omitting the **break** statement at the end of a **case** in a **switch** statement. Remember that, if a **break** is not included at the end of a **case**, then execution will continue into the next **case**.

```
int ch = 1 ;
switch ( ch )
{
    case 1 :
        printf ( "\nGoodbye" ) ;
    case 2 :
        printf ( "\nLieutenant" ) ;
}
```

Here, since the **break** has not been given after the **printf( )** in **case 1**, the control runs into **case 2** and executes the second **printf( )** as well. However, this sometimes turns out to be a blessing in disguise—especially in cases when we want the same set of statements to get executed for multiple cases.

[5] Using **continue** in a **switch**. It is a common error to believe that the way the keyword **break** is used with loops and a **switch**; similarly, the keyword **continue** can also be used with them. Remember that **continue** works only with loops, never with a **switch**.

[6] A mismatch in the number, type, and order of actual and formal arguments. Consider the following call:

```
yr = romanise ( year, 1000, 'm' ) ;
```

Here, three arguments in the order **int**, **int**, and **char** are being passed to **romanise( )**. When **romanise( )** receives these arguments into formal arguments, they must be received in the same order. A careless mismatch might give strange results.

[7] Omitting provisions for returning a noninteger value from a function. If we make the following function call,

```
area = area_circle ( 1.5 ) ;
```

then, while defining the **area_circle( )** function later in the program, care should be taken to make it capable of returning a floating-point value. Note that, unless otherwise mentioned, the compiler will assume that this function returns a value of the type **int**.

[8] Inserting a semicolon at the end of a macro definition. This might create a problem as shown here:

```
# define UPPER 25 ;
```

would lead to a syntax error if used in an expression such as

```
if ( counter == UPPER )
```

This is because, on preprocessing, the **if** statement would take the form

```
if ( counter == 25 ; )
```

[9] Omitting parentheses around a macro expansion. Consider the following macro:

```
# define SQR(x) x * x
```

If we use this macro as

```
int a ;
a = 25 / SQR ( 5 ) ;
```

we expect the value of **a** to be 1, whereas it turns out to be 25. This happens, because, on preprocessing, the statement takes the following form:

```
a = 25 / 5 * 5 ;
```

[10] Leaving a blank space between the macro template and the macro expansion.

```
# define ABS (a) ( a = 0 ? a : -a )
```

Here, the space between **ABS** and **(a)** makes the preprocessor believe that you want to expand **ABS** into **(a)**, which is certainly not what you want.

[11] Using an expression that has side effects in a macro. Consider the following macro:

```
# define SUM ( a ) ( a + a )
```

If we use this macro as

```
int w, b = 5 ;
w = SUM( b++ ) ;
```

On preprocessing, the macro would be expanded to,

```
w = ( b++ ) + ( b++ ) ;
```

Thus, contrary to expectation, **b** will get incremented twice.

[12] Confusing a character constant and a character string. In the statement

```
ch = 'z' ;
```

a single character is assigned to **ch**. In the statement

```
ch = "z" ;
```

a pointer to the character string "z" is assigned to **ch**.
Note that in the first case, the declaration of **ch** would be,

```
char ch ;
```

whereas in the second case it would be,

```
char *ch ;
```

[13] Forgetting the bounds of an array.

```
int num[50], i ;
for ( i = 1 ; i <= 50 ; i++ )
    num[i] = i * i ;
```

Here, in the array **num**, there is no such element as **num[50]**, since array counting begins with 0 and not 1. The compiler will not give a warning if our program exceeds the bounds. If not taken care of, in extreme cases, this code might even hang the computer.

[14] Forgetting to reserve an extra location in a character array for the null terminator. Remember, each character array ends with a '\0,' therefore its dimension should be declared big enough to hold the normal

characters as well as the '\0.' For example, the dimension of the array **word[ ]** should be 9 if a string "Jamboree" is stored in it.

[15] Confusing the precedences of the various operators.

```
char ch ;
FILE *fp ;
fp = fopen ( "text.c", "r" ) ;
while ( ch = getc ( fp ) != EOF )
    putch ( ch ) ;
fclose ( fp ) ;
```

Here, the value returned by **getc( )** will be first compared with EOF, since != has a higher priority than =. As a result, the value that is assigned to **ch** will be the true/false result of the test—1 if the value returned by **getc( )** is not equal to **EOF**, and 0 otherwise. The correct form of the above **while** would be,

```
while ( ( ch = getc ( fp ) ) != EOF )
    putch ( ch ) ;
```

[16] Confusing the operator **->** with the operator **.** while referring to a structure element. Remember, on the left of operator **.** only a structure variable can occur, whereas on the left of operator **->** only a pointer to a structure can occur. The following example demonstrates this.

```
struct emp
{
    char name[35] ;
    int age ;
} ;
struct emp e = { "Dubhashi", 40 } ;
struct emp *ee ;
printf ( "\n%d", e.age ) ;
ee = &e ;
printf ( "\n%d", ee->>age ) ;
```

[17] Exceeding the range of integers and chars. Consider the following code snippet:

```
char ch ;
for ( ch = 0 ; ch <= 255 ; ch++ )
    printf ( "\n%c %d", ch, ch ) ;
```

This is an indefinite loop. The reason is, **ch** has been declared as a **char** and its valid range is -128 to $+127$. Hence, the moment **ch** tries to become 128 (through **ch++**), the range is exceeded. As a result, the first number from the negative side of the range, -128, gets assigned to **ch**. Naturally, the condition is satisfied and the control remains within the loop.

Appendix **D** **ASCII C**HART

There are 256 distinct characters used by the IBM-compatible family of microcomputers. Their values range from 0 to 255. These can be grouped as shown in Figure D.1:

Character Type	No. of Characters
Uppercase Letters	26
Lowercase Letters	26
Digits	10
Special Symbols	32
Control Character	34
Graphics Character	128
Total	256

FIGURE D.1

Out of the 256 character set, the first 128 are often called ASCII characters and the next 128 as Extended ASCII characters. Each ASCII character has a unique appearance. The following simple program can generate the ASCII chart:

```
# include <stdio.h>
void main( )
{
    int ch ;

    for ( ch = 0 ; ch <= 255 ; ch++ )
        printf ( "%d %c\n", ch, ch ) ;
}
```

This chart is shown on the following page. Out of the 128 graphic characters (Extended ASCII characters), there are characters that are used for drawing single line and double line boxes in text mode. For convenience, these characters are shown in Figure D.2.

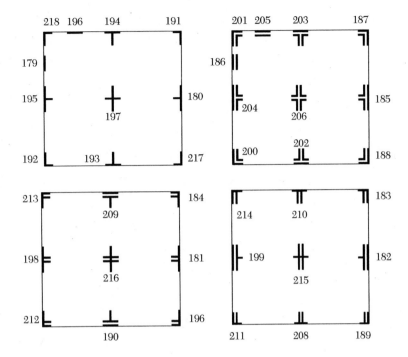

FIGURE D.2

Value	Char	Value	Char	Value	Char	Value	Char	Value	Char	Value	Char
0		22	█	44	,	66	B	88	X	110	n
1	☺	23	↕	45	-	67	C	89	Y	111	o
2	●	24	←	46	.	68	D	90	Z	112	p
3	►	25	→	47	/	69	E	91	[	113	q
4	♦	26	↑	48	0	70	F	92	\	114	r
5	♣	27	↓	49	1	71	G	93	]	115	s
6	♠	28	∟	50	2	72	H	94	^	116	t
7	●	29	↔	51	3	73	I	95	_	117	u
8	□	30	◄	52	4	74	J	96	`	118	v
9	○	31	►	53	5	75	K	97	a	119	w
10	▣	32		54	6	76	L	98	b	120	x
11	♂	33	!	55	7	77	M	99	c	121	y
12	♀	34	"	56	8	78	N	100	d	122	z
13	♪	35	#	57	9	79	O	101	e	123	{
14	♫	36	$	58	:	80	P	102	f	124	|
15	☼	37	%	59	;	81	Q	103	g	125	}
16	▲	38	&	60	<	82	R	104	h	126	~
17	▼	39	'	61	=	83	S	105	i	127	
18	↔	40	(	62	>	84	T	106	j	128	Ç
19	‼	41	)	63	?	85	U	107	k	129	ü
20	¶	42	*	64	@	86	V	108	l	130	é
21	§	43	+	65	A	87	W	109	m	131	â

Value	Char	Value	Char	Value	Char	Value	Char	Value	Char	Value	Char
132	ä	154	Ü	176	░	198	╞	220	▄	242	≥
133	à	155	¢	177	▒	199	╟	221	▌	243	≤
134	å	156	£	178	▓	200	╚	222	▐	244	⌠
135	ç	157	¥	179	│	201	╔	223	▀	245	⌡
136	ê	158	₧	180	┤	202	╩	224	α	246	÷
137	ë	159	ƒ	181	╡	203	╦	225	β	247	≈
138	è	160	á	182	╢	204	╠	226	Γ	248	°
139	ï	161	í	183	╖	205	═	227	π	249	∙
140	î	162	ó	184	╕	206	╬	228	Σ	250	·
141	ì	163	ú	185	╣	207	╧	229	σ	251	√
142	Ä	164	ñ	186	║	208	╨	230	µ	252	ⁿ
143	Å	165	Ñ	187	╗	209	╤	231	τ	253	²
144	É	166	ª	188	╝	210	╥	232	Φ	254	■
145	æ	167	º	189	╜	211	╙	233	Θ	255	
146	Æ	168	¿	190	╛	212	╘	234	Ω		
147	ô	169	⌐	191	┐	213	╒	235	δ		
148	ö	170	¬	192	└	214	╓	236	∞		
149	ò	171	½	193	┴	215	╫	237	ø		
150	û	172	¼	194	┬	216	╪	238	∈		
151	ù	173	¡	195	├	217	┘	239	∩		
152	ÿ	174	«	196	─	218	┌	240	≡		
153	Ö	175	»	197	┼	219	█	241	±		

HELPER.h FILE

```
LRESULT CALLBACK WndProc ( HWND, UINT, WPARAM, LPARAM ) ;

HINSTANCE hInst ; // current instance

/* FUNCTION: InitInstance ( HANDLE, int, char * )
     PURPOSE: Saves instance handle and creates main window
     COMMENTS: In this function, we save the instance handle in a global
               variable and create and display the main program window.
*/
BOOL InitInstance ( HINSTANCE hInstance, int nCmdShow, char* pTitle )
{
    char classname[ ] = "MyWindowClass" ;
    HWND hWnd ;

    WNDCLASSEX wcex ;
    wcex.cbSize        = sizeof ( WNDCLASSEX ) ;
    wcex.style         = CS_HREDRAW | CS_VREDRAW ;
    wcex.lpfnWndProc   = ( WNDPROC ) WndProc ;
    wcex.cbClsExtra    = 0 ;
    wcex.cbWndExtra    = 0 ;
    wcex.hInstance     = hInstance ;
    wcex.hIcon         = NULL ;
    wcex.hCursor       = LoadCursor ( NULL, IDC_ARROW ) ;
    wcex.hbrBackground = ( HBRUSH )( COLOR_WINDOW + 1 ) ;
    wcex.lpszMenuName  = NULL ;
    wcex.lpszClassName = classname ;
    wcex.hIconSm       = NULL ;

    if ( !RegisterClassEx ( &wcex ) )
          return FALSE ;

    hInst = hInstance ; // Store instance handle in our global variable

    hWnd = CreateWindow ( classname, pTitle,
                   WS_OVERLAPPEDWINDOW,
                   CW_USEDEFAULT, 0, CW_USEDEFAULT, 0, NULL,
                   NULL, hInstance, NULL ) ;
    if ( !hWnd )
          return FALSE ;

    ShowWindow ( hWnd, nCmdShow ) ;
    UpdateWindow ( hWnd ) ;

    return TRUE ;
}
```

Appendix F LINUX INSTALLATION

This his appendix gives the steps needed to install Red Hat Linux 9.0. In addition, a few commands have been indicated that are necessary to compile and execute the programs given in Chapters 20 and 21. Follow the steps mentioned below to carry out the installation.

(a) Configure the system to boot from the CD-ROM drive.

(b) Insert the first CD in the drive and boot the system from it.

(c) Press the 'Enter' key when the 'boot' prompt appears.

(d) Select the 'Skip' option in the "CD Found" dialog box.

(e) Click on the 'Next' button in the 'Welcome' screen.

(f) Click on the 'Next' button in the 'Language selection' screen.

(g) Click on the 'Next' button in the 'Keyboard' screen.

(h) Click on the 'Next' button in the 'Mouse Configuration' screen.

(i) Select the 'Custom' option in the 'Installation Type' screen and then click on the 'Next' button.

(j) Click on the 'Next' button in the 'Disk Partitioning Setup' screen.

(k) Select the 'Keep all partitions and use existing free space' option in the 'Automatic Partitioning' screen and then click on the 'Next' button. Ignore any warnings generated by clicking on the 'OK' button.

(l) Click on the 'Next' button in the 'Boot loader configuration' screen.

(m) Click on the 'Next' button in the 'Network configuration' screen.

(n) Click on the 'Next' button in the 'Firewall configuration' screen.

(o) Click on the 'Next' button in the 'additional language support' screen.

(p) Select a suitable option in the 'Time zone offset' screen and click on the 'Next' button.

(q) Type a password for the root account in the 'Set root password' screen and then click on the 'Next' button.

(r) Click on the 'Next' button in the 'Authentication configuration' screen.

(s) In the 'Package group selection' screen make sure that you select the following options—X window system, K desktop environment, Development tools, GNOME software development, and then click on the 'Next' button.

(t) Select the 'No' option in the 'Boot diskette creation' screen

(u) Click on the 'Next' button in the 'Graphical Interface (x) configuration' screen.

(v) Click on the 'Next' button in the 'Monitor configuration' screen.

(w) In the 'Customize graphical configuration' screen, select the 'Graphical' option and then click on the 'Next' button.

(x) Once the system restarts, configure the system to boot from Hard Disk.

USING RED HAT LINUX

For logging into the system, enter the username and password and select the session as KDE (K Desktop Environment). Once you have logged in, to start typing the program use the following menu options:

`KMenu | Run Command`

A dialog will pop up. In this dialog, in the command edit box, type **KWrite** and then click on the OK button. Now you can type the program and save it.

To compile the program you need to go the command prompt. This can be done using the following menu option.

`KMenu | System Tools | Terminal`

Once at the command prompt you can use the **gcc** compiler to compile and execute your programs. You can launch another instance of the command prompt by repeating the step mentioned above.

Appendix G

ABOUT THE CD-ROM

Included on the CD-ROM are simulations, source code, figures from the text, third party software, and other files related to topics in C programming.

See the "README" files on the CD-ROM for specific information/system requirements related to each file folder, but most files will run on Windows 2000 or higher and Linux.

INDEX